D1570573

# PRESIDENT JOHN F. KENNEDY & MARILYN MONROE'S SON,
## IN HIS OWN WORDS

# PRESIDENT JOHN F. KENNEDY
# & MARILYN MONROE'S SON,
## IN HIS OWN WORDS

JOHN F. KENNEDY

KILONOVA PRESS

New York, NY

President John F. Kennedy & Marilyn Monroe's Son, in his own words

Published by Gatekeeper Press
2167 Stringtown Rd, Suite 109
Columbus, OH 43123-2989
www.GatekeeperPress.com

Audiobook produced by Daryl Bolicek at Wildhorserecording.com
Book Trailer created by Joe Nuckols of AudioVideoBookPromo.com

Library of Congress Control Number: 2020944876

ISBN (hardcover): 9781642375206
ISBN (paperback): 9781642375213
eISBN: 9781642375107

www.johnfkennedyinhisownwords.com
contact: john@johnfkennedyinhisownwords.com

# CONTENTS

# PREFACE

**IT WAS A SPRING** day in Beverly Hills, California, a little chilly. My mother had picked up her last passenger. Next, on to buy snacks for our three-hour drive to Western White House to visit my dad. It was the last item left on her itinerary to do. She pulled into Ralph's Market on Wilshire Boulevard and Crescent Ave. She parked. Suddenly, we were blocked in by a car stopped behind us.

Everything took mere seconds to unfold. Two men came rushing out of the car that had blocked us in our parking space. The man with the blue eyes grabbed me and pulled me out of the vehicle. The other man had a gun to my mother's bosom. He told her, "If you scream, I'll kill your child." There was no time to say, "I'll see you later" to my mother. I looked at her and said, "If my father's family has anything to do with this, I will not stop. I give you my word!"

That was the last time I saw my mother alive. I walked among the elite to scrounging around for my next meal, day in and day out, fighting to stay alive!

This one day changed my life forever. It took more than half a century to write my biography. There are many people to thank for helping make this book possible, impossible to tell you about each one.

If it were not for my in-laws Felix and Mercedes raising a marvelous daughter such as my wife Hilda T. Kennedy, I might not be here today.

**PLAYBOY**

HUGH M. HEFNER
EDITOR-IN-CHIEF

October 3, 2006

William Henry Kennedy
1672 Grove Street
Ridgewood, NY  11385

Dear Mr. Kennedy:

If you have an unpublished book related to Marilyn
Monroe and your father's alleged kinship to her
and John F. Kennedy, I'll be happy to pass it
along to someone who might be interested in its
publication.

They would presumably require some real evidence
of that kinship.

Sincerely,

Hugh M. Hefner

HMH/aw

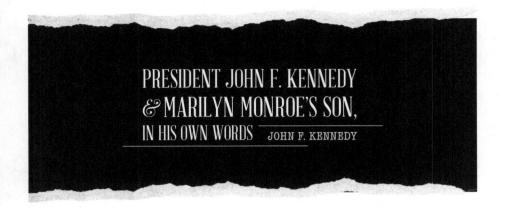

# PRESIDENT JOHN F. KENNEDY & MARILYN MONROE'S SON,
## IN HIS OWN WORDS    JOHN F. KENNEDY

**TODAY WAS GOING TO** be the day that I planned out so long ago. It has finally arrived. I still see that little boy ripped from his mother's hands. It was right after my mother sang happy birthday to Dad that my world changed. To this day, I still have that same feeling as when we stopped at the corner of Wilshire Boulevard and Crescent Dr. in Beverly Hills, California. The changing of the landscape did not help to erase the memory of the last time I was with my mother, Marilyn Monroe. It's forty-six years later, and I still see that little boy trying to return home to his mother's arms. There is no better way to return home. Then to see yourself standing in United Federal Court appearing before Judge William H. Pauley in Lower Manhattan, New York. I am suing the trustee of my late father for his last will, my birthright.

Being in the Daniel Patrick Monahan Federal Courthouse in downtown Manhattan did not faze or intimidate me at all. After all, 90 days earlier, I sent a letter to my sister Caroline Bouvier Kennedy Schlossberg stating we need to talk, and time is of the essence. Caroline attended law school, so she should understand the legal definition of time is of the essence.

Standing around the 14th floor, waiting for the courtroom doors to open was an exhilarating feeling. I knew this day would come. I did not expect it to take long.

When the courtroom doors opened, we walked into this dark oak room. The first thing I noticed was the carving of a bald eagle etched into the wood, the symbol of pride and justice in the United States of America. Am I finally going to receive my day in court, or is the federal court a farce like every other courtroom I have experienced? The first order of the court was roll call. The court clerk called out the cases to find out who was present. Wouldn't you know it, I was the first to be called: John Fitzgerald Kennedy v. the Trustees of the Testamentary Trust of the Last Will and Testament of President John F. Kennedy, Docket No. 08 Civ. 8889 (William Henry Pauley III). The attorney answered, "Here!" Once I heard that my heart sank to my feet. This judge wants this case gone. The court clerk finished the roll call; I was correct. Again, the court clerk called out, "John F. Kennedy versus the Trustees of President John F. Kennedy."

The attorney entered court proceedings first. He sat at the left of the table, and I sat to the right of him. With my back to the courtroom, I turned to look for my wife and son; they were sitting right where I left them. I looked around. I noticed that I was playing to a full house. There was not an empty place to sit on the benches in the courtroom. There was standing room only, and attorneys were standing on both sides of the courtroom.

Attorneys filled the courtroom. Perhaps some of them were friends of the Kennedy Clan of Massachusetts, the first family of the United States? How was all of this going to play out in their minds? Would people come to view the Kennedy's as I do? My day in court was what I had been waiting for, and it was here. There I was with just one attorney sitting to the left of me. Sitting on the left side of the courtroom were seven attorneys representing Caroline Bouvier Kennedy Schlossberg; talk about overkill.

The judge entered the courtroom, and I appear before the Honorable William H. Pauley III of the Southern District of New York. I had the pleasure of appearing before a judge before, but this was the first time he did not greet the courtroom. An unsettling feeling came over me; my stomach started knotting up.

I felt as if I was back in 1968.

> The judge asked me, "Which parent would you like to live with?"

*I answered, "These people are not my parents. I would like to go home."*

*The judge replied, "It is understandable that you would say that, son." Vivian and Maryann had made the same statement before my testimony.*

*"These are not my parents, and I do not know who to choose your honor." The judge looked on as Mary's attorney said, "What is going on?" The judge did not get through with his question when the attorney asked for an immediate recess. The judge granted it.*

*Mary's attorney took the four of us out of the courtroom. In the corridor of the hall, the attorney grabbed me by my shirt collar, asking me, "Who are your parents?"*

*I answered, "President John F. Kennedy and Marilyn Monroe are my parents."*

1968, I did not have any say. It appeared to be the same here in this courtroom in 2009. When a judge enters his court and does not say "Good morning," it is an indication that you lost your case on the onset. Is this what happens when your Uncle Robert F. Kennedy's name is on the Department of Justice Building in Washington, D.C.?

The court clerk called the case. "All parties in the matter of John F. Kennedy versus the Trustees of President John F. Kennedy; please rise."

The Honorable William Henry Pauley III entered the courtroom, sat down, and looked around. Judge Pauley glanced over at Marcy Harris, the attorney representing Trustees, and looked back at me. "I came here to dismiss this case, but it seems like both parties are here."

It was 1968 repeating itself. I was going to be locked out of the legal process again. How was I to trust any decision that the

Honorable William Pauley renders? Was he going to lock me out of the legal system? The same way my uncle, The Honorable Senator Edward M. Kennedy, did when Mary Joe Kopecky died? He locked the prosecutor out of the courthouse, made a deal with the judge, and got away with killing her. Well, somehow, someway I was not going to let this judge do the same thing to me.

I was going to go all the way to the United States Supreme Court. His attitude was what I had been fighting for 47 years. People do not understand just what kind of criminal organization my Grandmother Rose Kennedy, the Att. General Robert F. Kennedy, and the Hon. Edward Moore Kennedy created. And what that criminal organization has done to keep me right where I am. I was not going to let this happen to me again. I am tired of people taking a side when only one side has a say! This time, Marilyn Monroe and President Kennedy's son was going to be heard! This judge was not going to violate my constitutional right to a fair hearing.

> *Judge Pauley ordered that 4 out of the 7 had to leave the courtroom. Leaving Attorney Marcy Harris, representing my sister Caroline Bouvier Schlossberg. After all, Edwin Schlossberg is my brother-in-law and a trustee of my father's last will and testament.*

Attorney Marcy emphatically stated President John F. Kennedy and Marilyn Monroe, in fact, had a son. But he was given up for adoption at birth to the Burtons in 1955. The first time the Kennedy's heard of the son was in 1994. I listened to this and leaned forward, thinking, *That is a total fabrication.* She had not done her homework. If the Hon. William Pauley let this stand, then he himself was participating in this crime.

As Marcy was speaking, I turned and smiled at my son and wife. I was hoping that my Attorney would answer Marcy Harris's allegations; however, he did not. As I turned back around to face the judge, he murmured at me, "Where have you been for the last

47 years?" My attorney had instructed me not to say anything in court unless the judge asked me a direct question.

The Hon. William Pauley wanted to know what my residence was.

"Counselor, did Mr. Kennedy vote in the last presidential election?"

"Judge, he did not vote."

"You mean to tell me that Mr. Kennedy did not vote in this last great election that just took place?"

"Yes. Mr. Kennedy did not vote in this last historical election, Your Honor."

Once the Hon. Pauley said that the attorney should have informed the judge where I had been for the previous 47 years. What had been done to keep me in my place was still going on. It would have taken one phrase; however, Hon. William Pauley's murmur rang in my ears for an answer!

Today is Thursday, October 13, 2011; all my legal problems have come to an end. So, it is time for me to start writing about the injustice that the Kennedy's of Massachusetts have created. Their broken promise that the Kennedy's failed to keep.

What you are about to read are all facts and what I have experienced. As you read, you'll find that people in this story are true to life, and you may have heard of some of them. Perhaps you voted for them in a Congressional or Presidential race or seen a movie that he or she may have had a roll in. These facts are what historians do not know or do not want you to know.

I am the first grandchild of the most famous family in America. My father is John F. Kennedy, and my mother is Marilyn Monroe. My father was charismatic; he could command a room, but he was most at ease in one-on-one meetings. My mother, Marilyn, was like a white rose. You pulled back the layers, and there she was, just what you expected. I remember her kindness, the sweet sound of her voice when we spoke. She was the only one that could get me to change my decision. She had a knack for doing that. I can still hear her voice and feel her touch. I remember how safe I felt when I was with my parents.

The day our lives changed was when we had a family meeting. I still see that little boy standing there in his grandparents' living room, as has come to be known as the Kennedy Compound. I see myself on the couch, looking out the window, thinking, What is going to happen now? I could tell that it was not a party, lunch, dinner, or supper. It was different!

*My parents, grandparents, aunts, and uncles were all in the room. My mother and father took me aside and said, "We have something to tell you." My father spoke, "First, I hope that you understand why we are doing this. I am going to become the President of the United States, and some changes are coming."*

*At this point, his eyes started to well up, and his voice started cracking. My mother asked him, "Is this what you want to do?" He was holding her hand at this point.*

*He answered, "This is not what I want to do, but this is what I have to do."*

*By this time, he was holding both our hands as if he was trying to reassure us that everything would be fine—my Grandmother Rose F. Kennedy walked over and said he is going to be okay. My father replied, what assurances do I have? Is he going to be okay?*

*My uncle, Robert F. Kennedy, walked over and said, "Let's not turn this into something that it's not."*

*Marilyn turned to my Uncle Bobby, "This is my son, you stay out of this. Having this conversation right now isn't going to change anything. Sometimes I wonder whose interests you have in mind, Robert."*

*My father turned to Bobby, "Do not talk to my wife that way. Do you understand me?"*

*I asked my dad, "What is it you want to say to me?"*

*"Robert, she understands me and what I am trying to accomplish."*

*"Dad, what is it you want to say? What is going to change? Are you going someplace? Will you be back?"*

*"No! I'm not going anywhere. I'll be here with you and your mother. However, son, I do have something to tell you."*

By this time, I could feel the tension in the room. That feeling you get when something is going to happen. Something wrong is taking place. I could feel the knots starting to tangle in my stomach.

Dad turned to the room and said, "This is not easy to do. Jack is Marilyn and my son; this is a life-altering decision."

Aunt Eunice Kennedy Shriver weighed in on the conversation, "We have all agreed that this is what has to happen if John is to become president."

"No," my mother said to Eunice. "What if things start to go awry?"

About this time, my Grandpa Joe stood up in his calm, mild manner and said to me, "This is what we have been working to achieve. We are going to help your father become president of this country. I've had this planned out since before you were born, little Jack. Not to say that you should not be informed of what is going on; however, you are old enough to do what is required of you. I know that you understand just what is going on here. We are all willing to make sacrifices. All we are asking is for your cooperation."

*My father said, "Dad, it is up to me to tell Jack what needs to be said."*

*My father took my mother and my hands and sat us down. I was looking out of the bay window, out at the blue sky and down at the ocean. I could not tell if I was looking at the sky or mother's blue eyes. All I could see was the sadness in them.*

*The pain that she was in for what my dad was going to say. My father's reddish-brown hair and emerald eyes lit up the room. It was an explosion of color in the room emitting from my parents' eyes. With all that, I was hearing that my father wanted to become president. But what was still not clear was what my father had to tell me.*

*My father began, "My son, I love you and your mother. If I am to become president, I have to remarry."*

*"What do you mean you are going to remarry? Who are you going to remarry?"*

*It's a little more complicated than I thought.*

*"Son, your grandparents made a business deal with a man by the name of Jack Black. If I am to become president, I have to honor that deal."*

*"I know who Jack Black is; I do not understand what he has to do with you getting married, Dad?"*

*As I was sitting there looking at my father, it became clear just who Jack Black was. He was the man that lost most of his money during the 1929 stock market crash. He was the one my grandparents would discuss. Something about a business deal that my grandfather pulled out of at the last minute. Jack Black had lost money on the deal and ended up with a net worth of seven hundred and fifty thousand dollars.*

Mr. Black had always blamed the Bear for this. Yes, that is what his business partners called him: the Bear. But to me, he was just Grandpa! The Bear was one who always kept his word. He explained that in the business world, when one gives his word, it has more value than money. Sometimes you put a lot of time and effort into a business deal, but something just does not feel right. So, you walk away from the agreement. It has nothing to do with the person; it is just the deal. In this case, Mr. Black took it personally.

Mr. Black was the topic of conversation on more than one occasion. As Grandma Rose would tell it, things became heated. Mr. Black wanted to know why my grandfather felt the deal was not worthy of his time or money. He said, "Joe P. Kennedy, you have to make up my loss. You sold me out!"

"No! You don't understand the way things work at all." Mr. Black set out to ruin the Bear's reputation.

We were all at the dinner table one evening. I knew it was going to be a long, drawn-out dinner. It was chilly outside. We were all asked what our day was like and what we had done that day. There was nothing out of the ordinary that happened that day. Grandma Rose brought Mr. Black into our dinner conversation; it upset grandfather. She started by saying, "I ran into Mr. Black today, and he said it is time to live up to our agreement. I don't want to have to stop you two from killing each other again."

My father said to his mother, "To hear you tell it, you save the day. But what would our lives be like now, Mother, if you had not interfered?"

"John, you would be fatherless today, had I not stopped your father and Jack from dueling. Your father and Jack Black had it all planned out. They were going to duel! There was not a doubt in my mind which one was going to win that fight."

"Yes, that was the day that you came up with the idea! That one of us would have to marry Jacqueline. Why does it have to be me?"

Grandfather answered, "You're it, John. That's just the way things are."

"Dad, I have a son. How is this going to play out with him?"

"Jack is a big boy; I am sure he will understand. Besides, I have compensated him for his future," Grandfather replied.

"All this because of a business deal that went wrong. You are willing to alter our lives so that you can save face without any regard for *my* family?" Dad asked in anguish.

"You're going to go through with your so-called business deal!" Grandfather answered in an emphatical tone of voice. "YES!"

> *My father took me by my hand and sat me on his knee. I could see his eyes start to tear up. Tear droplets began to form on his eyes. His voice cracked in my ears as he spoke. "Son, I'm going to marry Jacqueline Bouvier. To bring peace to the family and to repay your grandfather's debt. I have to keep his deal, and someday you'll understand, JR. This marriage does not mean I will care for you and your mother any less. I will always love you both."*
>
> *Dad turned to my mother and said, "Do not worry; everything will be fine."*
>
> *Mother said, "How can we trust what is said here today? How will I know that my son will be safe when this is all over? John, can you assure me your father, mother, sisters and brothers, and their husbands and their wives are going to keep our son safe?"*
>
> *As I was looking around the room, I witnessed all of my aunts and uncles placing their right hands on the family Bible, swearing that if anything happens to me, they will use any means necessary to help me.*

My mother looked at my father and asked, "Are you sure this is what you want to do?"

"No, but this is what I have to do to keep peace in the family. I do not believe that they will betray us."

"If you trust in your sisters and brothers, I guess I have to as well."

# MEETING JACQUELINE FOR THE FIRST TIME

**IT WAS A BEAUTIFUL** spring day. I was with my grandparents on the Kennedy compound. I was coming down the stairs in the main house. My grandfather said, "Marilyn is here, your mother, JR."

I saw her pull up in the car. I watched her as she was getting out of the vehicle. She had on a sweater over a beige dress with light-colored shoes. She was walking as if she had something to say. Her head held high, chin even, and her shoulders back. My mother looked as if she was walking on a cloud. I could tell this was going to be a day of reckoning just by the way she was walking. It was her private side that was walking up the walkway.

My father had tried to get me to meet Jacqueline for about two months without success. My mother, being the peacemaker that she is, came to talk to me.

"Little Jack, I hear you are having an awkward time meeting with Jacqueline. Your father asked me to come and speak to you. Son, we cannot change what is going to happen; however, we can make it painless. This attitude you have taken is understandable but unacceptable. You are making yourself suffer."

"Yes, Mother, but I do not like her. I look at Jacqueline and do not see the same qualities I see in you. The sweetness when you look into my father's eyes, the feeling everything will turn out fine, your kindness, the tenderness that one feels when you enter a room. I feel as if we are going to lose all of that. You cannot ask me to sacrifice that. Just for something that my aunts, uncles, and grandparents want."

"Son, no one can take that away from us. That is who we are. Those feelings will be with you forever. I will always be your mother, the one you love."

The sound of my mother's voice let me know that I was in for a long chat. What was she going to talk to me about this time? She always said my father and I had what is called the father-son attitude. That was yes, Father, I hear you, and yes, I will do what you ask. But then turn around and do the opposite.

My Uncle Bobby would refer to bringing in the big guns when he was referring to my mother. She was the only one that could get me to change my attitude.

"Jack is never going to meet with Jacqueline or approve of her unless you ask his mother for help."

"Robert, I am working on it."

Mother was polite when she had to tackle any issue; she would sometimes call me Sugar, and this was one of those times.

"Sugar, sit down here with me. I hear you do not want to meet Jacqueline. She is not going to hurt you. All we are asking is for you to meet her. You will have to learn to tolerate her, that's all. There will always be someone here with you, so there's nothing to fear."

I could feel the pain I was causing mother that day. I could hear it in her voice and see it in her eyes. As I was looking into her eyes, I was thinking, How could I do this to my mother? She already knew my feelings. It was Grandpa Joe who could put an end to all this.

How do I reach my grandfather? It's not right to ask my father to trust this Jacqueline woman or to marry her. I wake up at night in a cold sweat. I can feel what is going to happen to us. I feel it right down to my very bones. Jacqueline is not a nice person. There is just something I do not like about her. I cannot tell you what it is.

"Mother, you cannot ask me to like her."

"I am not asking you to like Jacqueline. All you have to do is meet her."

"Oh! Next, you'll tell me I have to talk to her, too."

"No, just smile at her, that's all. That way, Jacqueline will not know your real feelings. I am going to stay with you to help you be that nice, polite boy that you are."

To hear my mother, Marilyn, tell it, she had to clean up the rough edges that all the Kennedy clan had. By the time Mother left, I was ready to meet with Jacqueline. The uneasy feeling that I was having had diminished, but it was not gone. Mother went back to New York. She let my dad know that the best he could hope for is that I understood what was going on, and I would do my best.

The day finally came to meet Jacqueline to give my approval and play nice. Am I welcoming Jacqueline into our family, or is she welcoming me into hers?

Here she was, this unassuming woman standing in front of me.

I did not let my mother down; I did what she asked of me. I walked up to Jacqueline and said, "Hello, it is a pleasure to meet you, and it would be our pleasure if you joined us for lunch."

She was unaware of what I was feeling. She began to speak, and I could hear this phony voice. She was trying to get my approval so that this business deal that Grandfather came up with did not fall through. I felt the room become more at ease once we were formally introduced.

My father was nice to Jacqueline, but his face did not light up like when my mother enters the room. It is just what Grandpa said it was—a marriage of business and nothing more. There were still feelings of uneasiness when I was around her. I felt as if my world was coming to an end.

We were having lunch. Jacqueline was sitting across from me. I did not utterly understand what was going on. My grandmother started discussing the wedding with my father. He said there would be a time and place for that.

Grandma Rose said, "This is a good time and place, John."

Dad looked at me, "JR, it is time for us to leave. You have met Jacqueline. It seems as if you are going to go along with the program, son."

I rose from the table, smiled, nodded my head, and said, "Goodbye."

As we were leaving the table, Jacqueline said, "What a well-mannered boy."

I tried that afternoon not to let anyone see just how upset I was. I still did not trust this woman; there was something that was not genuine about her. My father and I left the house and drove to get ice cream. As he was driving, he centered the conversation around the lunch meeting.

"Jr., now that you met with Jacqueline have you changed your view about her?"

"Well! Dad, is this something that you *have* to do or *want* to do?"

I could tell that my question was not easy for him to answer.

Son, there are just some things that you have to do. Marrying Jacqueline is one of them. I did not plan for this to happen; it just did. I am happy with you and your mother. It is hard for you to understand that. Your Uncle Joe was being groomed to become President of the United States, not me. All that is happening is I am the next in line to fulfill your grandpa's dream of having a son occupy the White House.

I could see that this was breaking my father's heart. I could see the sadness and the pain resonating from his face. The sorrow and uncertainty he was going through.

> *I could only imagine what he was thinking. How would all of this play out for the family that I already have? What will this do to my son and his mother?*

I sat quietly in the front seat of the car, thinking, How do I change these feelings that my father is having?

"Father! We could have had ice cream at home. Why did we come here?"

"Son, I did not want you to lose the taste of ice cream; that's why we left home."

"Dad, this had to be the longest ride I have ever had to get ice cream."

It seemed as if it was on the other side of the world.

It turned out to be a beautiful drive to the ice cream shop. Passing by the homes looking out onto the ocean. The grass bending ever so gently in the wind, blue skies just riding along the road with my dad. He finally decides on the farthest ice cream shop he could find. We had our ice cream; it was time for the ride back to my grandparents' home. On the way back home, dad filled me in on the family's next move.

"Jack, your mother, is coming to see you next week. She is going to ask how you liked meeting Jacqueline for the first time. I would like you to tell your mother about any misgiving you may or may not have. If you have any reservations, let her know. This marriage is something that I have to do to keep peace in our family. I will take care of you and your mother, as I always have. Your aunts and uncles will make sure that you and your mother will be fine. With that said, I hope that you will understand that I care and love you both."

When we arrived home, Jacqueline was no longer there. My grandfather was upset before we could even get our feet in the door.

He asked my father, "Why did you leave so abruptly? You are lucky; I stay to have lunch!"

"Mr. Ambassador, you do not seem to understand what you are asking me to do! Jack is my son; I am his father. I must care for him. You are asking me to put all my trust in this family and **damn** the consequences. I have to consider my wife's and son's welfare and feelings! I suppose you think this is a walk in the park for them as well. If this all goes awry, who will suffer the consequences? You? No, it will be me, my wife, and my son who will!" Dad shouted.

"Marilyn is right; there are no guarantees that any one of you will hold up your end of this bargain. We are playing with Jack's life here, Mr. Ambassador! When the time comes for me to marry this woman, keep in mind that this is a *deal*. This is what I am doing to get you where *you* want to go," Dad reminded him.

All this time, I was doing what I do best. Taking it all in and going over it in my mind to see how it plays out.

The only time my father called my grandpa, "Mr. Ambassador," was when he was upset. My dad once told me that Grandpa didn't like it when he called him Mr. Ambassador. I could see in my

23

father's face that he did not want to marry Jacqueline. It was as if his world was crashing down around him.

My father took me home and got me ready for bed. This was one long day. The only thing I knew was that my life as I knew it was going to change. My father was having trust issues. Was his family going to keep their word? How were they going to keep me safe?

# OUR FAMILY TIME

**BEFORE LEAVING FOR WASHINGTON,** D.C., my father arranged for me to meet him in New York City. Manhattan was our home away from home. It was there that my parents and I would go to become our own family. The good times we would have there. The walks in the park, dancing, and being a family.

My parents had two adjacent apartments in Manhattan. I did not understand at the time what was going on or why. For me, this was the norm. My father would come in one building, and my mother and I through the other. Just to see my father's face light up when he was with my mother and me is well worth the inconvenience. To see him hugging her and kissing her made me feel as if we were home. The love that they had for one another was something that could not be denied. You see, my father made us feel safe and secure. While in Manhattan, my mother always planned out our week. My father's job was to make sure that all would go according to her plan.

The day I arrived in Manhattan, the sun was shining, but it was still chilly out. I was taken to the apartment on the upper east side. I was the first one to arrive. Like always, there was someone there to walk me to the door and make sure that I was safe. The anticipation to see my parents was a feeling of total joy. My mother had always planned something special. To hear my father say, All days were exceptional when we were together.

It is hard for me to let go and share this story with anyone. I feel as if I am going to lose this part of my life. It is as if society will take my memories from me too. Mother would sometimes say, "Culture can be cruel."

When my mother came to Manhattan, she never looked the same. It was as if she was a new person. I knew it was her by the different walks that she had. The way she would walk let me know how she was feeling and what she was going to do. On this day, mother had her *I'm not in a hurry* walk. She was walking on a cloud, and she had all the time in the world. I could see that there was no business on her mind, just being a mother and a wife was all. My parents and I were together.

We spent the day in Central Park. This man was following us and taking pictures of us, as so often happened. My father was getting annoyed with him. He walked up to the man and asked him to stop taking pictures of us, but he just kept it up. Mother walked up to the man and said something to him in that sweet and girlish voice of hers. The voice that makes most men never say no to her. By the time she finished talking to him, he had handed her a roll of film. She came back and gave it to my dad, and he put it in his pocket.

"Darling, what did you say to him that made him give you the film?"

"Sometimes, you have to be a little more diplomatic about things, love."

The day ended on an upbeat. However, there was always something or someone who bothered us.

The next day, my mother decided we would go shopping on 5th Avenue. We were coming out of Saks Five Avenue Department Store. This tall and very distinguished-looking man walked up to my father and asked, "Mr. Senator, how is your little brother Teddy?"

Dad's facial expression changed; his jawbone became more defined and sterner. He was biting down on his teeth to control his temper.

"Ask my mother. I am sure she will let you know how my little brother is! At this particular time, I am with my wife and son, as you can see."

After the man left, Mother turned to my father and asked, "Why is it every time you see this guy you get upset?"

"Someday, I'll let you in on it, but this is not the day."

I had noticed that same stern look on my dad's face many times before. It meant there was going to be cane to pay. I knew that he was going to tell my grandmother something. This was not the first time Mr. Moore has upset my dad. He goes out of his way to agitate my father and me!

Despite the annoying intrusion, the weekend turned out to be a beautiful family vacation. It reminded me of my grandparents' place in Hyannis Port. That was where I stayed when I was not with my parents.

# THE WEDDING DAY

**WHEN I RETURNED TO** my grandparents' home, they were preparing for the wedding.

Grandfather Joseph asks, "Did your father inform you of how to address Jacqueline?"

"No, sir, he did not."

"What exactly did your father tell you?"

"He said when he comes back, we will talk. That is… when he returns back home from Washington, D.C., to let me know about the wedding. He will explain to me then how I am to address Jacqueline Bouvier, and what changes this woman is going to make in my life."

"Little Jack, you know better than that! You mean 'lady,' not 'this woman.'"

My grandfather only called me Little Jack when I was a hard head like my father.

The day finally arrived for the revelations I was waiting for, and dad sat me down to tell me what was expected of me.

"Son, Jacqueline and I are going to have an arranged marriage. That means that this is a business deal between two adults. Not that I'll care or love you and your mother, Marilyn less. Just that this is something I have to do to keep us together. Your grandfather made too many enemies over his lifetime. This is one of those times when the son has to pay for the sins of the father."

"Dad, what does this have to do with me?"

"Son, Jacqueline is going to become your stepmother. On some occasions, you'll have to call her 'Stepmother.' She is not going to take the place of your mother. However, this is going to change your life. That does not mean you have to call her 'Stepmother' all the time. You can refer to her as Jacqueline."

My father rose to his feet and walked into the next room. I heard him say in a grave voice to Grandpa Joe, "Sometimes, a man's life is not his own."

As the wedding day drew closer, the more apprehensive my father became. I would see his eyes well up, turning red. He would pick me up and whisper in my ear, "Please forgive me, my son, forgive me."

I could feel the beat of his heart, the trembling of his hands and arms. As he would whisper, "Son, I love you. Forgive me, forgive me," tears began to run down his face.

As he softly repeated, "Forgive me, son," I could see the sadness come over my father. It was as if his world was coming to an end.

"Dad, I am always going to forgive you. I know that you love my mother and me."

This man, who was my father, started to cry. It was not him, not the one that Mother called her rock.

I asked my father, "If you do not want to marry Jacqueline, why even entertain the idea?"

"Son, there are things in your life that you cannot control. This is one of those things. I just want you to remember that I do not wish to hurt you or your mother. It's your bedtime, so go upstairs, wash your face, and brush your teeth. I will be in later to tuck you in."

When my father came into my bedroom to tuck me in, he would always walk softly as if he did not want me to hear him come in. I could see the moonlight shining through the window. I was in-between awake and asleep. He would sit on my bed, whisper in my ear, and kiss me on my right cheek goodnight. My father made me feel that today is a good day, but tomorrow would be better.

On the day that Jacqueline became my stepmother, my father looked as if he had done something wrong. I could see that he was changed before my very eyes. His cheerful, greeting smile was no longer there on his face as he welcomed most of the guests. He shook their hands and nodded his head up and down to greet them, never uttering a word. My father was definitely not his usual self on this day. As the afternoon wore on, his attitude worsened.

By the end of the afternoon, my father took me by the hand. We walked into my grandpa's study, where he was waiting for him.

"Why is Jack accompanying you?" Grandpa demanded to know.

"Dad, he has every right to be in this study with us. This is all our lives you are asking me to alter. I want him to remember what went on in this room on this day. I do not understand how you want me to marry Jacqueline. But it's done! So, I am here. What is it you have to say?" my father replied.

He continued, "This wedding was not supposed to be this vast spectacle. You and my mother turned this wedding into this thing that it's not. How do you expect me to explain this spectacle to my wife, Marilyn? Just what should I say to her?"

All I could see was my father sitting there with his face in his hands, asking my grandfather, "How am I going to explain this? Just tell Marilyn this is the wedding that she and you did not invite us to, John."

I saw and felt the sadness on my father's face as we took a few steps away from my grandfather. I could see that lost look on his face as if he was losing all control of his life. Just what did all of this have to do with me? Why did he want me to hear all of this? To be a witness to what? I have never heard my father speak this way before.

"Dad, why did you want me to listen to this conversation? I do not understand what you want me to be a witness of."

"Son, you do not understand now, but someday you will. All I am asking of you is to remember this day. God forbid the day that you have to recall this day! Junior, it is time for bed. Brush your teeth, wash your face, and get ready for bed. I'll be upstairs to tuck you in and say our prayers."

I did what I was told. I tried not to doze off, waiting for Dad, but he took too long to arrive, so I fell asleep.

I thought I could hear his voice whispering in my ear, "I'll call you while I am on vacation."

I must have been dreaming. My eyes opened, and I caught a glimpse of dad, closing the bedroom door.

The next morning, I was up before the rooster crowed as Grandfather would always describe me. He was an early riser as well. Grandpa had his morning routine, reading the newspaper, and I usually sat and watched the sunrise. He said it was better to be well-prepared for the opening of the stock market instead of being caught by the seat of one's pants. Grandmother did the same mundane things every morning, like planning functions or shopping.

Grandpa Joe was a man who liked order. You did not just walk into his study unannounced. My father liked to say that my grandfather was in no man's land when he was in his studies. There were rules that everyone must follow, and you always had to make it known in advance that you wanted to speak to Grandfather before entering. It was hard for me to comply with this one rule that was strictly enforced. I was the only one who was able to enter into the study with him, but once 9 am rolled around, I had enough sense to leave, unlike my cousins who faced Grandpa's wrath.

My grandfather spent most of his time in his study, discussing with others how they were going to turn a diamond in the rough into the First Lady of the United States. It was some time before I understood what he meant by diamond in the rough; he was referring to Jacqueline Bouvier. How does a diamond in the rough become the First Lady?

# THE ROUGH DIAMOND
# RETURNS HOME

**WHEN MY FATHER RETURNED,** he was told that I had to become acquainted with my stepmother. My parents decided that I should call my father's new wife, Jacqueline.

He said that there would be no disputing who was who. Jacqueline was someone I must respect and be courteous to.

Like all kids, I came up with my own name for her. It was one sunny day. I'll never forget.

> *My parents and I were driving down a country road in a '57 T-Bird with the top down. My father was to the left of me, my mother to the right, and me in the middle. They were both wearing sunglasses as Dad drove down the highway. I could see the sunlight dancing off their hair. The wind was blowing my mother's hair out from under her scarf. There were cornfields on each side of the two-lane highway, and there we were, going about 60 miles an hour. Just us, without a care in the world.*
>
> *As I was sitting there, I could see where the corn met the sky. It was as if someone had taken a*

*picture and joined the sky, corn, and the road and us together. The car started to slow; we were coming to a fork in the roadway, and then we came to a full stop. As he began to speed up again, I looked over.*

*There was this thing hanging in the field, and I screamed, "Stop!"*

*I startled my parents. "What is it, Junior? What is it?"*

*"Stop–go back. I want to see what that thing is hanging in the field."*

*My father backed up the car and stopped.*

*I asked my parents, "What is that? Dad, what is that? That!"*

*We got out of the car to see this thing hanging on a stick.*

*I could see it was a doll the size of a person hanging there. It had cold, dark eyes; hair all mangled. Looking as if it needed a good night's sleep.*

*"What is it?"*

*My father said, "It is called a scarecrow."*

*"No," I replied. "It looks like Jacqueline when she gets out of bed in the morning." My parents laughed.*

*I said, "No, it's true. That is precisely the way she looks."*

*Mother educated me by saying, "Son, it's okay to think that, but it's not okay to say it. So never call her a scarecrow, please."*

*My father said it was time for us to get on our way. As we turned to walk back to the car, he took my mother's and my hands. I was on the left of him, my mother on the right. There it was again; that picture of the road meeting the blue sky and corn rising to meet it. All became one before my eyes. That feeling that my mother, father, and I were one. One of those days that would stay attached in my memory. When a boy becomes who he is with his mom and dad is when life becomes real.*

# JACQUELINE BECOMING FRIEND OR FOE

**MY STEPMOTHER AND MY** relationship started out polite enough. I did not know exactly how I was to treat her. There was nothing complex about her. She rarely had anything interesting to say or add to a conversation. The only thing my grandmother would say is that this woman would take some work. I didn't understand what my grandmother meant by that. Except that Jacqueline was not the person she made herself out to be. I guess what my grandmother was saying is my grandfather did not do his homework when it came to Jacqueline.

Jacqueline was a late riser, which annoyed my grandfather tremendously. My dad didn't seem to care what time of day Jacqueline was around. Grandfather, on the other hand, was upset continuously with my grandmother because Jacqueline was the last one to rise in the household. Grandpa wanted every family member at the breakfast table at the same time. He said it made for a pleasant family unity leading to a more productive day. At breakfast, Grandfather quarreled with my grandmother about how she was going to fix the problem. He became so bothered with Jacqueline's late rising, that he asked me, "What makes you rise so early in the morning?" I did not quite understand his concern.

"Grandpa, there is always something new to see, hear, and learn, and I want to see it all and learn what I can. I'm also afraid that I will miss something, but what I cannot tell you, Grandfather."

Right in the middle of breakfast, Grandpa said, "I have had enough of this, Rose. You have to do something about Jacqueline's sleeping habits."

My father laughed and said, "You mean her laziness. That is a job in itself!"

My grandfather had these rules: anyone not up by 6:30 in the morning could not accomplish anything throughout the day. He made it clear that Jacqueline was to be out of bed by 7 AM every day, including Sunday. This is where my stepmother and I started to have our differences.

The next morning, Jacqueline, my grandmother, and I were having a late lunch or, as Jacqueline would call it, brunch. Grandmother told Jacqueline that she did not understand how a small child like Jack could get out of bed at 6 AM and why she slept the morning away.

"Jacqueline, you have an obligation to the Kennedy family to start getting up at 7 AM. You are not keeping up with your part of the arrangement. Your sleeping late will no longer be tolerated in this household or any other. You are not here for your charm or your intellect; you are here to help us accomplish our goal for which you have been well-paid."

Jacqueline glared over at me and then back at my grandmother and replied, "Whatever does Jack have to do with me getting up early?"

The tone of her voice changed. I could see she was upset, but why with me? The tension at the table that afternoon was different. I could feel my stepmother was not pleased with me for what my grandmother had just explained to her. How was this conversation going to affect me? As Jacqueline was speaking to my grandma, she was looking in my direction. Why me? Her whole demeanor had changed.

I calmly requested, "May I be excused from the table?" before the conversation ended. As I walked away, I overheard Jacqueline say that there were too many rules in this house. I recall thinking the same thing. Wait until she figures out that not everyone has to play by them.

My mother would always say, when it comes to the Kennedy house, you play by the rules when they are looking at you. However, you do what you want when you are alone.

> *"Son, that does not mean there will be no repercussions. All I am saying is think before acting. Father, on the other hand, does not want you to get caught when you have broken the rules. You will not be scolded for the rules that you break. It is the blunder that you make breaking the rules that you are reprimanded for."*

From that day on, my stepmother's attitude towards me changed. We had this sort of love-hate relationship. Some mornings when we woke up, we would argue and fight. Mother always said that I should be careful because someday we may have to pay for this.

"Your stepmother is too vindictive. She is the kind of person that will bite off her nose to spite her face. Son, it is wiser for you to be polite and kind than salty. That does not mean that you do everything she asks you to. All I'm saying is to be careful. Your father always tried to get along with your stepmother. It doesn't work all the time; at best, the situation does not escalate at least. Learn from him."

I always tried to do what my parents asked of me. On this one particular morning, my stepmother and I both woke up irritated. Her in one part of the house and me in the other, trying to avoid any interaction. We had managed to maintain our distance the entire morning. By the afternoon, the stalemate had ended, we exchanged words, and it seemed I got the better of her. She grabbed me and backhanded me right across my face. Each time she struck me, I caught her forefingers in between my teeth. She kept slapping me, and the more she hit, the longer I bit down on her fingers.

There was blood coming out of her fingers, but I would not let go. I remember thinking, *I'm going to teach her who she can hit and who she can't.*

She began to scream, "Rose!" and the housekeeper ran into the room!

Grandmother Rose Kennedy started screaming, "Stop you two. Stop!"

I would not let go, and Jacqueline started screaming louder and louder to let go, let go. I still did not let go; I was biting down on her fingers as hard as I could. I wanted her to remember to keep her hands to herself.

The housekeeper screamed, "Stop, Jack, stop," as she pinched my nose in the hope that I would let go.

I knew I would have to take a breath sometime, so I decided it was time to let go. The housekeeper and Grandmother were still in a state of panic.

They simultaneously said, "Do you know what Jack Sr. is going to do to you? Do you have any idea, Jacqueline? You have just broken one of his Cardinal rules!"

"You do not put your hands on his son," Grandmother raised her voice at Jacqueline. "When you have to explain what happened, stay clear of Jack Senior, and hope for the best! I would like to know just what the hell you were thinking. Jackie, I hope you learned when you do something to Little Jack, he is going to make you pay triple. Go! Attend to your fingers; they are bleeding. Thank God Junior has rosy red cheeks. The redness will be gone by the time his father gets here. He'll never know the difference. But Jackie, never put your hands on him again!"

Later that afternoon, my grandmother called my father to inform him of what had happened. I heard one side of the conversation.

"Your son is raising hell. I want you to do something about his attitude. I am not going to tolerate this type of behavior. I had enough refereeing my own children. I'm not going to referee my grandchildren. Have I made myself clear?"

I snuck away as not to upset her more. I did not want her to know that I had overheard her conversation with my father.

The moment my grandmother hung up the phone, she sent for me. When the housekeeper finally found me, I was outside on the beach.

"I have been looking all over for you. You know you're not supposed to come out here alone. Your grandmother wants to see you."

I walked back up to the house. There she was, standing on the porch waiting for me.

"What is it you want, Grandmother?"

"I just got off the phone with your father. He said he would be here this weekend."

About three hours later, my mother called me. "Sugar, are you okay?"

"Yes."

"Jack, I want to know all the details on what had transpired this afternoon."

This is my mother being firm. She was not going to ask the same question twice. I explained what went on between Jackie and me.

Mother, being the peacemaker that she is, said that I should try to understand Jackie and not quarrel with her.

"Sugar, it's not healthy for you to lose your temper. You have to keep in mind what the doctors told you. Try to stay calm. However, I am happy to know that you are fine. Have you spoken to your father today?"

"No, I have not! My grandmother let me know he'll be coming to see me this weekend."

When my mother called me Sugar, I always felt special. It was the sweetness and the kindness that was coming out of her spirit; it came right from her soul. She made me feel as if I was the most important person in her life. It always made me stop in my tracks and listen to what she had to say. My whole world would stop just to hear my mother call me Sugar. It took the sting out of Jacqueline brutalizing me.

I saw Jacqueline later that evening. Her hand was bandaged; she looked as if she was still in pain. I did not feel sorry for what happened, and I felt the feeling was mutual.

# SETTING THE RULES

**FATHER WOULD EITHER ARRIVE** at my grandparents' house late Friday night or early Saturday morning. I don't know when he came home. When I made my entrance downstairs the next morning, my grandfather was having his first cup of coffee in the living room. He shared with me his good morning, but not much else.

"It is understandable that you are upset with me. I have disappointed you, Grandpa."

I knew that I would have to be responsible for my actions.

"Grandfather, I'll try to refrain myself next time someone irritates me."

"Jack, what are the odds you're going to keep your temper under wraps? Your father is going to have to deal with your anger issues."

Saturday morning breakfast was solemn. The one negative comment was when dad laid out his morning itinerary. There was only one item on it that he would be taking me for my morning exercise.

After breakfast, Dad and I went for a stroll along the beach.

"Son, there are always two sides to a story. I want to know why you bit Jacqueline. It's not like you to harm someone."

"Dad, it just happened."

"Son, this type of behavior doesn't just happen. You not telling the truth is not helping the matter."

I really did not know how to explain what took place. Dad somehow sensed that I was lost for an answer and told me to take my time and think about what exactly happened.

We walked a little further, and he said, "Son, I am waiting for an answer."

"Dad, I was doing what I usually do, but that day I was feeling irritable. I was going up the stairs, and Jacqueline was coming out of her bedroom. I could see she was not in a particularly good mood, so I tried to get out of her way. Jacqueline ran into me deliberately. She did not say, 'Excuse me' or 'sorry.' So I got upset, and I kicked her in the shin. She grabbed me and started to slap me. So, as she was hitting me, her fingers came across my face, and I bit down on them as hard as I could and would not let go. Of course, I did not like being slapped. I just couldn't let her get away with it."

I looked up at my father. "I am not going to say I'm sorry. I feel as if we were both at fault."

"Junior, I am not looking for whose fault it was. I am trying to find out what happened. I am going to talk to Jacqueline to see what happened and to stop this from happening again."

That evening after dinner, my father called Jacqueline and me into the living room to hear both versions of the day's event. Jacqueline had said that I was disrespectful and did not say, "Excuse me."

My father turned to me and said, "Junior, don't say a word."

He turned to Jacqueline. "Okay, you say he was disrespectful as you describe it to me. Why did you have to hit him? Did you run into Jack as he claimed at the top of the stairs?"

"I may have bumped into him, but that was all."

"Did you say, 'Excuse me' or 'I'm sorry?'"

"No! He is a child."

"Yes! Jack is my child, and I want him to grow up to be courteous and respectful of his elders. That's how you end up with adults who respect one another.

"I do not want this to escalate into an argument. Jacqueline, you should have said 'excuse me,' 'I beg your pardon,' or 'sorry.' That way, we could have avoided all this disruption. I hope you understand you are not to put your hands on my son again. I do not care what he has done. Do I make myself clear?"

"John, Jack doesn't look like he's suffering. *He* was biting *me*. Just look at the way my fingers look. They are still hurting and throbbing; he would not let go."

"You put your hands on him. Jacqueline, I do not think you quite understand what you did. Jack is not the kind of child that will forget this. He will find a way to get back at you. He will tell you not to do something once, maybe twice, but there will not be a third time. If you choose not to listen to my advice, the consequence will be on you."

As my father was speaking to both of us, Jacqueline was becoming upset. I was beginning to see a side of her that I did not know she had.

"Junior, you are going to have to find a way to control your temper. You have to consider the consequences of your actions. I am not going to punish you this time, but if there is a next time, you will be scolded."

Just as my father was saying that I could see Jacqueline turning red. She was upset to no end.

"Are you going to let him get away with biting me? You and your damn son are not going to treat me this way!"

She was irate and out of control. She threw herself on the floor and started rolling around and pulling her hair out. My father and I were stunned; we did not know what to do! It looked as if she was going into a convulsion. There were globs of Jacqueline's hair all over the place. It took her ten minutes to finally calm down. My father was still in a state of shock and did not continue the conversation.

"Jacqueline, we will have to continue this conversation in the morning. I'll not have you hitting my son. Marilyn and I never hit Jack; that was not our kind of parenting, and it will not be yours and mine."

The next morning, my father, Jacqueline, and I were having breakfast. My father began laying out the rules on what he expected from my stepmother.

"I do not expect that you will hit my child again. Jacqueline, if you put your hands on him again, he'll do anything he can to defend himself. He will not stand idly by and let you hit him."

"Yes, but I am your wife, let us not forget that."

"That does not give you the right to hit my child or any child for that matter! If Jack needs mothering, nurturing, and discipline, he has his mother, Marilyn and me, do you understand me?"

# FATHER AND SON TRIP

**LATER ON THAT DAY,** my father made plans to take me on a trip. The trip had something to do with how people lived. I did not understand what he meant by that. This trip was to be an eye-opener and a learning experience for me.

"Son, there is a whole world out there that you know nothing about. The only way for you to appreciate anything you work for or are given is to take this trip. I want you to experience what life is truly about."

I could not help thinking, *This is not going to be a trip of pleasure.* This trip is going to be a question-and-answer experience. Why didn't my father just become a teacher and not a senator? That would make things a lot easier.

I would be ready. Just knowing this trip was going to be an educational experiment was too much for one son to handle. Why does my dad have to do this to me? I guess this is his way of teaching me. But why! Why doesn't he just tell me where we are going and what he expects me to learn?

My father called my mother to let her know that we would be gone for two to three weeks, depending on how the weather holds up, and if I get sick or not. I still did not know where we were going. The only sign that we were going on a trip was our luggage placed on top of the vehicle. It had been tied down so that it would not fall off the top of the car. I have seen other people with their luggage on top of the vehicle, this was the first time for us.

As I was getting into the car, I noticed that there was enough room for more people. The car, to my surprise, was a station wagon. There were maps on the front seat and a picnic basket in the back. As we were driving off, my father began to explain that we were going on a road trip. "Son, I wanted you to see the country from a new perspective. It is not the road behind us but the road ahead of us. What you are willing to do for others and not expect anything in return.

"Attending church on Sunday is not enough; you have to meet the people that you are trying to help. When you are putting out money, you have to find out where it's going. You have to participate and make sure that we care for one another. I do not mean that you just care about your family, but others as well. These are people who struggle every day doing the best that they can. It seems as if they are standing stagnant in poverty, and no one cares. Sometimes it is the very people we deal with that do not let you prosper. It has nothing to do with where you come from but everything to do with what you are willing to do for others, without the expectations of being compensated for your efforts!"

I sat listening inattentively as we were going down the highway. I could feel the wind rolling through my hair, the warm breeze across my face as the sun was hitting it. I felt as if my father and I were becoming one with the universe. It was a feeling of one becoming one with nature.

In an instant, my father looked over at me, his son. "Are you listening to what I am saying?"

In a soft voice, I said, "Yes, I am listening to you. Would you like me to report back to you what you just said?"

"No."

I was listening to what my dad was saying, also hearing what nature had to say as well. It is not that I was tuned out. I guess I was tuned in to all of my surroundings. It is how I process information. Here's my father, here am I, we are together as father and son in nature.

By this time, we had already driven through the New England states. The night was falling. My father pulled into a hotel parking lot and checked us into a hotel. It was a small hotel with dinner. We had a shower and changed for dinner.

After dinner, my father read me the newspaper. That was one of his rules. Either he would read me the paper, or I read it myself. The world was our neighborhood, and the newspaper helped us stay in touch with them.

"Reading a neighborhood newspaper helps me to make the right decisions in the Senate. Reading a big city newspaper enables us to keep in touch with the world. Knowing what's going on when we travel allows people to understand we are concerned about their everyday problems."

He finished reading the newspaper and said, "It's time for bed." He laid out my pajamas on the bed for me. Once I was in bed, he whispered in my ear. "Son, think good thoughts, and have pleasant dreams. Tomorrow is going to be a learning experience."

We were up at about 5 am the next morning. To watch the sunrise over the trees was a magnificent sight. To see the rainbow of colors bursting through the trees as if this sight were just for us. Here we were, my father and I, witnessing the start of the day. I often asked my dad if God created this day and experience just for us. "Son, we share in this world, and it is designed for all mankind, not just us."

As we were driving away, I turned to look back at the beautiful colors that were coming through the trees; the reds, blues, yellows, and oranges.

"Jack, we are going to travel through the south of the country. We are going to drive straight through Washington D.C. on to West Virginia and down to Florida. You are going to see things you have never seen before. We are going to learn how we can become better citizens in this great country of ours. I want you to learn how to better serve your community. If there is one thing that I have mastered in the Navy is that our country is one community.

"The people that you are going to meet are not as fortunate as we are. We should make sure that all our citizens are treated equally. You and I are going to find out just what is needed to help every citizen succeed. We are in the land of plenty, but not everyone has everything."

We drove through Washington, D.C., on our way to the South. The driver turned off the main highway and let my father drive on another hour. From the road, you could see kids playing in the front yards of their homes. He would stop and get out of the car to talk to anyone willing to speak to him.

I recall two people sitting on their front porch looking at us as if we did not belong there. I watched as we walked by, someone said to my father, "What is a Yankee like you doing here?"

"I want my son to learn what America is all about. We cannot become better people without knowing who we are as a nation." The look on the gentleman's face changed. It seemed to become more relaxed.

"We do not have many of your kind passing through here."

"What kind are you referring to?"

"This place is a place that people try to get away from."

"I am here for my son and my job. To learn just what is needed to make a small town like this a place to return to.

"What do you mean when you say you're supposed to? May I call you, Sir?"

"Yes, that is how it's done around here."

"I am a Senator from Massachusetts; my name is John F. Kennedy. And I plan to run for president of the United States. I would like to know what I can do to help all the citizens of our country. I am traveling with my son John Junior so that he'll know what we're working for."

I could see the man that my father was conversing with was quite impressed.

He said to my father, "You look like a young man who cares for his family and his son, and fellow human beings. You do not speak like the typical politician, nor do you strike me as one. Most politicians think we are too far out of the way to visit us. But here you are sitting with your son taking the time to explain to me what your future plans are for the nation. If that is not the end-all to be all. You do seem genuine."

My father thanked the man for giving him his undivided attention.

It was time for us to move on. We drove for another three hours. My father asked me what I had learned.

Thinking about it, I explained, "Some people who worked hard all their life have little to show for it. Dad, the man's hands were rough and callous. His face was as if he worked in the sun all day. He had blonde hair, blue eyes, and spoke with a deep voice. As if he was tired of the wheels of life just spinning around and never getting ahead."

"Son, I believe today you learned a valuable lesson. Everyone, regardless of where they come from or where they live, should be given a chance to better their lives. I am not saying that the man we talked to this afternoon does not like his life, but I am sure he would like more time to spend with his family. It is not easy to work from sun-up to sunset. Not only is it not easy, but everyone should be able to enjoy the fruits of their labor." I would not know exactly what my father was saying until he drove further into the South.

My father would drive from sun-up to sunset. There was a lesson in this, and I am sure I was going to find out what it was. My father started looking for a hotel when the sun began to set.

"Son, are you tired?"

"Yes, I am."

"Are you tired of sitting in this car? Just think about the gentleman we met this afternoon. He's tired of working physically in the fields. There are different types of exhaustion. One is what you are feeling now; the other is what the gentleman was feeling this afternoon. Keep in mind that he doesn't stop working until the sun goes down."

The next morning at breakfast, dad prepared me for the day's events.

"In this country, there is something called segregation! This is something you have not experienced. Here in the southern states, it is more prevalent. You'll know it when you see it. It is the separation of people according to the color of their skin.

"Segregation is the result of a difference of opinions and attitudes. Discrimination is what narrow-minded people use to enrich their lives. From my point of view, segregation replaced slavery.

In this case, segregation is used to demean one class of people. It affects every aspect of their life. Here in the South, it is used across the board. Segregation affects wages, where you live, who you work for, and what type of job you can do.

"From my point, factory owners use it to pay lower wages to a man of color. This type of segregation causes a financial burden on the African American community. There is segregation when you cannot choose what water fountain you can drink out of and what public restroom you can use. All I am asking is that the African American community should be able to benefit from the taxes that they pay. There are some places throughout the South where people have to pay to vote. The real word for segregation should be 'discrimination.' It is something that is deeply embedded in the Deep South. I want you to witness this firsthand so that you do not partake in this indifference."

I was able to experience the meaning of segregation firsthand.

We came to a stop at a filling station. I asked the man pumping the gas if I could use the facilities, and he said, "Yes, but use the one for whites only." Then came the drinking fountain; "It's for whites only." I wanted to ask, Where does everybody else drink or go to the restroom if they are of color? Yes, there is a place, just not this place. I felt as if I was out of place. Everyone I ran into called me a boy. Father explained, "This is just the way people here in the South speak."

He explained something else to me. "Son, you do not like for strangers to touch you or shake hands. What you need to learn is when you meet a stranger, always tip your hat, not your head. That is another way to acknowledge someone. Greet everyone with the same facial expression. People who meet you for the first and second time will know that is who you are and not who you pretend to be."

My father called my mother just before we arrived in West Palm Beach.

"We are going to meet your mother here and then go to Miami Beach for a week. I want to know about what you learned on this trip and how you feel about what you have learned."

# MEETING MY MOTHER MARILYN IN WEST PALM BEACH

**WHEN MY FATHER AND** I arrived in West Palm Beach, it was late in the afternoon. We were exhausted, but with the anticipation of my mother coming to make things better, it was okay.

"Dad, why does my mother need to meet us here in West Palm Beach when she can land in Miami?"

"Son, let's unload the car, shower, and have dinner. I'll answer your question then." There were only two suitcases and some empty Pepsi bottles and discarded trash in the car.

"Dad, I really enjoyed this time together. I hope we do it again. I learned a lot; It is unacceptable to see what we do to one another for money."

We finished unloading the car and went inside. While we were having dinner, I asked my father again why my mother couldn't meet us in Miami.

"Son, it just makes things easy for your mother and me. We do not want the press to bother us. It makes a better experience for all of us. The fewer questions we have to answer, the more privacy we have."

"Dad, the press only bothers you if you let them."

"They have their place, and I have mine. You create boundaries between you and the news. If you don't, then you lose your privacy, and that is what I don't want to happen to us."

"Dad, may I be excused? I am tired, and I want to go to sleep."

"Yes, you may. I will be in later to say goodnight."

I got up from the table and went upstairs and got into bed. A short time later, my father came in to say goodnight. I had already fallen fast asleep when my father came in to say goodnight.

He pulled the covers up over me and whispered in my ear, "Son, you learned a lot on this trip. I hope that you take it with you throughout your life."

The next morning, we met my mother. To be reunited with both of my parents felt as if I were stepping into a movie. I never knew what to expect.

There she was, the lady I called mother and the rest of the world called Marilyn Monroe. I could never understand what the hoopla was all about.

I knew that she was famous and the people loved her. But the love that my father had for my mother was immense. She would sparkle as she was walking towards us, her shoes looking as if they never touched the ground. That sparkle was something my mother did just for the two of us. It was her way of making us feel that we are one family unit. No grandmother, grandfather, aunts, or uncles around to interfere. The three of us always had a group hug. My mother would pick me up, kiss me, and call me Sugar while all the time asking us how we were.

"You'll have to tell me about your trip. What did you think of it and what did you learn on your adventure? Jack, was your trip useful?"

"Yes it was, but more on that later. We need to get checked into a hotel. I had the reservations made for us already," Father answered for me.

We drove to Miami Beach. We checked into the same hotel that we always stay at. It was located on Collins Ave. Our room was located on the east side of the hotel that overlooked the ocean. It was our own oasis.

My mother did some shopping on Lincoln Road. When my mother shopped, my father always carried the bags. I noticed how people would look at them and tell them what a lovely couple they make. We were a typical family enjoying our vacation.

All my mother had to do was put on a scarf and dark sunglasses, and she would fit in. She still had the appearance of being someone special.

Most of the time, when people would see us together, they would stop us and say to my mother, "I know you from somewhere."

She would answer, "I'd like you to meet my son Jack."

That took care of the question.

Then my dad would say, "My wife is a mystery to me too. I sometimes have to ask myself, who is she going to be today?"

Dad took care of the same question when people asked him in another way.

"Yes, in the war, maybe that is where you know me from." I never heard him mention to anyone that he was a war hero. He would say, "I was in the Navy and lucky to have made it home, but how about the soldiers that made the ultimate sacrifice. They are the true heroes of the Second World War."

We did what most families did in Miami Beach. During the day, we would lie by the pool or on the sandy beach. Like all kids, I enjoyed it when my parents would run after me in the water, running back and forth from the waves of the ocean. To look down and see our footprints in the sand and watch the sea, and the water wash them away. This is a child's dream: to spend time with their parents. It made me feel as if I was the only one who had parents who cared for me and loved me.

By the end of the week, my father said it was time to return back to my grandparents. What kind of chaos would I find when we returned? Would my stepmother be upset, or would she even care? Jacqueline did not make it easy to transition between her and my parents. My mother said that Jacqueline was misunderstood. Dad had this nonchalant attitude when it came to Jacqueline…as if he didn't care if she comes or goes.

When it came time to leave, my parents would ask me the same question: whom would you like to travel with? By this time, I was becoming annoyed with having to choose between them. I understood why we had to take different flights, but I did not like it. My mother would land at LaGuardia airport, and my father at New York International Airport.

"Why is it when we travel here in the United States, we take different flights? When we vacation in Europe or Mexico, we go together on the same plane. This is our country; we live here. I am sure people will understand that you and my mother love each other. If the Americans forgave Clark Gable and Carole Lombard, they'd forgive you. I think Grandpa Joe is wrong in asking you to sacrifice our family for what he wants. For you, it is a business deal, but for me, it is my life."

My mother asked, "Son, do we have to do this now?"

"Mother, if we don't have this discussion now, then you tell me when. When would it be an appropriate time? You and my father are always busy."

I did not want to spoil the time that we had together.

"I am sorry, but I do not trust my aunts and uncles."

I did not believe that they care for me the way my dad thinks they do. My dad trusts them, but I do not; this is about trust.

"I am sure someday you will ask me who I want to go with. You are going to make me choose between the two of you. I know that neither one of you wants this, but that is what's going to happen. Unless you put a stop to what you are doing now!"

"Grandfather Joe, Grandmother Rose, and your aunts and uncles are asking you to trust them."

"If they were any kind of father, mother, sister, or brother, they would not ask you to do this to your family. Their one goal is to destroy us."

My father looked at me and said, "Jack, I am not going to let them destroy us the way you believe. I'll take care of you and your mother. I know that you have your concerns. I am sure that your Uncle Robert can be trusted to honor his word."

By this time, my mother was weeping. I could see the teardrops forming in her eyes. The way the blue reflected off her tears broke my heart. The pain and helplessness resonated from her face. I did not want to hurt her. All I was doing was trying to make my father understand that this is his family, and my stepmother could not be trusted.

I would not dissuade my dad regarding his opinion of the trust issues that I had for the family.

I could see that my mother was still crying.

"Jack, think about what you are saying."

Pleading with my mother, "It is not what I'm saying, but what I see in my dream. I see us abandoned and me alone."

"Son, I cannot believe that you think our family would abandon you! Where did you come up with this idea that our family will betray you?" Dad asked me.

"Just a feeling, and it's what's in my dream."

"Son, I do not know what I can do to make you feel different. You are letting your imagination run away with you."

"It is time for us to leave and return back home Dad, so are we going to fly together or take separate flights?" I asked in what I felt was justifiable anger.

"Junior, that is quite enough. Gather your things so that we can leave."

On our way to the airport, I continued my train of thought, *I do not want to end things on a sour note.* I brought up the road trip. "Dad, I was able to see the struggles that most Americans endure, and somehow, they manage to hold on to their dignity. Do you believe some day in this country, segregation will have an end?"

"Son, if we want to survive as a nation, we have to overcome discrimination."

When we arrived in New York, my father put me on a flight to Boston.

"Son, your grandfather is going to meet you at the airport in Boston. You are going to stay with your grandparents while I'm here in Manhattan."

"Dad, why does my grandfather have to meet me?"

"Son, the fewer people that know what is going on, the better control your grandfather has over any given situation. I'll be up to see you soon, so listen to what your grandmother says and try to stay out of dutch."

A few days later, when my mother came to Boston, I heard her talking to my grandfather. "Do you believe what the doctors say? That my son Jack Jr. has a 70 percent survival rate to the age of eighteen? Is that the reason you feel that you can cover the sun with one finger! It does not work! There is no way that Junior is not going to have his way, with or without your approval; he will have his say! I am sure the lot of you do not know the end result of you wanting Jack Senior to become president. I do not see anyone in this family giving up as much as Jack Jr. and I have so far. Once the Kennedy clan starts down the wrong path, they are all in, and there is no way to save them from themselves!"

Just when my mother was getting started, my grandfather looked at my father and said, "Can!" My grandfather was trying to say for my father to stop my mother.

Mother looked towards my grandfather Joe. My father answered, "No! I can't stop my wife. Even if I wanted to stop her, I would not. She is a part of this family and has the right to voice her opinion, and by the way, it is not an opinion; it is the facts."

All I could do was sit there and listen to what was being said. The only thing that I understood was that my stepmother Jacqueline was going to have a baby. Just what this had to do with me, I did not know. By this time, my Uncle Robert already had four kids and one more on the way, so what was one more?

Earlier that afternoon, my mother and I had a mother-son conversation. She informed me that this child that was coming is going to be my brother or sister and that I was to treat it as such.

"Do not pay attention to any rumors you may hear regarding your brother or sister. This child that is coming did not ask to be here. Sugar, what I want you to do is to be kind to Jacqueline. Try not to antagonize her. She is going to become easily upset and moody. I do not want to hear that you did something to upset her, and I have to come across the country to get you out of the mischief that you have got yourself into."

"Mom! I have cousins; they are fun to be around, but it would be nice to have a brother or a sister."

Across the room sat Jacqueline; she did not utter a word. Sitting there as if she did not have a thing to do with what was being discussed. She was going to give me a brother or sister; she was not half bad.

The only thing I could see wrong with this scene was my Grandma Rose's condescending look on her face. As if she was innocent of what was going on around her and had nothing to do with it. I knew that it would soon be my grandmother's turn to speak.

Here it comes, my mother asked my grandmother, "Are you just going to sit there in silence?"

"This was not supposed to happen. Jacqueline made it clear that she did not want kids."

"Rose, we are all sitting in the room for that very reason. All I'm hearing is this was not supposed to happen."

My grandmother was about to say something. Dad interrupted my grandmother, saying, "The only real concern I have here is how this is going to affect my son Jack!

"What are you going to do? Keep Little Jack and Jacqueline apart? Every time I call, it is something new. He said Jacqueline woke up on the wrong side of the bed and hit him for no reason. If you look at her fingers, it seems as if Junior was trying to bite them off. Is this the kind of parenting skills you have? It seems to me that you cannot come between an adult and a child. Mother, what will happen next if you have no control over your household?

"This is a question for every one of you. How is this child that is coming going to change the dynamics of your plans? Rose cannot control one child, how is she going to manage two?"

About that time, my uncle Robert spoke up and said, "She did a pretty good job with us."

"Robert, if that is the case, your mother would not have gone along with your brother, Jack, marrying Jacqueline when he already had a wife and son!"

"Marilyn, you did not have to take that tone of voice with me."

"Robert, you and I are what you would call water and oil. We do not mix very well together. You are the thorn in my foot, and that's putting it mildly! There are children in this room, so you take that Napoleon syndrome you have on down the road."

"Tell it to someone who cares, Marilyn."

Uncle Robert looked over at my father and said, "You need to control your wife."

"Little brother, you know very well when Marilyn gets started, she does not stop until she gets her point across. So, my advice to you is to let her finish."

From where I was sitting, I could see that my mother was starting to calm down. The rose color in her cheeks began to fade, and her clenched fists were relaxing.

It was as if my mother was beginning to live her own words. "Son, I want you to be a good brother to this child that is coming. Try to understand that it is not the child's fault that it is here, but the parents'. When God gives you a child, he's giving you a new beginning. So, take this child in your hands and into your heart and make a new beginning. That way, when the time comes, you can say you are a good brother, or at least you try to be."

At the end of the weekend, my mother went back to New York City and my father to Boston. Before my parents left, they explained that I would have to learn to get along with my stepmother. "This is going to be a long summer and fall for you. By the end of November or December, Jacqueline should have her baby."

I took my parents' advice and kept my distance from my stepmother. However, my Grandmother Rose was not so kind.

It was a beautiful July summer day. I could feel the soft ocean breeze across my face. Jacqueline and my grandmother were fussing. I really didn't understand what the argument was about, but I played nice. Jacqueline asked me to wear a blazer and short pants. I did not want to give her a hard time, so I did. The only thing I was sure of was that I was not going to be the one who brings her party to an abrupt end.

Jacqueline had been planning an afternoon social event. Her brother Jack and her sister Lee were the first to arrive. For some reason, the more people that came, the angrier my grandmother became. It was as if she had not received an invitation to the party.

There were women sipping tea, lounging around in their finery. They were wearing hats with flowers on them and white skirts, and some even had gloves on. The men were playing croquet, others tossing horseshoes. I noticed that my grandmother was not around. When I asked my stepmother for her, all she did was shrug her shoulders. This was one of those days that my stepmother and I enjoyed each other's company. This was something that my grandmother did not like to see: my stepmother and me at blissful peace.

How my grandmother was going to bring this pleasant afternoon to an end was anyone's guess. What cruel and vindictive plan did she have in store for Jacqueline? There she was, my grandmother, nonchalantly walking up to the guest tables to say hello.

She walked over to where Jacqueline and Lee were sitting. Placing her hand on Jacqueline, she said, "Isn't it amazing how far a lady of Jacqueline's stature has come?" I did not understand what my grandmother meant by that, but the women at the table got up and walked away. Grandmother's comment put a damper on the party. The guests started leaving.

Jacqueline sat there as if she was frozen along with her sister Lee for about five minutes in total silence. It was as if someone poured a glass of cold ice water down her back. She got up from the table and walked into the house without looking at anyone. Lee just stood there in silence.

Grandmother sauntered up the pathway back into the house, without even a goodbye. I did not dare say a word. I knew and felt it was something that should not have been told. Knowing my grandmother, she had her reasons for making that comment. This afternoon party that my stepmother had was the last one of the summer.

By the end of November, Jacqueline had my little sister Caroline. When she came back from the hospital, everything seemed to have calmed down. My father placed this small baby in my hands and said, "This is your sister. I want you to be a good brother to her, and I hope she will be a good sister to you." My father seemed to be happy, but I could tell he was preoccupied. As if something was missing.

My sister was not too old when I began to see this man named Aristotle Onassis around. He was a short, dark-haired man with dark circles around his eyes. I did not feel comfortable around him. There was this mistrust that I felt when he was around. Jacqueline said that he was a friend of her sister Lee, but that was debatable, in my opinion.

Sometimes I wondered who he came to see. Was it Lee, Jacqueline, or Caroline? One afternoon while I was alone with my stepmother and Lee, he came over. Jacqueline was feeling touchy all morning; she asked me to answer the door, and I obliged. When I opened the door, it was Aristotle. I walked back into the living room where Jackie and Lee were sitting and said, "Aristotle is here. Which one of you he came to see, I do not know, but he is here."

Jackie stood up, "What do you mean by that, Jack?"

"Just what I said, I do not know which one of you he came to see."

"Did you ask him?"

"No, I did not ask who he came to see, and I am not a doorman. Next time answer the door yourself! That way, you'll find out for yourself."

"You do not have to be so damn ornery, Jack!"

"Stepmother, you are not sick anymore, so I do not have to play nice. I am going to tell my father what you said. You know my mother does not like that kind of language. Why do I have to tolerate that kind of language coming from you?

"Are you trying to impress Aristotle? Is that why you are using vulgar language? And do not try to run after me because you will not catch me. It is better that you tell my dad what I said."

"To rat you out to your father does no good. Anything you say or do is good for him."

"Oh, Stepmother. If you think I am going to let you do anything to me, you're mistaken."

"Jack, there is no reason for you to get testy with me! Oh no, why is Aristotle here? What does he want?"

"He came here for a visit. That is apparent. I see him standing there, Stepmother."

"Jack, how many times do I have to tell you? Do not call me Stepmother!"

"Oh, okay, Jackie! I am going out to play, Stepmother. I just had to get that last one in." I always knew how to upset her.

I turned and strolled out of the living room. While all the time looking out of the corner of my eye. My stepmother had what my father would call a delayed reaction. If you did not have to duck, you would have to be quick to turn around. She would throw a stone at you and ask where it came from. Or did you see that? Today was one of the days that I made it out the door unscathed.

There were minor changes in all of us after the birth of my sister Caroline. I made it clear that I was going to be a good brother to Carol, as I like to call her. Dad said that he wanted me to become an exceptional brother, not just a good brother. "Try to understand her; we do not know what unexpected turns life will bring us or that we will create for ourselves."

My father seemed to have a newfound acceptance for my stepmother. That was a rarity to see: my father somewhat at ease around Jacqueline. He still did not light up like he did when my mother entered a room.

My mother, Marilyn, looked at me with her Caribbean Ocean blue eyes. With her classic honeysuckle voice, she said, "Jack, I would like you to be a kind and generous brother.

"What I mean is I want you to be noble and give Caroline your time. That way, she will always remember your generosity when the time comes. Always try to keep in mind that when something starts out bad, it ends up bad. This way, son, no fault will be bestowed on you."

I looked into my mother's eyes and took her words to heart. "I'll do what you ask of me, but we'll have to wait to see how all of this turns out." I guess the rest of the Kennedy clan will have to weigh in on how I should treat Caroline.

It was another typical Kennedy family Sunday dinner. When Uncle Robert, Uncle Edward, Uncle Sergeant Shriver, and all my aunts weighed in on how I should treat Caroline.

While we had our dinner, my father and mother assured my uncles and aunts that they had spoken to me. I understood that Caroline was to be treated like my sister. As always, at a Kennedy dinner, everyone has their say. This time, it was left up to my Uncle Robert to ask the questions. This never sat too well with my mother, Uncle Robert questioning me. She always said that my Uncle Robert was a thorn in her foot, the one she knew was there but just could not remove.

Robert, looking over at Marilyn, asked, "What was it that you said to Junior on the subject at hand?"

"Robert, in this household, there is always one. Why does it have to be you? My son Jack said that he would treat Caroline as a brother would treat a sister. Just keep in mind what we have done here will stay attached in his memory forever. Childhood is to learn and grow. Why is it you believe that he'll forget what we are asking of him? I am well aware that there is some kind of plan in place that you expect will turn out fruitful. I am saying you take a good look at what your nephew Jack is going to do.

"He is polite, smart, and rarely says a word. Jack has a knack for recalling what is said during a conversation. If need be, he'll use that conversation to his advantage. The best part of all is that I have not heard him tell a fairytale. So, with that said, he'll treat his little sister with kindness. I just hope that Caroline will do the same."

In typical Marilyn fashion, she turned to my Grandmother Rose. "Do you know where I come from we work?" With my parents' assurances that I was going to play friendly, the Kennedy clan was at peace. Their plan to make my father the President of the United States was still in play and things returned to normal. As usual, my mother returned to New York, and I stayed with my grandparents.

# SCARECROW TO FIRST LADY

**THE NEXT TWO YEARS** were spent watching my grandmother Rose trying to turn Jackie into a first lady and my grandfather Joe working with my father trying to make him presidential looking. My grandmother said to turn Jackie into the First Lady is to take a wool handkerchief and turn it into a silk scarf. A wool handkerchief you send to the laundry for cleaning, a silk scarf should be sent to the cleaners for pressing. That way, all the wrinkles, and kinks come out.

Jacqueline would say, the Fitzgerald charm school is more than one should have to handle. "Rose, you would think my upbringing was enough for the American people."

"No, Jackie. It's all about the polishing. We want to see Jack in the White House in the next election."

I laughed to see my grandmother and stepmother working together. It was like day and night or two separate worlds trying to join together. "Rose, that 18th-century charm just will not work in the 19th-century world."

"It worked for my father, Honey Fitzgerald, and it's going to work here. Jacqueline, keep your head high, your chin level with the floor, eyes to the bridge of your nose. If you have to look around, move your eyes left to right, up and down. If you insist on wiggling your head when you walk, twist your neck and tilt your head lightly. It will give you the feeling that you are as graceful as a

swan moving through the water. Jackie, it is the feeling that I need
you to grab hold of and don't let go."

Jackie turned and looked at Rose to send her to a place of fire.

"Jacqueline, that's not the look I was looking for! Jacqueline,
you are good with sending me to where you want me; however:
that is definitely not the swan look I am after.

"We are going to move on to your torso. Jackie, now that your
head is in line with your shoulders and straight with your neck.
Make the top of your head the center between your shoulders.
Keep the spine straight, your shoulders even. You should feel your
head and torso becoming one unit. Jackie, you are learning. Your
form is beginning to take shape. We still have to work on the way
you should walk."

"Rose, you are trying to make me the First Lady, not a queen."

"No, Jackie, I'm trying to make you feel like a queen; that way,
you can feel like a lady. From that feeling will emerge a first lady, one
that this family can be proud of. You'll take pride in yourself. This
is something that will stay with you for the rest of your life. Jackie,
you are going to be surprised how poise and grace open doors, and
people from all walks of life will welcome you into their world!"

"Rose, do you think the West Palm Beach elite will welcome
me in?"

"Jackie, my dear, that is a pedestal even sometimes out of
reach for me."

"Why is it that Marilyn is welcome in West Palm Beach elite,
and it is hard for me to be accepted there?"

"Jacqueline, West Palm Beach elite is a group of busi-
ness-minded people. They prefer to socialize with someone who
is going further themselves, someone who contributes to society
like Marilyn.

"Marilyn makes other women think outside of womanhood.
It is nice to be married, but as a woman, you should be willing to
work for yourself. She is no man's property and is very independent; Marilyn believes in equality for all women and is not afraid
to express her opinion. That is why she fits in with the West Palm
Beach crowd; they find her fascinating.

"Now Jackie, just keep your head held high, eyes in line with the bridge of your nose, shoulders straight, your torso straight, and start to walk. Remember heel to toe, heel to toe. You should feel as if you are walking on air. As if the earth is a soft cushion beneath your feet."

"Rose, I am beginning to feel as if I am walking on air."

"Jackie, you are not quite there yet. With a little more work, you'll become that swan peacefully moving through the water."

This transformation that my grandparents planned for my stepmother Jacqueline took time, money, and an array of staff. It was all done behind closed doors. This is the part that my grand-father was willing to invest in to achieve the ultimate goal to have one of his sons President of the United States, before his death. My grandfather often said, "If I could not become President of this country, one of my sons damn well better be. Rose, with your help and my money, I believe I will make it." I would sit there listening attentively to what grandfather was saying.

I always had that same burning question in my thoughts, *Do you understand what you are doing?* There were times when I just blurt out, "Do you know what you are doing!"

Grandpa always gave me the same answer. "Yes, I understand what I am doing, Junior." I felt as if Grandpa did not understand the question or had any clue how this was going to affect the family. The expression on Grandpa's face showed some doubt and reluctance to answer the question at times. How could he ask my parents to give up so much?

My grandparents still felt that Jacqueline needed to work on her social skills and her appearance. It was as if she was a debu-tante in preparation for her debut. But this time, she was going to be the First Lady of the United States. All the work that Rose and Jacqueline put into this project was beginning to pay off.

Jacqueline's demeanor and attitude were transforming her into a different person. She was turning into that swan that my grandmother was telling her to become. With the grace and ele-gance of a swan, she was floating on water. Jacqueline, turning into Rose in the Victorian age in the 19th century, has finally emerged.

The Victorian era does have something to offer to the middle 20th century. It's not all about how to extend your pinky finger when sipping tea, but being graceful about it.

# MALIBU

**AS ALWAYS, MY PARENTS** were rushing me off from one place to another. This time, I was to meet them in California. Sen. John F. Kennedy wanted to know how well he would do in California if he were to make a run for the presidency. My father, Sen. Kennedy, made sure that I would tag along with him. It was no surprise to me to know that my mother, Marilyn Monroe, was going to be there.

Everything had been arranged before I left Massachusetts. My mother called me and said she wanted me to be on my best behavior because I was going to meet some fascinating and significant people. "Junior, you are going to make new and old friends. One of them is your hero, the man you most respect and admire."

My father, Sen. John F. Kennedy, and I arrived safely into Burbank's airport for the stars. There was no fanfare upon arrival like there was when I visited with my mother. There was always someone there holding my hand to shelter me from the crowd. My mother explained that she wanted me to have as much as a normal life that a child could have. It was easier for me to travel with my father; no one really knew he was Sen. John F. Kennedy unless he mentioned it. Otherwise, we were just a father and son taking a trip.

That was in comparison to when my mother Marilyn and I took a trip. She would wear a hat, scarf, and dark sunglasses so that no one would notice she was the movie star, Marilyn Monroe. She would always sit by the window, giving me the aisle seat, that way she would not be recognized. She created a world for us that was all our own. Marilyn was a wife to my father, a mother to me, and an icon to the world. The best part was she knew how to keep them separate. There was Marilyn Monroe, who worked for a living, and there was the Marilyn, who was my mother.

The Marilyn that I called mother was sweet, kind, caring, and giving. The ability that she had to express herself. To hear her call me Sugar, I would drop what I was doing and run to her. She never had to call me twice. I was there Johnny on the spot. When I heard my mother calling me, it was as if an angel was calling for me. That sweet, soft hum of her voice always made me feel special. It was as if a drop of water was bouncing ever so gently off a white rose. I could still hear and see it. Her voice made me feel like I was the most important person in her life.

My uncles Robert Kennedy and Edward Kennedy would often ask me, "How does it feel when you hear your mother Marilyn calling you?"

"To listen to her calling you is to know that she loves you."

"Your grandmother Rose never called any one of us the way that your mother, Marilyn, calls you. You do not know how lucky you are to have a voice like that calling you, Jack! I have not once heard your mother raise her voice to you. It is always 'Jack, Junior,' or 'Sugar.' Never 'John' or 'come here now!' What I would not give to hear and feel what you feel. What do you feel, Jack!"

The Kennedy household always had an atmosphere of competition and competitiveness in it. We were trying to see who could outdo who or who could achieve more. It was not 'let's win together' but 'who'll cross that finish line first?'.

"Jack, your mother's voice inspires me to achieve my goals. She brings calm and stability to the family. She makes an outsider feel as if they are indeed family. Your mother says I'm the thorn in her foot. Too bothersome to ignore but too troublesome not to remove. Thank God she uses that cliché when you are around, Junior." I understood why my uncle Robert and my mother did not get along. He always put his nose where it did not belong. Uncle Robert had a bad habit of meddling in our family matters.

My mother has a no-vulgar policy when speaking and when spoken to. She would say, it is not your lack of education that makes one use profanity, but a lack of imagination. She would finish up by adding, "learn to use a thesaurus. That way, you will be heard, and your opinion will have more meaning."

My mother and Uncle Robert were like water and oil; they did not mix well together at all. There were times when my mother would ask my uncle, Robert, "Have you ever questioned why you are referred to as Bobby and not Robert?"

"No, it is what I have been called since birth."

"No, Bobby. It's because you need to grow up and stay out of grown-ups' business." There were times when my mother would insist Robert leave the room while she was there. When it came down to it, my mother had no confidence in Uncle Bobby.

I learned at a young age not to trust him too. I guessed when it came down to it, he was looking out for himself. When he placed his hand on the Bible and swore he would take care of me as if I was his own, my Uncle Bobby was lying to himself.

This trip was not about my father; it was about what was going to happen to me. We were in the car when my dad tapped me on the shoulder and asked, "Are you okay?"

I was lost in my thoughts before I realized he was talking to me. "Oh, yes, Dad. I was just daydreaming."

My father and I were on our way to Malibu to meet with my maternal grandfather, the industrialist Howard Hughes. I could see the ocean as we went along the Pacific Coast Highway. We were in a black four-door sedan sitting in the back seat. The driver made a right turn and drove up some hills. He pulled into a long circular driveway. We stop in front of this two-story home that had four columns in front of it with four stairs, a landing, and four more stairs that you had to walk up before entering the house.

As we entered the home, I could see the ocean from the foyer. There was a circular staircase going up to the second floor. The butler took my father's hat and said, "Follow me this way, please." We went on to the patio that revealed this magnificent ocean view of the Malibu Bay. My mother was there with some of her friends. There were my grandfather and hero Howard Hughes with a team of lawyers.

Father said, "This is going to be an interesting meeting," as we walked over. Mr. Hughes greeted us as he always did with a warm welcome. Mr. Hughes was a man that would not give you his time if you did not have something interesting to say or business to conduct. He believed that life here on earth was to be productive and not wasted. When I heard him speak, it was always something meaningful. I considered Mr. Hughes not just my hero, but my mentor and grandfather. He has always fascinated me; I never understood why he was so misunderstood. Howard Hughes was a man that had given so much for so little.

I walked over to the pool, took off my shoes and socks, and placed my feet in the water. I could hear the conversation in the distance that my parents and Grandpa Howard and his lawyers were having. Mr. Hughes was doing most of the talking. He was concerned about my mother's and my safety. "What provisions have you made to protect my daughter and grandson, Jack?"

"The Ambassador has taken care of all of that."

"Yes, but what are you doing to make sure that Marilyn and Junior will be safe? That is what I meant. Not what is Joe doing about their security?"

"Jack, I did not go out looking for fame; it found me. That is something Marilyn did not understand. When you find the kind of recognition that she has achieved, you lose your privacy, and there is no way to get it back. How is it that when Marilyn is walking in the street with Junior, her stunt double has to tell the news reporter that Junior is her son and not Marilyn's? You think I do not know what is going on with my own grandson and daughter?

"Jack, you are going to dig yourself a bottomless pit that you'll not be able to escape from. You are placing all your trust in the Kennedy Dynasty without a single thought of what harm it could bring to your own family."

I was sitting on the edge of the pool—my head down as if I was looking out at the ocean. Still, my eyes were fixated on my father sitting there without uttering a word. He looked like a man who has just been handed his hat! My father was not a man who would let anyone talk to him that way, but Grandpa Howard did. This time, my father was lost for words. Was it out of respect for Grandpa Howard that my father sat there in uttered silence, or was it something else?

"Howard, I am well aware of your concerns, but I don't believe that the Kennedy Dynasty will harm my son or wife."

"What you think and what can happen are two different things. Jack, have you taken into consideration the Ambassador Joe Kennedy's age?"

"My father is in good health and is well cared for."

"Yes, for now, the Ambassador is in good health. But do you understand all the stress that he is going to be under? Trying to hold all of his planning and scheming together just so that he can say his son is President of the United States?

"The American public is forgiving; it seems that your father, the Ambassador, does not remember Clark Gable and Carole Lombard's love affair. Marilyn is your first wife; that is a vastly different situation. What are you going to do when the public finds out what you did? The public forgave their shortcomings. I'm sure they will forgive you too."

"So far, Mr. Hughes, I have not done anything to be ashamed of."

"Jack, I have watched you introduce Junior and Marilyn to the bourgeoisie as your son and wife. I am concerned with the public and what they will do or say about all of this deception. Just the fact that your brothers and sisters are taking part in this deception says that they do not care about the consequences. So long as it is not them who will suffer the outcome of this endeavor that your father planned out."

"Mr. Hughes, you had known my father all the way back to his Hollywood days. You have been in the same room with him when he wanted something. The Ambassador is like a runaway locomotive; you know it's going to run out of steam. You just don't know where it's going to stop and what casualties will lay in its aftermath.

"Mr. Hughes, I believe that I have something to offer the country, and my wife Marilyn and son Jack will come out of this unscathed. As far as the public is concerned, I have my plans to inform them when the time is right. I will not leave Marilyn or my son blowing in the wind like a handkerchief. As far as my brothers Robert and Edward are concerned, I put my complete trust in them as I do in my sisters and their husbands. I have total confidence in the Kennedy Dynasty. First and foremost, we are a family that trusts one another."

"Senator Kennedy, that is what I mean; we do not know who is going to remain standing when all this is over. I fear that you are headed down the wrong path with this plan to make you president. It would be in everyone's best interest to inform the public you and my daughter Marilyn had a biological son together!"

"Senator, I told you before you married Jacqueline that you should let the public know about Jack Junior, and now you have a daughter. Just what the hell did you think Jacqueline was going to do to keep a foothold on your throat?" I could still hear Grandpa Howard's voice while he was speaking to my father and mother. I looked up directly at my father. His face was as red as an apple. The sunlight was hitting his hair precisely right; I noticed the sun streaking through his hair.

My mother was sitting there listening attentively, looking very businesslike. It was as if she knew what was on the agenda before we arrived. She was looking at Grandpa Hughes with her blue eyes, that color blue that you see glowing in the dark. My mother asked, "What is it you are proposing, Howard? Are you asking us to adopt Jack, my son?

"For you to ask us to give up our parental rights is preposterous. I would never relinquish my parental rights to anyone. When a child is conceived, he or she does not know who their parents will be. I have no intention of walking away from my responsibility as a parent. I work for my son to have a better life than I had as a child."

"Marilyn dear, I am not trying to take away your parental rights, and I can see that Jack Jr. is well cared for. What I am asking is to ensure that he will be safe, or at least you and the senator keep all options open."

I turned back around; more guests were arriving. They were the same group of people that I would see at my aunts' and uncles' homes. There was this one man I do not recall ever hearing him call my mother, Marilyn. He always called her his doll.

This same man at my grandfather's party was the comedian at the party. He had a way of making things funny. He and my father would try to one-up each other to see who would get the most laughs. I did not understand the jokes; however, I did enjoy laugher.

I asked him why he called my mother his doll. He said, "Look at her. She looks like a doll; she is childlike, a little angel; the only thing that your mother is missing is wings."

There were greetings and hand-shaking. I was watching Grandpa Hughes. He stood up to greet the comedian; he calls him Bob. There was a mutual respect for one another. Mr. Hughes's temperament did not let him stand up for just anyone. So, Bob had to be big!

Bob and Howard Hughes were more alike than not. Hughes bought up Las Vegas, parts of Malibu, and El Segundo, California. Where Bob would buy land around small cities and towns and hold on to it until the land value would increase, to later build on the property or sell it. That way, both Howard and Bob would maximize their profit.

To hear these two men talking together was an excellent learning experience. To look around and witness the adults eavesdropping on Hughes's and Bob's conversation in itself was comical. What I was waiting for next was the eavesdropper to pull out a pen and paper and begin to take notes! The code of ethics did not allow for that to happen. But what a sight to see if that did happen!

The noon sun was turning into a cool afternoon breeze. My mother called me over to put a beach shirt on and change out of my wet swimming shorts. The afternoon event was also starting to wind down. People began leaving, but there was still that one question that needed to be answered.

Howard Hughes was not a man that you kept waiting for your answer. My parents came to a consensus on how to turn down Grandpa Hughes without just saying no. That was the dilemma that my parents were faced with. My father and mother both said that it was a kind gesture and noble of Grandpa Hughes to want to adopt me. They would have to choose their words carefully before they began to speak.

My father and mother walked hand in hand over to Grandpa Hughes, where he was reclining in a lawn chair. They were now sitting side by side. In his Senator fashion, my father sat up straight with both feet planted firmly on the ground.

The Senator leaned forward and began to speak, "Howard, I understand that you are incredibly fond of Jack Jr., and I know that you are concerned about his safety. I assure you that your concerns will be front and center; however, to ask my wife and me to give up our parental rights is a bit premature. Not at any time, have my wife and I entertained the notion of giving Jack up for adoption. I have guarantees from my immediate family that they will always have Jack's security and well-being first and foremost at hand."

As my father was finishing up, my mother smiled at my grandfather before saying a word. "I thank you for your concern, Howard, but I would never relinquish my parental rights to anyone." My mother took Howard Hughes's hand. In a soft voice, she began to speak. She was consoling him so as not to be misunderstood. "I have always wanted to be a mother, and my son John Jr. is a blessing. I am doing what I have to do so that my son stays with me. From the day he was conceived, I have cared for him. I hope that if I ever need your help that your door would remain open."

"Marilyn, you and your family will always have a place in my home. You and the senator have put me at ease somewhat.

"However, you are placing your trust in the Kennedy Clan Dynasty. The question remains, what will come first, your son Jack or the Kennedy Dynasty if something goes awry? The consequences will have a catastrophic effect on your political career, and it may come to an end. When you make it to the White House, what happens to Jack?"

"Howard, I plan to take my son with me wherever I go, which means the White House too. I am going to introduce Jack to the same Heads of States."

Once my father said that Howard Hughes smiled. "Senator, it seems that you are letting me know something that no one else is aware of."

"That is correct; I have not laid out my entire plan to anyone. You and my wife are the only two that I have told what I have planned out for Jack." *Does my father want me to become president?* "I want my son to enjoy the benefits of my work, as well."

With that out of the way, it was time for us to leave. From the adults' point of view, this was what you call a productive meeting of the minds. My dad was not going to leave me blowing in the wind like a neckerchief. My dad's question-and-answer section seemed to have made my mom and Grandpa Hughes content.

My mother changed me and her clothes while my father waited for us. She always liked to dress me in shorts, I could not understand why. She would say that little boys belong in shorts. "When you are old enough, you will appreciate it."

Once we were dressed, we said, "I'll see you later."

We drove down the hill to Highway US 1; I could see the sun to the left of us starting to set. The sun was shining brightly through the car windshield; reddish-yellow colors were emanating from the sun, which turned the inside of the car orange. The bright colors stayed with us as we turned onto Sunset Boulevard on our way to our hotel. By the time we arrived at the hotel, the sun had gone down.

Someone from my Grandpa Joe's Chicago office had made all our travel arrangements. The driver pulled up to the hotel door and got out to check us into the hotel. This time, my dad was not having any part of that. He was determined to go through the hotel lobby. He opened the back door of the car and helped my mother out of the vehicle. He waited for me to climb out of the back seat and took us both by our hands. One of us on the left, the other on the right side of him, we walked into the hotel hand in hand. It made me feel as if we were back in Europe, not that no one knew who my parents were; it was just that people left us alone. The bellhop took the keys and our bags. Off we went to our cottage.

We spend the next three days there, resting, eating, sleeping, and swimming. We were peaceful and blissful. No one was around to take my hand for my mother and say that I was their child or asking my mother for her autograph.

This kept everyone happy, the heads of the studios that mother worked for, and my Grandfather, Joe Kennedy. At the end of the week, it was time to leave. My mother and I went on to New York City, and my father left for Washington, D.C.

# LOOK WHO'S GLOWING

**WE ARRIVED IN NEW** York City; it was late in the afternoon. We went immediately to our apartment, no stops along the way, which was unusual for my mother and me to do. Mother would have the driver stop at a friend's or my Aunt Patricia's place just to say we arrived fine and hello. That was her way of keeping peace in the family. This time, she was lost in her thoughts. It was as if she had something to tell me, but she just did not know how to start the conversation. She would turn to look at me and turn back to stare out the window as the driver was driving.

I wanted to make it easy for my mom. I made sure I did not ask a direct question. "Mom, what are you thinking?"

"Sugar, I'm going to call your Uncle Robert and have him take you to your grandparents. They're here in New York, so you will not have to go to Boston." I did not know if she was asking me or telling me. I always found it easy to say no to my father, but when it came to my mother, it was 'yes.' When mom starts out by calling me Sugar, it was hard to say 'I'm not going.' There was that motherly tone that she would use; it was like a soft hummingbird was singing to me, letting me know that this is in my own best interest.

"Jack Jr., I have some planning to do. I hope that you understand that what I have to do is in our best interest. I have to take your Grandfather Hughes's words into consideration. I would never give up any child of mine for adoption. That goes against everything I believe in. I'll make sure that your father will take you with him to the White House when he becomes President. That way, you'll be safe and secure. The Secret Service provides for the immediate family members of the President; you are your father's firstborn. You are the first grandchild born into the Kennedy Dynasty.

"You are going back to your grandparents' home in New York. Uncle Robert will be picking you up in the morning."

"Mom, do I have to go with Uncle Robert? Every time Kathy and Joe see me, they start to cry or wet their pants. Joe is constantly wetting his pants, and I'm not doing a thing to him."

"Son, you just have a stern persona, and you speak too direct. You should try to be more childlike, Sugar."

"Mother, I'm not a baby. I am a child; if I try to be any more innocent, I'll be a baby."

The next morning, Uncle Robert whisked me away to my grandparents' home. Uncle Robert was asking me about my trip to Grandpa Hughes's place. "Uncle Robert, I enjoyed myself. Grandpa Hughes and my parents talked about grown-up things. I did not pay too much attention to their conversation."

Uncle Robert took my answer to mean if you were not there, you should ask one of my parents. He was well aware that one of the rules that my parents had was: never repeat what you heard. Especially when you were not part of the conversation or contributed to what was being discussed. When it came down to it, Uncle Robert was the ears and eyes of the Kennedy Dynasty.

"Junior, did you meet any interesting people while you were in California?"

"No! No one of any interest." I was becoming annoyed by all of Uncle Robert's questions. I turned to look at my uncle, "If you have any questions, why don't you ask my father or mother? They'll be able to inform you about our travels and with whom we met." Just about that time, we were pulling in front of my grandparents' townhouse.

I walked into the living room. "Is Grandpa Joe here?" I felt safe when I knew he was around. That sense of security that I had, just knowing that he was close by meant no harm would come to me. I could hear Grandma Rose's voice, "He is in the back." Grandma Rose and Jackie were still working on what a first lady should be.

Grandma Rose was telling her that she was a hard shell to break, but my God, this is going to work. My grandmother wanted Jackie to be better than an average conversationalist. She wanted her to be able to hold her ground. What my stepmother Jackie did not understand about my grandmother was that there was no pleasing her. She should just do her best and stop trying to satisfy my grandmother's every whim. It worked for me. That was something my father taught me. The best way to please my grandmother is not to!

My grandmother finally turned around and noticed I was in the room.

"How long have you been standing there watching us?"

"I just arrived here, Grandma. I came in to say hello and to ask how you are feeling."

"I am beautiful; let your grandfather know you are here."

All these little formalities that I have to go through are nerve-wracking. Why is it that my grandmother is so strict? It has to be that proper Bostonian upbringing she is so proud of. I've heard other friends say their grandmothers are nice. Just what happened to mine? The only thing I needed was to listen to her screaming at the top of her lungs. Why doesn't my stepmother just put her in her place? She should learn to be a fast runner like me. Do what you have to do and exit on the quick.

The next few months were spent working on trying to help my father become President of the United States. Most of the people that my father was working with would come to our home, or we would go to their home. My father had said Ronald Reagan was the one who introduced him to Marilyn Monroe while he was in San Francisco working for the United Nations. He was not sure if Ronald would work on his campaign.

Whenever Ronald did not see me with my dad, he would ask him where his shadow was. My dad would say, "He is right here." Where he was, I was. My father had a love for all children, not just his own. We were inseparable, and this upset a lot of people, especially my uncles. My father had told anyone who asked, "This is my son, and he is staying right here with me. That is not going to change anytime soon, do you understand me!"

This was becoming a problem for Uncle Robert. My grandfather had told him to keep any unflattering articles out of the news. His job was to prevent the press from printing any reports about me and to say I was his son or one of his sister's kids. It always amazed me the things people would do for my father to become President of the United States.

Sometimes my uncle would have to pay news reporters not to report what they saw. There were times when I was with my uncle, and reporters would walk up to him, asking him questions. All he would tell them is, "You can't report that," and they would oblige him. It was as if we could do no wrong.

This time, my uncle Robert was going to have his work cut out for him.

My grandfather had called Uncle Bobby into his study and told him to close the door behind him. This had to be something big!

The lower my grandfather's voice was when he spoke, the more severe the problem. My uncle could not have been in my grandfather's den for more than 10 minutes. When he came out all red-faced and stomping his shoes, I knew to get out of his way! This was not the time to try and find out what was going on.

He scurried by me and almost made it past my grandmother and stepmother. He stopped, looking at the both of them, and said, "I did not sign up for this, and now I am right in the middle of it all. Just what do you think I am going to do? Watch Marilyn for the rest of my life?" Neither my grandmother nor Jacquelyn had a chance to answer him. He was still on his way out the door. He did say goodbye. I have learned from past experience, when Uncle Robert is in a huff, get out of his way, but it was amusing to see him this upset!

I could hear my name being called by my grandfather from his study. "John, come in here now!"

As I was entering the study, I noticed the look on his face. He was not happy. "John, sit down! I want to talk to you." As he began to speak, I started to get a lump in my throat.

"John, I want to know about your trip to California."

"Sir, you have always told me not to inform others about personal matters. You are aware that my father does not like me to discuss what is going on in our personal family life."

"Oh! Right. I'll just ask you this, did you stay in the same hotel?" This is the same question just formed differently. "John, your father taught you well. You are not going to answer any question, are you?"

"No. If I do not have to, I will not."

My grandfather's facial expression changed. He was calming down. "Your parents have made their lives more chaotic with one small act. They will have to let you know what is going on."

"Grandfather, should I wait for them to tell me what is going on, or may I ask?"

"I'm going to take my own advice. You'll have to wait for your parents to let you know about the dilemma they are facing."

This edgy feeling that I was experiencing made me feel that I could not just get up and walk out of the den. This was going to take all of the charm I could muster up. Leaning forward, head held high, I asked Grandpa, "May I be excused?" He looked at me in the same way I've seen him look at my father as if we could do no wrong.

"Yes, you may be excused."

I rose up out from the chair and walked calmly to the door. I turned to ask, "Would you like me to close the door behind me?"

"Yes, please."

As I was closing the door, I recalled my father's advice. "Son, when my father, your grandfather, calls you into his den and tells you to close the door behind you, he is going to get down to business. Be attentive and respectful, and hopefully, he will not bring the walls of Jericho down on you." My dad would have been proud of me the way that I conducted myself in my grandfather's den. I felt as if I was the most important person in the house for the rest of the day!

Later that afternoon, my mother called to see how I was doing. She asked if I made it back okay and how I was feeling and if I was being treated well. "I am fine, but my grandpa Joe says you and my dad have something to tell me about our California trip."

"Yes, but the trip had nothing to do with what we have to say. Your father and I will be there in a week or two to let you in on what's going on."

"Mother, I think that this is going to be an Oh-my-God moment!"

"Sugar, I want you to remember that your father and I love you very much."

"Mom, did something happen while we were in California that I am not aware of? Uncle Robert and Grandpa both asked me about our California trip."

"Sugar, don't worry! We'll be there to explain what is going on."

When I placed the telephone receiver down, I felt an emotion of joy. As if something special was going to happen. I felt it while I was talking to my mother.

For the next two weeks, I spent time with my little sister Caroline. She was already walking and talking. I began to notice that when I called her Carol, she would smile and come running to me. When Jacqueline witnessed Caroline running towards me, she said, "It is the sweetness in your voice that your little sister hears and likes." I enjoyed getting to learn how to be a big brother. There was always someone around to share your time with.

Father instilled in us the importance of being a good brother and sister.

"I'll not tolerate any sibling rivalry in this family from either of you." He said to have a durable family foundation, my sister and I would have to work together and not against each other. His words made sense to me; I decided to take his words to heart. Caroline made it easy to be a kind and understanding brother; she was so little and sweet anyway. How could I ever mistreat a baby? I did not have it in me to be jealous or envious. Besides, I did not understand the meaning of these words. I was sure that I did not want to know their significance either.

Whenever Jackie was told that my mother was coming to visit, she would take a trip. Sometimes she would stay away for 2 to 3 days, leaving Caroline with dad and me. My father was good to Caroline, but I felt he was closer to me. He said that he divided his time equally between my sister and me, but I think that he spent more quality time with me. He did!

It was not my place to ask Jackie where she was going or with whom she would be staying with. When I asked my dad where Jackie was, he always gave me the same answer, "Ask your Uncle Robert. I have my hands full with you, Caroline, and your mother. I can't worry about were Jacqueline goes."

Sometimes, it was better not to ask and to leave well enough alone. My dad never said that it was not my place to ask about Jackie's whereabouts, but his facial expression spoke volumes. It was as if he was asking for forgiveness for things yet to come. Was he questioning himself? Asking, is this all worth what we may or may not go through? He once said, "People will help you jump into a boiling pot, but would they give you a hand to get out?" Did he need a helping hand now? The only thing I could do was try to make him see that I was going to be a good brother to Caroline.

My dad has said, "Anyone can skip a stone across the water. How far and how high you want it to go is up to the trick."

He told me, "Junior, you are like a rock; you will finish what you start and go a long way. Somehow you'll make it all the way to the top, never forgetting to dance along the way."

It was the end of summer. My grandparents and I were on our way to Hyannis Port. We were there to meet my parents. Grandpa Joe was not in the best of moods; he had something on his mind, something that we were all waiting to find out. As in all large families, it was hard for everyone to meet in the same place at the same time. This time, Grandpa Joe did not want anyone's schedules conflicting with this family gathering!

It was Grandma Rose's responsibility to make sure that everyone was there and on time. This was to be an extended weekend gathering if need be. No one was leaving until Grandpa Joe had his say. It was Saturday afternoon, and my mother was the last one to arrive. Grandpa Joe, Grandma Rose, Dad, and I were all waiting for my mother on the front porch.

Caroline and I were sitting on the stairs; my grandparents and dad were standing next to us, looking out towards the ocean. I could see them out of the corner of my eye.

I heard a car pull up, so I turned to look. It was my mom. The car pulled around and stopped; I watched her as she was getting out of the vehicle. It was as if Marilyn was making her grand entrance, the kind of display that every director tries to capture on film, but somehow it gets lost. The sun was hitting her hair and legs just right as if to say, "Here I am." It was a mesmerizing moment for the five of us. Watching Marilyn walk up the walkway with all of her ladylike charm and beauty, it was a fairytale moment playing out.

I heard my grandfather's voice in the background saying to my father, "Jack, I can see her glowing from here. Anyone with half a brain can see that she is with child."

Mother had brought me a lollipop, the kind of candy that is as big as my face. I took the candy and broke it in half, giving a piece to Caroline. As I was giving Caroline the candy, Mother said, "He is a good brother; Carol did not have to ask for a bit of his candy. I'll have to remember to bring something for both of them on my next visit."

Mom, Dad, and grandparents went into the house while my sister and I stayed sitting on the porch. It was sometime later that Uncle Robert came to let me know my presence was required. Oh! I could tell just by the tone of his voice he was upset, and I did not want to exacerbate the situation by lollygagging around. I immediately stopped what I was doing and went into the house with him.

I walked into the room, looked for my parents, and sat down between them. It was as if I put my bare feet into a nest of red ants. I could not help but think, *What have I done now?* Dad began to speak first.

"Son, your mother, and I have something to tell you. We want you to try to understand that there is going to be a new addition to our family. We do not know if it is going to be a boy or girl. The only thing we can say now is that you are going to have another sister or a new brother. What do you think of that, son?"

Taking a line from my mother, I asked, "What does this have to do with me?"

"Son, at this particular time, nothing, but it will affect you in the future. Your mother and I thought it would be an ideal time to let you know what is going on. We feel it is our place to tell you about the new addition to the family. We want this news to come from us and not someone else."

"Dad, if there is one thing that I have learned from you is that there are two sides to every story."

Mother was all smiles as if she had hit the Irish sweepstakes. "Jack, how do you feel that you're going to be a big brother again?"

"Mom, I'm going to be a good big brother just like I am now. I do not expect anything to change except that there will be four of us now." Mother was quite pleased with my response; she hugged and kissed me and told me to go outside and play.

Before I left the room, I could hear the naysayers. "Do you really believe that Jack is accepting of all this?" "Caroline is less than four years old, and now Jack Jr is going to have a little brother too! This time it's his mother Marilyn that is with child, and the father is the same as Caroline. How in the Sam hell are we going to explain all of this? How are we going to explain all this when the time comes?"

Simultaneously, my parents said, "We are going to tell the truth." Upon hearing their answer, I picked up the pace and hurried out of the room.

Why is it that everyone in this family has to have a say? This time would be no different. The doors closed behind me, and voices were raised. Everyone's opinions and grievances were heard and resolved. Yes, we were all supposed to fall in line with the grand patriarchy plan.

The next seven months were spent on the child that was coming, keeping the public from finding out that my parents were having another child, and dad becoming president. Mom and Dad were going to have to meet with Grandpa often. To inform him of the status of mother's health and what was going on at the studio. Oh! And there was my dad's presidential campaign status report.

Grandfather requested Uncle Peter Lawford's help in keeping my mother's condition under wraps. "It's an asset to have you as a son-in-law and working in Hollywood, Peter. This way, I have some control over Marilyn and the press.

"Peter, Marilyn is her own person! She is going to do exactly what she wants when she wants and damn the consequences. If she were more like some of the characters she portrays in the movies, our life would be much more comfortable not only on us but on the male species as well. We should have put an end to the women's Right to Vote. No! Hell, we should have stopped the women's rights movement before we gave them the right to smoke!"

It made me snicker to hear how upset Grandfather becomes. Just discussing mother with someone upset him. Sometimes I think Grandfather's inability to control my mother was going to cause him to spontaneously combust. Father said that Marilyn was the only woman that Grandpa ever met that he could not control.

Between Uncle Robert and Uncle Peter, Grandfather had a handle on what information would be released to the public. If he had to pay a reporter or two, so be it, but overall, it was the influence that my grandfather wielded that helped out the most. Grandpa Joe said, "If it was not for the back-door deal, I would not be where I am today."

Mother was becoming weary. Just what was she going to do with two kids? How was all this going to play out? I understood my mother's concerns; I had my own. *What makes parents think that a child does not understand what is going on around them? Would we all make it through the other side of Grandfather's plan? Especially now that Mother was going to have a baby?*

Mother and Father had decided that when the child was born, he or she would live with my father. Mother's work schedule was too hectic on her, and father had a bigger support group, meaning that all of the Kennedys' husbands and wives would lend a helping hand.

There were times when I would run up to my father or mother and called them Mom or Dad. One of my aunts or uncles would grab me and say, "Come on, son. Over here." If it was someone my parents did not trust, I was whisked away. It was easy to deceive someone by inaction or with words and sometimes both. In the case of this child, there was nothing to hide.

If someone asked Dad if I was his son, he answered, "Yes, he is my son. Why?" And smile. It made me laugh when someone asked that very question. Here my dad was telling the truth, and no one was the wiser. Dad would say, "Be truthful, son, but people still don't believe you. You're better off telling the truth, that way you do not clutter your mind with unnecessary information that you probably will not remember."

It was mid-autumn when my mother gave birth to a baby boy. As planned, my father was the primary caregiver. All was going fine until my stepmother began to interfere. She was upset that she had to care for a child that was not hers. By this time, she was already the First Lady of the United States. To hear my father, "When it comes to Jacqueline, all bets were off." She was not going to cooperate in any way, shape, or form. That was fine with my parents, but she was interfering with the domestic help. She would not let the babysitter take care of my little brother.

When Jacqueline became furious, she would throw herself on the floor, roll around, and pull her hair out. She was now using my little brother JonJon to get my father's attention.

While all this was going on behind closed doors, people were beginning to refer to my stepmother as Jackie. For some reason, they felt that 'Jackie' suited her. But people did not know the Jackie that I knew. I can say at best we had a love-hate relationship. It just depends on who was in the room with us and what time of day it was. We would start out the day with smiles, or we began with throwing stones at each other, and by the end of the day, they would turn into boulders.

Jackie seemed to gain some independence once she became First Lady; she was not going to help rear my little brother. Jackie had told my father, "I'll not be a slave to a child that is not mine! You find someone else to care for you and your first wife's child. I am unwilling to play mother to anyone else. Still, Caroline and Jack Jr. If you and Marilyn are planning on having more kids, you better damn well leave me out of your situation. I was paid to marry you, not play nursemaid to another one of your children."

"I'm not asking you to play nursemaid to anyone. What I am asking is that you stop interfering with housekeeping. I leave one set of instructions for them, you come along and change them. What you seem to forget is that John is my child and not yours; I'm his father, and you are not his mother." What my dad and stepmother were really arguing about was who was going to care for JonJon.

Not in the sense that who was his parent, but who was going to clean up after him? Just who was going to feed him, bathe him, and clothe him? That is where my stepmother was interfering. She was playing with the life of a child. A newborn baby that was not hers. I understood that this was a problem for my father, but I didn't know what to do about it. My dad was trying to be a father to Caroline, JonJon, and I and Jacqueline was undermining him. His authority was not an easy thing to go through.

Dad came up with a solution as to who was going to care for my little brother, JonJon. It was going to be me, his big brother. We had one of those 'come here and sit down' conversations that fathers and sons have when they tell you 'you're going to do something' and not 'are you willing to do it!' I could feel by the tension in his voice and his demeanor this was going to be a one-way conversation. This was one time that I was going to hold my ground. I did not care what he had to say, I was going to stick to my guns.

"Son, I need your help with your baby brother, the kind of help a brother like you sometimes has to do. You are a lot older than your brother, so it should be easy for you to do what I am going to ask you to do."

All I could do was sit there looking into his green eyes and wait for him to finish what he had to say. As he was speaking, I was thinking, I'm ten years older than my brother; I already knew what he wanted me to do.

I was in the room a few days earlier when he was talking to my mother on the phone telling her what he was going to have me do. I never understood why it is when parents speak; they think that children do not understand? They act as if we are not in the same room or on the same planet as they are.

"Son, you are going to have to step up to the plate and help me with your little brother."

"I already help out with JonJon. How else do you want me to help him?

"Dad, I am a child myself. How do you expect me to help you care for him? That is a father's job not to be left or handed down to his son. The answer is no!"

"Son, I need your help; this is a critical time in a baby's life when it needs to feel loved and cared for."

"Dad, the answer is still no. It is not that I do not care for my little brother, but he is your responsibility, not mine. Please do not ask me to do this."

I saw his eyes start to tear up, and he bowed his head while still looking at me and said, "Okay, son. Okay." Once he said that I knew what was coming next.

Dad was going to bring my mother into the picture, and what she was going to tell me was no big surprise. My mother called to tell me that she was coming to the White House to see me. What son can say no to his mother? It's a low blow when your father has to tell your mother to make his son do something he cannot. I guess it goes back to what my Grandpa Joe would say. "If I can't make your father do what I want, his mother sure as hell can."

Needless to say, my mom came to see me about my reluctance to cooperate with my dad. When she walked into the room, I could see she was not pleased with me at all. She had that no-nonsense walk and attitude about her. I know from past experiences; I was fighting a losing battle. This time, I knew whatever mother was going to say, I was going to do.

As always, when my mother entered a room, it was hello, how are you, and how have you been. She was not one to start off with a negative comment. The only thing I could see was that she was disappointed in what I had done or failed to do. I knew that she was here to talk to me about my lack of cooperation with my dad. I could not help but think, *why did my dad have to bring my mother into this*?

Just as Mother was sitting down, a nanny came into the room with my little brother and gave him to Mother.

"Sugar, I want to know why you refuse to help your father with JonJon?"

"Mom, I feel that it is not my place to do Dad's job. He should be the one to clean up after JonJon, not me."

"JonJon is your only brother!"

"But he is Dad's son. Why should this fall on me? JonJon is my dad's responsibility, and you want to make him mine!"

"Jack!"

Once mom called me 'Jack,' I knew this was one-sided.

"You are going to do what I tell you to do. I had to come all the way from California to take care of something that you should have been willing to do on your own. JonJon is family, and you should be ready to help out with your brother's needs. Jacqueline is not letting his nanny give him the care that he needs. You should not be willing to take part in Jackie's shenanigans. What she is doing is undermining your father's authority, and I will not tolerate you doing the same thing. Young man, you better have a good reason why you made me come out here. Do you have a reasonable explanation of why I am here?"

If I tell Mom the truth, it may hurt her feelings. Or will she understand my point of view?

"Jack, I'm waiting for an answer."

"Mom, first, I don't know how to take care of a baby. And second, I am afraid of what it is going to do to me."

Mother began to change her demeanor; it was as if she knew what I was going to say before I said it. "Sugar, come over here. Sit next to us. Tell me what is really bothering you."

I walked over to where mother was holding JonJon and sat down. She placed him in my arms. All I noticed was the sadness in my mother's eyes. I could not help but think I should have done what my father asked me to do.

"Sugar, I do not understand your unwillingness to help out with your brother, which is a part of being the older sibling. The older child is always ready to step in when the parents are at work. That means that you have to be willing to give your brother or sister the required care that is needed. In this case, it is your brother that needs your attention, and I cannot always be around. That is where the oldest of the family comes in, and that family member is you. So when JonJon needs to be fed, bathed, or have his diaper changed, that is where you come in."

"Yes, Mom, but I don't feel that way. I feel as if he is going to leave me blowing in the wind like a discarded handkerchief. He'll not even want to know that I exist, much less stop to say hello."

"Sugar, do you know what you are saying?"

"Yes, I do, Mother. I do." I could see by the look on my mother's face that she did not like where I was going with this.

"Mom, someday I'll ask JonJon for five minutes of his time, and he'll not even give me that, no matter how many times I change his diapers or feed him. That is exactly what he is going to do. I'm sorry for saying these things to you, and I know that you do not want to hear it, but this is what is going to happen if you and Dad do not stop and think about what you are doing to us. I do not feel safe here with my stepmother Jacqueline. I do not trust her, and it is not just her; it is also my aunts and uncles too. They say that they will take care of me, but what about when you or dad are not around? What happens then?"

"Sugar, you are getting way ahead of yourself here. Let me take care of one issue at a time. The issue at hand is, will you help with JonJon. I'll work on the rest of your concerns later. I want you to take a look at this before you answer my question."

She lifted the diaper off JonJon's backside, and there was an open wound on his buttock. I could see the pain on my mother's face, and the tears start to roll down her cheeks.

"Mother, this he can survive. But the next thing you are going to ask me to do for him, I am going to say NO! So please think before you ask me to do this."

"Sugar, helping care for your brother will bring you closer together."

"I'm going to do what you are asking of me, only because you are asking me and not for any other reason."

"I believe this will help you to be better brothers. JonJon is going to do what he wants to do when he is old enough. He will never want to hear what we are talking about here today. Never!"

"I'll put my fears and indifference aside to do what you asked me to do." We left the White House with JonJon for West Virginia.

We stayed in my dad's home that he had there. For the next two weeks, my mother gave me a crash course in baby care.

She said that the first thing you have to learn is to listen to a baby's cry. The sound of a baby's cry will let you know what it needs or wants. That does not mean that you wait for the baby to cry; it just means that a baby does not grieve for any reason.

The first time I listened to my brother cry, I could hear the difference. It was because he was hungry. This was the first time I really listened to the way a baby cries! A baby does indeed have a different need for each sound of its cry. I knew that it was time to feed him.

Mother showed me that you place a baby's cold bottle of milk in a saucepan with water and heat the bottle of milk. "Do not let the water come to a boil; it will overheat the milk, and you may burn your brother. The way you test to see if the liquid is too hot for your brother is to turn your wrist upward and sprinkle two to three drops of milk on your wrist. If you are burned, the milk is too hot for your brother."

It took a few tries of warming the baby bottle before I could get a handle on this baby feeding task. The crucial part in all of this was to not let the water boil; if you do, you will get burned.

Yes, just as much as a baby can eat, even more comes out. That is the hard part of this baby care thing, changing my little brother's diaper.

The first time I changed my brother's diaper, Mother gave me a thimble to place on my finger. She had me put the thimble on my fourth finger so as not to prick my finger with the safety pin.

"Jack, in time, you will learn to be an old hand at changing diapers, and you will not need the thimble." She left out the part that babies move, and sometimes you stick your finger with the safety pin. *Who came up with the name safety pin?* There were times that I had forgotten to use the thimble when changing JonJon's diaper. Still, I never stuck JonJon with the safety pin. My finger was another matter.

By the end of the second week, I was learning to give JonJon a bath. I believe mother was making up the rules on how to bathe a child as she was going along. The smaller the infant, the smaller the object you use to bathe the child in. Unlike a nanny, Mother starts out cleaning the kitchen sink. She cleans the kitchen sink until she sees her reflection in it. Once that was done, she ran the water, making sure that the water was not too hot or cold. She did not let the sink tub fill to the top, just enough so that she could place her elbow in the water to test the warmness of the water.

"Jack, this method does two things: make sure that you have enough water to bathe the child and that the water temperature is fine."

She placed my brother on my left arm face up and soaped up a washcloth.

"Jack, don't rub the baby with the washcloth. You wipe him gently. Do not scrub your brother. If you scrub him, you'll give him a rash, or worse, you'll break the skin, and it will start to bleed.

"Sugar, the more cautious you are when you are caring for a child, the fewer problems you will have down the line."

As always, Mother made everything complicated simple. "Jack, this is a life learning experience, and someday you'll use what you have learned here on your own children. It will help you to be a better-prepared parent. Your future as a parent is well on its way. The better care you give to your brother, JonJon, the more you will appreciate this learning experience. These kinds of experiences you never forget. This is what is called memorable moments.

"Sugar, I have arranged for you to have your riding lessons for tomorrow afternoon."

"Mom, that is a good idea; the weather is beautiful out this afternoon. Let's hope that it is the same way tomorrow."

"By the way, Jack, your father is coming to stay the weekend, and I'm going to be leaving Sunday."

# HORSES

**THE NEXT MORNING, I** was up at about 6:00 AM. That is the usual time that I like to rise. Mother placed a list of instructions on the nightstand for me sometime during the night. It instructed me what to do first for JonJon.

> *Good Morning, Sugar, I left this list for you to follow to make your morning less hectic. First, check on your brother to make sure he is still sleeping, shower, have your breakfast. By this time, it should be about 7:00 AM. By 7:00, JonJon should be awake. Check to see if he needs to be changed. If so, change his diaper. Move on to wiping the sleep from his face, remember to wipe gently, not rub. Once you have done this, it is time to feed him. If you keep a list and check off each item as you complete the task, you make fewer mistakes.*

I followed the list exactly the way it was written. To my surprise, Mom was preparing breakfast for the two of us. We sat down to have breakfast at about 6:30 AM. "Mom, I thought that I was on my own this morning?"

"You are. I'm only here as an observer to see if you follow the list and help if you're not sure what to do. So far, you are on target, which is a good thing. This way, by noon, you will be ready for your riding lessons."

"Mom, it is nice that you are here to guide me through this list, but you're here because this is what you do! It's time for me to check on JonJon." Mother was right; the list worked out fine. Right up until my riding lessons.

It was early afternoon. I was getting ready for my riding lesson when the equestrian pulled up in the drive. I had my riding boots on and hurried out the door. I did not get past the threshold of the door before I heard my mom.

"Jack, I know that you do not have your riding boots on in the house."

"Mother, I'll remember not to put them on in the house next time."

"Jack, be sure to remove your riding boots before you enter the house. I do not want you to make a mess or bring a smell back."

"Okay, Mom!"

"Love you, see you later!"

The one thing about living with my dad in Washington, D.C., you don't have to drive too far to be in no man's land. Which was an excellent place also to be surrounded by Mother Nature!

Knowing that the founding fathers of the United States passed through these woods makes me appreciate the area even more. I feel as if I could see history unfolding as we passed through these woods onward to our destination. I felt as if General George Washington could come passing through on his Great White Stallion at any moment. I could hear the gallop of his stallion in the foreground and the marching footsteps of his troops. What a magnificent and astounding feeling to know that I am here, where greatness once passed. God, I love my country! I now understand why it is said in a war to the victor go the spoils. This was not the first time I had been on this road; however, it was the first time I experienced our country's history.

We pulled up to the stable. As I was getting out of the car, a man walked over to me and asked if my name was Jack, and if I had a sister named Caroline and a brother named John.

"Sir, I believe you are mistaken! I know that I have a sister named Caroline but not a brother named John. What brother? I don't have a brother."

"Yes, what is his name?" This guy really believed I didn't know that he was a reporter. Like my father, President John F. Kennedy, would say: Never ask a question when you already know the answer. I walked away from the reporter with a smile on my face.

I was having a pleasant day until I saw that the scarecrow was here.

"Oh, hello, Jackie." It makes for a better day to call my step-mother 'Jackie' instead of 'scarecrow.'

"So, where is your brother, Jack? I have not seen him for a while."

"Stepmother, just what are you trying to say?"

"Oh, just making polite conversation, Jack."

"Jackie, it will take more than your appearance here today to upset me." I could see that Jackie was getting flustered.

"Jack, you have not answered my question. How is the babysitting working out for you? Do you like changing diapers!"

"Oh, Stepmother, what kind of rhetorical question is that?"

By this time, Jackie had climbed up on to her horse. She was rubbing me the wrong way. "Jackie, someday, in the far-off future on a day like today, you are going to feel carefree. It will be a beautiful, warm summery day. You are going to fall off your horse. You will be spatial, and you are going to make the worst decision of your life. You will see everything you have done and everything you're going to do before you hit the ground.

"I will not be there to see you fall, but I will see the landing. This fall will be the beginning of the end for you. I'll hear of your untimely demise by your own hands."

"Jack, do you have any idea how long I have been racing horses?"

"Yes, I do. You are quite the horsewoman. But that doesn't mean what I just said is not going to happen. All I am saying is it's going to happen. So it is up to you what you are going to do about it."

"Jack, do you still need help climbing up on to your horse? You place your right foot in the stirrup and bring your left leg over its backend. Make sure it is its backend and not its front end, Jack.

"Jack, you are small for your age; that horse may be too high for you."

"Oh, Stepmother. I do believe that it is time for you to ride away. Keep in mind that it is a horse you're on and not your broomstick."

"Jack, you do have a way with words!"

"Well, Stepmother, you do bring out the best in people.

"You sometimes forget that we have met some of the same people. Unlike you, I am absorbing and analyzing what is being said. So that I can find the true meaning behind any conversation that I am having with someone. In your case, you speak only because you have a tongue. Not that you ever had anything interesting to contribute to a conversation!"

My stepmother's facial expression looked as if she was ready to explode; this was my signal to exit the scene. "It's time for my riding lesson. This show is over. You have a good afternoon, Stepmother." I rode off to the riding range and spent the next two hours riding and jumping over fences before I brought the horse to a smooth stop.

On the way back home, I was in the back seat of the car, looking out the window. The ride back brought me back to that same sense of history. This time, it was even more. I could not get the thought out of my mind of just what took place here. What battles were fought here during the Civil War? It was as if some army regiment of soldiers would come walking through the woods at any moment. The sound of the car's tires on the road started turning into the echoes of soldiers' footsteps marching off to war. The sunlight came streaking from behind the tree trunks, branches, and leaves. It was a rainbow of colors, gold, red, blue, and orange, sparkling as if I was looking through a kaleidoscope!

I was in tune with the mirage that was unfolding before my very eyes. Then I noticed off in the distance houses coming into view. My eye happened to catch a glimpse of some automobiles that were parked in the driveway that were not there when I left. The changing sights brought me back to my present surroundings. There was a car parked in the driveway. That could only mean one thing, my dad was there waiting for me!

We pulled into the driveway and stopped in front of the veranda. Dad was standing there, waiting to greet me while holding my little brother in his arms. Dad's war injury did allow him to pick up my sister, brother, and me too often, but this looks like something that he wanted to experience. To hold one son in his arms and greet the other son as he arrives home.

"Hello, son. Did you have a joyful afternoon?"

"Yes, I did."

He tried to pick me up to kiss me on my forehead with JonJon in his arms. My weight, together with JonJon's, was too much for him to manage. "Son, you are taller and heavier. Pretty soon, you'll be as tall as me."

Dad always found a way to encourage me.

"Dad, I was with Jacqueline today at the stables."

"And how was she, son?"

"She was her usual self."

"You did not upset her, did you, son?"

"Oh, no! Not me, Dad!"

"Jack, that will be the day that you do not bother her." We turned to walk into the house, my brother in his arm and my hand in his. As we entered the house, my mother said the image of the three of us could be a Norman Rockwell painting. "Sugar, before you take another step in this house, please kindly remove your riding boots and get ready for supper."

"Mom, do I have enough time to shower before supper is ready?"

"Jack, you are well aware that cleanliness is one of my rules at the dinner table." *I guess that means yes.*

"Jack, sometimes you're impossible."

"By the way, Mom, what is for dinner?"

"Jack, you'll find out when you make it to the table."

Supper time finally came around; it was the same thing as if we were at my paternal grandparents' dinner table. There was always a conversation, and everyone was expected to participate in it or comment on the topic. The topic was set by the patriarch of the family, this time, my dad and President of the United States of America. I was expecting the conversation to be on domestic or world affairs. But no, the subject topic was my new experience of being a responsible big brother.

"Dad! Mother explained that this was what a big brother does. He fills in when the parents are unable to care for their child."

"Son, that is absolutely correct. The question remains, what are you feeling on the matter? Are you still reluctant to lend a hand?"

"No, Dad. Mother and I came to an understanding, and I'm willing to give my full support in the care of my little brother."

"Jack, I am elated to hear of your willingness to step up and support our family!"

"Jack, your father and I have been talking, and we have decided that you'll be meeting some people he will have a meeting with at the White House."

"Dad, what does Mom mean by that?"

"When a world leader comes to visit in the Oval Office, you are going to meet that person too."

"How are you going to manage that when Caroline and I cannot just walk down the stairs to your office? There are too many rules governing the White House."

"Son, it just depends on the door that you enter through and exit out of. Some protocols and regulations must be followed. These rules were set up by people who were ruled by Kings and Queens of Europe. The same etiquette that was used for them is used in the Oval Office protocol.

"The White House Residence, where we stay, is off-limits to the CIA but not the FBI. The CIA is to investigate international crimes that have occurred or may occur. The FBI only has the right to be up there if a crime has been committed. The Oval Office is where I conduct the country's business. When foreign dignitaries visit the Oval Office, they are there to represent their countries and trade. So they enter the office through particular doors. It's called following protocol."

"So the visiting dignitaries come in the front door, and I come in the back door?"

"Yes, son. You will be there as an observer that is allowed so long as we follow the protocol.

"You will be the first child of a United States President to say 'I was there.' What I want is for you to say I met some of the same people that my father did. This way, no one can say I kept you in the dark. You will be front and center!"

Mother sat there gleaming like a well-lit Christmas tree the first night that someone flicked on the switch. My dad sat back in his chair as if he was a general of some Army who had just laid out a well thought out plan to conquer his enemies. It was a father ensuring the safety and security of his son and family.

"Son, I know that you had a long day. You look as if you are going to fall asleep right here on the table."

"Dad, may I be excused from the table?"

"Yes, you may, son. Make sure you brush your teeth and wash your face. I'll be in to tuck you in and say our goodnight prayers."

It was not unusual for both my parents to come into the bedroom and tuck us in. The thing that made this night different was that I noticed when my mother left the room.

My father walked over to JonJon's crib and leaned over to whisper in his ear. I thought, *What could he be saying to a baby?* He finished whispering and picked up JonJon's hand and kissed it, and said goodnight.

He turned and walked gently over to where I was sleeping. He sat on the bed and whispered in my ear and kissed me on the forehead. Dad is truly a father in every sense of the word. He treated us as equals, doing for each of his children what needed to be done. He did not play favorites.

The weekend was ending; it was time for Mom to return to California and Dad to D.C. As planned, I stayed with my dad. There were school days and tutors, and between all of this, I cared for my brother the best I could. That is what Mother expected of me: to do my best. She always said, If you don't place the spoon all the way to the bottom of the pot to stir the stew, it will stick." Meaning if you do not change your brother right the first time, I'll have to do it all over again. So if you do not intend to do the job well, don't do it at all.

Being in the White House residence was like visiting a museum. So long as you stayed in your assigned area, you were okay. Try going outside the designated territory, and there was always someone to stop you. A foot soldier is lurking in every corner of the Executive branch of the White House. I named these places 'the forbidden zones.'

What helped me to cope with all the rules was that everyone needed a hall pass, including the First Lady Jacqueline, to enter a forbidden zone. What made the forbidden exciting was that it was closed off to everyone. They would all give me their version of why it was forbidden. Still, when it came right down to it, it was because it was the Executive Office of the United States of America.

The White House staff made me feel welcome, but there was always that sense that I was a guest in my own home. Equal to being in your favorite aunt or uncle's house: you are welcome, but soon you will have to go back to your parents' house, so don't wear out your welcome. I was always polite and respectful of my elders, as to not embarrass my parents or myself. Plus, there was that musical baton that was in the back of my mind that Grandma Rose used on us. The one she used to tap me on the shoulder with to let me know that I was not on my best behaver. If there was a tap on my shoulder, I knew that she was annoyed, but if she poked me with that damn baton, her wrath would come later.

The explanation Mother gave me was, "Your Grandmother Rose comes from the last century, where the only thing a girl had was her poise and charm. They were expected to have large families and smiles and make-believe that they were content with their life. Whatever you learn from her, it will become useful to you someday. You can capture your audience's attention by how polite you are. So always be courteous and respectful of those around you." Mother was right; it did me no good to be ornery or mean. It only makes matters worse.

Speaking of making matters worse, father received an urgent call from Grandpa. He was in a huff over something that my mother had said. When Grandpa Joe was upset, and I mean angry to the point of livid, I could hear what he said while he was conversing with my father by the telephone.

Grandpa's words and voice could bring down the walls of Jericho all over again. This time, he was upset with what mother had said to the cast and crew when she returned to work. Someone had replied, "Marilyn, you're looking good, like always, but it looks like you lost weight. What did you do, have a baby?"

From what I could hear, Grandpa Joe said, "John, your wife Marilyn turned around and answered, 'Yes I did, and it was a BOY!' It looks as if there is no controlling Marilyn, and she is going to be a force to be reckoned with."

"Dad, you do understand that Marilyn is doing what is best for our children? If she wants to inform her coworkers that she and I have another child, that is fine with me.

"Marilyn has made it clear to you that she does not need, nor does she want, anything from the Kennedy family as a whole. All that she needs is for you and Robert to stay out of her family rearing."

"Jack, you are the President of the United States. Do you know what can happen if this gets out? We will be unable to control it."

"Dad, maybe it would be for the best that the public was aware that Marilyn and I have children together."

"Son, if the public ever found out that Robert helped to cover up the fact that you and Marilyn were married, his political career would be over."

"Dad, have you ever thought what we are doing to Jack Jr. and JonJon is wrong? Marilyn has every God-given right to do what she has to do to protect her family. Look at this through her eyes. You are one of the most influential men in the United States, and just look at what you are asking of her. There are no guarantees that this family is going to live up to their obligations and do the right thing for our children. In Marilyn's eyes, we are all not trustworthy. She is still having a hard time understanding how a family like ours can ask her to give up being a wife and a mother. She is not going to play ball with you and Robert. If you believe that you and Robert are going to stifle my wife, Marilyn, you are mistaken!"

I had never heard Dad speak to Grandpa Joe like that before. It was not a lack of respect but more of a firm husband and father speaking to his father. The feeling of euphoria came over me to hear my father defending this family. It was one of those moments as if I was a mouse in a trap, understanding these two giants defending their actions. I was keenly aware that Dad wanted me to overhear his conversation with Grandfather Joe. The calmness that I heard in my dad's voice, I still hear today. It is just as surreal now as it was then. It is one of those rare moments in time that brings back this event.

To see my dad leaning back in his chair, holding the phone to his ear to make sure that his father understood what he was going through. There was no smiling or laughter on my father's face, just sadness. As if to say to his dad, do you have any idea what you are asking of me? His pain was cutting through me like a thousand little paper cuts. Each paper cut was etching his pain into my memory so that I would never lose sight of what was being said.

I do not recall if my father said goodbye, just that he hung up the phone and asked me to come closer to him. I was too old to sit on his lap, but not too old to be kissed on the forehead, and that is what he did. He kissed me on my forehead. It's a feeling that only a father can give to his son. He made me feel safe and secure, and that everything that he and my mother were doing was in the best interest of our family.

My dad was true to his word; he had me come down from the White House residence to the Oval Office to meet with some of the same people that he was meeting with. This was his way of introducing me to history in the making.

# WITNESSING HISTORY

**THE PREPARATION WOULD TAKE** hours, days, or weeks; it just depended on whom I was going to meet with – some president, dignitary, or a leader of some cause. Dad would give me some material to read and asked me some questions about the person that I was going to meet before meeting them. These were people who were out to change the world or bend it to his or her will. Dad made sure that I knew the name of each president and which country they came from. As for dignitaries, I had to know which post they held in their government. The most interesting were the leaders of a cause.

Meeting some of these people was proving to be more comfortable than others. President Charles de Gaulle of The Republic of the French was a tall, thin man who spoke and carried himself as the general that he once was, but now he was the President of France.

When I entered the room to meet Mr. de Gaulle, I felt a sense of respect and admiration. Here were two men that helped to end World War II, each in their own way. President John F. Kennedy said to President Charles de Gaulle, "I would like you to meet my son John Junior. He is here to meet you so that he'll learn that fear is easily overcome. What stories Junior will be able to tell! When Junior is in school, studying world history, he will be able to say 'I shook hands with Pres. de Gaulle.'"

In response to what President John F. Kennedy, my dad, had just said, Pres. de Gaulle replied, "Well then, let us not reveal any government secrets." Once Pres. de Gaulle said that, it put the room at ease, something only a great general could do. There is something to be said when you are in a place with a General like de Gaulle.

President de Gaulle was quite surprised to learn that I knew the role he played in World War II and that he was, in fact, a General in the French Army. Now, Mr. de Gaulle is the Pres. of France, and his goal is to return France to being a significant player of substance on the world stage. Not that France would play second fiddle to anyone, just that he wanted the French people to have a say in world events. For me, it was fascinating to meet someone whom my grandparents and parents have spoken of around the dining room table. Here I was, meeting one of the many people who helped to end World War II.

Meeting Pres. de Gaulle helped me understand why my grandfather was adamant about having a meaningful conversation at the dinner table. When meeting someone of de Gaulle's stature, the image sometimes does not live up to a person's expectations. Here he was, the general of an Army. He was standing in front of me. All I could think was, *He is just as tall as my father.*

Perhaps I would have been more impressed if I would have met him in his youth or with his army standing behind him. All in all, the best thing to do is not embarrass yourself or the country and keep your opinions to yourself. As my mother would say, "Jack, you do not have to comment on everything. Some things are best left unsaid."

President de Gaulle had already been informed that I would be meeting with him, if only for a few minutes. He was asked if it would be okay with him. This was to be a learning experience for me and something I would keep with me for the rest of my life. Whenever my dad used those words, 'learning experience,' I knew that during dinner, there would be a question-and-answer session with both parents. Meeting President de Gaulle would be no exception.

As always in the White House, what door you enter depended on who you were going to meet. It is all about the door. Did I just meet the President of France or the general of the French army? Or is de Gaulle just a citizen of France? This would be one of the questions from my dad at the dinner table. Not what role did de Gaulle play in World War II? Instead, who did I meet?

Like clockwork, my mother called me at five o'clock that afternoon. She asked how my day was and how I liked meeting Pres. de Gaulle.

"Mom, it was great, but I was expecting something more of an Army type of a person. Who I met was a gentleman in a suit and tie. His shoes were shined so much I could see my reflection, and he seemed kind enough."

"Son, you have to put more emphasis on his achievements and not your expectations."

"Mom, I'll have to think about that one."

"Jack, just put more thought into who you are meeting and their accomplishments, and it will help you to understand what is going on around you. It is not all about the world you live in, but the world around you. Your father and I want you to learn about different people and about their culture and how they interest you. It will give you a different perspective on life and help you treat all people with the same respect and attention."

"Mother, I did not mean to upset you, but what more can I say about a person that I spent no more than ten minutes with? If you are this upset with me, what do you think I am going to have to come up with when Dad asks me that same question at dinner?"

"Jack, I do not know, but you better come up with a meaningful answer. You have time to come up with something interesting to say at the dinner table tonight. Your dad will call you on it.

"If the only thing you could come up with is de Gaulle's shiny shoes, it may not be entirely your fault. The French are very conservative people and don't have the same sense of humor us Americans have."

"Mother, Dad is going to ask me some off-the-wall question about de Gaulle at the dinner table, and I'm going to have to come up with the answer he wants to hear. It is time for me to go. I'll speak to you later."

As I placed the telephone on the hook, I thought Mother was right. If I were going to take anything away from meeting the head of state, I would have to put more emphasis on the quality and accomplishments of the person and not my expectations of them. How does my mother do that? She makes me reconsider my opinion but did not come right out and say, you need to say this or that.

It was back up to my bedroom to put my thinking cap on. I was well aware of what the dinner conversation topic was going to be on. However, what was I going to bring to the table? Surely it could not be about de Gaulle's high-gloss shoeshine. Dad will blow a gasket if I bring that to the table. I could hear him now. "Jack, this is not about some high-gloss shine on some roadster. This is about a man who helped to liberate his country from occupying forces! You'll have to do better than that!"

There is nothing worse at the dinner table than to not bring some substance to the conversation. Hopefully, we'll have a late dinner, and that will put an end to my dilemma!

As always, someone comes along and slashes your hopes for salvation. "Dinner will be served at 7:00 PM. Do not be late to the dining room table." Wow! That gives me 45 minutes to come up with some excuse not to have dinner this evening. If I am a no-show at the dining room table, Dad would have to leave the dining room to find out for himself just what is wrong, and there will be Cane to pay if he finds that I'm faking it.

I'll shower now; that way, I will not have to shower before bed. Showering now will be my bird in the hand. Next, I'll lay out my dark blue jacket, light blue knitted pullover, and khaki trousers with black shoes. Hopefully, Dad will get the hint that I do not want to get involved in any stimulating conversation about meeting de Gaulle! I headed into the dining room at 6:50 PM. *That way, I'll be the first one at the table and the first to be excused from the table. That's a well thought out plan! I just hope it works.*

Not to put Dad wise to what I was doing, I sat down at the dining room at 6:51 PM to appear as if I was waiting for him to arrive instead of Dad waiting for me. I could count on Dad's internal clock to work to my advantage. He entered the dining room at 7 PM sharp, not 1 minute early or 1 minute late.

"My mother has taught you well; you are at the dining room table, not keeping your elders waiting. Son, you are making my generation of Kennedy's look bad. That seems a little out of place for you to be at the dinner table on time. Since you believe that eating is a waste of time." I could not help but feel the cat was out of the bag. I know with what Dad had just said, I had to manipulate the conversation in my direction.

"No! Dad, I'm excited to have met with the former General and now President of France Charles de Gaulle."

As I was speaking, I reached for the linden napkin and placed it on my lap. Hoping all the while Dad's presidential mode would kick in and that, since he is the leader of the free world, hopefully, he'll take the dinner topic in another direction.

I could easily say I outfoxed the fox, but here it comes! He pulled his chair in, sat up, and leaned back with his shoulders parallel to the painting on the wall. His green eyes looked at me as if to say, I'm aware of what you are trying to do! "So you find President de Gaulle fascinating?" There it was! The feeling of being a mouse caught in its own trap.

"Son, I am not an avid hunter, but your facial expression does resemble a deer caught in the headlights of a car." Only my dad could bring a cartoon character to the dinner table, and he was right, the game was over.

"So, son, what do you find fascinating?"

"Dad, his life resembles Napoleon; here are two extraordinary men in history living the same experience. The only thing that separates the two men is time and circumstances. Napoleon Bonaparte trying to create an empire, President Charles de Gaulle restoring France to pre-World War II glory as a force to be reckoned with."

"Jack, that was well-stated; you did not bring substance to the conversation. You managed to echo his cause. The French Empire is giving way to independence. Still, I do not believe that her influence on the world stage will ever diminish or has diminished."

I have attended enough of these dinner conversations to know that two things were going to happen. The topic was going to become more detailed, and I was in way over my head. I had to come up with a legitimate reason to leave the dining room table. The only thing I could come up with was that I did not like to eat dessert. I preferred to eat most of my vegetables, but for me, dessert is one of life's pleasures I could do without. Since I was at my own table and not an invited guest to dinner, I felt I could say no to dessert. Dad was well aware that I did not like dessert after having dinner, so this would be a good reason to leave the dinner table before dinner had ended.

"Dad, I do not feel like having dessert. May I be excused from the table?"

"Yes, you may, son."

About that time, Jackie asked, "You're not going to sit through dessert with us? We are having strawberry shortcakes."

"No, thank you. I had a long day. You have cake." Stepmother sat there for a second or two with this blank look on her face.

The next thing I noticed, her face was turning red! She started questioning Dad, "Do you understand what he is saying?"

Dad turned to me. "I don't think he knows what he is implying. Jackie, my dear, you are blowing his comment out of proportion. Jack, if you are done with your dinner, it's time for you to turn in."

It was customary in the Kennedy household not to leave the dining room table without being asked to be excused, and mother always said to have a peaceful meal at dinner is to be one with God. But I just had to bring up Marie Antoinette let them eat cake. I do not know if Antoinette said to 'let them eat cake,' but it sure fits in here. After all, I did meet de Gaulle earlier today. Besides, Jacqueline knows me all too well. We can't resist taking a jab at each other; it's what we do. I guess she turned red-faced because she left herself wide open for that one. I could not help but chuckle as I was walking away.

Dad came into my room to tuck me in bed and say goodnight. He had a ritual that he would not whisper the same phrase twice. I often witnessed him whispering into Caroline and JonJon's ear too. Was he whispering the same phrase to the three of us, or was he changing it up? If I was going to get a meaningful answer, I would have to wait for the right time to ask him.

The next two dignitaries that I met were of the same substance but unique to themselves. One was the hammer and the other the sickle. Premier Nikita Khrushchev was what I would call the Hammer. He would clench his fist and raise his right arm to drive his point home. I've seen him do this in person in the United Nations in New York City and on television. It was quite a spectacle to see Khrushchev in action, and his action was always an attention grabber. When I met him in person, he was not that same overbearing man.

I recall that Khrushchev had a grandfather feel about him somehow. This man cares about the children. He was not that overpowering figure that I had seen from afar. When I entered the room, Khrushchev said to my father, "So this is your son, Jack." I don't think it was a real question, but more like 'it's about time I meet your eldest son in person.'

"Am I meeting your son Jack as a social call or as the son of the President of the United States?"

"Yes, as the son of the President of the United States."

"So this is the son of Marilyn Monroe, the movie star?"

"Yes, he is her son, and I am the father."

"Mr. President, what makes you believe that we did not know how many children you father?"

"I never meant it to be a secret that Marilyn and I have a son."

"Mr. President, Jack Jr. is the worst-kept secret that I have come across in a very long time.

"People have to be closed-minded or not aware of their surroundings, not to notice the way you look at Marilyn. To see in the flesh what that look produced, it's an honor and pleasure to meet your son Jack Jr. firsthand. What a head of hair he has and not a bad-looking child if I do say so myself."

To see my dad and Khrushchev talking as one father to another was astonishing. One the leader of the free world and the other the leader of Communist Russia, talking to one another as if they did not have a care in the world. It made me feel as if these two men could solve any world crisis.

They are so close but yet so far apart. If all that is in between these two leaders is their ideology, why can't they resolve their differences? This is too much for one person to handle. How do these two come together for me but cannot find common ground for peaceful coexistence? The baffled look on my face did not go unnoticed. By either my dad, President John F. Kennedy, or Premier Nikita Khrushchev, it was as if both men knew what I was thinking.

"Jack, it's time for you to turn to your studies." I shook Premier Khrushchev's hand, "It was nice to meet you. You are more of a kind giant than the ferocious Russian Bear that I expected to meet today."

"Jr., I see that you have done your homework. We *are* ferocious; do not let the Russian Black Bear kindness fool you. We believe that if you take care of the young in our country, they will take care of when you're older."

As we said our goodbyes, I could see that my dad had a sense of accomplishment on his face. It was as if he knew that I would always keep some part of this meeting in my subconscious mind.

I walked out of the room, thinking, This is not the end of my encounter with Premier Nikita Khrushchev. There would be a dinner conversation that I would have to prepare for with my dad. I could not for the life of me understand why we had to have a discussion at dinner. The dinner table is to enjoy your meal and be one with God. Most of the time, the Kennedy clan try to one-up each other, not that anyone had anything new to bring to the table, just mindless, meaningless conversation.

I have to get my thoughts on something else.

Grandpa Howard Hughes's dinner table was an adventure in itself. Grandpa Hughes's dinner table was always more interesting, like the story of the Spruce Goose. To hear how he came up with the idea to fly that big bird that he created. To hear him tell how he took off in the Spruce Goose, for lack of a better name. How he fired up the plane's engines one by one. He could feel the contact of spark to the Pistons and the fuel combusting in the engine's cylinders. One by one, the propellers had made contact; it was time for him to show just what he had accomplished. Was this Goose going to fly? He pulled back on the throttle. He could feel the plane start to shake and the belly of the Goose skimming above the water as if the Spruce Goose was a bird on a pair of jet skis rising out of the water. The front of the plane lifted out of the water first. He was gliding across the water. Next was the tail of the aircraft that lifted out of the water. "I am airborne; this big bird is flying."

The joy that Grandpa Hughes had telling us that one act of accomplishment left us feeling that we were in the company of someone who still had more to achieve in their life. There was more to come from Grandpa Hughes, and not just the Spruce Goose. This was a man who loves aviation. To hear him tell it, he was not done with flying or building planes.

Now that is the kind of dinner conversation I enjoyed having. It was as if I was in the cockpit with Grandpa Hughes from the moment he envisioned the concept of the Spruce Goose until its one and only flight. Not this meaningless, mindless chatter that is so often discussed at the Kennedy compound. When the same topic comes up, I would often sit at the dinner table, thinking, What is going on? I'm going to have to come up with something exciting and meaningful just to have a seat at the dinner table tonight. Why?

It's better if I just go upstairs to check on my brother JonJon; he may need changing. If my dad expects me to come up with something witty, intelligent, or meaningful at the dinner table tonight, I'll have to enlighten him on my duties as a big brother. This topic should be suitable for all parties at the table.

As luck would have it, my dad had other engagements that evening, and my brother and sister and I would be dining alone. One thing I could always count on was my mother calling me like clockwork at 5:00 PM to find out how my day was and to check up on my little brother. She was the one who informed me that my dad would not be joining us for dinner. Now I was going to get away with not having to have my opinion heard on Premier Khrushchev. No! That topic was going to be discussed at a later date. As my dad had explained in great detail, dinner conversation will improve my communication skills. And an ability to carry on a meaningful dialogue with my counterparts, whomever they may be.

By some design, my parents came up with, I was to meet Andrei Gromyko from Russia. I found him somewhat like the Russian sickle, sharp. I did not know in which direction he would swing his sickle, only that he would. He was more formal in attitude, unlike Khrushchev. He had this no-nonsense attitude about him as if he did not like to be in the same room with children.

My dad seemed more presidential to me as if this was the first time these two have met. My father introduced me to Mr. Gromyko.

"Jack, this is Andrei Gromyko; he is the Foreign Minister of Russia." Gromyko's handshake was firm and gripping, the kind of grip that would not let your hand go. There was this cold chill in the room; I can still sense it. It was as if he was holding the Cold War together. President John F. Kennedy was standing tall and firm as if he was still the Commander of PT 109 in the middle of World War ll. But this time, he was the Commander in Chief of the Armed Forces of the United States of America. His posture was saying: I'm not going to give one damn inch.

When he was talking to Mr. Gromyko, I noticed indecisiveness in his voice. That could only mean one thing: President John F. Kennedy did not want to let on what he had in store for Mr. Gromyko and Khrushchev. The encounter with Mr. Andrei Gromyko was one of those no-nonsense meetings. It was a hello and goodbye type of introduction, no small talk.

Why is it that parents think that children do not have questions? Life is a learning experience, and it starts from the moment we are born. Each time some event takes place in our life, we feel as if we experienced that event before, or it is new to us. I was aware of my surroundings, and I understood just who I was meeting. However, in my subconscious mind, there was that nagging question! Just what does all this have to do with me? How was it going to play out in my life? Would meeting all of these heads of states and dignitaries have a positive or negative impact on my life? These are real concerns that children have that adults think are nonexistent in their children. But we can feel and recall as they do. Was meeting Gromyko a positive or negative thing? Only time will tell.

My dad, President John F. Kennedy, introduced me to Dr. Martin Luther King Jr. Would meeting Dr. Martin Luther King Jr. be lost on me? I recall the morning I met Dr. King.

I looked like a shiny new silver quarter. My dad made sure that I had a high gloss shine on my belt buckle and shoes the night before. "Son, you are going to meet someone tomorrow morning that is going to change the way that men respect one another. Dr. King is going to put an end to segregation, and we are going to help him. I want you to sit in silence and absorb as much information as you can in tomorrow's meeting. Someday you'll be able to say you were there in the room when discrimination and segregation started to crumble. You are going to step out of the class bubble that you live in and enter into the real world."

The next morning, I was going to meet a man that was larger than life. The kind of man that was going to make history and change the way I viewed the world. I could feel knots in my stomach, and the knots were getting tighter to the point that the only thing I could do was stand straight and tall as I entered the room to meet Dr. King. It was the longest four steps I have ever taken in my life to meet someone. The feeling that I had was as if I was going to spontaneously combust. I knew that I was meeting someone that was determined to bring change to the injustice that was being done to all people, not just African American people. Dr. King was going to do all this through non-violence.

As I walked up to my dad, he said, "Dr. King, I would like you to meet my son Jack Jr. Son, this is Dr. Martin L. King, the leader of the civil rights moment."

Dr. King shook my hand as if to say we are on equal ground; it was a feeling of real honor to be standing with Dr. King. I said hello and sat down next to Dr. King. I did not say a word.

President Kennedy and Dr. King began to strategize just what course the civil rights movement was going to take and what part President Kennedy was going to play. Dr. King assured the president that the civil rights movement was and always will be nonviolent, so long as he was at the helm of the campaign. Dr. King started off talking about the three branches of government and their workings. There is the executive branch, legislative branch, and the judicial branch. They discussed how they were going to bring about real change that would reflect the makeup of the United States.

"Dr. King, as long as you do not advocate for any changes in these three branches of government and stay within the framework of the United States Constitution, you have my full support and backing of this administration."

"Mr. President, I'll keep your advice in mind and do my best to adhere to it. Mr. President, you mentioned in our phone conversation that you had something personal to speak with me about."

"I did have a favor to ask of you, but the opposition that you are encountering is too much to trouble you with my personal problem. You have already helped me just by agreeing to let Jack Jr. sit in on our conversation. I am sure he'll not forget what we have discussed here today. Dr. King, I'll be with you every step of the way. I'll be the shadow behind the man in your movement for civil rights."

With that said, I was rushed out of the office. As always, I would go out one door, and someone else would come in the other.

I had no time to reflect on who I just met or what had been said. I had been whisked away as if I was not supposed to be there with Dad and Dr. King.

I did not understand at the time what the fuss was all about. This was just men planning and strategizing how to make America a place where all people can enjoy the fruits of their labor and to live freely. I guess I'll have to bring this topic up at the dinner table. This was indeed an exciting and educational experience I had this morning. I have the rest of the afternoon to find out more about Dr. King. The first thing I have to do is check on JonJon.

Once my chores were done, I was able to concentrate on the morning events. Being around Dad's work was like a set of encyclopedias were playing out in front of me; all that knowledge coming together in one room was impressive. Most parents believe that their children do not comprehend what's going on around them. My aunts and uncles never felt that kids remember or can recall some events. They need to know that if a child participates in their surroundings, it makes for a brighter future for the child.

Just how was I going to use Dad's and Dr. King's meeting this morning, I didn't know. But with time, I'd figure it out. I just had to wait and ask Mother her opinion on what happened this morning. She always had excellent insight into what was going on in the world.

Later on that afternoon, Mom called, and we talked about the meeting that Dad and I had with Dr. King earlier that day.

"Sugar, how did you like meeting Dr. King?"

"I like Dr. King. He and my dad seemed to work together well. Something about trying to change the Jim Crow laws in the Southern states."

"Son, do you recall the trip that you went on with your dad through the southern part of the country? Do you remember the sign that read 'people of color are not allowed?' Jack, in some states, discrimination is based on the color of someone's skin. It is prevalent and legal. The best example I can give you is when an entertainer performing the same work that I do is paid less than I make only because of the color of their skin. When a segment of society sets out to discriminate against anyone for the color of their skin or national origins of their religion, it should not and must not be tolerated.

"Sugar, if you do not understand any of the words that I just mentioned, look up the definition in the dictionary. Break it down to their simplest terms. Do not only read the first line in the description but read the whole definition of the word. This way, you'll have the entire meaning of the word and not just assume what the words mean. Get a thesaurus and look up the synonym and antonym of the word, that way you'll fully understand the meaning of Dr. King and the Civil Rights movement."

"Mom, you and Dad are going to cause me to take off in orbit; this is just too much to absorb in one day."

"Jack, just think of all this as a learning experience. I guarantee you'll be a better person for it. This is what life is about: learning and growing so that you'll have a better tomorrow."

"Dad is going to expect me to participate in dinner conversation, and what do I have to offer?"

"Sugar, you have an abundance of information and experience to bring to any discussion, not just at the dinner table."

"I guess you're right, Mom! I'll just have to brush up on the Civil Rights Movement. I'll wait for you to call tomorrow."

"Love and kisses, Sugar."

"You too, Mom." As I hung up the phone, it occurred to me that she was right. I was all worked up over nothing.

Dad had not asked me my opinion on any of the people that I had met with at dinner; however, I knew it was coming. He was going to wait to see how I was going to utilize the allotted time he had given me to prepare. Dad liked to see just how well one was prepared on any given subject that came up at the dinner table. It was his way of 'schooling me' as he would say.

I made it through three nights without one question about anyone I had met or what had transpired in his office. That was not like him. I had been by my dad's side too long not to be prepared for what was coming next. I always kept in the back of my mind what he would say, "I want my kids to be well-mannered, polite, and above all, well-informed on world events." I am going to make my Dad proud. This is going to be the one time I dazzled the adults at the table with my opinions and make Joe and Kathy red-faced with envy. There was no way I was going be caught in the outhouse with my pants down, as my dad likes to say. I had three days for rest and relaxation. I was going to be prepared.

The weekend had snuck up on me. It was Friday, and my dad and I were on a train to Hyannis Port to meet my mother for the weekend. Dad's mood was somber; it was the same look he had when he was thinking about our future. He sat in silence, staring out the window out into the far distance. If I spoke to him, it would bring him back from the bewilderment that he was in.

I wanted to say, "Dad, don't worry. Everything will turn out fine." Better yet, I wished that some stranger would interrupt us so my dad would snap out of it. Here we were, the President of the United States and his son taking a train ride home. The passengers had no idea that their president was taking a train ride with them. I wanted us to remain inconspicuous. I looked out the window and started counting telephone poles to myself as we were passing them.

Having a large family, there was always someone there to meet us at our final destination. This time it was Uncle Steve. Dad and Uncle Steve did not say too much to each other on the ride to my dad's home. Dad still had not shaken that bewildered look that he had. We got out of the car. Dad, taking me by my hand, looked over at my grandparents' home, shook his head, and walked into the house. It made me feel as if he did not want to see his extended family.

The next morning was Saturday. Mom had arrived sometime during the night. Knowing that my mother was here made watching the early morning sunrise breaking over the horizon from my bedroom window more enjoyable. I felt if I did not witness the dawn of the sun that I was going to miss out on something. Observing the sun break through the horizon felt as if there would be some spectacular event during the day. To feel that warm morning sun embracing my face as I look out the window with my arms on the windowpane and my chin resting on my arms took me into my own enchanting world. Mom said I look like a Norman Rockwell painting sitting there looking out the window. The way the sun's rays streaked through my hair, turning it red.

The day started out like any typical Saturday at the Kennedy compound. Kids running in and out of the house and adults doing what they do. Grandmother asked Dad where Jacqueline was. "Will she be joining us this weekend?"

"I believe she is in Virginia horseback riding or may be floating around the Mediterranean with her sister Lee and Aristotle Onassis."

"Son, there is no need to get testy; all I did was ask a question."

"Mother, that is like asking me who was holding Dad's hand while he was in California. Or yours, for that matter while you were here alone."

Mom said to both Dad and Grandma Rose, "I did not come here to hear anyone in this family rehash the past. It is the future that we need to concern ourselves with; there are young lives here that we have to take into consideration."

Mom and Dad spent the day walking and talking on the beach. I could see that whatever the topic of conversation was, it was intense. Mom was telling Dad something he did not want to hear. I did what I do best: just sat back and went along for the ride. This was one afternoon that I was happy to see come to an end.

We did the usual Sunday morning thing, to attend morning mass. We waited to have breakfast three hours before worship or three hours after worship. What the reasoning behind waiting to eat is I did not know. I was taught it had something to do with Catholicism. Grandma Rose, on the other hand, said we come from the land of plenty: therefore, we should sacrifice ourselves to a light Sunday breakfast after mass. That meant that we were all going to have two eggs and two slices of bread without butter and jam. I guess this was Grandma Rose's way of teaching us humility, either way, I always felt eating was a waste of time.

After breakfast, Mom and Dad were still in their own world talking. I still had no idea what they were talking about, but Mother was doing most of the talking and Dad, well, he was just listening. Anytime anyone tried to eavesdrop on their conversation, Mom or Dad would shoo them away. It was like the children's song, There are flies in my buttermilk, shoo fly, shoo! You are not wanted around here. Sometimes adults just don't get it; kids will keep coming back to irritate them.

It was around 12:30 in the afternoon that we were told to start getting ready for lunch. That meant that it was time to change into something more formal. It would be khaki pants, a white shirt, tie, and a navy-blue blazer with gold buttons. It seemed like it was going to be more of a formal lunch gathering with some special guests, but it turned out it was just the immediate family.

Grandpa Joe started out the afternoon meal by saying grace. "Thank you, Lord, for what we are about to receive." During the blessing, we were not allowed to raise our heads, but there was no rule on looking around the table with our eyes. That is just what I did: raised my eyes to take a look. Here we were, all sitting around the table as if we were all soldiers, and Grandpa was the general of his army. This meal was enough to make up for the morning toast without butter and jam. If Grandma ever figured out what I was doing or thinking at the table, she would have asked me to leave the room.

All at once, the napkins came off the plates and onto our laps. It was like clockwork. Mom was a little faster; she placed my napkin on my lap, looking over at Grandpa and taking a glance at Grandmother. By the expression on their faces, it was as if Mother was going to drop a bomb. That one act gave the adults an indication of what my parents had been discussing all morning. It was my mother being defiant. Dad saved the day! "Junior, which of the gentlemen from Russia did you find more appealing?"

"I found Khrushchev to be more receptive to children. It seemed to me that you found him easy to work with. It was a nice touch that he invited me to visit the Kremlin. He was not at all like the man that I had seen on television. He did not throw his weight around, although he is an important man. When you meet someone like Khrushchev, you feel that he walks with a sickle in one hand and he swings a hammer in the other hand.

"Khrushchev represents Russian ideas, and Gromyko implements Russian policy. They represent the Russian people very well. One is the hammer and the other the sickle."

"That is a good point, son; however, what exactly is it you mean by that?"

"Khrushchev seems to want to keep the Cold War going. It works for him. Gromyko, on the other hand, looks like a man that understands that some kind of change is needed. Just what kind of change is anyone's guess. Who is going to make the change? We will have to wait for the outcome."

As I was speaking, I focused most of my attention on my parents. They were beaming with pride, as well as my grandfather. It was my aunts and uncles who did not look too happy. Uncle Robert was envious and looked like a volcano ready to erupt. He was not the only one at the table whose face was red. There was Uncle Edward, Sgt. Shriver, Uncle Steve, and even Uncle Lawford were all pinkish with surprise about whom I had met. Uncle Robert was the only one to speak up at the table.

"Jack, it seems as if you are grooming Junior to be the president of the United States."

"Bob, is there a question in there someplace, or are you trying to dominate the topic of conversation? That is a rhetorical question that does not need an answer, Bob.

"What I am doing is preparing Junior for his future, and if that means someday he would like to be president, then so be it.

"Robert, I hope it is not handed down from one brother to another as it was done to me. Our bother Joe should be standing here now, not me."

"Don't take my words out of context, Jack."

"Robert, I'm calling it the way it is. If Jack wants to be president of this country, that is his decision."

"Mr. President well said. Is there anyone else that we should know about that Jack has met with?"

"Robert, he'll let you know by the end of lunch if you decide to make the conversation flow in that direction."

Just about that time, Grandpa Joe spoke up, "I will not have dissension in this family. You understand that, Robert. If John wants to steer Junior to a political career, no better time than the present to start."

My dad was doing the right thing carrying on the Kennedy family tradition by starting me out in politics at such a young age. Uncle Bobby was not going to let the topic of conversation go in another direction. What he was after was to find out who exactly Dad was introducing me to.

When I had let on that I had met President Charles de Gaulle of France, Uncle Bobby became more enraged. I could see the tips of his ears turning red from where I was.

"Junior, do you even know who President de Gaulle is?"

"Uncle Robert, President de Gaulle was a general in the Second World War. He helped to liberate France from occupied Germans. He would like to return France back into a World Power. However, the days of the great empires of the world have sadly come to an end, not that France will ever take a back seat to any nation. The world indeed had changed."

I felt as if I was in my element sitting at the table having an adult conversation. As I was speaking, I would glance at each uncle, aunt, and cousin. Grandpa Joe, looking over at Dad and Mom, said, "It seems as if you have the makings of a real statesman there."

It was a surreal feeling to know that I had the attention of my audience; it was as if I was having an out of body experience.

The conversation at the dining room table was going back and forth from one person to another. Grandfather kept bringing the conversation over in my direction. I felt as if he was testing me on my knowledge of world events. What events had happened, and who was responsible for what. "Junior, you seem to have met several European leaders. Have you met anyone in particular from here?"

"Yes, I have Grandpa."

Again, all eyes were on me.

"I met Dr. Martin Luther King, the civil rights leader."

"Junior, you have been very busy meeting people. What can you tell us about Dr. King? Do you believe he'll achieve equality for everyone in America?"

The word equality was my grandpa's way of throwing me off my guard. He used the word equality to ensure that I was not guessing at what he was saying. He wanted to know that I did my homework on the topics at hand. I did not let his grasp for the English language dissuade me. I understood that equality for all and the civil rights movement are one and the same. You cannot have one without the other.

"Dr. King, by far, is the one who impresses me the most. He is a man who wants to change things for all people, not just one group of people. The Doctor is asking that people from all walks of life should be able to come to any table and must be treated as an equal. He would like to see the same books that I read in school are available to all children. Not like the books that I had seen when I was going through the South last school year. The books were all out of date. Without proper education, how does a society pull itself out of poverty?

"When I was visiting Miami Beach, I noticed there were separate restrooms. It read 'white' or 'colored only.' That in itself is racist and discriminatory. If we truly live in a free society, this cannot stand. There can be no separate but equal in a free society."

As I was conveying my opinion, I glanced around the table. I could feel that I had captured my audience once again. I could see the envy on the faces of my aunts and uncles. Dad was the first one to ask, "Son, do you believe meeting Dr. King changed your views on Civil Rights? In other words, would you support the Civil Rights Movement?"

"Yes, Dad. I think we will become a better nation for it."

Here I was, having lunch with my dad, who just happens to be the leader of the free world. I was having an out-of-body experience. I was well aware that I had the attention of the room, and my body and soul were one. It was as if I could see my own spirit standing on the right side of me, looking at myself, saying, "Excellent job." The feeling lasted for a moment, gone the next.

Mom asked, "Sugar, are you ok?"

"Yes, Mom, I am fine." It was as if she was seeing and feeling the same thing I was.

Grandpa Joe said to my dad, "Jack, I believe we have the makings of the next generation of politicians. Junior knows how to captivate his audience."

*I have to admit, having long, drawn-out conversation parties are not all that bad.*

Uncle Robert and Uncle Edward were not too happy with my performance. They came to the conclusion that my father was wasting his time introducing me to people like Dr. King. Uncle Robert believed that I would not remember meeting Dr. King, much less remember what Dr. King had said in the meeting. This was just another reason my mother and Uncle Robert could not be in the same room for too long. She told Uncle Robert, "We can do without your negativity or your jealousness of a child.

"Which one is it, Robert? Don't tell me you have that Napoleon syndrome going on with your own nephew. I personally do not have anything against men of your stature. I just don't like your attitude and your attitude towards my son. I have no idea if that is your opinion or your wishes, but I am sure of one thing. What we do today, Jack Junior will remember tomorrow, and someday he'll write about it. So my advice to you: treat Jack kindly. He is your nephew, but all children too. What goes around, comes around, Robert."

I did not understand why Uncle Robert and Uncle Edward were so adamant that I would not remember Dr. King, but they were.

Grandpa Joe always said I had a bright future, but mother, on the other hand, believed that Uncle Robert and Uncle Edward were going to destroy that future. It all came down to trust. Mother did not trust anyone who was at the table besides my dad. The lunch ended on somewhat of a somber note, but I was able to hold my own.

Mom and Dad went off to talk. I still had no clue as to what they were conversing about. Anyone could see that their topic of conversation was heavy. Mother had left the Kennedy compound later that afternoon. She said, "I'll see you later." That was Mom's way of saying goodbye. Dad looked as if Mom had left him with some heavy decision to make.

No sooner than Mother drove off, Dad, Grandpa Joe, and Uncle Robert went into Grandpa's den and closed the doors behind them. The three were in the study until dinner was being served. When they came out for dinner, there were no smiling faces. We all sat at the table without uttering a word. The only thing that anyone said was Amen after grace. Whatever Mom was discussing with Dad, Grandpa and Uncle Robert now knew.

"Junior, we are going back to Washington D.C. tonight, and your mother is going to meet us in Manhattan in a week or two. It seems your mother had made some plans of her own. I am going to have to go along with it. In any case, she is going to let you know what her plans are."

Grandma Rose spoke up and asked what her plans were.

"Mother, this is between Marilyn and me, but I'll let you know when all is said and done."

After dinner, Uncle Peter drove us to the train station. Dad and I were wearing baseball caps pulled down to our eyebrows. Dad had his sunglasses on too. Uncle Peter said my dad looked like some mean sob guy that was going to rob the train with his sidekick.

# GOING HOME

**WE ARRIVED IN D.C.,** still wearing sunglasses and our baseball caps. The funny thing about this was that Dad did not like to wear a hat or cap of any kind.

The White House was within walking distance of the train station. We were going to walk to the White House, but Dad changed his mind. Someone who worked for Grandpa Hughes was waiting for us to drive us to the White House.

"Sir, Marilyn will be here sometime this week. No later than Wednesday next."

We enter the White House through the service entrance. The next week and a half, I follow the same schedule that Mother had laid out for me. Attending school and taking care of my brother. The day finally arrived when my mother came to talk to me.

She laid out her plan for what she was going to do. How she did not like the way that things were. It was not working out the way that she and Dad had discussed years earlier.

"Jack, you are getting older. I want to know if you are willing to come to live with me in California."

"Yes, I would like that."

"Jack, I'm going back to work to make a movie with Dean Martin in a picture called Something's Got to Give. I am in the process of buying a home for us and revamping my career. It's on the fast track again, but this time I'll be working in Las Vegas. I want you to know that I am working to give you a safe home life."

"Mom, I'm a bit confused, but I've always believed I was going to live with you someday!" About that time, I turned to see who was entering the room. It was Uncle Robert.

"It's you. Are you here as the Attorney General of the United States?" He never answered me. I knew Robert well enough to know that he was there as acting A.G. of the United States. It was quite clear to me that he was here for his own best interest.

"Jack, have you made a decision on which parent you are going to stay with?" I was infuriated by the very question.

"Uncle Robert, I have always tried to make it clear that if I have to choose a parent, it would be my mother!"

I turned to my father, "Dad! I'm going to stay with my mother. You have your parents, brothers, sisters, Caroline and Jonjon. My mother only has me to stand up for her. So I am going to stay with my mother. It is my choice. And besides, it gets too cold in D.C. in the wintertime.

"I'll be able to visit you when you are in the Western White House. It's not too far from Los Angeles. Mom and I have driven it before to see you and JonJon, so there is no difference."

Robert said, "Marilyn, why would you make this decision to take Junior now? The Kennedy Patriarch Ambassador, Joe Kennedy, worked out a deal with Junior's father and me that he would give him $400,000,000 in a trust fund. Marilyn, that has been done!"

"I'm well aware of that, Mr. Attorney General. The part that is being ignored is you still have not informed the public that John is Jack's father."

"Marilyn, what is the rush?"

"Bobby, you have the naivete to ask me that question? Just who the hell do you think you are? Your brother is my sons' father, and you have no right butting in where you do not belong."

My father chimed in, "Bobby, why do you always manage to upset my wife, Marilyn? We have discussed it, and we are going to inform the public that Marilyn is my wife, and Jack is my son."

"John, have you thought of the fallout that you would have to endure? Will you be able to govern this country with all the problems we are going to have?"

"You ask me that now!? Hell, I've been doing just fine up until today, and tomorrow looks better than today, Robert!"

"John, this should be a family matter where we all have a say in when to inform the public of Jack's existence."

"No, Robert. That is your misguided confusion. This is between a man and his family. Where do you think you fit into this scenario?"

"Jack, I just think you should give some more thought on the upheaval you are going to cause."

"Robert, I never intended to put my life on hold for the last nine years. This is not what my wife and son signed up for."

"Jack, all I'm asking for is some more time to find the best possible outcome for this scenario."

"Robert, most of the government, friends, and some support-ers out there know of Jack's existence. If they have accepted it, I am sure the public will too."

"John, you act as if you are going to hold a press conference today and tell the world what is going on right now!"

I looked up at Uncle Bobby, his face and ears were as red as overripe apple falling from a tree. "Robert, the sooner, the better. Just not much longer. Do you think that I should wait? Robert!"

"Over my dead body are the two of you going to do such a thing as to inform the media about Jack; now is not the time."

I have been waiting for this moment! When my dad was so upset that he would give me the answers I am looking for. Here I am standing between the President and the Attorney General of the United States of America.

"Dad, why did you give my brother and I the same name?" I was keenly aware of what I was asking.

President John F. Kennedy, my father, looked at me and said, "I gave both you and Jonjon the same name to save one of your lives, and it's not you I'm worried about!"

My mother chimed in. "I have had enough of the two of you discussing what you think should or should not be done with Jack. I am leaving the two of you to rehash this issue by yourself. I am taking Jack with me now to California." As we were walking out the door. Mother turned to both my father and uncle and said, "I will be back for Jonjon."

Mother and I left the room united. We waited for Uncle Robert and Dad to finish up their heated conversation upstairs.

I did not feel as if I was leaving with Mom as much as she was leaving Dad. We were going to start a new life in California without my dad. There would be no more cold winter days or nights waiting for Mother to come and pick me up in Hyannis Port, Massachusetts. This was going to be the last long goodbye.

Dad was a good father who did his best not to make the same mistakes that his father made with him. There were only two things that puzzled me about my Dad. The first one was when he would watch Mother and me interacting as mother and son. Dad would ask me, "What is it like to have a mother?"

Grandmother Rose was not the most caring or giving person. I noticed she was less so with Dad than with any of her other children. I could see the pain in his eyes when he asked that question, and I tried to be kind and thoughtful when I answered.

"Dad, when Mother enters a room, I feel the room fill with sunshine, and that makes my day. Just by her being here. She gives it life. I thank God that she is my mother, someone as loving and caring as a mom should be."

Out of my aunts and uncles, I do not know which one I would miss the most. The Kennedy clan called competitive achievements healthy. From my standpoint, this was nothing more than outright sibling rivalry that ran amuck at times. This was one of the things that I would not miss about living with Grandpa and Grandmother. It is one thing to have your sibling help you achieve your goal; it is another when you are asked to sacrifice your family to obtain that goal. It was not difficult for me to leave this rivalry behind me. What was worrisome was to know that I had to leave my dad and brother JonJon behind, at least for now!

My suitcases were packed the night before. All I had to do was walk from my father's doorstep to my grandparents' main house. As I walked in the door, I could see the two suitcases waiting for me. All that was left to do was say, "I'll see you later."

Mother and I were on the plane; we landed at Burbank Airport in California. Mother preferred to land in Burbank; she said it was less fanfare, and that's where most people landed when they did not want to deal with the crowds of people.

She hailed a taxi. The driver took our suitcases and placed them in the trunk of the car. The driver asked Mother, "May I take your valise?"

"No, thanks. I'll keep this with me."

"Lady, where would you and the boy like to go?"

"Brentwood off Sunset Boulevard."

Mother, not being one to waste time, told me to pick out landmarks along the way to our new home. "This way, if you get lost, you'll know where you are and how far away from home you are." So I did what I was told to do.

"Junior, Los Angeles is more spread out than Hyannis Port, Boston, Manhattan, or Washington D.C. Those places have one central point that you can find your way home from, not like L.A. Los Angeles is one large city with municipalities within the City of Los Angeles. If you memorize that, you should not get lost."

The driver took us out on the road. Burbank was as if we were in another world. As we were driving, I asked Mother, "Isn't this where Bob Hope lives? The comedian that calls you his little doll."

"Yes, it is Sugar; you are absolutely correct." No sooner did we come out of Burbank were we going up one hill and down the other side of that same hill. The driver stopped at the bottom of the hill. To the right of me was the Hollywood Bowl.

"Sugar, I want you to make this one of the landmarks that you memorize." I was already familiar with some of the places that we were passing through. We came upon Sunset Boulevard. Where the carhop was that my parents and me frequent when visiting L.A. The driver turned right onto Sunset Boulevard; the ride gave the feel of going from a metropolis city to the countryside. The trip down Sunset Boulevard led into a residential area. On top of a mountain was Will Rogers's house and a small stream of water running in front of us. The driver made a left onto a street and stopped at this front gate with two large wooden doors. He stopped and waited for someone to open them.

This was the first time that I saw the home up-close. The only other time that I had seen this home was when my parents and I picked it out. The first time I was there, my dad said that it was gated and closed in. My parents agreed that it was a safe neighborhood. I was excited to know that we had chosen such a warm and cozy community for my brother and me. All I could see was the Spanish architect from the back seat of the car.

As the gate was opening, I noticed over the front door was a mural; it was a lady dressed in her best ascending from heaven. Mother reached over and hugged me and said, "Son, this is yours. I promise we will never be apart again. This is going to be our home. How do you like it?"

"Mom, I love it, but no matter where we are, so long as I'm with you, it's home."

I walked in the frontdoor and saw a wide-open space.

"Mom, where is the furniture!"

"Sugar, it's on its way. The furniture should be here before JonJon arrives. So, for now, you have your room, and it is furnished. We'll have to make do with what we have now."

I walked into my bedroom, and my mother was right. Boy! Was she right! I noticed on the desk was a dictionary and thesaurus with my name inscribed on them: Jack Jr., in big, bold lettering. My heart dropped to my feet. Returning to Mother, I said, "I guess you have enrolled me in school?"

"Yes, I did, Junior. As a matter of fact, we passed the school that you'll be attending on our way here."

"Mom, when will I start school?"

"Monday!"

"That soon?"

"Yes, that soon, Sugar."

# THE UNSAID GOODBYE

**MOTHER AND I SPENT** the weekend shopping and preparing me for school. We started out shopping in Westwood and ended up in the Magnum's Department approximately 16 miles from home. Living in L.A. was a significant change from the East Coast; there was no change of seasons. That's where I had a problem. Mother had her idea of what I should wear to school, and I had mine. It was not her choice in the style of clothes, but it was the short pants that I could not handle. It was not my temperament to throw a tantrum, but how else was I going to change her mind on dreadful short pants?

I could see by the expression on Mother's face that she was enjoying herself. It was funny to me to see everyone who was shopping was dressed as if they were going to a garden party. Women wearing hats, gloves, makeup, and fingernail polish as if they had nothing better to do but shop. The men had more of a look on their faces that said, What am I doing here? But they too were clean-shaven, had pressed shirts, slacks, and some even had sports jackets.

Yes, there were also some of the guys walking around with their wives and girlfriends in shorts. I was not going to get out of this one. Mom believed that if you could keep boys in short pants, they were less likely to grow up and become a stuffed shirt. That was her way of saying, My boy will not be so damn ornery. For me, I think Mom just wanted to keep me a child for as long as she could.

We finished up our shopping and had lunch at the Sheraton West Hotel right down the street from the Bullocks Department

Store on Wilshire Boulevard. It was strange for me to find that here I was shopping and having lunch with mother, and no one knew what she did for a living until she signed the check. There were no crowds of people or fans interrupting our lunch like Grandma Rose said there would be. I can still see Marilyn as her fans called her, sitting having lunch in the Sheraton West Hotel. The way she had a scarf wrapped around her platinum blonde hair with big round sunglasses. I sat there thinking, *This is my mother.*

This image is what every director wanted to capture on film.

"Junior, you are in deep thought. You look as if you are spellbound."

"Mother, I am." Her voice brought me back into the world around us. In school, the teacher called it daydreaming, but this is reality. There I was, sitting with the most famous woman in the world, and she is my mother. This was the first time I gave it any real thought; her magnificent charm and beauty.

Sitting with my mother, seeing her gleaming like a star in the blue daytime sky, brought a sense of being to the both of us. I still hear the gentleness of her laughter and see the joy of her peaceful spirit. This is a memory that I keep hidden for myself. I know it's there, but why should I share it with anyone now? I see that little boy with his mother walking hand-in-hand, talking and laughing without a care in the world. It was as if a whole new world was opening up for the two of us. There was no more chaos in our lives, only blissful peace. If only the Kennedy's would have left us alone. We left the restaurant for home.

Mother did not like driving all the way down Vermont Ave to the Santa Monica Freeway; she preferred to take Wilshire Boulevard. She found more enjoyment taking the scenic route, which for her is Wilshire Boulevard. That way, if she passed another department store or spotted a child's boutique, she could stop and shop. There was not a boulevard that mother drove down on our way home that did not have a store on it. We crossed La Cienega Boulevard into Beverly Hills; I was getting an uneasy feeling. I asked Mother if there was a different street that we could take.

"Yes, Sugar, there is, but this is the fastest and easiest way home. It's a straight line from where we are to the house."

We made it back without any incidents, but I really did not like going through Beverly Hills via Wilshire Boulevard; it gave me the heebie-jeebies!

Mother and I arrived back at Brentwood late in the afternoon. We took the packages out of the back of the car into the house. I went into my bedroom with the packages in-tow. I hung up the clothes that we had gone shopping for. Mother said that we needed to rejuvenate. It was more like a power nap or, for lack of better words, a 15-minute rest.

Marilyn, or mother, in other words, was the conventional mother. When I arose from the nap, Mother was preparing dinner. She had all of the ingredients laid out on the kitchen counter for split pea soup. There were cube-cut carrots, sliced celery, diced and chopped onion, garlic, bay leaf, rosemary, and diced bacon. I sat watching as she started placing the bacon in the heat pot with a dash of oil. She rendered the fat from the bacon, leaving enough bacon fat to coat the onion and split pea.

She added the water, bringing it up to a simmer. Once the water started simmering, she added the rest of the ingredients in intervals, explaining the cooking process as she was going along. "The carrots and celery should be added in the last 10 minutes of cooking time to keep their crunch. At the end of the 10 minutes, turn off the heat. The vegetables will continue to cook, and they will not be crumbling and mushy." I noticed my mother kept stirring the soup.

"Mom, why is it you are continually stirring the soup?"

"Sugar, if you don't stir the vegetables, some will cook faster than others. By stirring them, they will cook evenly and will not stick to the bottom of the pot."

Mother was not one to waste her time; in fact, she utilized it well. Once she removed the pot from the heat, she started setting the table for dinner. "Mom, may I help you set the table?"

"Yes. Place the butter on the table."

As I was doing that, Mother was slicing the loaf of bread that we had purchased on our way back from shopping.

"Mom, is that the bread we bought at the farmers market this afternoon?"

"Yes, it is, Junior. The very bread."

"Why is it we have loaf bread instead of regular store-bought sliced bread?"

"First, the bread was baked this morning; second, it tastes better, and third, it's aesthetically made for an impressive looking dinner."

"Mother, are you sure that you don't want someone to think you baked the bread yourself?"

"Well, that too, Junior." We both started laughing!

"Mom, this split pea soup is delicious. I especially like placing the bacon on the bread. It makes for an excellent bite-sized bacon sandwich."

We finished dinner, and I cleared the table while Mother washed the dishes.

Mother's rules were very different from what I had been accustomed to at my grandparents' home. There was no getting up from the table and leaving your dishes and utensils on the table for someone else to pick up after you. She said that household chores would help me become a responsible adult. I was expected to clean up any mess that I made. There is such a thing as an occasional spill or accident, but even then, I was supposed to lend a hand with the clean-up. Whenever I stay with my mother, I understood that she worked, and I did not want to cause her any undue hardship, so I learned early on to lend a helping hand.

This was the first time in a long time that I did not have to be annoyed by someone's disturbance. I felt that this was going to be a new beginning for my mother and me. The only thing that was missing was my little brother JonJon. It would only be a few months before he would be joining us.

I did not mention to Mom how I was feeling. I didn't want her to know that I was missing my brother. Besides, it had only been one day. No sense in whining like a spoiled brat; it was too soon for that. So I said goodnight and Mom reminded me to brush my teeth, wash my face, and comb my hair. Now, who combs their hair before they go to bed?

She said, "By combing your hair before bed, it helps you when you wake up, looking fresh and ready to start a new day."

"Mom, but you just have to do it all over again in the morning."

"Sugar, it's just less work in the morning if you do it now."

The next morning, we attended church one block off of Wilshire Boulevard. It was out of the driveway, left on the corner, down the street, another left around the bend, and we came to the stoplight. Mother made a left onto Wilshire Boulevard; she drove up to the top of the hill and made a right across the street from where she once had an apartment on Wilshire Boulevard.

It was a small Roman Catholic Church. Mom had asked the night before what church I would like to attend. "Any Roman Catholic Church; that is where I feel more tranquil," I answered.

She said, "That will be fine with me."

I understood Mother's feelings; I sometimes felt the same way. It is not the Catholic Church, but the people who attend the church that she could not deal with. As we were getting out of the car, Mother uttered a statement as if she was speaking to herself, "We come seeking God, his forgiveness, and the ability to forgive" before we entered the church.

The rest of the day was pretty uneventful. There was a small gathering at a restaurant in the farmers market on 3rd and Fairfax. It was some guy from the movie studio setting up appointments for the week.

Now she was going to inform the public of my brother and me. Mother said that "truths should do just fine." The fixers from the movie did not look so happy with her answer.

"If that works for you, then we will have to go with it." I could see it was as if someone shoved a tablespoon of castor oil down his throat, and there was nothing he could do about it but take it.

"Marilyn, the studio can only do so much for you, but you have to take care of yourself and Little Jack here. When you have an interview in the future, the movie studio is going to send a double with you. That way, the double can say Jack is her son; this is only going to be until Little Jack's unveiling."

"That is so gracious of the studio executives to have my best interest at heart!"

That was a bit of sarcasm coming from Mother, and it did get a laugh. The rest of the afternoon I spent in the pool while mother read the newspaper. Mom made sure that I stood on the shallow end of the swimming pool. I was not the best swimmer. Mother was afraid because doctors told her I was too small for my age, not only that, I would probably not live to see my 18th birthday, so she was a little overprotective.

Dinnertime came. Mother had made roast chicken with herbs. She pulled the skin off the chicken, rinsed it, patted it dry, and rubbed olive oil over it with herbs, salt, and pepper too.

This evening there was no rice, potatoes, or white bread. Mother had removed any starch from this evening meal. It was 100% whole-wheat bread, minus the butter. This night it was going to be olive oil. Mom did not need the American Government Food Pyramid to figure out what healthy eating was. Mother's philosophy was to read up on a healthy diet, and if you can do that, the next best thing to do is cut your portions in half. Add in less red meat and more vegetables to your diet. You'll feel healthier and maintain your weight.

I have only one problem with vegetables, and that is zucchini, Italian Squash, I don't care what name you add to Zucchini Squash. I was not going to eat it. Mother and I went around and around on the subject of zucchini. I explained to her that one type of squash has fuzz on it, and I was not going to eat it. I don't care how it is prepared or what you smother it in, I was not eating it. I just could not get it down. Zucchini, no way! I would conjure up the image of the fuzz growing into long strands of hair and choking me. There was just no way I was going to eat that stuff.

"Jack, you have overdramatized this zucchini thing."

I was old enough to pick up on what Mother was really saying. When she called me Jack, it was her way to let me know that I was pig-headed like my dad; all I could do was smile and laugh.

Dad had a problem with carrots, and I had a problem with zucchini. There was no way I was going to eat zucchini, even if it was shredded into a soup. I preferred to go to bed without eating instead of eating zucchini. Unlike Dad, Mom would shred the carrots, and Dad was none the wiser, and what you can't see you will eat. I believe that Dad was well aware of the shredded carrots in his soup; it was just his way of keeping the peace in the family.

Once dinner had ended, Mother and I cleaned up. The last thing to do was to dry the dishes and put them away. It was time to prepare for school. Mom picked out the outfits that I would wear for the next five days. Three out of the five days, it would be short pants with a short-sleeved shirt. After all, it is Sunny Southern California. To my surprise, Mom pressed everything except the socks. Mom finished up the pressing of my clothes, and it was time for bed. Mother made sure that she heard me say the Lord's Prayer before she left the room and turned the lights out.

The next morning, Mother had prepared a light breakfast consisting of two poached eggs, two slices of wheat toast, and oatmeal. The milk had to be warm, not boiling, but warm enough so that it would warm the belly as it goes down. We had breakfast, and Mother insisted that I shower before going to school. She laid my attire out on the bed.

"Sugar, this is your first day attending school in California. If you make a good impression, it will reflect well on both of us."

I came out of the shower, and Mother gently towel-dried my hair and used her fingers to fluff it up.

"Mom! What are you doing?"

"Sugar, I don't want your curly head of hair to lay flat. It looks better when the sunlight streaks through it." I did not wish to upset her, so I let her finish.

"Jack, I want you to play nice with the other children at school today."

I did not answer her, but if I could hold my own against my cousins, the schoolyard should be a breeze.

Mother did as all mothers do, she took a picture of my first day of school for my dad here in Sunny Southern California. Once the picture taking was done, she drove me to school. While on the way to school, Mother again reminded me to take notice of any landmarks that would help me remember the way home. The only thing that I recall was the streets had the same name and that there were more than five numbers on every house address.

We came to the top of the hill and made a right turn onto Sunset Boulevard. Not too far away was Will Rogers' Ranch and a small stream that ran across Sunset Boulevard. She made a left and stopped in front of the school.

Mom got out of the car and walked me to the door of the school. I could see the euphoric joy that she was displaying. Mother made me feel that this was something she genuinely felt for the first time. Something she always wanted to do, but for some reason was unable to do, and that was being a mother to her son once again. To see the radiance of her happiness beaming from her meant the world to me. In that instant, I knew that I made the right decision to live with my mother. Mom was getting what she wanted, and that was to be a mother to her sons. With Mother and me, it was always 'I'll see you later' and never 'goodbye,' and this time was no different.

The school day flew by. I was surprised to see Mother waiting for me with all the other mothers! It never dawned on me how I was going to return home from school. I just assumed that she would send a car and driver to pick me up, but she came herself; it was a real treat to see Mom in the school parking lot, waiting for me.

Mother and I fell into the same daily routine; it was get up and go to school, and she would go to work. She said it was my job to be a student, and her job was to provide for us. I only recall once or twice that I did not attend school due to her work.

She had a meeting with producers in the St. James Hotel in West Hollywood. Mother did not want anyone but her picking me up from school, so I had to attend this meeting with her.

She was going to sing happy birthday to my dad in New York City at Madison Square Garden. There was some argument as to whether or not the studio executives were going to let mother have time off work to attend the party, much less let her sing for Dad. It had to do with studio overhead. What would it cost the studio if they closed down production on the film that my mother was working on? Mother being Marilyn, which is sometimes one and the same, was going to do what she wanted.

What she said to the executives was, "I am going to sing to my son's father, who just happens to be President of the United States and my husband, so YES I AM going to sing for him!" It just so happened that this was studio business, so there was a studio stunt double with us. She was there to keep the news photographers at bay. There were a lot of unanswered questions when we left the meeting. Mother was going to sing for Dad, but would she have a movie deal to come back to?

As luck sometimes goes, things went from bad to worse. We had walked out of the hotel and up the hill to Sunset Boulevard, where some freelance photographers were milling around on the corner. Mother leaned over to her stunt double and asked, "How did these guys know where we were going to be?"

About that time, one of the photographers asked her, "Is that your son, Marilyn?"

"Yes, he is!"

Simultaneously, the stunt double said, "No, he is mine."

I could see the bewilderment on their faces. They were not sure who to believe, and some things were better left unsaid. We did not get across Sunset Boulevard to the restaurant for lunch when this woman named Eleanor stopped us and asked mother how she was.

This was not the first time we had run into Eleanor, and it wouldn't be the last time that I would have to deal with her. I just knew that I did not care for her; she did not seem trustworthy. At least, that is the way Mother made it look. Eleanor seemed to pop up whenever Mother and I were together. However, my mother did exchange pleasantries with Eleanor.

I was amazed to see Mother was all business when we would encounter Eleanor. This was the first time I had given any real thought to who Norma Jean Baker was. When we would run into Eleanor, she always insisted on calling my mother, Norma. They are the same person, but one was all business; the other is the character that she created. As my mother would say, Don't misconstrue one with the other, or you'll be fooled.

The three of us finally made it across Sunset Boulevard to have lunch.

We had our lunch, and this time, the stunt double, Mother and I climbed into a chauffeur-driven limousine home. Mother entered into the back seat of the car first, I was next, and the stunt double was last. Here I was sitting between Marilyn Monroe, the movie star, and her coworker, and that I had just witnessed Mother at work.

Mother was going to sing for my dad, and nothing was going to stand in her way. It was becoming clear why Grandpa Joe wanted my mother to be more like the character that she created. The character that the theater audience fell so in love with.

For the next few weeks I spent attending school, Mother was working on her movie. There was nothing mundane about our day. If Mother was not working, she was studying her movie lines, and I had homework.

I was a tribute to a one-sided telephone conversation between Dad and Mom. They were working out the New York trip and when JonJon was coming to California. Mother was to sing for Dad, and JonJon would join us a week or two later.

Things looked as if they were on track. Mother was going to have her two sons under one roof with her. This trip to New York was going to decide our future. This was the happiest I've seen my mother in a long time. Bringing her family together was the one thing that was going to make her whole. She was finally going to have the family that the Kennedy patriarch had taken from her.

Jacqueline had already decided that she was going to continue seeing Aristotle Onassis. Still, the question remained: What was Dad going to do? Was he going to keep up the charade with Jacqueline, or was he going to leave her? This time, it was up to Dad what he was going to do.

From my perspective, Mother was willing to accept whatever conclusion Dad came too. She was fed up with everyone else making decisions for her and her family. This time, no one and nothing was going to come between her and what she wanted. Not even the movie executives who threatened to fire her.

She said, "If I made it this far without your support, I could do without you. A woman will fight for her family, so what is so wrong with me fighting for mine! I'm going to New York at any cost, do you understand me?" And with that said, we were going. It was no movie character talking; it was my mom.

Mother and I flew out to New York; she was going to sing Happy Birthday for Dad, who just happened to be the President of the United States. No sooner did we arrive at our apartment, in comes Uncle Robert interfering in our family's affairs. But this time, my mother told him to take a step back.

"Robert, which are you concerned with? The scandal the country will go through or your own political ambitions! Look, Mr. Attorney General, that is a rhetorical question. We both know it's your political career you are worried about."

"What is it going to take for you to understand that someday we'll have to answer to our families?"

"One red moment is worth a thousand dark nights. It is time we take responsibility for our actions and face our fears. I want Jack Jr. and JonJon to experience what it is like to be brothers, to give them some kind of childhood together. If that means I have to do it by myself, I will. I do not want anything from your family, and I don't need it. I am going to work for my sons, do you understand me, Robert!"

"Marilyn, there is no way anyone is going to stop you. How are we going to explain why you are singing for the president, and where the First Lady is?"

"That is no concern of mine. However, I am sure you'll come up with something. You always do. If you are up for suggestions, just say the president's wife is singing for him, the mother of his two sons.

"By the way, my only concerns I have right now are my two sons at this juncture, Robert. As I said to you in the Oval Office, I'll be back for my other son, and I'm back. If I were you, I'd start making plans for that."

Mother sang for Dad; it was their way of killing two birds with one stone. What the movie executives and the public failed to consider was that this was two people celebrating their birthdays together. Maybe that's why the First Lady was not in the audience; she knew her place. Grandmother Rose did mention the First Lady's whereabouts; she was not discrete with the details.

Mother and I were headed back to L.A. It was my understanding that Mother and Dad had worked out the details of where they were to meet and give JonJon to Mother before we left New York.

When we returned to L.A., Mother had been fired from her movie job. That was fine with her. The concern she had was for the people who work behind the scenes. She said if the movie studio starts production on the movie Something's Got to Give, she will return to work as soon as possible. Otherwise, she was looking for other projects to work on, and the Vegas deal was coming up fast. She still has to deal with bringing my brother home.

Mother had agreed to resume working on the movie Something's Got to Give, and that she would not cause any more delays. The one thing she had left to do was drive to the Western White House to reunite with my brother. This time we were going to become the family that Mother wanted, even if it was just the three of us.

The euphoria that was beaming around our home was electrifying, just knowing that JonJon would finally be coming home to join us. Mother had made all the arrangements to drive us to San Clemente in the morning. She asked me to prepare the wardrobe that I would like to wear on JonJon's homecoming the next day.

The next morning, Mother was up earlier than usual. She looked radiant as always. Mom had on a white-flowered dress and sweater covering her shoulders with flat-heeled shoes on. She was bubbly and happier than I had ever seen her. It was like before Grandpa Joe disrupted our lives with his presidential plans for my dad. I could not have been more content myself. Miss. Murray, the housekeeper, handed Mother her itinerary for the day. Miss. Murray told my mother to adhere to the agenda, or she would be late.

I opened the front door, and I noticed it was early morning. The splendor of the day was just beginning, the dew rising off of the grass bursting into the sky. It was as if I had opened the door to an enchanted forest. The rosebuds looked as if they were ready to break into full bloom this morning. California lived up to its splendor.

Mother strapped me into the front seat of the car, and we drove off. As she was driving, she paid close attention to the itinerary that the housekeeper had given her earlier. We drove past La Cienega Blvd to pick up some of her coworkers and friends that were going to accompany us on our trip to the Western White House. Once mother picked up everyone, she had me sit in the front between her and another passenger. She had one last thing to do, and that was to pick up some snacks, milk, and soft drinks for the trip.

Mother headed back down Wilshire Boulevard. She said it was the fastest way to go out of town without going through Downtown Los Angeles traffic. Marilyn, not being one to waste time, came up to North Crescent Drive between North Canon Drive on Wilshire Boulevard, made a right turn into Ralph's Market, and stopped the car.

As she came to a complete stop, this car stopped directly behind us; we were locked into our parking space. I turned and looked out the rear window and watched as two men casually walked up to the car. There was one to the right of the vehicle and one on the left side. The man on the right side of the car was a medium-height, blue-eyed, thin-haired white man with a foreign accent. The man on the left side of the car was tall, well-built, and had brown hair and glasses, and he spoke with a southern drawl. I could feel my heart racing, and I knew that my worst fears were unfolding. Today was the day that I told anyone who would listen; this was going to happen!

The man on the right side of the car grabbed me and started pulling me through the open window in the front of the vehicle. The other man on the left side of the car placed a gun to my mother's chest and said, "If you scream, I am going to kill your son!"

Mother said, "Please don't take Jack! I'll give you this." She pulled off the ring that Dad had married her with. The man said, "I'll take the ring and him as well."

All I could do was look at mother and say, "Mother, he means what he is saying. He'll kill us both, please! I love you, Mom. If the Kennedy's have anything to do with this, I am going to stand by you." The man on the right side of the car pulled me all the way out of the vehicle.

While all this was going on. The store manager was coming out of the market to see what was going on. He noticed that the man on the right side of the car had a gun. The store manager stopped in his tracks! Everything was unfolding with such precision that anyone could figure out this was a well laid out kidnapping.

The man on the right side of the car placed me in the back seat of his car with a woman wearing a nurse's uniform. The man who pointed the gun at my mother's chest got into the back seat of the car as we drove off.

I saw two figures standing behind a tree just across Wilshire Boulevard on Crescent Drive. I recognized them both. They stood behind a freshly planted tree on Crescent Drive, watching their handiwork unfold. How did Jacqueline B. Kennedy, the First Lady of the United States, and Aristotle Onassis feel to witness their work in progress? I turned back around to take one last look at my mother so that her memory would stay attached in my conscious and subconscious mind.

Mother was outside of her car, talking to the man that came out of Ralph's Market. It was still early morning. The traffic was light as we headed down Wilshire Boulevard. The man driving the car did not say much, but I recall his voice having had a distinctive sound to it. The kidnapping took only moments, but it played out in slow-motion as it was happening. We headed to the central rail-road station in downtown Los Angeles.

As we were getting out of the car, I tried to break away from the woman in the nursing uniform. I was screaming and yelling that she had taken me from my mother. No matter how loud I cried, no one could hear me. I felt as if I was yelling into the air. A policeman stopped us and asked, "What is going on here?"

The nurse replied, "Officer, the child is incorrigible; his mother asked me to take care of him. As all children do, he's throwing a tantrum."

"No! She took me from my mother just now! I don't know who she is! I've never seen her before! My mother would never leave me with this woman. Please, I don't want to go with them."

The policeman said, "I understand. Children will do anything to stay at home these days."

The man who placed the gun on my mother's chest and the nurse seemed to know one another. They acted as if they were husband and wife, making as if I was their child.

We had gotten onto a train going north; we had our own cabin so we would not be disturbed. The nurse gave me something to calm me down and fall asleep.

We got off the train in San Francisco. We stayed in a hotel, not the kind of hotel that I was used to with my parents, more like a rooming house or a better description would be a flophouse. The woman who was dressed in the nurse's white uniform changed into her street clothes. She kept me drugged for days, and when I was not drugged, the man with the southern drawl was hypnotizing me. He was trying to get me to forget what had happened and what was happening.

I was in the boarding house, sitting looking out the window. In the distance, I could hear planes take off and land, a lake, and some factories. It was a working man's neighborhood, not at all what I was accustomed to. The day was beautiful; the sun was shining, but it was breezy outside. The day was filled with mundane activities.

I was beginning to feel alone, not that I was by myself. I wondered if I would ever see my parents again. Who was going to help us now that we were on our own? By now, I have learned the name of the man with the southern drawl. His name is Tom, and his wife is just a nurse. I don't know how long it's been since the last time I have seen my mother.

The man with the European accent came running up the wooden stairs in the boarding house, shouting, "Tom, we have to get out of here now! The boy's father called the law on us, and they are on their way."

Tom and the nurse wrapped me in a blanket and carried me out the back door down the wooden stairs into a waiting car. The man with the European accent regained his composure and went out the front door as if nothing was going on. As he was going to the front door, the police and men in black suits and ties were entering the boarding house.

The man driving the car was the same guy that drove the car to the train station. This time, the nurse jumped into the front seat, and Tom was to the right of her. She shoved me in between the dashboard and the floorboard of the front seat. Tom was holding me down, and the nurse was holding my back while the driver held down my feet as he drove off with the other hand. The driver of the car asked Tom, "What are we going to do now if we're caught?"

"We're going to jail for a long time."

We headed back down to Los Angeles. On the way, the driver stopped, and Tom made some calls. We arrived in Los Angeles and stayed in a seedy part of town. It was the driver who chose this part of Los Angeles. The man with the European accent called it the Red Light district. I was in between Bunker Hill and N Beaudry, just to the right of the Hollywood freeway. I began to think, *Is this going to be my world now?*

The woman in the white nurse's uniform wanted to go home. Tom asked her to stay until we were settled in. The next day, I was watching T.V. by myself in a dark room with the shades drawn, and the news came on that Mother had died. I could not believe what I was seeing! The next thing I knew, my arm was gushing blood; I don't know what happened! The television screen was gone, and my arm was bleeding.

Tom's wife came running into the room, and she began to nurse my arm. I was in total shock. I could not speak; no words would come out. Nothing would come out. All I could do was cry dry tears without a sound, just sitting there thinking my mother was looking for me. While all the time, Tom's wife was taking the glass out of the gash on my arm. She cleaned out the glass and stopped the bleeding. I still did not say a word; there was still silence in the room. She did not say a word; instead, she gave me a glass of water and a pill to take.

The world around me had fallen apart, and there was nothing I could do about it. I did not know if I would ever see her again or be able to say goodbye to my mother. The only thing left was a lot of tearful nights!

Tom's wife became increasingly uncomfortable around me and wanted to go. I overheard the four captors discussing a plan that someone else had hashed out for them. I was to stay with Tom and his family. The other three of Tom's partners in crime were to return to their lives. Tom and I stayed in the same general area around Bunker Hill off the 101 Freeway.

# CHANGED IDENTITIES

**TOM HAD A FAMILY** of his own that he mixed me in with. I blended into his family exceptionally well. The problem was when I spoke, people said that our dialects were not the same. Tom's family had more of a southern drawl, and I had a northern dialect. I also had command of the English Language well for my age and environment. His answer to any question was that he was caring for me for a friend. Tom was not a cruel man, just someone who did not like to work and was looking for a free ride. From the moment that Tom kidnapped me from my mother, he stayed one step ahead of the law.

I don't recall how long I stayed with Tom, only that the Federal Bureau of Investigation (FBI) was looking for him. I could not distinguish if the FBI was looking for him for the crime of kidnapping or something else that he had done. There was one thing for sure, I would not stay with him and his family for long. The question remains, What was he going to do with me? It would not take him long to find someone to leave me with.

The area around Bunker Hill was a criminal haven. Tom's criminal past was catching up with him; he did not want to be found with me. He dropped me off with the Sanchez family on the other side of the 101 Freeway and left town with his family. The Sanchez family lived on Hill Place and Sunset Boulevard, which is within walking distance of Bunker Hill.

This was an exceedingly difficult time to understand what was happening. I began to question if every child goes through this at my age. Was this the norm? What was I expected to do? Would I ever see or talk to my dad again? I was not even sure what the meaning of death was or how it would affect me. The uncertainty and chaos of this ordeal of being kidnapped were taking its toll on me. Where was I going to end up, and who was going to care for me?

It's not that I went along with this crime; it's just that people tend to do anything for money.

It was becoming apparent that I would have to do it alone, so I would have to get along with these people. Did this kidnapping become a part of life because of me, or is it what happened to everyone? Rodolfo and Emily Sanchez and their children treated me with respect and kindness; the only thing is, they are not family.

Eventually, the surrounding neighbors started inquiring where I came from, and why it was that I was there day and night. Unable to articulate to the neighbors why I was with the Sanchez family, I would say I'm waiting for my mother to come and get me. I felt as if I was running on an eight-cylinder engine. When was all this chaos going to stop? Would I ever see my father and brother again?

The Sanchez's neighbors became increasingly apprehensive about why I was there and who I really was. I could sense that they knew something was wrong, but they did not know what. It came to a head when the neighbors started questioning why a parent would leave me for so long with people like the Sanchez family. We just looked too different from one another. "His parents have to be looking for him."

While Rodolfo worked, Emily stayed home with her children and me. The neighbors kept questioning Emily, why was I there? The questioning started to take a toll on Emily's nerves; she wanted me out of her home. I would not be settled in one place when I would have to move to another. Rodolfo and Emily stayed in contact with Tom all the time I was with their family. I heard Rodolfo telling Tom that I could not stay with his family any longer. The boy's skin color is the problem. He is too white, and we are too dark.

"The neighbors! He has to go! The police are coming around the neighborhood more than usual. I believe that some of the neighbors found out who he is, and they are going to turn us into the FBI."

Soon after that conversation, Tom came back into the picture. He assured them he and his other partners would come up with a solution and asked him to be patient. The solution that Tom came up with was suitable for all parties involved in the kidnapping, including the accomplices.

I was out with Emily shopping. We were out most of the morning. We were having lunch when I heard a car pull up outside. I walked from the kitchen to the living room. I stood there as Tom opened the screen door and walked in. Behind him was my stepmother Jacqueline Bouvier Kennedy and Aristotle Onassis.

The first thing I said was, "I want to go home, Jacqueline."

But Jacqueline did not answer me.

Emily picked me up and held me in her arms. She asked them, "What are you doing here? You know you are not supposed to meet here at my home. That is what we have all agreed to: no meeting would be held in this house!" Rodolfo's mother was lying on her bed in the living room.

She asked, "What are all of you going to do with this child? He'll remember all of this, and what will all of you do then?"

Rodolfo's mother was the only one who had shown any concern for my well-being. The living room of this small Victorian home was getting smaller by the minute.

I could see Tom walking up the wooden stairs through the screen door. He was with a heavyset woman whom I had seen around N. Beaudry Ave and N. Temple Street in the Red Light District of Los Angeles just down the street from where we are now. She was the woman who ran a boarding house. She was not very friendly, but from what I could tell, the woman had met with Jackie and Aristotle before arriving here.

Jackie and Aristotle hand-picked this woman to be my next caregiver. Emily did not like the idea that this woman was going to care for me. Emily made her opinion be known. "This woman you want to leave Jack with is a known Madame and runs a brothel.

Mary has been a lady of the evening and progressed to become the Madame of the establishment. She sometimes rents the boarding house rooms by the hour and chooses the clients that suit her.

"How could you leave this innocent child with her? Mary's sons are the local hoodlums of this section of the Red Light district. They are the strong arm behind Mary's illegal activities.

"Jackie, how are you going to hand your stepson over to this woman? He is Marilyn Monroe's and President Kennedy's son, Jackie. Think about what kind of person Mary is!"

"Emily, I assure you I have no intention of leaving Jack with Mary forever; it is just for the time being. His father is sparing no expense to find him, and believe me, if we do not do something now, we'll all go to jail."

I pleaded with my stepmother. "Jackie, I want to go home. I do not want to stay with these people! Please don't leave me here!"

"Jack, as I said, it will be for the time being. Stop being so childish; you are too old to act this way." My words fell on deaf ears. I knew this was going to be my fate.

Aristotle began to explain to Rodolfo, Emily, Mary, and Tom what they needed to do to keep my father from finding me and to keep their criminal organization out of jail. Tom was to bring me to Rodolfo and Emily Sanchez's home in the morning and pick me up in the late afternoon for the next three days. This should stop all the questions that the neighbors have. I heard Tom say, "I'll work on what to do next. If we all keep our heads, we should be fine."

Aristotle's plan may have worked if it was not for Tom getting into trouble. To make matters worse, Mary's sons had legal problems of their own. The decision was made that I finally stay with Mary. I don't know why I was left with Mary or why Tom had to leave Los Angeles.

It was a sunny afternoon when Mary arrived to take me to her house. We took a yellow cab down Sunset Boulevard. The driver made a left turn onto Bellevue Avenue. We continued on Bellevue Avenue until we came to East Edgeware Road, where we came to a complete stop to make a right turn. I was sitting in the back. I looked out the window over at the fire station that was in the middle of two streets. He made a right and pulled out in front of a two-story Victorian home.

I looked up to see this raggedy girl sitting on the front stairs of the house. She was the spitting image of a rag doll with a pageboy haircut. She had on bobbysocks with black and white wingtips, girl's shoes, and she looked as if she had not had a decent meal in her life.

This was a catastrophic change that I was experiencing at the sight of this girl. How could a mother treat her child this way?

I did not understand what was going on or what was happening to me! There were all these questions running through my mind. Does this happen to all children, or was it just me? Do all parents lose their children this way? Is this what people do to their own children? Leave their children for someone else to care for them? How and why did I end up here?

Just to see this girl changed my entire perspective on life. My mind was racing, and my body was starting to tense up. All I wanted was to go back home! I felt as if I was losing consciousness. Something was grabbing hold of me and not letting go, as if to say, "Do not enter that house. You'll not return."

The closer I got to the door, the heavier my feet became. I did not like the uncertainty of meeting Mary's daughter Yolanda. I walked through the door of that Victorian House. It was as if this was going to be my life, and here is where I was going to stay. I don't recall ever seeing such a tragic mess, much less having to stay in one.

It was more of the look of despair on Yolanda's face that ran through my veins that made me feel alone. The hopelessness of her sitting on the front veranda ran throughout Mary's house. There was no warmth in the home, nothing welcoming me in. I felt as if evil was choking me and running through the house. How was I going to come out of this? Just how long are my stepmother Jacqueline and Onassis going to leave me here? Is this temporary, or is this going to be a permanent stay? Onassis did give Mary a hand full of hundred dollar bills to feed and care for me.

Yolanda was around 14 to 16 years old and as thin as a rail. She was not a very pleasant person to be around, not at all the kind of person I was accustomed to. It was some time before I met Mary's sons; they were either in jail or juvenile hall except for Robert, who I believe was married. One by one, they were released from their incarceration.

I recall meeting Mary's first son when he was released from the county jail. He called me Little Kennedy, as did the hoodlums that he associated with. If it was not Little Kennedy, they called me Little Jack. Charlie and Gilbert were held in a reform school, and Daniel was in Juvenile Hall. It was difficult for me to understand exactly what was going on and what this all meant for me.

Mary and her family members began to have the same problem the Sanchez's had. Just where did I come from? Where were my parents, and why was I staying with Mary? Mary tried her best to keep me sedated and locked in her house. She had to contend with her sons and daughter. Mary decided that it would be best if I went with her to work.

Mary's sons Richard and Robert's last names were Gomez. Charlie, Gilbert, Daniel, and Yolanda's last names were Gonzales. Paul was the father of the Gonzales family; he had just started a television repair shop where Mary did the bookkeeping and answered the customers' calls.

Mary let it be known that I was President John F. Kennedy and Marilyn Monroe's son; it was no secret. In fact, it was common knowledge in Mary's social circle. The public did not know that President Kennedy had two sons with my mother. That's all she was able to tell people.

I was sitting in Paul's business one day when this woman walked in by the name Josephine. She lived around the corner from the shop. "Mary, who is this beautiful little boy you have sitting on that milk crate?"

"He is the son of Marilyn Monroe and President John F. Kennedy, and I am babysitting for them."

"Mary, are you kidding me! Mary, what is his name?"

"Jack!"

She turned to me. "Jack, are you really President Kennedy and Marilyn Monroe's son?"

Mary answered for me. "Yes, he is, and I'm babysitting him."

"Oh, so when is your father coming to get you?"

"I do not know if they know where I am," I answered.

"Mary, are you up to no good?" asked Josephine.

"You know me, you tell me!" she answered with a smiling smirk on her face. Mary and Josephine laughed.

About that time, Cleo Cresson, the woman who owned the beauty shop next door, came in. "What are you laughing about?"

"Mary is up to no good, Cleo."

"You mean she told you who the boy is sitting there on the wooden mike crate?"

Josephine said, "She did, Cleo. Who would believe that the son of the President of the United States would be here sitting in Paul's shop? Cleo, he even looks like President Kennedy!"

"Yes, he does, Josephine."

No sooner had Josephine and Cleo left the shop when I noticed this girl and man around Richard's age come running into the shop. They could not have been more than a half a block away. They could barely breathe, much less be able to speak when they entered the shop. They look at me. "You are President John F. Kennedy and Marilyn's son?"

"Yes, I am their son!"

"So, you met our mother?"

"If the thin woman with the black hair that was just in here is your mother by the name of Josephine, yes; however, we were not properly introduced."

"Properly introduced, what do you mean?"

"Just what I said. I had to describe your mother to you to know which woman was your mother. Your mother, Josephine, was not the only woman who was just in here; there was also Cleo. She had red hair. Now, what is your name if you do not mind me asking?"

"I am Josephine, and this is my brother Larry. I am called Josie."

"Well, Josie, it is nice to meet you. I'm John."

"Gee! You really are their son! I can tell just by the way you speak; you even stood up to introduce yourself and nodded your head. That is amazing. What sophistication you display at a young age. Mary, he does not belong here; how long are you going to babysit him?"

"I beg your pardon! I'm not babysitting for anyone! I'm watching him. I do not have time to take care of my own. I'm not going to babysit someone else." With that said, Mary told Larry and Josie to go home.

It was hard for me to understand if every child in the world had to experience what I am experiencing. *Is this part of life, or is this just happening to me?* I keep asking myself these same questions. To be here with Mary gave me a feeling of insecurity. I feel as if I was alone, that there was no one I could depend on for comfort or security. Not the way that I felt with my parents. That caring, loving feeling that my parents had showered me with was missing.

There were days when Mary would leave me with her sons Richard or Robert to watch me. Mary paid twenty dollars to watch me and twenty dollars for food. The meal was baloney, cheese, or peanut butter and jelly for lunch. That was for four people to live on until dinner. I don't recall if Mary made dinner when she arrived back from work. I am not sure if I even ate dinner.

Mary was still encountering the same problem that Sanchez had meddling neighbors. The questions were the same. Where did I come from, and what was someone like me doing in a place like this? How long would her neighbors accept that she was babysitting me? She knew that she had to do something, but what?

She had decided to take me to work with her again; she never left her house before 10:00 AM. We walked the two blocks to the bus and headed towards Downtown LA. We'd get off at the last bus stop and take the streetcar for another six blocks and get off right in front of the shop.

When we arrived at the shop, she turned on a TV and told me to sit down and watch TV. Something I did not like to do was watch TV. I believed it was a colossal waste of time. I had no choice but to do what I was told.

As I was sitting there watching television, the news came on that my mother Marilyn Monroe's death was a suicide. The next thing I knew, I was standing up, and my arm had a burning sensation on my left arm and a gash on the right side of my torso bleeding profusely; there was glass on the floor around me. There was light powdery smoke coming out of the TV.

Mary was stunned. She grabbed some shop work cloth and wrapped my arm to stop the burning and bleeding. I could not move. The only thing I could do was stand there crying in silence; there were no tears, just cries of silence. My mother had everything to live for; we were on our way to pick up my little brother. We were going to be a family! Why! Why would someone say that she committed suicide?

Mary had taken me to the back of the shop to clean up the cut on my arm and side, but I still could not feel a thing. I was in a state of shock! Unable to utter a sound, I did not feel any physical pain, just the mental strain that I would not see or talk to my mother again. Mary gave me a pill to take with a glass of water to stop me from shaking. I could not speak; it was as if my life was over. What was going to happen to me now! Was I going to die like my mother? Why was my dad not there to save her?

Still, I was crying in silence, not wanting anyone to see my pain of the loss of my mother. My hands were so cold to the touch. I felt my legs to make sure that they were not frozen as well. My hands felt as if I had placed my fingers in icy cold water, but my legs were warm to the touch. All I could think or say was that I wanted to go home. I want to go back home! I don't know if the words came out or if anyone heard them. The feeling of loneliness was more than I could stand. Was this going to be the last time I would ever see Mother? I fell asleep. When I woke up, I was back in Mary's apartment.

I was not allowed to watch TV or go outside of the apartment. I was kept drugged and hungry. I do not recall for how long, just that time seemed to move slower after hearing that Mother committed suicide!

Mary still had to deal with the neighbors meddling into her business as Mary called it. Mary brought two female children into her family, Vivian and Maryann. Vivian resembled Robert;

Maryann looked like Danny, Mary's son. I had no idea why Mary and Paul were adding more children to their family, but they were.

Richard and Robert were from Mary's first marriage. Charlie, Gilbert, Danny, and Yolanda were from her second marriage to Paul. I do not know where Vivian and Maryann came from, only that they arrived after my arrival. Tessa, the owner of the two-story Victorian house, was not too happy having ten people living in her downstairs apartment. Mary was also fearful that someone in her neighborhood was going to call the police on her. She found a single-family house within a six-block radius from the two-story Victorian home.

It was a perfect place to hide a kidnapped child. There was only one way in the cul-de-sac and one way out. It was the third house from the top of the hill and the third house from the bottom of the hill; it was the house in the middle of the block.

When I arrived at the new house Mary had purchased, it was the middle of the night, and Sally Cynthia Celeste was added in. She was the latest member of the household.

Sally had reddish blonde hair with brown eyes. She was about 6 to 8 years old. This was all too confusing to me; I did not understand what was going on. What purpose would all these new children serve? Vivian, Maryann, and Sally started calling Mary mother' right off the bat. I knew full well that Mary only had six children when I arrived.

Why were Vivian, Maryann, and Sally calling Mary, Mother? I began questioning myself; is this what happens to all children when their parents are no longer with them? For good or bad, this is where I am now. What do I do about it? Am I supposed to forget my parents and where I came from? What was going to happen to me?

Mary kept Vivian, Maryann, and me locked in the house. We were not allowed out to play. She had hired a babysitter named Amalia for the five of us, and Mary took Sally to the shop with her.

Amalia was hired to do the cooking and cleaning and to take care of us. Amalia would arrive at about 10:00 AM Monday-Friday. Yolanda and Daniel left for school before Amalia arrived. Amalia had her own ideas on what her caregiving duties were.

She assigned Maryann, Vivian, and my daily duties. Vivian and Maryann did the morning dishes and mopped the kitchen floor, and I had to clean the bathroom. Yolanda usually returned at about 3:45 PM, but no later than 4:00 PM. Daniel, whom we now called Danny, would leave school and help out at Paul's Gonzales and Sons business.

Amalia spent her day barking orders at us, and when she was not barking at us, she was hitting us. I had never been physically abused before for not doing what I was told to do, but I was scolded. My parents never hit me, what gave this woman the right to? This kind of physical treatment was very unusual for me; Jacqueline hit me, but I did defend myself. I defended myself even when I was with Mary. Mary was cunning. She could use it to her advantage. She said that I was violent. I had no concept of what was going on!

By the time Yolanda arrived home from school, it was time for us to make the beds. There was a living room that was converted into the master bedroom and one small bedroom and one large bedroom for a total of 3 bedrooms. The master bedroom consisted of one King-sized bed; the small bedroom had two beds, and the large bedroom had four beds.

Amalia would nap right around the time Yolanda would arrive back from school. Amalia made it clear she wanted the beds made before she rose from her nap. There would be severe punishment if our assigned duties were not completed. It became apparent that I would have to comply with my assigned tasks. Danny was not aware of just how lucky he was. Not to have to put up with Amalia's abuse.

One afternoon, Paul and Mary came to the house unannounced. Amalia jumped up from the small bedroom bed where she had been napping. Amalia grabbed the broom out of Vivian's hand before Paul and Mary entered the house. She pushed Vivian to the side, making it appear as if Amalia was doing the house chores herself.

When we tried to inform Paul and Mary about what was going on, they neither cared nor did they pay any attention to us. The two of them did not understand what took place. I was too small for my age, and I could not fight back. Not that Amalia was a big woman, but she was more of a significant size than me, and my parents raised me to respect my elders. How was I going to stop this tyrant?

Mr. and Mrs. Gonzales seemed to believe that you spare the rod and spoil the child. I was never going to become accustomed to this kind of physical abuse, but how could I stop it? The only thing I could do was ask my Guardian Angel to help me endure this ordeal that I am going through. One afternoon, my prayers were answered. Salvation came from a Russian woman next door.

Danny did not follow his daily routine. He arrived at the house immediately after school. Amalia and Danny had never mixed well, they argued quite a bit. This one afternoon, Danny had had enough. Amalia told Danny, "If you do not work for your keep, you will not eat." Danny started using profanity, and Amalia did not take it lightly. I have never heard anyone speak to anyone the way that Danny spoke to Amalia. To tell the truth, I did not understand the language that Danny was using. Judging by Amalia's expression, it was horrendous profanity.

Amalia grabbed a broom and began to strike Danny with it. They went from the living room to the kitchen while all the time, Amalia was hitting Danny with the broom. Yolanda, Vivian, Maryann, and I tried to stop Amalia, but it was to no avail. Danny started to strike Amalia with a closed fist, but somehow they ended up out on the back porch. Danny, with his back against the rail and Amalia with a stick in her hand, they continued to fight. The six of us were all on the porch when a woman screamed, "What are you doing? Why are you hitting that poor child with a stick? You do not hit children, especially with a stick." At about that moment, she realized that there were more children in the house!

"Oh! How many children live in that small house!? Oh, my goodness! Are you children attending school? I can't believe that there are so many of you!"

Amalia hit Danny one more time with the broom, and the Russian woman screamed. "If you hit him once more, I am going to call the police on you!"

The woman asked, "Are you kids attending school?"

Amalia played as if she did not speak English. To tell the truth, Amalia's English was broken and even hard for me to understand. I do not recall what the neighbor's name was, only that she was going to find out why we were not in school.

The next morning, Los Angeles police came knocking on Mary's door. Mary looked out the window and had Danny take me into the bedroom closet and close the door. I was in the closet in the small bedroom and could hear everything that was being said. Danny had his hand over my mouth, muffling my screams for help!

The policeman said to Mary, "One of your neighbors reported that you have school-age children residing here who are not attending school. Why is it that your neighbors just found out you have more children living here? Madam, why is that?"

"Officer, I just moved into the neighborhood and have not had the time to register them for school. I have a new business that I just started with my husband, and things are hectic; however, I plan to register them for school next week."

"Well, Mrs. Gonzales, we will be back to check in to see that these children are all registered for school in a week."

The police left, and I came out of the bedroom closet. I walked into the front room and could see the look of satisfaction on Mary's face as if to say, I pulled one over on you again!

Mary went into action. She started making calls. Was Mary going to enroll me in school? She called Tom first. Next, we met with Aristotle Onassis and my stepmother Jackie in the Echo Park just down the street from where I was being kept in plain sight.

Aristotle told Mary not to panic. He and Robert would take care of everything. The first step was to get Vivian Gonzales enrolled in school since she was the oldest. I was to be registered next, and last would be Maryann. Onassis and my stepmother assured Mary that she would not have any problems with the school officials. My stepmother handed Mary some money for her troubles and told Mary, "Take good care of Jack."

I began to argue with Jackie. "You are going to keep me here for as long as you possibly can. Someday I'll make you pay for what you have done. I'll be the cause of both your deaths. Keep in mind what I told you when you were getting on your horse. You'll be spatial when you make your decision to take your life. As for you, Aristotle, I will make sure you receive full payment for your part in all of this!"

Mary and I got into a taxi, leaving Onassis and Jackie walking through the tennis courts in the park.

Mary followed Onassis's instructions to the letter. Mary enrolled Vivian in school first. When the police returned to Mary's house, she informed the officer that she indeed enrolled Vivian in school and that Maryann and I would be attending soon. "Mrs., why are the other two children not enrolled?"

"Well, sir, as I explained, I just moved here. I misplaced my son's birth certificate, and without that, I can't register him for school."

"Mrs., I'm going to give you another week to make it to the hall of records where you should be able to get one immediately."

The following Monday, Paul and Mary drove me to Rosemont Elementary School to register for school. Paul stopped the blue panel truck in front of the school. Mary and I got out of the panel truck and walked up the stairs and into the main office. The office secretary walked over and asked, "How may I help you?"

Mary replied, "I'm here to register my son for school." That was the wrong thing to say.

"Mrs., I am not this woman's son; she is not my mother!"

"Son, if she is not your mother, then who is she, and where is your mother?"

"My mother just died; it was on the News. This woman is not related to me in any way."

Just about that time, a thin woman with purple hair came out of a door to the right of us. "What is all the commotion about out here? What is going on here?"

"Mrs., Mary is calling me her son, and I am not her son. President John F. Kennedy is my dad, and Marilyn Monroe is my mother!"

"Allow me to introduce myself. I am the Principal of Rosemont Elementary School. My name is Mrs. Barnum, and this is my secretary Mrs. Richards.

"Now, what is going on here? Why is this child insisting that you are not his mother?" The secretary, Mrs. Richards, suggested calling the police. She said, this child does not resemble this woman; maybe there is some truth to what he is saying. The woman with the purple hair, Mrs. Barnum, said, "Let's straighten this out now before calling the police.

"Mary, I'm the principal here, and I have to ask you some questions. What is causing this child to say you are not his mother? I hope you have a reasonable answer."

"Mrs. Barnum, look at me. I'm a 350 lbs woman with light skin, dark hair, and Mexican descent. He has light skin with freckles on his face and arms, and his hair is reddish light brown. He looks White American. He has always been ashamed of my appearance."

With that explanation, Mrs. Barnum was satisfied with Mary's answers. Mrs. Richards, the school secretary, still insisted on calling the police. "Mrs. Richards, you and I experienced this kind of behavior before; someone is always trying to pass for something they're not. I sympathize with Mrs. Gonzales."

Mary handed Mrs. Barnum a white document with the word 'baptismal' inscribed on it.

"Mrs. Gonzales, I cannot accept this baptismal certificate to enroll him in school. You need a birth certificate to make sure he is an American Citizen."

"Mrs. Barnum, I just moved into the neighborhood. I can't find his birth certificate."

"Mrs. Gonzales, I am sorry, but those are the rules. You'll just have to come back when you have all the correct documents."

I stood there thinking, *How could she do this to me?* What did she mean that I was trying to pass? Pass for what? What is it that I'll be learning here in this school if a child does not have his or her say? Mrs. Richards was adamant that she wanted to call the police; however, Mrs. Barnum refused to do so. Why? Mary was upset; we turned and walked out.

We returned to Rosemont the next week. This time, Mrs. Barnum immediately came out of her office. As if she was waiting for us, she stood next to Mrs. Richards in silence. We seem to be going through the same motions as last week. This time, Mary handed Mrs. Richards a white document that read 'Birth Certificate.' Mrs. Richards read the document and said to Mrs. Barnum, "There is no first name on it."

## CERTIFICATE OF LIVE BIRTH
STATE OF CALIFORNIA—DEPARTMENT OF PUBLIC HEALTH

| | | | | |
|---|---|---|---|---|
| STATE FILE NO. | | | REGISTRATION DISTRICT NO. | |

| THIS CHILD | 1A. CHILD'S FIRST NAME | 1B. MIDDLE NAME | | 1C. LAST NAME Gonzales | |
|---|---|---|---|---|---|
| | 2. SEX Male | 3A. THIS BIRTH SINGLE, TWIN, OR TRIPLET Single | 3B. IF TWIN OR TRIPLET THIS CHILD BORN 1ST, 2ND, 3RD | 4A. DATE OF BIRTH—MONTH, DAY, YEAR July 22, 1955 | 4B. HOUR 6:45 A |

| PLACE OF BIRTH | 5A. COUNTY LOS ANGELES | | 5B. CITY OF | | 5D. INSIDE CITY X OUTSIDE |
|---|---|---|---|---|---|
| | 5C. FULL NAME OF HOSPITAL OR INSTITUTION LOS ANGELES COUNTY GENERAL HOSPITAL | | LOS ANGELES 5E. ADDRESS 1200 NO. STATE STREET | | |

| LOCAL RESIDENCE OF MOTHER | 6A. STATE California | 6B. COUNTY Los Angeles | 6C. CITY OR TOWN Los Angeles 12 | | 6E. STREET OR RURAL ADDRESS 226 North Beaudry Avenue |
|---|---|---|---|---|---|

| MOTHER OF CHILD | 7A. MAIDEN NAME OF MOTHER—FIRST NAME Mary | 7B. MIDDLE NAME Rae | 7C. LAST NAME Lopez | 8. COLOR OR RACE OF MOTHER White |
|---|---|---|---|---|
| | 9. AGE OF MOTHER AT TIME OF THIS BIRTH 37 | 10. BIRTHPLACE STATE OR FOREIGN COUNTRY Colorado | MAILING ADDRESS OF MOTHER | |

| FATHER OF CHILD | 12A. NAME OF FATHER—FIRST NAME Paul | 12B. MIDDLE NAME | 12C. LAST NAME Gonzales | 13. COLOR OR RACE OF FATHER White |
|---|---|---|---|---|
| | 14. AGE OF FATHER AT TIME OF THIS BIRTH 35 | 15. BIRTHPLACE STATE OR FOREIGN COUNTRY Texas | 16A. USUAL OCCUPATION Repairman | 16B. KIND OF BUSINESS OR INDUSTRY Television |

| INFORMANT'S CERTIFICATION | 17A. I HEREBY CERTIFY THAT THE ABOVE STATED INFORMATION IS TRUE AND CORRECT TO THE BEST OF MY KNOWLEDGE | 17B. SIGNATURE OF PARENT OR OTHER INFORMANT Mary Rae Gonzales | 17C. DATE SIGNED BY PARENT OR OTHER INFORMANT July 23, 1955 |
|---|---|---|---|
| ATTENDANT'S CERTIFICATION | 18A. I HEREBY CERTIFY THAT I ATTENDED THIS CHILD AT THE TIME OF THIS BIRTH AND THAT THE CHILD WAS BORN ALIVE AT THE HOUR, DATE AND PLACE STATED ABOVE Geo. A. Wright M.D. | | 18B. ADDRESS L.A.County General Hospital |
| REGISTRAR'S CERTIFICATION | 19. DATE RECEIVED BY LOCAL REGISTRAR AUG 8 1955 | SIGNATURE OF LOCAL REGISTRAR George M. Uhl, M.D. | |

Mrs. Barnum asked her, "What color is the seal on the Birth Certificate?"

She answered, "A bluish-purple."

"Mrs. Richards, you can register the child for school."

I have just had my identity changed from John F. Kennedy Jr. to Boy Gonzales, and I am now 7 years young. How was this going to affect me in the future? How will I get back home! Will Dad find me, or will I have to stay here with this evil woman Mary?

Not only did this birth certificate change my name, but it also gave me new age, saying I was born in 1955, taking years from my life. I'm seven years old all over again! My weight and height worked against me too. Am I going to live to be eighteen years old and die like the doctors have told my parents? I should be attending junior high school.

My father will never find me now. The feeling of helplessness came over me, something that I never felt before. How was I going to survive all that is happening to me and around me? I was lost in thought when an African American woman entered the office wearing a light blue uniform. She was thin and well-mannered. Mrs. Barnum formally introduced us. "Ruben, I would like you to meet Mrs. Kurt; she is the school custodian, and she'll escort you to your classroom."

"Nice to meet you, Mrs. Kurt." I immediately took a liking to Mrs. Kurt. I could never imagine that she would play a pivotal role in my survival.

# NOVEMBER 22, 1963;
# COMING OF AGE

**MRS. KURT AND I** walked up to the second floor of the main building. She had something to do in one of the classrooms. Then we walked out onto the schoolyard, up to a first-grade class for seven-year-olds. The teacher took one look at me and said, "Mrs. Kurt, are you sure you are in the right classroom?"

I took my seat. I stared out the window almost the entire day. I did not want to participate in the class curriculum. I was uncomfortable in the classroom and accustomed to fewer students in a classroom. I was totally out of my element. There was no beautiful grass or trees, no branches swaying in the wind. It was as if I was a caged bird taking in the sights from behind bars. My whole life was caving in around me, and there was nothing I could do.

I had one last hope that my father would come to rescue me from this nightmare that I was in. How could he find me if he does not know where I am or what my name is now? How was I going to make it through this day? By the time I came out of this subconscious travel that I was in, recess came around.

It was nothing like I had experienced before. The trauma that I was experiencing was overwhelming. To this day, I cannot recall if that first kindergarten teacher I had at Rosemont Elementary School was male or female. (Because of my size, they put me in kindergarten for a day. By lunchtime, the kindergarten teachers were complaining to Mrs. Barnum that I was not 7 years old. In fact, I was speaking as if I had already been to school.)

The one thing that I was sure of was the window. There was no stained glass to marvel over.

I was assigned a student to take me to the cafeteria for recess snack. I had no idea what was in store for me, but this was going to be a whole new learning experience. The teacher had us line up at the door, boys on one side of the door and girls on the other side in a single file but separated. We walked out the door as if we were robots walking heel to toe, our backs straight, and our heads held high with our shoulders back. We were released onto the school playground. Joel, my escort, told me to walk fast, but do not run. You do not want to be the first one in the cafeteria, and you do not want to be the last one to arrive.

"Joel, why do you want me to walk fast?"

"Ruben, okay, this is the way it works in the cafeteria. If you are one of the first in line, you may get the leftovers from the day before, and if you are at the end of the line, there will be nothing left for you to snack on."

"What are you talking about, nothing to snack on? Why?"

To my surprise, we had to line up to enter the cafeteria. If that was not bad enough, there was no assigned seating. This was something I was not accustomed to.

"Joel! This is more of a race compared to a recess with snacks. I'm not accustomed to this kind of atmosphere. Recess is to enjoy your snacks, not all this loud chaos. This cafeteria is more of a dungeon, and we are expected to eat here?"

"Now!"

He said to take what you want. There was nothing to take. It was all sugar and pastries. Where was the cereal with milk or warm oatmeal? The pastries consisted of a slice of toasted white bread buttered with a mixture of sugar and cinnamon. How could anyone call this a breakfast snack?

I took a glass of milk and came up to the cash register. I had no idea what was in store for me next. The cashier looked at me and asked for payment. "Payment for what may I ask?" The cashier smiled and began laughing.

"I don't see what is so funny, Mrs.!"

"Where did you come from that you don't have to pay for what you have in your hand?"

"My parents pay for this sort of thing. I've never carried money with me before."

"What is your name, son?"

"I am John F. Kennedy, Jr."

"Yes, and I'm Jackie. Now, what is your name?"

"Oh, try Ruben Gonzales." She picked up the roster and read the names to herself.

"There is no Ruben Gonzales here. So, if you don't have the money to pay for the milk, put it back."

"Madam, this is all new to me; you do not have to be so rude!"

Mrs. Kurt was in the cafeteria, and she paid the nickel for me.

The cashier said, "Mrs. Kurt, are you going to help out every child that forgets to bring their milk money with them to school?"

"It's only a nickel, and besides, you had a good laugh at this child's expense."

I thanked Mrs. Kurt and turned to my escort. "Joel, where are our assigned seats?"

"Man, where did you come from there are assigned seats? Ruben, sit anywhere there is a space, hopefully for the two of us. We have twenty minutes for recess, and we just spent ten of it in line. Let's go."

"No, you go on, Joel. I am going to stay here and finish drinking my milk."

"It would be better if I stay with you. I don't want you to get lost; besides, we have to line up to go back into class."

"Joel, you mean to enter into class."

"Man, Ruben. You are weird."

"Joel, if my mother or grandmother heard me misusing the English language the way that you are doing, there would be a price to pay. I'd have to rewrite what I had just said if I had spoken the way that you just did."

As we left what looked to me like a picnic table, Joel said, "This way."

I followed him up the stairs and out the door onto the school-yard. The morning sun was blinding.

"Ruben, we have to line up according to our room number."

"Joel, I'm right behind you." We lined up in two lines, the girls on one side and the boys on the other side. The teacher stood between the boys and girls at the front of the line. As we walked into the building on our way to the classroom. As we were entering the building, I began to feel that we were more like cattle herded from one place to another.

The remainder of the morning I spent trying to cope with the changes that were occurring all around me. The most drastic change was my name from John to Ruben. I did not answer when I was called on to answer a question. The only way I could have a conversation with someone is if I initiated the conversation myself. And then I would have to look directly at the person. It became a huge problem whenever the teacher called on me to participate in the classroom curriculum. My inability to answer to the name Ruben branded me a daydreamer.

"Mrs. Phermint, I am not a daydreamer. I am accustomed to being called Mr. Kennedy, I am not here to make friends. I attend this establishment to broaden my education. I understand that you are the teacher here, and that, out of respect, I have to refer to you as Mrs. Pherment.

"You would receive the response that you are looking for if you would use my correct name."

"Mr. Gonzales, I don't care what you are accustomed to. Your registration card reads Ruben Gonzales, not John Kennedy. I am going to give you one warning. If you continue to disrupt this classroom, I am sending you to the principal's office."

Lunchtime could not come soon enough. It seemed that no matter what situation I was in, it turned into unexpected trouble. The embarrassment that I had experienced in the cafeteria for recess reared its ugly head for lunch. Where was I going to get the money? To pay for what I was going to place on my tray?

When I came to the cashier, she asked if I was new to the school and what my classroom number was. That was easy enough. "I'm in Mrs. Pherment's classroom. I do not recall the classroom number."

I had forty-five minutes for lunch. In that allotted time, I had time to play on the school grounds. This morning's snack was awful; the afternoon was horrendous. A hotdog and a bag of potato chips with milk all for .35 cents? I reluctantly handed over the thirty-five cents that my babysitter gave me.

How was I going to survive on this meal? The Rosemont Elementary cafeteria hotdog was no comparison to a New York City dog with sauerkraut and mustard on a steamed bun. This hotdog was raw and cold, the bread hard and dry. To top all that off, who in their right mind would put mayonnaise on their dog?

Claude was a school mate and a neighborhood friend. When he heard me ask for mustard, he repeated, "MUSTARD? Ruben, you are a white boy!"

"Why, Claude? Because I like mustard on my hotdog?"

"Yes, that's it. At my house, we never put mustard on sandwiches; it is strictly mayonnaise."

The cashier told us to move along and discuss our eating habits at the table, boys!

Claude and I sat down to have our lunch. By the end of our meal, we became friends. He seemed kind enough. We left the cafeteria together and went to play on the school playground. Claude introduced me to some of the other boys and girls that were in the same classroom as us. Each grade had its own assigned area to play in; we were awarded the foursquare area.

The object of the game is to have four people standing in a large square painted on the ground, tossing the ball to others. The other players try to keep the ball within the square and off the yellow line. The game was easy enough, but some of the other kids were masters of the foursquare game. They knew how to make the ball slide, and it would bounce twice in your square, and you were out. The real trick here was that 26 kids were to have their turn at playing the game; however, the clock always ran out, and some kids were left out of the game. It was the same routine; you line up in single, double lines, boys on one side and girls on the other side, and like soldiers, we were escorted into our classrooms.

It was forbidden to interact with anyone while we were being escorted into the classroom. All that I could hear were the shoes of the other children echoing through the school grounds.

My hands clenched into a tight fist, I said to myself, What am I doing here? This is not what my grandpa Joe said he would do. He was to take care of me. Is this care? Is this going to be my life from now on? Will I have to go along to get along?

There was not a cloud in the sky. The sun was shining, and the skies were blue, but why am I here? As I was stepping out of the sunlight into the dark school, I felt the warm sunshine leave my back. While still hearing the sound of marching shoes hitting the floor as we ascended onto the second floor.

Was the memory of my parents going to do the same as the sun, turn to darkness? It was as if I started school all over again, this time with a new name and a different culture. Why was it that my words kept falling on deaf ears? I can still hear the shuffling of my classmates' shoes ringing in my ears as they were taking their seats. I had to walk to the last row, closest to the window, to the sixth chair. The rest of the afternoon went off without a hitch.

Mrs. Pherment was an exotic dresser. She wore a leopard skin sweater, black trousers, and high heels. She had what beatniks would call a 'cool vibe.' I took a liking to her. She made me feel as if I was going to make it out of the devilish nightmare I was in, or at least get through it.

Mrs. Phermint called on me to come to the blackboard. Solve long division. It was easy enough, and of course, I got the answer right. As I turned to walk back to my seat, she handed me a note and told me I had to turn it back in the next morning signed.

"Ruben, you can read that on your time, not on mine. Fair enough?"

2:30 came around soon enough, and it was time to go. I started to walk out the door when Mrs. Phermint asks me, "Where are you going? It is not time to leave yet. Don't just rise out of your seat and walk out the door."

The room filled with laughter. "Mrs. Phermint, I am not a child that I have to wait for you to walk me out the door."

"Ruben, I don't know what prep school you attended before arriving here, but we line up, and I walk you out of the classroom."

Mrs. Phermint walked the class out the school door onto the sidewalk, where, on the corner, Vivian was waiting for me. We had to wait there on the corner for the teacher to give us the okay to cross the street.

Vivian and I walked the eight blocks back to the house. The place that I knew I did not belong, but where I had to stay. There was no one to greet us; we were on our own.

When Mary and Paul arrived around 8:00 PM, I gave Mrs. Gonzales the note that Mrs. Phremint had given me to have my parent or guardian sign. Mary became enraged when she read the letter.

"Who gave you this note?"

"The teacher, Mrs. Phermint, gave it to me to have someone sign it."

"She wants me to provide you with thirty-five cents a day for lunch? Where does she expect me to get that from! Oh, and you need pencils, pens, and paper. Well, you can do without like I had to."

I do not recall if I had dinner that night, or if I just went to sleep.

The next morning, the bowl of the warm oatmeal I had for breakfast killed my hunger pain. I asked Mary for the note and the money. She signed it but did not give me the lunch money for the rest of the week. She told me to come home for lunch. As far as the school material, she would bring it when she returned from the shop.

"That's fine, but what do I do for now? What do I use for a pen, pencil, and paper?" Mary's language had become more abrasive as the conversation continued. I do not know if it was her lack of education or if it was her upbringing, but what she said next was uncalled for and not worth my time hearing it.

"God damn it! I told you I would bring it when I returned home."

"Mary, this is not my home; this is your home. Keep that in mind. I do not have to put up with that kind of language, you hear me! I did not ask to be here, and I am not one of your kids for you to talk to me like that, you hear me!"

Paul was leaving at the same time Vivian and I had to be in school, so he gave us a ride to school. I noticed that Paul was upset, not about what Mary had said, but, in fact, because he had to provide Vivian and me a ride to school. Mary and Paul had the same attitude towards me, Vivian, and Maryann. The closer we were to the school, the more he began to run his mouth.

"You are not my children. Why do I have to go out of my way to drop you off at school?"

We were at the doorsteps of the school in no time. I could not get out of the panel truck fast enough. How lucky am I that these two want to play my parents?

We arrived early. I decided to borrow a pencil and paper from a classmate. I still had not done my work from the previous day. I completed all twenty-five math questions in the twenty minutes that I had before lining up for class. It was not like me not to double-check the answers for correctness. It would be better if I skipped going to the cafeteria and rechecked my math homework.

Mrs. Phermint arrived on the school playground. Where we had lined up to be taken into the classroom at 9:00 AM on the dot. The curriculum started with reading, writing, and history. Mrs. Phermint first had the class read out loud. Once each student finished reading their part of the story, she asked us to elaborate on it. She was impressed that I knew what the word 'elaborate' meant.

She split the classroom into two groups. A is where the more advanced students sat, and B is where students who needed more attention sat. It continued like this throughout the day, then recess break, lunch, and playground break, and we were let out of school for the day.

Mrs. Phermint called me up to her desk and asked, "Have you a tutor at home?" She was surprised I answered no.

"Ruben, you are ahead of the class, and I would like to have you moved up to the next grade level. First, I would have to have your parents agree with the move. Would you be fine with that?"

"That would be fine with me, Mrs. Phermint; may I return to my seat?"

"Yes, you may, Ruben."

The school bell rang no sooner than I had taken my place.

I was up and in line to be escorted out the door and down the street by the teacher. Vivian was waiting for me at the corner, as usual. As we were walking to the house, I explained to Vivian what Mrs. Phermint had told me. Vivian was extremely excited that we would be in the same grade. We started making plans for how we would help each other academically.

When I arrived at the house, there was this older woman there. She was thin, medium-height, with salt and pepper colored hair. Her name was Lena Richard; she lived in Bunker Hill. She took one look at me. "So, you are Little Kennedy?"

"Yes, I am, and who are you?"

"I'm Lena Richard. You look like your father, but you are small, like your mother."

"Mrs. Richard, you know my parents?"

"Who doesn't know your parents, Ruben!"

"Well, it is nice to meet you, Mrs. Richard. May I be excused?"

"Yes, you may, son."

That evening when Mary arrived, she prepared dinner for herself and Paul. After dinner, she had Yolanda do the dishes while Vivian and I did our homework. Mary called me into the bedroom where she and Paul were sitting.

"I had a call from your teacher. It seems that you are some kind of a smartass. Well, let me tell you, you are going to stay in the grade that you're in now. Do I make myself clear?"

"Did Mrs. Phermint explain to you that if I do not advance to the next grade level that I will not achieve anything?"

"Listen to me, you are going to stay in the grade that I put you, do you understand me? Just who do you think you are! You are not better than anyone else. No one is going to tell me how I am going to treat you or raise you. You are in my house, do you understand that? You are nobody in this house, is that clear?"

I walked out of the room into the room where Vivian, Maryann, Sally, and Yolanda were. Yolanda saw how distraught I was and added fuel to the fire.

"That is just the way my mother is. You learn over time to get over her abuse."

For the next week or two, Mary kept me from attending school. She would lock me in the room and drug me while Tom was back at hypnotizing me. He and Mary were trying to get me to forget who my parents were. This treatment went on for the entire time that I was not attending school. Drugging and hypnotizing had affected my sense of time. It was not until Mrs. Barnum, the school principal, threatened to send out a truant school officer to find out why I was not in school that they let me go back.

When I returned to school, I had no idea where I was or what year it was. It was as if my sense of time had vanished. Almost as if I had started a new life. I knew the life I had lived was back there somewhere. Would it be better for me to leave it in my subconscious mind, or should I try to retrieve my memories?

There was that one persistent issue I had: I would not answer to the name Ruben. I know what Mary and Tom Proctor were trying to achieve, but it did not work. Where the drugging and hypnotizing worked was, I had a hard time with the third person when I was writing. I had forgotten the mechanics of writing and the spelling of words. It was as if they erased it from my memory banks. Also, it was as if they knew that I would not be unable to write a book about my ordeal. Eventually, I knew that I would find a teacher to help me overcome this obstacle that Mary and Tom put in my path.

It was November 22, 1963; the assignment for the day was to watch the televised Dallas trip of my father. Mrs. Phermint and the teachers on the first floor joined the class to attend the event. Everyone in the room was filled with anticipation to see what President John F. Kennedy was going to do in Dallas, Texas. I was seated in the first row, the second to last child when it came on the T.V. *President John F. Kennedy was killed.* I stood up and gasped for air!

I shouted, "They just killed my father! They just killed my father!"

By the third time I said, "They just killed my father!" a teacher had grabbed me and started to shake me.

"What are you saying?"

"They just killed my father."

She backhanded me right across my face from left to right.

I could see the whole class was in shock because of what they had witnessed on tv and what I had said. I started crying and repeated, "Someone killed my father." The teacher was still shaking me.

The door was opening, and in comes Mrs. Kurt dressed in her blue smock with a white handkerchief crying and wiping the tears from her eyes.

They rushed me into the principal's office on the same floor. I was told to sit and wait for the Principal, Mrs. Barnum. I was crying uncontrollably.

After I had calmed down, Mrs. Barnum had Mrs. Kurt take me back to join the rest of my classroom, where I remained the rest of the morning in shock. The school closed early; I had never felt so alone in my life! Was I going to meet the same fate as my parents? Who was going to care for my brother and me? It was up to me to keep us both alive.

JonJon had always been in the back of my mind, but now we were both without parents. How were we going to survive all of this tragedy without a parent? Would he ever talk to me again? Would I see him again? Would he remember that he has a brother?

For the next week, Mary kept me out of school. The day I returned to school, I was called into Mrs. Barnum's office. She asked me why I was not in school.

"Mrs. Barnum, Mary kept me out of school."

"Why? Were you sick?"

"No, just upset. My dad had been killed."

"Look here, Ruben; if you do not stop calling President John F. Kennedy your father, I am going to call your mother."

"Mrs. Barnum, as I told you before, my mother is no longer here."

"Ruben, if you keep saying Mary is not your mother, I am going to call the police."

"Mrs. Barnum, that would be fine with me!"

"What is your mother's telephone number at work?"

"Mrs. Barnum, for the last time, Mary is not my mother, so stop calling her that!"

"Young man, don't you take that tone with me."

"Why don't you ask Vivian what the phone number is. She may know. That is if you are going to get to the bottom of this."

"Ruben, you have been in trouble from the very moment you put your foot in this school."

Mrs. Barnum gave me a hall pass and had me take Vivian out of her classroom. Vivian and I were walking back to the office.

"Ruben, what have you done now?"

"The purple-headed Barnum wants your mother's telephone number."

"What, you did not memorize the phone number to the shop?"

"No, I did not; why would I?"

"You were told to memorize the telephone in case you are lost."

"What makes you believe I want to come back here if I get lost?" We made it to the principal's office and were told to sit and wait for Mrs. Barnum.

Mrs. Barnum was sitting behind her desk when Vivian and I were told to go into Mrs. Barnum's office. Mrs. Barnum was placing the phone on the hook when we walked in. She stood up and told us to have a seat. "Now Vivian, what is your mother's telephone number?"

"It is area code (213) 555-1927."

Mrs. Barnum jotted down the telephone number and proceeded to dial the number. I heard Mary's voice saying, "Gonzales and Sons TV Repair Shop at 1552 West Pico Street; how may I help you?" Why is it she had to be there early today? Just my luck!

"Mrs. Gonzales, I need you to come to this office to discuss your son Ruben."

I told her, "Look, Mrs. Barnum, I'm going to tell you for the last time: Mary is not my mother."

I heard footsteps behind me and turned to see Mrs. Kurt and Mrs. Richards in the doorway.

"Have you been standing in the door the whole time?"

"Yes."

I could hear Mary asking Mrs. Barnum, "What the hell are you doing bothering me at my place of business?"

"Mrs. Gonzales, we have a problem with your son, and I want to get to the bottom of it before it gets out of hand."

"What problem is that?"

"Ruben kept saying that Marilyn Monroe and President Kennedy are his parents! The staff and teachers are distraught due to the circumstances that have occurred over the last week. Before I let him back in school, we need to resolve this matter."

"Okay, I'll send someone to pick him up now."

Mrs. Barnum sent Vivian back to class, and I had to sit in the outer office waiting area.

It took all of forty-five minutes for Paul and Mary to arrive. Mary came into the office and demanded that I get in the blue Chevy panel truck. She told Mrs. Barnum that she would return with an explanation in two to three days.

"Hey, wait a minute here. Why does Vivian get to stay in school and not me? That is so unfair! Just for telling the truth."

"I told you to go outside and get in the truck; do you hear me? I am not going to tell you again."

"Mary, why is it going to take you two to three days to give me an answer to my question?"

"Mrs. Barnum, I have ten kids to support, and I dropped everything to come down here. I don't have a secretary or a technician to handle everything for me so that I can step out. I had to close my place of business."

Mary had me by the collar of my shirt as she was pulling me out of the office. She continued to hold on to my shirt collar as we were walking out the schoolhouse door onto the street. She finally let go when we got into the truck. Paul pulled away from the school as fast as he could.

Paul was upset with me.

"Do you know I had to close the shop just to come to get you?"

It was hard for me to understand what Paul was asking. He spoke with a heavy accent. "I'm informing you that you must remember I have a business to run. I do not have the time to take care of you."

"Paul, I did not ask to be here!"

We pulled into the back of the shop and went inside. Mary had this frantic look on her face as she was making phone calls. Paul did not look too well. It was as if they both were afraid of going to jail. It was the same look when the police came to Mary's to question her about all of us not attending school. I could not hear who Mary was talking to, only that she was to meet her in a few days. Mary had made it clear to the person on the other end of the receiver that they had to respond within the week. I could not believe that I was sitting here in the shop on the same milk crate. It was a never-ending cycle, one thing after another!

# GRANDMOTHER ROSE VISITS

**MARY STILL HAD MOST** of us kids locked inside her home. She left me locked in my room and went about her daily chores. I don't mean that she kept a clean house, only that she did what she usually did.

There was this woman who would come to Mary's home on Wednesdays to read tarot cards for her. Her name was Lily, and she lived around the corner from the shop. Whenever Mary had a crisis, she always turned to Lily for advice or to learn the outcome of her plight. From what I figured out, Mrs. Barnum requested some information that frightened Mary.

Lily had advised Mary that if she held her nerve, she would come out on top. "Just do what you are told, and all will be fine."

It was a cold California dark morning when Mary had me dressed in my Sunday best. She had called for a taxi around 7:30 AM and asked the dispatcher not to be later than 8:00 am. Mary had forgotten that the taxi drivers always had a difficult time finding her address. They complained that her address was hard to locate. This time would be no exception; the driver arrived late. Mary had to call the dispatcher several times to make sure the taxi was on its way. By the time the cab came, it was 8:30 AM. Mary was furious.

He pulled up to the curb and honked the horn of his cab. We climbed into the back seat of that taxi and drove off. "Where are we going?" the driver asked.

"We are going to Echo Park."

The driver shouted, "Echo Park! You could have walked there. It is right down the street."

"I know that. If I wanted to walk, I would have. Just get me there. I am late! I'll make it worth your while!"

"Okay. But all the streets around here are dead ends. What is the quickest and easiest way to get there?"

"Go out there, make a left, go down to the corner, make a left, go about two blocks, and make another left on Glendale Boulevard. Once you are on Glendale Boulevard, stay in the right lane; you'll make a right onto Bellevue Ave. Stop in front of the tennis courts and let us out."

It would have been faster for us to walk, but with Mary's size, it would have probably given her a heart attack. Instead, we had to take a taxi which took more than ten minutes. When we came to a stop, there, sitting on the far side of the tennis court, were three people. They looked as if they were hiding in plain sight. I recognized them. I was crossing the tennis court in no time at all.

There sitting was my Grandmother Rose Fitzgerald Kennedy with her back to the street. Jacqueline Bouvier Kennedy and Aristotle Onassis were sitting opposite my grandmother. I walked up to them and sat down.

"Grandmother, what you are doing here! You mean to tell me you have known of my whereabouts all this time and did not come to get me? Now both my parents are gone, and you're here! You and my grandpa Joe promised me. You said you would take care of me. We trusted you! I want to go home. I want to go back! Grandmother, I am waiting for an answer here."

No sooner did I say that when Mary walked up and began to speak.

"Rose, I am having a lot of problems with the school principal. She wants to know why I have Jack. I'm having a meeting with her and her staff on Monday. What do I tell her?"

Aristotle began to answer the question for my grandmother. "Mary, I'm taking care of things as we speak. Do what I instructed you to say, and you should not have any more problems."

Mary turned to my grandmother Rose. "I need some money to care for Jack."

"Mary, you say you love Jack as if he is your son, so work for him like he is your son!"

I pleaded with my grandmother. "Grandmother! She is not telling you the truth. Mary keeps me hungry, cold and refuses to furnish me with school supplies or send me to school. I have to come up with my own 0.35 cents for lunch. She is mean and cruel. Mary has her children do her misdeeds for her. She pays them with the money that you and Aristotle give her. She is treating me miserably, and I want to go home. They have tortured and beat me. Please, I want to go back home. I'll be a good boy. Take me home."

"Jack!" Mary shouted.

"I'll be back for you soon, don't worry. I'll be back."

Aristotle handed Mary a stack of hundred-dollar bills and told her to take care of me. I broke away from Mary's clutches and tried to follow them into the car. Jacqueline had pushed me away from the car and told me to stand back. They pulled away from the curb and drove onto the Hollywood freeway. I broke away from Mary again. I ran after the car, but they were long gone. I ran across the street into the park this time. I was on the lakeside and began to cry.

I sat in the park, gazing out across the lake, watching the ducks gently float by. I knew that I was on my own and that I had to come up with some plan to survive. With the death of my parents, especially my father, I would be fighting his legacy in the court of public opinion.

Perhaps Mary was correct, who was going to listen to me? I don't recall how long I had sat there thinking when I heard Charlie and Danny calling.

"Ruben! Ruben, where are you!"

I did not answer; I waited for them to come around the bend for them to see me. Charlie saw me first.

"Didn't you hear me calling you?"

"No. I did not."

"Yes, you did. Why didn't you answer me?"

"You know Ruben is not my name!"

"What do you expect me to call you? Little Kennedy? Get over it! Let's go!"

We walked across Glendale Avenue up the wooden stairs through the pathway crossing Belmont Ave. Up the one block to 510 N Burlington Avenue to that two-bedroom house where I was now going to have to call home. I knew full well; this is where my grandmother was going to leave me. I had one hope left.

What was Mrs. Barnum going to do? How was Mary going to convince her that I was her son? Would I have to go along to survive this ordeal, or would Mrs. Barnum call the police?

Monday morning finally came around, and Mary and I were in the principal's office of the school. Mrs. Barnum's office was just to the right of the counter in the main office. All I had to do was turn my head to the right, and there she was. The School Principal, Mrs. Barnum, was the one person who holds my fate in her hands.

Mrs. Barnum looked a little more confident this morning; Mary was displaying a more subdued attitude, more of a victim instead of the perpetrator. I could see that Mrs. Barnum and Mary were playing off of each other's attitude big time. We waited less than 10 minutes but no more than 15 when Mrs. Richards told us we could go into Mrs. Barnum's office. As we entered the office, Mrs. Richards closed the door behind us.

Mary and I sat on one side of the desk, and Mrs. Barnum sat on the other side. It was a very professional, orchestrated meeting. Mrs. Barnum starts the meeting off by asking me how I was feeling, and if I have overcome my anxiety. The moment she said that any hopes of her helping me were going to be none to nil.

Mrs. Barnum looked at Mary and began with, "I'd like to make time for you to speak with the school psychiatrist regarding this matter with your son Ruben. I am going to let you talk first, and I'll give you my assessment."

"Mrs. Barnum," (that was a rarity for Mary to call anyone of color. Mary did not even speak to law enforcement with that kind of respect.) "You teach about the founding fathers of the United States here in this school, am I correct?"

"Yes, we do."

"Well, what is the problem? Ruben thinks of President Kennedy as his father."

"You make a valid point, but something has to be done to stop him from saying the president is his father."

"I cannot agree with you more, Mrs. Barnum. What is it that you want to do about it?

I shouted, "But he is my dad. He is!"

"Look, if you do not stop referring to Pres. Kennedy as your father, you'll have to see the school psychiatrist."

Once Mrs. Barnum said I was going to have to see the psychiatrist, I decided to go along with her decision.

I recalled my dad and how hard he tried to bring my Aunt Rosemary home from the Sanitarium. He'd argue with my grandmother that it was not right, leaving Rosemary in a sanitarium. Dad said that Aunt Rosemary was our responsibility and not someone else's. Dad believed my grandmother did not want to deal with Rosemary's disability. Which had been exacerbated by the doctors giving my Aunt Rosemary a lobotomy.

It was my understanding that people who had visited a psychiatrist had some kind of mental impairment. There is a stigma that comes along with seeing a psychiatrist, and I did not want that stigma to follow me through my life. Sense Mrs. Barnum only gave me that one option to see a psychiatrist, that meant that she was not going to do anything about my kidnapping.

I tried to convince Mrs. Barnum to call the police.

"Ruben, you are confusing the founding fathers of this country with your own parents. It would be in your best interest to see a psychiatrist."

"Mrs. Barnum!"

I asked, "Why a psychiatrist? What is that going to achieve? There is nothing wrong with me mentally."

Mrs. Barnum turned to Mary. "Mrs. Gonzales, I will need your permission before the department's psychiatrist can speak to him."

"Mrs. Barnum, if you think that he needs a psychiatrist, that is fine with me. Why spend the money unnecessarily?"

The terror that came over me by mentioning the word psychiatrist.

"Mrs. Barnum, I believe there will be no need for that now, but if necessary, I will give my consent at a later date, but for now, the answer is no."

Mrs. Barnum was satisfied with the outcome of the meeting. As the school principal, she made it seem as if she fulfilled her obligations as a principal and a law-abiding citizen. Mrs. Richards, Mrs. Kurt, and the teachers were not too happy with Mrs. Barnum's decision not to bring the police into the matter. Mrs. Barnum's decision was final, and I was sent back to class. I was made to understand if I were going to survive, I would have to go along with this criminal organization. That Uncle Robert F. Kennedy, Edward M. Kennedy, and Grandmother had created. Mary and Mrs. Barnum made it clear that I was in their clutches from that day on.

# SURVIVING

**THE ONLY WAY I** was going to survive the kidnapping was to learn to get along with my captors. Not that I was held in chains or even locked in the house under lock and key. It is society's indifference towards me that I would have to endure! Everyone who came in contact with Mary was either paid or a willing participant in this crime. It was as if to say, How dare you say you are the beloved president's son? Not only that, but Marilyn Monroe is your mother to boot? How does one survive the depths of who your parents are or have become? That was the dilemma I was faced with.

Survival was my main concern.

Lena Richard would sometimes babysit me. She made me feel as if she cared for me. Like a real grandmother should.

One conversation I recall having with her was she was going to teach me to care for myself.

"Little Jack, I'm going to show you how to cook, clean, and mend your clothes. In Lincoln, Nebraska, where I come from, every farmhand has his specialty. You, on the other hand, are from the city and are all alone. By the time I get through with you, you'll be a well-rounded young man."

The first thing that Lena taught me was to boil water. She said that water boils at 216 degrees, and once it started to boil, it was not going to get any hotter. "Jack, once the water boils, place two eggs gently into the water. If you just drop the eggs into the water, you'll crack them, and all that will be left if you are lucky is the yellow yolk of the eggs. So be careful."

Once Lena was sure that I could make soft- and hard-boiled eggs, she moved on to baking. Baking was easy; all you had to do was follow the directions on the packages. The baking was easy, not like she was going to teach me to bake from scratch.

It was not long that I was threading a needle and sewing my britches, as Lena would call pants. The hardest thing about mending my own clothes was getting the damn thread through the hole of the needle. Lena was surprised that I was familiar with the thimble. When I explained to her that I used a thimble before, she said, "Your mother, Marilyn Monroe, is quite clever. I would have never thought of using a sewing thimble when changing a baby's diaper; it makes sense.

"Jack, there is no good reason why you should run around looking like you are alone. I am going to teach you to iron your shirts and trousers." Lena was true to her word. In no time, I was cooking, cleaning, mending, and ironing my clothes. She always said, "Put a little elbow grease into your work, and you can accomplish anything."

Lena tried to put some of that old-fashioned Nebraska religion in me. I still look fondly on the days when she would take us to the Midnight Mission to hear the preacher preach. We'd walk down to the Midnight Mission on Temple Street and Beaudry Ave.

There it was, the Mission, looking like something out of the depression era. You could see that the people who were sitting in pews had not had a decent meal in a long while. Men with hard, thin, elongated faces. Women with their children with no place to go. I have never seen such despair in all my days. I heard the preacher preach. I do not recall what the message of the sermon was. The thing that sticks with me to this day is the loneliness that was all around me.

After the sermon was over, the people filed into one single line; there were women, children, and men. All of us waiting patiently for a cup of coffee, bread with butter, and a slice of bologna to eat. The sandwich tasted as if it was made the day before and sat in the hot sun. Lena said if I ever need a hot meal, this was the place to come. "Everyone is welcome, and you'll never be turned away. All religious denominations are welcome here."

Lena gave Yolanda and me .15 cents each to take the bus back home. Lena lived within walking distance of the Midnight Mission. Of course, Lena lived at the top of Bunker Hill. She said she enjoyed walking.

Lena was the one person who was true to her word. She helped me to stand on my own two feet. She said, "Don't let what's going on define you; you define it. I want to give you something that you can use for the rest of your life.

"Jack, your dad's death had taken a toll on you. His demise has left you with a speech impediment. I want you to think before you speak; the words will come to you. You should have no problem. Once you gather your words and thoughts, it will be easy for you to speak. Soon, you'll be able to speak clearly, and your tongue will not get twisted.

"I know that Charlie striking you in the back of your head when you are doing your homework does not help."

"Lena, it is as if someone taught Charlie to place a ring on his middle finger and hit me in the back of the head. When he hits me, the shock sends lights through my brain that I feel come out of my eye sockets. I asked Charlie, who taught him to torture me this way? But he did not answer me. I told him, 'if you do not stop torturing me, I'm going to find a way to make you think twice before you lay another hand on me.' I could tell by the expression on his face that he knew I was serious, but as he said in the past, who was going to help me?"

With the Gonzales and Gomez clan, action speaks louder than words. I became keenly aware it would take action to resolve this issue with Charlie. It would have to be drastic, something so extreme that he would keep it in the back of his mind for the rest of his life.

The solution came to me one morning when Charlie came home from school early. I was in the kitchen, making myself breakfast when he walked in. Charlie was wearing his football letterman's jacket. This day, he felt as if he was a badass!

I do not recall what set him off, but he started arguing with me. We ended up outside of the house. Almost as if to say, I'm going to beat the living hell out of you, and I do not want to have to clean up your blood. Charlie had me by the collar of my shirt with one hand and hit me with the other. He was hitting me as if I was a grown man.

I could see my blood on his right hand. I began to yell for help. Unable to defend myself, as he had me standing on my toes, I thought of kicking him in his shin, but that would not work. I would lose my balance, and we would both go over on our backsides.

"Go ahead, Ruben, yell for help. Who is going to come to your rescue? Who?"

In my moment of agony, I stopped crying. I just stopped. Charlie drew his right arm back as if he were going to throw a football, but instead of a football, his fist was clenched.

"Why did you stop crying and yelling for help? Why did you stop crying!"

I could feel the tears roll back into my eyes, and the pain was gone. "Charlie, you are right. Who is going to help me? I have no one. You're right."

By this time, our eyes were locked as if I was looking into his soul, and I said again, "You are right!"

I guess sometimes the right words were my salvation. Charlie finally let me go. Once Charlie let me go, I understood that I was alone, and I would have to learn to defend myself against these wild beasts.

I did not know what a son of a bitch was, but it was the nickname that the Gonzales and Gomez clan gave me. I came to accept that these beasts did not have any respect, and lack of education was no excuse.

I looked dead at Charlie.

"You are going to pay for this. I don't know how or when, but I am going to make you fear me! You're not going to terrorize me every time you have a bad day! You have to go to sleep sometime, Charlie. And when you least expect it, I'm coming after you. Do you understand me? And I mean what I say. I'm coming after you, you hear me!"

That evening when Mary came home, I told her what Charlie had done to me. In her vulgar, uneducated manner, she said, "You god damn people just can't get along."

I came away feeling that there was no hope for these people. It was confusing to me. Just what did God have to do with Charlie physically assaulting me? I have never felt so insulted in my life. I began to question if all children go through this, or if it was just me. I did not want to let Charlie become complacent with himself, so I decided to act that night. I went to bed early and sensed Charlie, Gilbert, and Danny were asleep.

I waited until around three o'clock in the morning when the three of them were in their deepest sleep. I got up out of bed without making a sound. I tiptoed out across the wooden floor out of the room. Making sure that no one could hear the crackling of the wood under my bare feet, I made it out of the room without making a sound. I rounded the door and went into the kitchen, still trying to remain silent.

I opened the kitchen drawer and looked for the most significant and sharpest butcher knife I could find. There it was, the butcher knife that I had been sharpening earlier that day. I crept back into the bedroom. As I entered the bedroom, the moonlight flooded the room with enough light to see the contours of Charlie's face.

I crept up to Charlie's bed. The moonlight was beaming across his face. I could hear him breathing; I was that close to him.

I gently pulled the blanket cover down, so as not to wake him. I placed the butcher knife to his chest, I bent over him, and I shook him. He opened his eyes without gasping a word. I could see the terror on his face as he looked down at his chest. I whispered into his ear.

"Don't say a word." I could see the reflection of the blade beaming in Charlie's eyes.

With the soft whisper of a child, I said, "I told you if you ever put your hands on me again, I'll kill you. Do you understand me! Do I make myself clear, Charlie?"

I was holding the butcher knife with my left hand and had my right hand on top of the knife. I tapped on the knife ever so lightly, just enough to break the skin. Charlie was still in a state of shock! I gave the knife another light tap on its tip until a drop of blood was on the knife. I showed Charlie the end of the tip of the blade with his blood on it. "I told you I'll find a way to make you understand that you are not going to terrorize me anymore."

I pulled the covers back over him and walked back to the kitchen and placed the knife in the sink. The next morning, Charlie told his mother what I had done.

I did not fully appreciate my action until Mary's reaction to what I did during the night. Mary had taken all of the knives from the kitchen drawers that morning. There was not one decent knife in that house from the day that I showed the courage to stand up for myself. Not that the brutality ended with what I had done to Charlie, just that the knife was no longer a means of protection.

The only thing I could do to get through this was to go along with what the Kennedy clan had in store for me. I was going to try and keep in my memory every good and bad thing that was done to me in the name of the Kennedy family and its matriarch in hopes that someday I would overcome society's indifference towards me as well.

Mary was the perfect candidate to do the Kennedys' bidding; she turned out to be a vulgar, vile reprobate in every sense of the word, and her family was no better.

It was not soon after Dad was assassinated that the Gomez and Gonzales clan went to work trying to annihilate any memories of what I would now have to call my past life with my parents Marilyn Monroe and President John F. Kennedy. I guess that was the first time I really began to understand what Mary and the Kennedy's were doing.

Charlie Gonzales had to marry Ernestine Rodriguez because she was pregnant. Her nickname was Chita. The best way to describe Chita was to say she was the stag of the neighborhood; at least, that is what her soon-to-be husband Charlie called her. She was mean, cruel, and Mary's confidant and enforcer.

# FINDING HOPE AGAIN

**IT TURNED OUT TO** be one of those days of being in the right place at the wrong time. The newlyweds' reception was being held up the hill from Mary's house at 510 N. Burlington Ave. A young adult, Roland, around the same age as Charlie, crashed the wedding gala.

He grabbed a bottle of champagne off the dining room table. He and Charlie were having a staredown as he was reaching for the champagne. It wasn't until Chita screamed, "Get the hell out of here!" at him, did anyone pay attention to him.

As she was screaming at him, he popped the cork on the bottle of champagne and took a big swig.

I couldn't be experiencing a Deja vu moment.

John, the chef, and Louis Rodriguez, Chita's father, pulled the guy out of the living room front door. The guy staggered to the middle of the third tier of stairs.

Chita and her parents were right across from Roland. Charlie and I were standing on the second tier of stairs, watching, waiting for what Roland would do next.

Roland raised the champagne bottle to his lips and took another gulp. I was waiting for some reaction out of Charlie, but he just stood there. Roland drew his right arm across his mouth to wipe his lips. He leaned back and pointed directly with his index finger at Chita and said, "The baby Chita is carrying is mine." It was no secret that Charlie was forced to marry Chita.

Roland is the brother-in-law of Marjorie, and his brother is Dooly. Marjorie babysat me over the summer when Amalia was abruptly asked to leave. (Mary believed that there was some hanky-panky going on between Paul and Amalia.) So she hired Marjorie to babysit us. Marjorie's husband, Dooly, called me Little Kennedy. They told Mary that I do not answer to the name Ruben. To get my attention, they preferred to call me Little Kennedy. Dooly said I looked like my father, President John F. Kennedy.

In the summer of '63, Richard, Mary's oldest son, married Minta. Minta has a young sister named Yolanda, who is a friend of Chita. Yolanda had told her sister Minta that Richard was in jail, and she should do the Christian thing and go to visit him.

Richard was supposedly some gang leader. He had been discharged from the Army because he was a thief, and old habits die hard. I recall when Richard came back from Germany, some rival gang members kicked his ass. To me, Richard was a dog with a loud bark and a small bite. When Richard was discharged from the Army, Paul did not want him to live in the same house with him.

Around that same time, Thomas Proctor came back into town. He pulled up in a candy apple red Buick Le Sabre. I was playing in front of Mary's house when out of the car comes this red-headed, blue-eyed girl. She could not have been more than 30 years old.

I could hear her say to Tom, "Is that him?"

"Yes, that is him; he is President Kennedy's and Marilyn Monroe's son."

Tom called me over to meet his new wife, Linda, who was from Dallas, Texas. I couldn't help but notice that she looked much younger than Tom. She was sweet enough, but I could see that she was not compatible with Tom. Most of the time, I called Tom by his last name: Proctor. He is one of the people who kidnapped me from my mother, but he treated me with more respect and kindness than I have received from Mary or her family.

There was some discussion going on that maybe Proctor and Linda would adopt me and raise me as their own. Mary did not take too kindly to the idea of me going with Proctor and Linda. It was decided that I would stay with Mary. By this time, I had been so physically and mentally abused that it had taken a toll on me.

I decided it is better to go along to get along if I was going to survive. So I started saying, "You are talking about Mary, not my mother."

Not that Mary was even capable of being a mother to her own children, I just wanted the pain and suffering to stop. At least, that is the way I explained it to Linda.

I like Linda; she made me feel as if she really cared about my well-being. "Ruben, how are you doing in school?"

"Well, when Mary lets me attend school, I always manage to upset the teacher. If that was not bad enough, Richard Noriega and I had a fight during recess. We had a fight on school grounds, and I got expelled. I can't help it if the school is backward and does not teach history accordingly."

"Ruben, are you sweet on any of the girls in your classroom?"

"Yes! There is one girl, her name is Maritza. She is beautiful, has big brown eyes with long black hair. Maritza does not like boys with freckles on their faces. I have some freckles on my face, but they are not as noticeable as yours are Linda. I can tell that Maritza likes me, but she is shy. Maybe if there is a school dance I'll ask her to dance with me. The May Day school dance is coming up. I'll ask Maritza to dance then."

"Ruben, you know how to dance?"

"Yes! My mother taught me to dance."

"Your mother taught you to dance?"

"Yes, my mother! Not Mary, my mother!" I always assumed when I emphasized my mother, people understood I meant my real mother, Marilyn Monroe. And not Mary, who pretended to be a mother.

Linda just happened to be one of those people who understood when I stated 'my mother.'

Linda and I finished up our chat, and she walked into the house. I was well aware that it was ill manners to eavesdrop on someone's conversation. However, as Linda was walking way, she and Tom started discussing me.

"Tom, the way Jack talks about his mother, he drives home the point that he is referring to his real mother and not Mary!" As Linda and Tom entered Mary's home, the last thing I heard was Linda saying, "Tom, how could you have this child live in this deplorable condition?"

I dare not follow them into the house. I knew it was not my place to interfere with any discussion Mary, Tom, and Linda were going to engage in. It was not customary for the kids to speak openly and freely what their intentions were. It was almost as if I did not exist, or at least I had no feelings.

It was not long after meeting Linda that Mary's son Richard decided to get married. He was still in the early stages of his discharge from the Army. It seemed that Richard had a hard time keeping his hands off of other people's property. Mary's motto was, I don't have to be jealous of anyone, I have all kinds in my family.

There was some disagreement about who was going to be in the wedding. It turned out that the only one that Minta wanted in the wedding party was Sally. It seemed that Richard's own sister Yolanda did not meet Minta's standards as a bridesmaid. Sally was a last-minute replacement for a flower girl at the wedding.

To put it bluntly, Minta believed that by marrying Richard, she had married beneath her. She always gave me the impression. That she thought that out there in this world, there was someone better for her. But Richard would do for now. When it came right down to it, Minta thought her fecal matter did not stink, but her gastrointestinal discharge gave her away.

Richard had a difficult time adjusting to marriage, it seemed. He did something that would not let them have a peaceful night's sleep. He arrived at Mary's home all hours of the night. I was awakened by his knocking on his mother's window to let him in the house. Richard's stepfather Paul would become so enraged at Richard's behavior he would leave the house and stay away for 2 to 3 weeks at a time. Unbeknownst to Mary, everything that Richard was discussing in the confinements of her bedroom, I could hear.

Mary was not the type of person to keep her criminal activities private. It was as if she wanted the world to know what was going on and what she could get away with. She used her family as pawns in a chess game.

Richard's conscience was tormenting him. One early morning, he woke up the whole house. Paul told Mary, "If Richard comes here and wakes me one more time, I'll leave you. Just what the hell is bothering him?"

Paul had left the house that night, and Mary and Richard went into her bedroom and closed the door to talk.

The house became eerily quiet as I was lying in bed. I could hear Richard begin to sob uncontrollably. Minta was threatening to leave Richard if he did not stop leaving her alone in the middle of the night.

He was gasping as he began to speak. Richard would say to his mother, "I can see him, I can see him. I see the life leaving his body, the surprised look on his face at what I had done." He was telling Mary what had happened to a rival of his, how he pulled out the gun and fired off one shot, killing someone. I do not recall the name of the young man that he killed, only that I was hearing how the event unfolded and what it was doing to his conscience.

Richard was going into great detail how he placed the gun in Edgar's hand amidst the chaos in the bar. Making it seem as if Edgar himself had fired the fatal shot that killed the guy.

"Richard, if you do not pull yourself together, you are going to go to jail. I have done everything I could for you to avoid going to jail.

"Richard, I had to ask for favors to get you into the Army and look at what you did. You have a dishonorable discharge for the thievery in Germany. The moment you were removed from the Army, you fell into the same habits and began socializing with the same people that got you in trouble in the first place. How are you willing to undo all of my work just to ease your conscience? Do you understand just who is under our roof? We can all go to jail!

"Our sacrifices will all be for nothing, just because you cannot man up, Richard!"

I was lying in bed looking out the window at the moon, hearing the sternness in Mary's voice and the weeping of Richard echoing in my head.

It was not unusual for Mary and Richard's conversation to last until the sun came up. But this time, Richard had to be home before Minta rose out of bed for work.

Mary was true to her word; it could not have been more than a week or two when Paul returned from his hiatus. Mary had a

Sunday barbecue to bring Minta, Richard, and Paul together for a meeting of the minds. As always, Mary held the meeting in her bedroom behind closed doors.

Turns out, Mary met with someone named Ramos. He had a business on Evergreen and First Avenue on the Eastside of Los Angeles. He was going to help Richard overcome his fear. She laid out her plan on how Ramos was going to help Richard.

I met Ramos sometime later. He was a short Spanish man with slick black hair and moles on his face. He was always dressed in a white shirt, black or gray slacks, and black shoes with a mirrored shine. Whatever plan Ramos and Mary came up with seemed to work. Richard's midnight visits diminished until his conscience no longer plagued him.

The only solitude I could find was either in school or at the park. The school day started out like any other school day. I scrounged around for breakfast and looked over my homework from the previous Friday. I was in the habit of not having breakfast before leaving for school and arriving without my schoolwork. Going without breakfast was something that Mary had done even to Richard and Robert, her older sons when they attended school. So I felt that I was treated as their equal. And who was I going to complain to? Complaining seemed to bring on a beating from either Richard, Charlie, or Daniel, so it was less painful to just go hungry.

Arriving at school without the homework assignment was another matter entirely. How was I going to make Mrs. Cobb understand that the house that I was in was morally corrupt in every sense of the word? If someone was not ripping up my homework, they were tearing out the pages out of the books. There was no way I could turn in the assignment if I did not have the reading material to complete the homework. To top it off, Charlie was still hitting me in the back of my head when I did my homework.

The solution I came up with was to try and do the homework before class. This did not always work. Where was I going to come up with a pencil and paper to do the assignment? The next best thing was to read the chapter that I was assigned and memorize it. This way, when Mrs. Cobb asked me a question, she would know that I did the assignment but did not have the material to finish it.

I arrived at school early, and there was my classmate Walter. He was from Germany and the smartest kid in the classroom. I asked him if he had a pencil and paper he would lend me, and I wrote a quick history of Central America.

The particular country I found most interesting was Guatemala. For some reason, I found this country and its history and people fascinating. I don't know if it was the bright colors displayed on the front cover of the history book or the ancient Mayans that fascinated me. All I can say is from this country rose hope.

As I was studying over the weekend, I felt a kinship with its culture. Mrs. Cobb assigned Monday mornings for oral history. She made sure that everyone in the classroom turned in the topic that they were assigned.

Mrs. Cobb started in her usual way, randomly picking who she wanted to hear from. When she pointed at me and called 'Ruben,' it took her two to three 'Rubens' before I stood up. She looked at me, with that calm authority in her voice and asked, "What did you learn in your readings over the weekend?"

"Mrs. Cobb and classmates, the topic that I'll be discussing is the Country of Guatemala and its culture. My question is on the Republic of Guatemala. Guatemala is bordered by Mexico to the north, El Salvador and Honduras to the south, Belize and the Atlantic Ocean to the east, and the Pacific Ocean on the West.

"Guatemala has ancient people there called the Mayans, and because Christopher Columbus was looking for India, we referred to this ancient society as Indian. However, the Mayan culture has been around just as long as the Egyptian culture. Although Egyptian culture did not have human sacrifice, the Mayan Culture was as advanced as their counterparts. Human sacrifice was ended by the Spanish once they conquered the Mayan civilization.

"The national bird is the Quetzal; it's green with a red chest and a tail that is about a foot long. Their main exports are coffee, fruits, and vegetables. Its economy is similar to ours here in the United States. It is primarily a Catholic country. The country celebrates November the first as a national holiday. It is what we Catholics call All Souls Day. The whole country celebrates by visiting their departed loved ones by high noon and serving Fiambre for lunch, which is the main meal of the day."

I turned the book around I was reading, giving the class a snapshot view of what Guatemala looks like today. An indigenous Mayan was sitting with her knees bent under her. With a child sitting next to her and one bundled around her back. The green grass was rising all around her; off in the distance was a river. The image in the picture was bursting with colors; it was as if I was there, and I could hear the water from the river softly running across rocks. I had no idea what made me say, "This is the country that my wife is going to come from."

"Ruben, your emotional display of the history of Guatemala makes me want to visit Guatemala. However, I doubt very much if you can say at such a young age that your wife is going to come from Guatemala."

"Mrs. Cobb, I don't know if you believe in divine intervention, and maybe you're right. The difference between you and I is I believe God takes care of his own. I now have hope that I will not have to stay here forever."

I sat down. I could feel the eyes of my classmates staring through me. Someone in the room shouted out, "Does that mean Maritza does not have a chance, Ruben? Or you don't have a chance with her?" The boys in the classroom laughed, but the girls were a whole other story. They were smiling at me as if to say, You are thinking of starting a family at your young age?

Mrs. Cobb had the classroom put their materials away and line up for recess. She had this displeased look on her face at what I had said in the history report. So far, she was the first teacher I had a harmonious relationship with. I enjoyed her after school music class. I hoped that I did not do something inappropriate or say anything to offend her.

Recess was over soon enough. I was back in the classroom. Mrs. Cobb called me up to her desk and handed me a note and told me to take it to the office. I took the notice and walked out of the class. By this time, going to the Principal's office was old hat. I was either in trouble for distorting history or my political views.

Why should it be any different being sent to Mrs. Purple-Headed Barnum's office now? It was not my fault that I knew my future wife was going to come from Guatemala.

I entered the office and handed Mrs. Richards the notice.

"Ruben, not again!

"Cynthia says you are such a nice boy. She says you are sweet, kind, polite, and thoughtful, so why are you here now?"

"Mrs. Richards, how do you know Cynthia? That is if you don't mind me asking?"

"She is my daughter."

"Now, that makes sense since you both have the same last name."

"Well, that is usually the way it works, Ruben."

Mrs. Barnum came out of her office, took one look at me, and said, "Not you again! You are turning this into a habit, always in some mischief! What did you do now?"

"Mrs. Barnum, the note should be self-explanatory; it would help if you read it before you accuse me of doing something wrong!"

"Ruben, don't you take that tone with me!"

"Well, read the note and find out what I did!"

"Do you want me to get my paddle out, young man?"

"Mrs. Barnum, I read a report that I wrote this morning before class. I gave an oral account of what I have learned about Central America. What is so wrong with that, may I ask?"

I could see the steam coming out of Mrs. Barnum's ears. She was upset, and I had no idea why.

"Ruben, you have a condescending answer for everything."

Mrs. Barnum blamed that on my parents.

"I met your parents, and they do not speak as you do. It's as if you come from a different planet."

"Mrs. Barnum, I don't think you ever met my parents. So how did you come to that conclusion? You have met Mary and Paul, and I already told you they are not my parents, and if you don't like the way I speak, there is nothing I can do about it. This is me!"

Mrs. Barnum finally read the note. There she was, this tall, larger-than-life, purple-headed ostrich turning red. She never told me what the note said, but I would have to return to her office in the morning.

The next morning, I arrived in the principal's office at 8:55 am. I could see Mrs. Kurt in the supply room, setting up a student's desk. Mrs. Richards called me up to the front desk.

"You are going to take a series of six tests. Three this morning and three tomorrow morning. You'll be taking these tests in the supply room. This way, no one will disturb you, and you can focus on the test and only the test. You'll be timed on them. Your first test will be 45 minutes long; you'll be given your usual 20 minutes for recess."

I took the first test that morning at 10:00 AM and had recess. I returned on time to finish up the other two tests.

The next day, I finished up the other three parts of the test. They were the same standardized test that was given early in the year to chart your learning progress.

The tests were easy enough, but the cane that I was going to have to go through for passing them was more than anyone could handle.

At the end of the third day, Mrs. Cobb handed me a note to take home to Mary. She said that I have to bring it back signed. On my way home, I opened the letter and read it.

> 'Mrs. Gonzales, according to Ruben's test results, they showed he should be moved to a higher grade level. If he remains in the current grade level that I am teaching, it will hinder his interest in school and impede his ability to want to learn. What we are proposing is that he be moved immediately to the next grade level and reevaluated once he is comfortable in the classroom.
>
> Thank you,
> Mrs. Cobb

As I was walking, I pondered what was written in the note. I know that if I handed it over to Mary, there would be three possible outcomes. One, I would stay locked in a room with Maryann; two, I would be left alone by myself; or three, if I'm lucky, she would sign the note. The second choice made more sense. Mary was going to force me to stay in the house by myself. She was going to do what comes naturally for her: lie. She will say that I ditched school.

I thought about how my vocabulary was changing. It was as if I was drowning in stagnant water. I did not know what the word ditch implied, much less have to use it in writing or speaking.

What a change I was experiencing. Do all kids my age go through this experience? Is this what it takes to become an adult?

I made it to the house within 45 minutes. That's a long time for me. It had taken me less than 10 to walk the same eight and a half bocks to the house.

As always, I opened the front door, and there was no one to greet me. *Maybe I'll have an afternoon snack.* I walked into the kitchen, opened the refrigerator, and the light comes on!

That was a miracle in itself, thank God. But still, from one corner to the other, it was open space and cold air coming out of the refrigerator. Gone were the days of plentiful food. Opening the door to the fridge made me appreciate my mother more than I ever could express to her. If one thing came to mind, it was that I would now have to fend for myself. I've heard Mother say to Dad, "If you aren't willing to get going, you can stay put." I finally closed the refrigerator door and walked outside onto the veranda.

Looking out past the palm trees into the blue California sky, I thought it was time to toughen up. I guess I would have to become entrepreneurial. I skedaddled back into the house, looked around for a shovel, a fishing pole, and a bag. I walked out to the back yard, dug up some worms, placed them in the bag, and headed to Echo Park Lake.

I got down to the lake and spent the rest of the afternoon fishing. I caught three decent-sized fish, or so I thought. I returned to the house as quick as I could to prepare the fish. I guess living within walking distance of a lake paid off.

I cleaned the fish and cooked it as if I was an old hand at all of this. Boy! Was I surprised! The fish shriveled up to the size of a potato chip. There was not enough meat to make a meal out of them after cooking them.

All in all, it was an afternoon well spent. It was nice to be treated to a meal out of your own work. Besides, Mary would be back at her scheduled time between 7:30 PM and 10:00 PM, so perhaps I would have more to eat.

It was around 8:00 PM when Mary and Paul arrived. She prepared dinner for her and Paul. While she was finishing up having dinner, I mustered up the courage to enter the kitchen and show her the note that Mrs. Cobb had given me earlier that afternoon. I handed Mary the letter, and boy! She started raising cane!

"What the hell have you done now! Just who the hell do these people think you are, Ruben? You are not going to be moved to another grade just because someone in that damn school says it will hinder your learning abilities! Do you understand me?"

Well, that was the end of that, and for the next two weeks, I was to stay home alone. Hell is where Lucifer lived, so what does he have to do with me?

Was this a new form of language that I would have to learn to survive? My mother would be appalled if she heard me speak the way Mary does! I guess it goes to Mary's upbringing!

I was not allowed to leave the house until 2:30 PM for the next two weeks. I did return to school after those two weeks. Mary had informed Mrs. Barnum that I was not to be moved up a grade, or she would remove me from Rosemont Elementary School and find a school that would let me be.

When I returned back to school, Mrs. Barnum told me it was okay, and asked me would I like to join the school choir? She explained that I would have to stay after school Tuesdays and Thursdays for an hour with the rest of the school choir.

We had our music time, which was 45 minutes long during the day, but I would have to meet with the choir for practice. I figured since I enjoyed music and it took me to a place of peace and tranquility, I would join.

"Ruben, you have a child's voice for singing, and you have a knack for reading and understanding musical notes and their measurements. It is as if you have had vocal training before, but I have met Mary. I believe it is a natural ability that you have for music. I think you would make an excellent vocal student. You are the kind of vocal student that a teacher dreams of having but never finds. Now here, one of you is standing right in front of me.

"I have watched you help Mrs. Kurt clean the school auditorium after school, and you stay until the job is finished. Apply that same work ethic to your love of music, and you'll go far."

Mrs. Barmun was right. I do love music.

What Mrs. Barnum did not know was that I was helping Mrs. Kurt clean the auditorium so that I would have the money to pay for my lunch.

Mrs. Kurt and I worked out an agreement that I was never to tell anyone that I was working for my lunch money. I never felt as if Mrs. Kurt was taking advantage of me, or it was child labor. It was just something that I had to do to survive.

There is an art to pushing a janitor's push broom. It was pushing the broom and lifting it and shaking the dust off. Mrs. Kurt was impressed by my ability to master the push broom. There was one last skill to learn, and that was to mop the wooden floor in the school auditorium without making a mess.

The school supplied Mrs. Kurt with all the materials she needed to keep a hard, clear surface coat on the wooden floor in the auditorium. She and I would start out by removing the dust and grime from the floor then moving on to putting a high-gloss shine on the floor using a clean mop. The school auditorium took all of 45 minutes to clean right. At the end of the 45 minutes, we would end up at the light switches.

"Ruben, turn on the light switch and look across the floor of the auditorium."

When the lights came on and lit up the hall, I could see the lights reflecting from the hardwood floor. I was surprised to see my reflection on the wood floor and all the wood grain highlighted in the wood.

She said, "Ruben, this is a job well done; you should be proud of yourself," as we were standing there admiring our work.

I looked up at her and said, "Thank you."

I do not know if I was thanking her for teaching me a skill or that I was going to have lunch the next day. When it came right down to it, I guess it was both. As Mrs. Kurt reached over my head to turn off the light. She said, "Just think, come Christmas, you'll be up there on that stage singing, and you can be proud that you cared enough to make this auditorium presentable."

I looked up with a smile on my face. "Oh! Mrs. Kurt, Christmas is a long way off." But inside of me, I felt something that I never felt before, and that was a job well done. I had taken care of lunch; now what am I going to do for dinner?

It was hard keeping up with schoolwork when you had to think about where your next meal was coming from. If I was going to survive this ordeal that my stepmother Jacqueline and Aristotle had placed me in, I would have to fend for myself. I came up with a plan that on Monday, Wednesday, and Friday, I would look for some type of work.

Any place I asked for a job, they said I was too young, or I did not look needy enough.

I was walking back to Mary's house, which was becoming my new home. Not that it was a home-like. My mother had made a home for us.

Gonzales and Gomez were not the most congenial people to live with; it was a whole another world. There was always chaos going on in the Gonzales household, and if that was not bad enough, I had to learn a new language.

I was supposed to know that when someone is named Ramiro, I had to roll the R when annunciating Ramiro. When I was with my parents, I had no difficulty enunciating Cesar Romero, the actor's name. Still, Ramiro was just too hard to say by itself.

My best friend, Ramiro, was heck. For some reason, it always came out Medo. Medo did not mind the mistake; he said that I was highfalutin, and that was no fault of mine. Medo did not understand that I knew the difference between being disadvantaged and being impoverished. "Being disadvantaged means there is the hope of pulling yourself out of poverty. Being poor is that you lack the skills to pull yourself out of poverty, Medo."

"See Ruben, this is what I mean by highfalutin. Where do you come up with this stuff?"

Medo and I were walking home from school when he stopped to buy a Coca-Cola. We had walked into Johnny's liquor store. The Coca-Cola cost .15 cents, and the store owner charged him .16 cents. I asked the store owner Johnny what the extra penny was for. He said there is a one-cent deposit for the bottle!

"You mean you give money back for the empty bottle? Empty as in nothing inside the bottle?"

"Yes, that is definitely what I mean."

"Wow!"

Johnny, the store owner, looked at me with a surprised look on his face.

"Where did you come from, kid?"

"I just did not know that someone would pay for an empty pop bottle, that's all."

"What's the big deal? It sounds like you are not from around here, son."

"If I tell you where I come from, are you going to help me to get back there?" Johnny looked at me and shook his head.

Medo said, "Ruben, do you always have to get so sarcastic with people?"

"Look, Medo, I am not sarcastic. I am just asking a question, that's all."

On the way back home, Medo was astonished by my interest in the Coca-Cola bottle incident.

"Ruben, what is your fascination with the Coca-Cola bottle?"

"Medo, who can believe that someone is going to pay you for an empty bottle, that's all! Look how many bottles people toss in the trash. Medo, are you aware that they are throwing money in the trashcan? Keep in mind Medo what we place in the garbage. It's cans, newspapers, magazines, cardboard boxes. And they are all bundled into neat packages and placed at the curb for trash pickup. All some-one has to do is walk up and take the bottles and sell them."

"Ruben, do you realize how many bottles you would have to pick up to make a dollar?"

"Yes, I do, but it's free money, Medo. Are you aware of that?"

"Ruben, you cannot be that poor that you have to pick up bottles out of the trash."

"Medo, I prefer the phrase 'discarded bottles.' You make the word trash sound demeaning. Medo, nothing is humiliating about free money! This is money that someone does not want, and you're working for it. One thing that my mother taught me about money is there is nothing wrong with money that you work for, but there is something wrong with ill-gotten gains." About that time, Medo turns down the street to his home, and I continued on my way home.

As I was walking across the footbridge on my way home, there were some discarded pop bottles, so I picked them out of the cans and took them back with me.

Collecting bottles on my way home from school was turning out to be a real learning experience. I would have never thought that there would be a mathematical problem and an issue with the bottle exchange itself.

The small size of the pop bottles was no problem to exchange for money. The bigger size Royal Crown soda bottle was worth three cents. It was the RC bottle that was giving me a problem. The deposit was three cents, and people just did not discard them. So when I did find an RC bottle, it was like hitting pay dirt.

I never believed that two cents would become an issue with the store owners. The BCD Market on Temple Street sometimes refused to take the RC bottle, especially if I had more than three. It turned out that the owners of BCD Market did not want to relinquish the deposit money. The owners of the market were from the far east; their names were Larry, Bruce, and Lee.

Larry would take the bottles, but only up to five, and it depended on how much the bottle was worth. Bruce did not care how many bottles I had so long as I spent the money in the store. Lee, however, was a totally different character altogether. There was no way he was going to take any bottles unless I could prove that I purchased the soda in his store. So I hatched a plan: when I bought a pop bottle in BCD Market, I made it a point to get a receipt. I saved the receipts, that way I could outsmart Lee. But he was the type of person who just did not give in; besides that, he was the brawler of the store. At any sign of someone trying to lift something without paying for it, Lee was Johnny on the spot.

I found some Brew 102 beer bottles; they were brown in color and held 32 ounces of beer. The funny thing about Brew 102 brewery was that it was located at the last turnoff leaving downtown LA. I can't tell you how many times I passed this brewery with my mother to see my father in the Western White House. There were two tall barrels about two stories high and about 20 feet wide. Now I was collecting their bottles so that I could survive. Boy! Did I hit pay dirt when I came across an empty 32-ounce beer bottle; the value was 5 cents. With five empty beer bottles, I could have a meal. The only problem was the store owners did not like to take them, and I would have to walk as far as the Pioneer liquor store, and that is eight blocks away.

How was I going to split up these bottles for deposit? I decided to take a few bottles to the BCD market, which was a three-block walk, and come back for the rest of the bottles. I stood at the cash register, waiting for my turn. Bruce took the bottle and gave me the money.

Lee started shouting at some kid in the store. "What are you doing? What you are doing!" Next thing I knew, he was screaming and clenching a meat carving knife in one hand and a butcher knife in the other, screaming at one of the neighborhood kids. "Get the hell out of my store and never come back!" It was like something out of a cartoon, and I didn't even watch TV.

I took my $.13 and got the heck out of there.

As I was walking out of the store, Lee started shouting at me, asking me to check my pockets to see what I had.

Bruce shouted at him. "You know who he is, leave him alone. He is the only kid in the neighborhood that you do not have to worry about. He won't take anything without paying for it."

It never occurred to me that I could take something to eat without paying for it.

I hurried back to where I left the other three Brew 102 beer bottles and decided to walk to Pioneer. It was a nice walk, anyway, down the big stairs to Glendale Boulevard and across the street into Echo Park.

I was walking on the side that the lake was on with my brown shopping bag from the central market from downtown LA with the last three bottles. I was trying not to let the bag and the bottles hit the ground; if they did, it would all be over with.

As I was walking, I wished that I was a foot or two taller; that way, the bag would not hit the ground, and the bottles would not break. I could not help but think what a joke God had played on me. Was I going to be as tall as my mother?

I had made my way to the Lilly pads that Aimee Semple Mc Pherson brought back from one of her worldly adventures. It is said that Aimee brought back some seeds and tossed them into both sides of the lake. It always looked to me as if she placed the best seeds closer to her Temple. That is the side of the lake that the Lilly pads grow best. Aimee had built Angeles Temple, and that was a short walk from the Lilly pads. In all honesty, on a beautiful California day with the blue sky, I could see the Temple and the Lilly pads blending into one. I could visualize way back in the 20s when Miss. Mc Pherson was gathering her flock into the lake to be baptized.

I made it out of the park, and it was back to reality with my brown shopping bag. I hoped I did not chip one of the bottles or break one entirely. I had only four more blocks to walk, which made this endeavor palatable. I just hope that I would be able to cash them in.

Crossing Sunset Boulevard would be challenging. There were too many automobiles and pedestrian traffic, and the bottles were getting too heavy to carry. *Hopefully, I don't run into any of my smart-aleck friends and hear about my adventures at school.*

There is no shame in being hungry; there is when you are not doing anything about it.

I finally made it across Sunset Boulevard, home free; Pioneer Liquor was at the end of the block.

I turned in the bottles without a problem. With money in hand I walked across the parking lot to Pioneer Chicken. I Purchased chicken wings and French fries. I walked back to Echo Park. I came across a bench where I sat to enjoy the scenery of the lake, the Lilly pads, Angeles Temple, and lunch.

As I was enjoying my surroundings, I began to toss French fries to the ducks. As these fine specimens of nature were gliding so gracefully on the water. There was this question that was coming to mind. *What would one of these ducks taste like if I was to cook one up?* The only tricky thing about having duck for dinner would be to catch the thing. I have seen these ducks running off and taking flight for a good hundred feet. Besides, the hobos in the park have not been able to pot one of these ducks, how would I?

I decided to scurry on back to the house, not that anyone cared or was waiting for me. I was only tired of getting a walloping every time any of the Gonzales's, Gomez's, or the Rodriguez's felt it was their duty to do so.

I made it back to the two-bedroom house, where one of two things was going to happen. One of the girls was going to ask me, "Where have you been? I am going to tell my mother that you did not come straight home from school." Or it would be Mary's same old song. "If I told you once, I've told you 1000 times. Just who the hell do you think you are?"

By this time, I had learned to stand across the room when Mary started to get vulgar. I have seen many instances where she would grab Charlie, Gilbert, or Danny by the collar and strike them. There was no way on God's green earth that I was going to let her do that to me.

It looked as if this evening was going be another night of dreaming of dinner instead of having dinner. Either way, with any luck, Paul and Mary would not get back there until 9:00 PM or 10:00 PM.

I made it through the next day without getting my backside beaten for trying to become self-sufficient. I knew that I would have to devise another plan to support myself. This scavenging for bottles was not going to last forever, and the store owners were threatening to call Mary. That was getting old, too.

A classmate of mine had a paper route; his name was Richard Noriega. I was learning that if you want to succeed in life, align yourself with the top of your class. Richard was not a Poindexter type of guy, but if I needed help with schoolwork, he was the go-to guy. He lived 4 blocks from me, and that was far enough so that I was not being watched by the Gonzales's and especially them good-for-nothing Rodriguez's.

Richard and I were in the after-school choir together. His singing voice was higher quality than mine, so there was no reason why I could not tag along with him on his paper route. How do I casually work my way into Richard's paper route? The next after-school choir meet was in two days; I'd talk to him there.

Mrs. Cobb, the music teacher, took a liking to me. She had the kids in the chorus learn to read musical notes. Mrs. Cobb evaluated the entire choir. We were separated into groups by our vocal talent and our ability to read music. Richard had the voice, he was designated as the male lead singer in the choir. I had a knack for understanding the music notes. Mrs. Cobb said that was my niche in life.

"Mrs. Cobb, my mother had a piano in our home, and she was teaching me to play the piano and read music."

"Ruben, you are a fortunate child to have a mother who understands music."

There was always someone to rain on my parade. This time it was Richard. He said, "Ruben, I've been to your house, and there is no piano."

"Mrs. Cobb, there was a piano in our home."

"Oh! So you have a babysitter, and you attend school here."

"Yes! Mary is my babysitter, and at one time, I lived in a home that had a piano in it."

After choir practice, I walked with Richard to his house. There were two bundles of newspapers for him to deliver. It was the evening Herald-Examiner News Paper.

"Richard, who delivers the morning paper?"

"I do not know."

Richard took the two bundles of newspapers and instructed me on how to put the paper in order. "Place the advertising in the center of the newspaper." He would place the paper in a cloth bag with a pouch in the front and back. This way, the weight of the newspapers was evenly distributed as Richard delivered them.

As we were walking, Richard would toss the paper onto the front porches of the houses. If the newspaper did not land where he wanted it to, he would retrieve it and place it in its correct area. His route went as far as the Frosty Freeze soda shop. As we were delivering the paper, I was scrounging around for bottles.

"Ruben, what are you doing?"

"I'm taking the bottles so that I can turn them in for the deposit."

"Deposit!"

"Yes, Richard, the deposit. I want an action figure, a G.I. Joe, so I save money to buy it."

"Are you aware of just how many bottles you would have to collect to buy a G.I Joe action figure?"

"Yes, I did the math."

"This newspaper route pays me $25.50 a month plus tips."

"I could make that in a week if I find the right bottles. Anyway, it's my own money, and I can do with it what I want."

"Ruben, I am saving up my money so that I could buy me a car when I get to high school."

"Richard, I'm worried about the here and now, and you're planning out for high school?"

On the way back, we were walking down Sunset Boulevard and up Bonnie Brae Street, praying as we walked along the way. After we prayed, Richard sang as he was tossing the newspapers to the homes. I happened to notice that there were newspaper stands that you put a dime in and take a paper. That gives me an idea; I did not mention it to Richard. We kept on walking, Richard went on singing a Beatles song, Yesterday. He was quite good, and he knew all the lyrics to the song.

As we came to some of the homes of his customers, he sings loud enough so that his customer could hear Richard come.

"Richard, you sing as you place the paper at the doorstep, why?"

"There is a strategy for delivering newspapers; sometimes, the owners are home and hear me singing and ask me to stay until I finish the song. Sometimes I get a tip right at the end of the song or an even bigger tip at the end of the month, either way, I make out. So it is all in a day's work."

We had passed by Tom and Timmy's house. Richard lived right around the corner from the two friends of mine. Richard made a right turn on Kent Street and made a left at the corner. I took the long way back to my house. I was walking along the street that was closed off to vehicle traffic.

I could see the tall buildings in downtown Los Angeles as I walked the closed-off street. It was not easy for me to hide my activities with so many eyes around. Not that anyone cared; it was just that Mary made sure that I did not make friends with anyone. If I did make friends, Mary made sure that one of her children would destroy my friendships. It was bad enough to hear the people in the neighborhood say, "What are you doing with those damn Gonzales's? Do your parents know that you are socializing with these people?" or "You and those damn kids do not fit together."

I arrived at Mary's house before I knew it. I still had not gotten over the reality that no one was there to greet me when I arrived. I walked to the kitchen and opened up the refrigerator, and like usual, I could see the four corners of emptiness; this was a good day because the light came on. That meant that we would have electricity and hot water. Walking in the house and opening the refrigerator door you'd think was disappointing. Still, it was more a ritual than a disappointment.

One by one, the rest of the Gonzales family would come rolling in the house, taking their turn opening the refrigerator door. I don't recall if they ever put their hand in the refrigerator to move anything around. It was just a ritual that everyone went through.

Once in a while, Mary's oldest son Charlie would take the mustard and mayonnaise out and have a mustard and mayonnaise sandwich. He was the lucky one. I tried a mustard and mayonnaise sandwich and puked my guts out. The problem was I did not like the taste of mayonnaise; it was just too slimy for me. And that was if there was bread.

Gone were the days that my mother would take a slice of bread with sprinkled sugar on it and wrap it in a napkin and place it in my pocket to have something to eat while I was outside playing.

Whether or not this would be an evening where Mary would arrive and prepare dinner was anyone's guess. Would it be enough for 3 adults and 5 children? Would this be a night where I dreamt of having dinner, or would I actually partake in the meal? To ease my hunger pangs, I decided to do my homework; wouldn't you know it, I had three sheets of paper, and I started writing an essay.

I first had to read one chapter on General Custer and write an essay on what I had read. I finished up reading and started writing the essay. I really do not recall what the piece was about, but the fury I was going to cause the next day was not going to be easy. I made the mistake of bringing the knowledge of Gen. Custer that I had heard discussed in the Kennedy household. It was my understanding that Custer, although a great general, killed women and children needlessly. That is what I remembered learning at home so, why not tell the truth about the man? I finished up writing the essay; it has to be about nine o'clock, and Mary has not arrived to make dinner.

Vivian is vindictive and calculating. She became agitated and tore up my homework. This tearing up my homework was becoming a rite of passage in the Gonzales household.

I was down to my last sheet of paper. I decided to take a brown paper bag and cut it using it to write on. I used the same dimension that any essay would be written on. I even drew the straight lines across the brown paper bag.

Vivian was not going to stop me from turning in my homework on time. The only thing I did not know was how this was going to be perceived in class.

I was so exhausted from the labor of the day, and it was late, so I crawled into bed. The next morning, I rolled out of bed, and the next thing I knew, I was on my way to school with my history book and essay in hand.

Arriving at Rosemont Elementary School, I saw there were kids from all over the world. It reminded me of the United Nations. I had friends from across the globe. There was Walter from Germany, Joe from the Philippines, David from Korea, Susan from Japan, and José from Mexico. Of course, there were the kids that were born here in the good old USA. I always tried to align myself with kids from all walks of life. Kids that I could grow with.

Grandpa Hughes said, "Having the right attitude brings people together." He always said, "If you do not have anything interesting to bring to the table, I do not have time for you."

When the teacher called me up to her desk, she asked me, "What's the meaning of this?"

"What is the meaning of what, Mrs. Phermint? That is my homework, the assignment for last night."

"I know that. What did you use for paper? A brown paper bag?"

"Yes, that is absolutely right. I used a brown paper bag."

"Ruben, in what book did you read that Gen. Custer massacred women and children?"

"Mrs. Phermint, you are confusing me. Don't you remember what your parents taught you? I remember what my parents taught me. If you like, I can go to the library after school and bring you proof that Gen. Custer killed women and children."

The next thing I heard was Rusty's voice. "I told you Ruben is a communist sympathizer! I told you!" As Rusty was shouting, Mrs. Phermint was speaking with me.

"Yes, Ruben, but you do not learn about things like this until you're in a higher grade level. By the way, Ruben, you cannot be in such dire circumstances that you cannot afford notebook paper. Take this note and essay to Mrs. Barnum, the principal. I cannot have you turning in homework that will disrupt the class."

The only thing I had going for me was that it was the end of the school day, and I would be out of here in 30 minutes.

I took my lovely time getting to the principal's office. I did not even bother to read the folded note that Mrs. Phermint wrote. I wanted it to be a surprise when Mrs. Barnum read it. That way, when she asks me, "What do you have to say for yourself now?" I'll say, "What do you mean?"

As I walked into the office, I noticed that Mrs. Barnum's office door was closed. Usually, the closed door was a sign that she did not want to be bothered by the school business. But truth be told, I believe she was just tired of dealing with the Gonzales bunch, as she called us.

I was coming through the door; my favorite person was there, Mrs. Richards. She smiled at me and asked me, "Is there ever going to be a week when you're not in this office for something you did or did not do?"

"Mrs. Richards, this time, I have no idea why I am here." I handed her the note that was still folded.

Mrs. Richards said jokingly, "Should I be expecting Vivian and Mary? Your imposter sisters as you call them."

"Not this time Mrs. Richards. I'm on my own this time."

"Ruben, take a seat."

I took three steps backward and sat down. Mrs. Richards knocked on the door of Mrs. Barnum's office. I could hear Mrs. Barnum say, "What is it this time? Not him again."

Mrs. Barnum kept me waiting for 15 minutes; it was 2:45 PM when I was called into her cave, as I like to call her office. Mrs. Barnum did not even offer me a chair. The first thing out of her mouth was, "What are you doing here now?"

"Mrs. Barnum, you have the note in your hand, and I am sure you can read. What does it say?"

"You don't have to get snippy with me, Ruben."

"So why do you ask such a ridiculous question? If you are holding the note in your hand!" What was this purple-haired witch going to say next?

"Ruben, you can't be that poor that you cannot afford paper. So what is the meaning of you turning your homework in on a brown paper bag?"

"Mrs. Barnum, every time I try to do my homework, one of Mary's kids comes along and disrupts me."

"Ruben, those kids are your brother and sisters."

"Mrs. Barnum! You call them what you want, and I'll call them what I want! Right now, it's my convenience to call them Mary's kids. You are not going to torture me in any way, so why not tell you the truth?"

"Ruben, just how many of you damn Gonzales's are there left that will be attending this school?"

"Only Sally and she is a demon in sheep's clothing."

"Ruben, how would you like me to call your mother and tell her that you are disrupting the classroom?"

"Mrs. Barnum, do what you please, but before you do that, know that her family does not do anything to me without Mary's approval."

"Ruben, return to your classroom. The school will be out in 10 minutes." I walked back to class, stopping off at the boy's room to kill some time.

It was the same routine: form two lines, the girls on one side, the boys on the other. The teacher was walking us out of the building on the street. This time, I was not going straight to the house.

I walked from school to Sunset Boulevard to the newspaper stand to purchase a newspaper. I had $.10. I dropped it into the metal box that held the newspapers. I took out four papers and walked to the corner of Echo Park and Bellevue to sell them.

I had decided this would be the right spot to try and sell the newspapers. It was a three-way stop before getting on the Hollywood freeway or heading down one block to Glendale Boulevard.

I chose the ideal spot, selling out of newspapers within 20 minutes to the passing motorists as they were going by. My initial .10 cent investment netted me a 175 percent profit for the papers. I walked back to the newspaper stand to buy more newspapers. I took the scenic side of Echo Park Lake, the side that had grassy hills and a boathouse to admire, on my way back to Sunset Blvd.

It took me all of 10 minutes to arrive back at the newspaper station. I deposited .80 cents in the slot and took out five newspapers. I walked back to the same spot and sold the papers that I had purchased. I had made a total of $1.40 in tips for less than an hour's work. It was walking back and forth that got me. I took the money and rolled it up in my pants pocket; that way, I would not lose it. Thank God it was only a three-block walk to the house.

Walking on Bellevue Avenue brought back memories of the last time I saw my Grandmother Rose, Jacqueline, and Aristotle. Across the street, over by the big swings. It was where Mary took me to meet with them. What a memory! I walked across Glendale Boulevard up the wooden stairs and back to the house.

What chaos was awaiting me there, God only knows. I walked into the house, and it all started. "Oh, you are going to get it. Mrs. Barnum called. You are in trouble. You are to going to get it good."

"What's it to you if I get it good or not, Sally?"

"Listen, Freckle. You're going to get your ass beat good."

"Sally, do you have to shout to get your point across? Someday it will be your turn, but I will not be dancing around with joy and glee like you; that is what makes us different."

"There you go with all your high and mighty talk."

"Sally, it is not high and mighty; we just come from diverse backgrounds. You believe Mary is your mother, I don't. Or should I say you want me to think she is something to me."

"Ruben, who is going to believe that you are the son of President Kennedy and Marilyn Monroe? Who? Ruben, I am never going to help you get back to where you came from, you understand?"

"Sally, there is no doubt in my mind that you mean what you just said, but you are not the first one to tell me that, and you will not be the last."

There was nothing left to do but weather the storm that Sally had mentioned.

When Mary arrived home, she questioned me about what took place in Mrs. Barnum's office. It was hard for me to play nice. The alternative would not play out well, either. If I had to make Mary believe this charade that she is my mother, so be it. It is what you call surviving, and it beats receiving some retribution in the future.

With Mary, there was always one of her kids ready and willing to brutalize me. If not with a fist, it would be with words. With a beating, the pain will eventually subside, but words stay with you forever. The less I remember about these brutal beatings, the better off I'll be.

The next morning, Mary and I were off to see Mrs. Barnum; it had to be around 8:30 AM when we arrived at the office. For some reason, unbeknownst to me, Mary always had a condescending attitude towards authority figures, and this time would be no different. We entered Mrs. Barnum's office, and the first thing out of Mary's mouth was, "What is it that Ruben has done? That you could have taken care of yourself without bringing me down here. I have a business to run!"

"Mrs. Gonzales, have a seat. I'll explain the situation as clear as possible. Ruben turned in his homework assignment on a brown paper bag. In his essay assignment, he called one of America's heroes, General Custer, a murderer of women and children. I went over his textbook last night, and there is nothing mentioned in his history about this massacre in the assigned book."

Mary, being one to manipulate the situation in her favor, started with how impoverished she was and how caring for ten kids was hard work. I could see that Mrs. Barnum was taken in by Mary's manipulation. It was no longer about me and why I had to use a brown paper bag to do my homework, but how hard it was for a woman with ten kids to raise. It did not make a difference that only six out of ten were Mary's kids.

"Mrs. Gonzales, the fact is Ruben went outside of the scope of the history book."

"Mrs. Barnum, Ruben has a mind of his own. I once watched him take a four by four and pound a nail through the other side. He did not stop beating the nail even to take a lunch break, so when he wants to know something, he'll find the answer."

At the end of the conversation, Mary had Mrs. Barnum in her corner, and there was no way I was ever going to turn Mrs. Barnum around to my side. Mrs. Barnum wrote out a note, handed it to me, and instructed me to go to class.

I arrived in class about 20 minutes late. I handed Mrs. Phermint the note that Mrs. Barnum had given me and sat in my assigned seat.

The moment I sat down, Leroy whispered, "What happened in the office?"

"Nothing happened in the office of any importance. I'll tell you on the playground at recess."

Recess was at 10:00 AM, and 10:00 AM came quickly. No sooner were my classmates and me on the playground when Leroy came running up to me and asked what happened in the office.

"Ruben, I saw you sitting in Mrs. Barnum's office. Who was the heavyset woman sitting next to you? Was that your mother?"

"No, Leroy, that was not my mother; how many times do I have to tell you my mother is deceased."

Just then, I could see Catherine Brown running towards me, so I ended the conversation. She asked me the same question, "Who was the heavyset woman sitting next to you in Mrs. Barnum's office?"

Before I could answer, Leroy answered for me, "Ruben wants us to believe that it was his babysitter."

"Leroy, do we look similar to you? That woman is not related to me."

"Yes, but I heard Mrs. Barnum call her Mrs. Gonzales."

"A lot of people have the same last name, Leroy, that is not family."

"I'm telling you he is a honky and not a Mexican."

"Look, you two. I have had just about enough of this 'what am I' stuff. Leave it alone. Let's go to the cafeteria. Catherine, I made some extra money yesterday."

We stayed too long on the playground, discussing my nationality. By the time we made it to the cafeteria, there was not a snack to be had. We made our way back up to the playground. As in all schools across America, the boys were on their side of the playing field. The girls on their side of the playing field.

The only time the boys and girls were able to intermingle was in the school cafeteria. It was hard for me to understand this separation of the sexes. The school that my parents sent me did not have this separation of boys and girls. It made for a better building of a community.

I finished out the school day and walked down to Sunset Boulevard to the newspapers stand. I noticed that there were more newspapers in the box. I dropped $.10 in the slot and pulled out five papers, then I turned and walked down Echo Park Ave to Bellevue Ave, stopping there to sell the newspapers.

I was getting surprisingly good at my new enterprise; I sold out of my newspapers in no time. Not understanding the supply and demand side of my new enterprise, I decided it was better not to sell too many of the papers. Fifteen newspapers would be my set goal to sell per day, and that would be enough so as not to attract attention. I did not want Mary to find out what I was doing; I knew if she did, she would find a way to put an end to my business.

All of this is just too much to deal with at one time. I did not want the memories of my Grandmother Rose, Jacqueline, and Aristotle Onassis coming back to haunt me. I decided to walk in a different direction to Mary's. I headed down the path leading to the lake and made the sharp right along the lake. There was a little hill with green shrubbery and tall trees, and behind the trees were beautiful trimmed green bushes that blocked my vision to the other side of the park.

As I walked along this magnificent façade that Mother Nature has supplied, my memories of so long ago had transformed into my sanctuary. Walking this oasis, I felt as if someday I would make it back home. Walking through to the other end of this place, my tranquility was always short-lived, but it was still a place of hope for me. It was that left turn that I had to make that brought me back to reality. I stopped and turned in the middle of the pathway to take one last look at the splendor of the park. I walked out of the park following the same walkway back to the house, trying to hold on to the peace that being alone gives me.

Topping the hill on Burlington and Bellevue, there were police cars parked on both sides of the street. For some reason, Gomez and Gonzales did not know how to get along with their neighbors. It seemed that Mary's oldest sons, Richard and Robert, were some kind of gang members, and their reputation followed us to 510 N. Burlington Street. It was becoming routine that at least 2 to 3 times a week, the police were investigating something that the Gonzales kids have done. If they were not throwing rocks at cars, they were stealing from the neighbors or harassing them. I was always the one that the police held responsible for what was going on in the neighborhood. It was as if the police could sense that I was older than the rest of the Gonzales but did not want to accept it.

I tried to stay at the top of the hill, but Maryann called me, and I was drawn into their conflict. It was difficult for me to understand why the Gonzales and Gomez family did not fear or respect the police. It would seem that Savaniy (Chita's sister), Yolanda, Vivian, Maryann, and Sally were fighting with Millie, the neighbor from around the corner, and she called the police. I told the police that I had nothing to do with their argument; I was just an innocent bystander. The police officer said, "You stood back and watched this argument escalate?"

"No officer. I was not even here, so I do not know what went on." The police officer asked me my name, and without hesitation, I said, "John F. Kennedy Junior."

"If you are John F. Kennedy Junior, what are you doing here?"

By this time, the police let Savaniy go up the hill to her mother's house.

The rest of us kids went to the house. A policeman opened the door of the refrigerator, blurting out, "With all of your kids in this house, there is no milk!"

"Sarge, this kid says that he is the son of President Kennedy and Marilyn Monroe."

The next thing I knew, I was in the back of a police car headed to 1552 W. Pico Street. We arrived at Gonzales & Sons radio and television repair shop.

I could see Mary through the glass window of the police car until it came to a complete stop in front of the shop. If there was one thing in the Gonzales household that Mary made a definite point to pay was the telephone bill.

When the police officers and I walked into the shop, the police officer said to Mary, "Is this your son?"

Mary turned the tables on the officer. "What has he has done now? He is always in some kind of trouble!"

"Mrs. Gonzales, he has not done anything wrong; however, he said that he was kidnapped and that Pres. Kennedy and Marilyn Monroe are his parents."

"Sir, you have been to my home at 510 N. Burlington Ave. You have seen how small the house is. Who would not want to live someplace else?"

"Yes, but I noticed that your daughters do not look as malnourished as the boy does."

"Sir, that is because he does not like to eat what I prepare for dinner. I have ten other mouths to feed, not just him."

"Mrs. Gonzales, I opened the refrigerator, and there was not even milk inside."

"Sir, I do not have the time to keep the pantry full, much less the fridge with ten kids to feed."

"Mrs. Gonzales, you may be correct, but he looks different and speaks differently from the rest of the children."

"Officer, he looks like my father, who was French. That is where his red hair and light skin comes from.

"As far as Ruben speaking differently, he just pays more attention to his school courses. Most of the older neighborhood called him Little Kennedy because they say he looks like President Kennedy."

About that time, the phone rang. Mary answered the phone and said, "Hello, Fazio."

I knew who she was talking to, but what I did not understand was why she called him Fazio. It was a short conversation, just to say, "I do not have the time to speak with you, so call back later." Mary hung up the phone and continued her interview with the police.

"Officer, as I was explaining, some of my friends and family members call him Little Kennedy because they think he looks like the late president."

The only thing I could do was tell the officer that Mary was not telling the truth, but for some reason, people believe what she says.

So the two officers left me with Mary.

Just as the police were driving away, Paul and Danny were coming back from a service call. When Paul entered the shop, he said to Mary, "What is he doing here!"

"Them damn kids got into some kind of trouble with one of the neighbors, and she called the police."

"Ruben, what neighbor called the police?"

"It was Millie, Bobby Faulkner's mother."

"What happened that she called the police?"

"I don't know. I was playing in the park. I was not there this time."

Neither Mary nor Paul looked too happy; they looked more nervous and scared, I would say. They started to speak Spanish to each other; the only time they did that was to make sure I did not understand what was being said. Not that I knew what Paul was saying when he spoke English. Most of the time, his words got lost in its meaning.

Friday was one of the busiest days of the week at the shop, and I had to be here. I had to stay until 9:00 PM, that is the regular closing hour.

Mary had given Danny some money to make it to the house on his own. He had left two hours before us. As Danny was walking out, Tom came in.

"Mary, what was going on! Why did the police bring Jack down here?"

"Tom, you know that you are not supposed to refer to him as Jack! I called you Fazio to let you know that the police were here and to confuse people as to whom I'm speaking to. Never Jack or Little Kennedy, only Ruben. It is about him, Fazio. Ruben, got that? How did you find out so quickly that he was here?"

"John F. Rudley called me. He was working in his garden. He saw Jack in the back seat of the police car as it was going by. Mary, this can't keep happening. Why is it always him? The one who bores the brunt of everyone else's deeds?"

"Tom, it is time to close up; we'll discuss this later."

Paul locked the front door; Mary and I got into the blue panel truck that was parked in the back lot. We went to one of Mary's favorite restaurants, Lee Me Lou's. It was an old Chinese restaurant that had been around since the '20s. Mary seemed to know the restaurant owner exceptionally well. I guess she started coming here way back in the Old Days. It looked as if we took an actual step back in time.

I have even heard rumors that there was a gambling hall in the basement at one time. There was an ornate Chinese themed bar to the right of the restaurant. The bar looked like a replica out of a movie. It even had the beads hanging in the doorway, and it was too dark to see inside.

Mary ordered from the à la carte side of the menu as if Paul was one of her patriots. The camaraderie between Lee and Sue, the owners, gave me a feeling that they knew each other's dirty little secrets, the kind of secrets that would land them in jail to this day.

We were eating Chinese, but what were the other kids going to have for dinner? I could not help but think this is what they do when we are at home fighting for our next meal.

Mary was eating as much as she could, and Paul had to undo his pants to fit even more into his belly. I, on the other hand, took only enough to sustain myself. At the end of dinner, I asked Mary if she was going to order takeout for the other kids. That seemed to have upset both Mary and Paul. They did, however, pack up what they did not finish and took it with them.

This would not be the last time I asked myself this question. Just what was I doing here with these people? Looking back on all of this, I often wonder if my mother, Marilyn Monroe, had ever been in this restaurant like so many other movie stars whose autographed pictures lined the walls, signed 'Thank you, Mr. Lee' or 'good luck.' I got up the nerve to ask Mr. Lee's son David if Marilyn Monroe had visited his establishment, but Mary gave him a look that could kill, and he never said yes or no.

On our way back to the house, Mary was agitated. When she was upset, she could be very vulgar. She rarely used profanity, her anger came through in her voice.

I knew that there was going to be retribution for what the kids had done earlier in the day. Mary started yelling the moment she entered the house. There they were, Yolanda, Vivian, Maryann, and Sally Cynthia Celeste, getting an ear full.

Mary screamed at the top of her lungs, "Do you know what would have happened today? We could have all went to jail, all of you!

"All of you! When are you going to understand that we would all go to jail!" This was just one of those 'if I go you go' moments. I have become accustomed to hearing these people say to one another, If I go, you go.

"We are all going to have a serious talk about just what you people want to do. I have told you time and time again, I do not want the police here in this house!" I knew the inevitable was coming. When

Mary said, "You sons of bitches are going to get us in a lot of trouble if you keep pulling the same stunts that you pulled today."

All I could see was this 350-pound woman throwing her voice and weight around. The only one who spoke was Sally, and all she said was, "Savaniy did it. Savaniy, she did it! Savaniy did it!" Mary told everyone to go to bed now!

The next morning Tom came over; he usually brought groceries with him for Mary to prepare breakfast, or sometimes he made pancakes.

This morning, Mary, Paul, and Tom were discussing the events of the previous day and what Tom was going to do about it.

Paul said to Tom, "I am going to treat these kids the way you treat your kids, Tom."

"Paul, if that is the case, that would be damn good, but look at the way you have them living."

Paul was so enraged, he got up from his breakfast and walked out the door, slamming it as it closed. He slammed the door so hard that the window in it broke; the glass was just replaced.

I laughed, knowing it would be another six months before it was fixed. So much for a Saturday morning. I did not know what the conclusion was, but I knew that it had to do with what they were going to do with me.

For the next three weeks, Paul was on one of his alcoholic odysseys; it was his favorite thing to do when he wanted to get away for a while. The remainder of the weekend was uneventful.

Monday started out the same as the end of the weekend: boring. But the moment I dropped the .50 cents for 5 newspapers, things went downhill. This man in a pickup truck with three kids inside followed me to Echo Park Avenue and Bellevue Avenue. He parked just down the corner. He watched me sell the newspapers. When I was done, the three kids with him followed me back to the papers stand. I dropped $.40 in the slot and walked away.

I was not paying attention to my surroundings when the man and two boys jumped out of the truck, stopping me in my tracks. He asked me, "Just what the hell do you think you are doing!"

"Excuse me, sir, what are you talking about? You do not have the right to speak to me that way."

"You have to work for me in this neighborhood if you want to sell newspapers."

"Just who are you?"

"This corner is in my designated area, and you cannot just pick up newspapers and sell them. I should have my boys here teach you a little lesson and take your earnings."

I could see that his boys were nervous. One of them began to speak up and said, "Joe, he is a scrapper. I have seen him fight in school, and he can hold his own. It would not be in our interest to fight with him or try to take his money because he will get us back. If not here, it will definitely happen in school."

I turned to the man and said, "Sir, I take it your name is Joe, he is right."

"I will get my money either here or in school, so you make the decision."

"Whatever newspapers I take out of the box, I replace it equal pay, so what is your problem?"

"The problem is you buy the paper from me for ten cents and resell them for $.10."

"I still do not see a problem here."

"I need you to be on my payroll; it looks good for me."

"That is your problem, not mine.

"The first thing you are going to have me do is get a signed permission slip to work for you, and that is just not going to happen."

"Young man, who do you know that works for me?"

"Joe, I don't know anyone that works for you, or at least I think I don't."

"I'm entitled to a percentage of what newspaper boys receive. You have to know someone who sells or delivers the paper. Look, kid, if I catch you back here tomorrow selling newspapers, there is going to be hell to pay."

It was just too lucrative to walk away from this enterprise that was funding my recess and lunch. How could I just walk away? The next day, I was in the same spot when Joe came out of nowhere with three of his cronies. The only thing I heard was, "Get him, boys!" Newspapers went flying everywhere. I looked around to see what I could grab to defend myself with, but there was nothing. So I grabbed a hand full of hair and swung with the other and hit one of them upside his head.

I was swinging and punching for dear life; it was the same two guys from yesterday. They were putting on a brave front now. The third boy was the biggest out of the three. This was the first time I saw him. He was the one that I chose to unleash my rage on. I was not going down without getting my share of licks in. I have been in enough fights with my Kennedy cousins and the Gonzales's to know you do not lie down. I came out swinging or run like hell if you don't want your backside beat. So I kicked and punched my way out of there.

I did what my dad taught me. I stood up straight, planted my left and right foot firmly on the ground, and stood my ground. I went after the big guy; first, he made that one crucial mistake. When I slugged him, hitting him in the stomach, he bent over, grabbing his stomach with his arms crisscrossed. That is when I kneed him in the face. "Hey, boys! If you come after me, I'll see you at school."

I ran as fast as my legs could carry me. I was in the wind.

As I was running, I was plotting out what direction I was going and dodging traffic to get across the street to the wood stairs. I hauled ass up the stairs. I could feel the wind on my face and streaking through my hair. I finally came to a stop at Bellevue Avenue, Belmont. I leaned against the white wooden railing to catch my breath.

I had to laugh. It took me all of 3 minutes to make it one block, up the wooden stairs, and through the pathway and out of sight. I turned to see if Joe and his boys were still there. All I saw was the lake on one side of the street and the playground on the other side. Joe and his boys were nowhere in sight.

I finally caught my breath and ran all the way to the house right into the bathroom. The first thing I did was look in the mirror, and yes, the face was saved one more time.

The next day, I was gunning for Eddie. I watched him go into the boy's bathroom alone at school. This was my chance. I casually walked into the bathroom, waited for him to finish up, and said, "Wash your hands. We are gonna talk.

"Eddie, don't you start crying! I'll whip your ass right here right now." I grabbed him by the shirt collar and laid my right fist into his left cheek. "Eddie, if you tell Joe where I live or come after me again, I'm going to teach you how to be a man. Understand me?"

"Yes, Ruben! Yes, Ruben!"

"You're not so badass now, are you, Eddie?"

Ramiro walked in and said, "Ruben, do you need some help?"

"No, I have it taken care of."

"Ay, Ruben, looks like you made him piss twice, once in the toilet, and once in his pants!"

Do you threaten me, Eddie, again? "I mean it, Eddie, you tell anyone about this, I'll beat your ass." I let him go, and that was the end of that. That was the end of my newspaper days, but I still had bottles to sell.

I continued going to school and collecting bottles. My love of music was starting to take hold of me. I was learning to read and write music. The best part of all of this was I was learning to conduct the orchestra. Mrs. Cobb, the school music teacher, said that I was born to love music, or I had been schooled in the art of music. It was the hours of music time that my mother and I spent together. But either way, Mrs. Cobb was going to make a music conductor out of me, and I was thrilled with the idea. Mrs. Cobb had me read the music first and wave the baton to the notes on the music sheet, trying to look at the orchestra at the same time.

"Do not lose sight of either one; it's your eye following the music notes; the baton will lead the orchestra. It is the beat of the music that you are setting, the tempo. Think of yourself as a general in the army and the orchestra as your troops. They will follow your lead. At the end of all this preparation, Ruben, you are going to lead the Christmas show. Ruben, try not to miss any more school days."

"Mrs. Cobb, I do not miss school because I want to. It is because they will not let me come to school. I love school. I know that I need to learn the three Rs, but Mary sometimes keeps me in the house."

"Ruben, what do you mean Mary will not let you come to school?"

"She does not want me to learn or receive an education. Her family has continually badgered me, but it is okay for everyone else to go to school." After having that conversation with Mrs. Cobb, I was no longer being bothered or ridiculed at the house. It was anyone's guess why.

It had to be October of 66 that the Gonzales's had a big Sunday barbecue; it was bigger than usual. This time, Mary's whole family was there. Richard, with his wife Minta, Robert, with his wife Lillian and their kids Little Lillian, Rory, Bobby Junior; Charlie, with his wife Chita and their son Raymond all gathered together for a Sunday barbecue, along with Tom and Linda. To my surprise, even John F. Rudley showed up to the barbecue, the first and only time I have seen him in Mary's house.

Mary had spent the morning preparing potato salad and had Danny cut up the chicken. Paul started the barbecuing at about 2:00 PM, and everyone arrived by three o'clock. I could feel there was a little tension in the air by listening to some of the conversations the adults were having.

There was a picnic table in the backyard next to the barbecue full of the usual things that Mary served. There were coolers filled with soda, bags of potato chips on the picnic table, and more food inside the house. All of the adults were sitting around the picnic table, discussing what they were going to do with me. I just happened to be at the kitchen window looking out to see what was going on. It seems that they were concerned about what I had said to the police that I was President Kennedy's and Marilyn Monroe's son. Danny, Yolanda, Vivian, Maryann, and Sally kept getting in trouble with the police. Once I heard that I knew it was time for me to ease away from the window without being heard.

By the end of the barbecue, Mary had us kids clean up the kitchen. Everything was clean and put away neatly, or should I say as neatly as could be. I finished up and went outside to play. I did not like to be around or socialize with anyone in the household, I just could never bring myself to do it. I always felt like the outsider that I was in a place that I had no right to be in.

I didn't get up to the corner when Raymond came running after me telling me that my mother wanted me. I knew that Raymond didn't know any better. I couldn't yell at him and say, "You know damn well, Mary is not my mother." Raymond was just a child, so it was better to just leave it alone.

I walked back down to the house and into the kitchen. Sitting around the table was Paul, Mary, Richard, and Linda. Tom was still outside in the backyard, talking to John. Mary hollered, "Fazio, come inside; he's here."

While we were waiting for Fazio to enter the kitchen, I asked Linda if she would attend my orchestra recital. Linda reminded me of a Texas Rose. She said, "Yes, I would love to be there, and thank you for the personal invitation."

"Linda, it is my pleasure."

'Fazio' came in and sat next to his wife, Linda. I was looking into Linda's eyes when she asked me if I would like to live with her and Tom.

"Ruben, if you need some time to think about it, feel free to say so. I don't want to make you feel as if you have to make a decision now."

"Linda, that sounds like a good idea, and I don't need time to think about it. I just have one demand, and this is to remain a Roman Catholic. This is the only thing that these people have not taken away from me."

"Son, that is not a problem. Tom here is a Roman Catholic. He can take you to church if that's all it will take for you to come to live with Tom and me."

My answer reverberated throughout the house, "Yes!" I could see the unpleasant looks on the faces of Mary, Paul, and the rest of the Gonzales family. Even Raymond didn't like the answer. Richard spoke up for the group as a whole.

"Mother, are you really going to let Little Kennedy go with Linda and Tom? Are you really going to let this happen?"

"Richard, what choice do I have? The damn kids keep getting into trouble. Someday, this perfect crime is not going to be so perfect. We are all going to end up in jail, do you want that? How are we supposed to explain why he is here? Remember, your father has a lot to do with him being here."

Mary looked at me, "Go outside and play."

The dirty looks I was getting as I left that kitchen and passed the living room were frightful; it was as if all of these evil people wanted to physically harm me. I scurried out of the house and ran the rest of the way to the playground. I stayed playing on the swing until the sun started to go down. I was apprehensive about returning back to Mary's house. I knew that if I stayed out any longer, I was only going to make matters worse. It seemed that the Gonzales/Gomez family were not happy with my choice to go with Linda and Tom.

Charlie's wife, Chita, took a tone of voice that was borderline envious or even hateful. She asked me, "Just who do you think you are to choose Linda and Tom over Mary?"

"Chita, what business is it of yours who I have decided to go with?"

She tried to hit me, but I was not going to let her brutalize me the way she did with the rest of the kids. Charlie noticed that I was looking around for something to hit her with. He hollered at Chita, "Leave him alone. You do not know what he is capable of doing to you."

I could hear Mary call someone 'mijo.' I had no clue who she was calling. She kept saying, "Mijo, come here. Mijo, come."

In one loud burst, Mary hollered, "Ruben, come!"

I asked her, "What is it with this 'mijo' stuff? Why are you calling me mijo? I am not your son. You call Richard, Robert, Charlie, Gilbert, and Danny mijo, not me.

"I am not your mijo; you understand me?" Just as I was finishing up, I felt this wisp of wind through my hair. It was Richard trying to hit me. I took off like a deer running through the forest to escape a gunshot. I was leaping over little children as I was making my getaway. I was so gone. I did not stop running until I arrived at

Glendale Boulevard and Bellevue Avenue on the lakeside of Echo Park.

I skedaddled down the little dirt hill and sat on the built-in bench. I rolled myself up into a ball, brought my knees up to my chest, and folded my arms over my knees, resting my chin on my arms and sitting there looking out over the lake.

No one came looking for me, and why should they? I had nowhere to go. It had to be around 9:00 PM when I returned to the house the Ed Sullivan Show was on. I was exhausted from the day's activities; I just went to bed. Being in a place that I did not belong, I learned to sleep with one eye open and one eye closed. It was never a sound sleep, just enough sleep, so that I would not wake up more exhausted than when I went to bed.

It was Monday morning, and the sun was shining through the window on to my face. I was the first up and out of bed.

One of the things that no one knew was that the walls separating the bedroom where I slept and Mary's bedroom are paper-thin. I could hear Mary's conversations with Paul or when she was on the telephone. I knew that there would be a repercussion for my choosing Linda over Mary.

Mary had sent Vivian and Maryann to school while Yolanda, Sally, and I stayed. Yolanda and Sally were still sleeping, and Mary called me into her room. I went into her room to hear what she had to say. She was sitting in her recliner. "I have something to explain to you and show you.

"Ruben, you see this piece of paper? It's a birth certificate. It says a baby boy named Gonzales - date of birth 7/22/1955. You are not going to leave this house until you are twenty-one; do you understand me? If you leave before your 21st birthday, you have no idea what I am going to do to you! I have the backing of your grandmother, uncles, aunts, your stepmother Jackie, and also Onassis, so you are not going anywhere, do you understand that? You are stuck here with me no matter what you do or whom you ask for help, absolutely no one will hear your cry for help. There will be no justice for you; do you understand that? No one will help you!"

I rose up from the corner of the bed where I was sitting and walked out of Mary's bedroom. Mary's scheme did not dash my hopes or dreams. I still had my little sister and brother to hold on to. Perhaps someday they would remember me, and the three of us will be reunited.

The rest of the day was pretty much uneventful; I spent it coming up with a long-term plan. What was I going to do for the next ten years? How was I going to survive all of the hate, destructiveness, evil, and above all, society's indifference towards me? Why am I held responsible for who my parents became? They were my parents before they became icons.

I waited until after 2:30 PM and started looking for bottles; that way, the neighbors or police would not bother with me about not attending school.

I was looking forward to the next day of school. It was the same thing, but this time, I threw myself into the music.

Music took me to another place. It was an escape out of the brutalities of the real world. I was picking up everything that Mrs. Cobb was teaching me. I was trying to find that human compassion that I had lost when my mother passed away, that is what I found in music. COMPASSION!

I had that same feeling when Linda was around; she was a compassionate person. I could feel it resonating with Linda.

It was about three weeks before the Christmas show. Linda came to see me. I asked her if she was still coming to the recital.

"Ruben, I'll be there. Ruben, is there anything that you need for the concert?"

"Linda, I have to wear a white shirt, tie, black pants, and black shoes. Mary said she did not have the money for them. I'm working and saving my earnings to purchase my attire myself."

"Ruben, don't worry!"

Linda turned to Tom, "Let's go to buy what he needs now."

The next thing I knew, the three of us were on our way to Sunset Boulevard to buy what I needed.

Tom came to a stop right in front of Jerry's Department Store, and the three of us got out of the car and walked into the store.

Jerry's Department Store would not have been my choice to purchase a wardrobe. The clothes are too expensive, and I was not into Hang Ten or Ocean Pacific Style. Then again, I am not the one paying for them.

The brief moment I spent trying on clothes took me back to the days with my mother. I could picture Mother side by side with Linda asking each other, "What you think about this?" or "What you think about that?"

When Linda laid the black and reddish tie across the white shirt, I could almost hear my mother saying, "What do you think about this combination of shirt and tie, Sugar?"

I could not help myself; I started to cry.

"Ruben, what's wrong? Why are your eyes beginning to well up and turn red?"

I could not tell Linda that she reminded me of my mother, Marilyn; I did not want to spoil the moment. "Linda, thank you. I am happy, that's all." Linda smiled as if to say I know what you are feeling.

The shirt and tie were an easy find, but the black pants, well, that was another thing entirely. I was too small for the young man's size pants and too big for the boy's size pants. I had to buy pants that had to be altered. Linda suggested that we buy the shoes first before having the pants altered.

Jerry's Department Store did not carry shoes. We crossed the street to the shoe store, I picked out a pair of black Wingtip shoes. Tom added his two cents in. "Linda, you don't think Little Kennedy is too young for Wingtip shoes?"

"No, Tom, he'll feel like the orchestra conductor that he wants to be."

The three of us walked back across Sunset Boulevard back to Jerry's. I had to try the pants on again at this time. I had the black Wingtip shoes on.

The tailor came over and had me stand in a three-way mirror.

"Sir, I do not want cuffs. I want straight-leg pants with a half-inch fold in between my ankle and shoe with a half-moon cut at the bottom of the pants. I want the pants to cover the back of the shoe just above the heel."

"Mrs., where did this kid come from? A boy his age is not supposed to know what he wants when it comes to slacks, but he knows. Why?" I could see the pride gleaming from Linda's face in that instant.

Linda said to the tailor, "He is going to be my new son if everything works out."

Tom paid for the clothes. I would have to come back for the pants next week. I had just one problem: I did not want to take anything with me. I knew that if I took the shirt, tie, and shoes with me, I would not find them when it came time for the concert. I asked the store manager if I could leave all the items until the tailor finished altering the pants. Everything was okay with him so long as I came in with the receipt.

When we left the store, Linda turned to me and said, "Thank you. Now I know what it feels like to have a son. Thank you again, Jack."

"Linda, I felt as if my mother was watching us, and she seemed pleased with what you are doing for me. She would want me to thank you for her if she were here. I thank you for your kindness and generosity; thank you, Linda."

Tom drove me back to Mary's house and dropped me off. Before I got out of Tom's green four-door Ford automobile, I asked Linda one more time if she was still going to attend the Christmas Concert.

"Jack, I would not miss it for the world." I was out of the back of the car. Tom pulled the vehicle away from the house. I waved and said, "I'll see you later," as the car was rounding the corner.

The next two weeks were going to school and learning to conduct the orchestra. I was amazed at just how much work goes into conducting an orchestra.

As the orchestra leader, I was able to distinguish what instrument and what chorus singer had made an error. The conductor places the instruments where he wants each of them. The instrument and singer are set where his ear hears the sound and where it rings the clearest to him.

Of course, Mrs. Cobb made her opinion noted. As the teacher, her view out-ruled mine. Conducting the orchestra was the most peace and tranquility that I had since the death of my parents. On the last day of rehearsals, I felt as if I found my niche in life.

The day of the Christmas concert was here. I had some last-minute pointers and rehearsal after lunch. By 3:00 PM, the bell had rung. It was time to go. In 4 hours, I would have to be back in the school auditorium. There was no time to waste. I arrived at the house in 20 minutes. I walked into the house into a vast silence, the kind you hear when you are alone. I quickly stepped into the bedroom, where I slept and started looking for the receipt for my shirt, tie, pants, and shoes.

I kneeled down on both knees and looked between the bed railing and the box spring of the bed. It was right where I left it, folded nice and neat like I left it. I did not want to waste time, so I walked to the big stairs; it had to be a six-story walk down. In the past, I took my time walking down these stairs, but not today. I was in a hurry.

I had no time to enjoy the spectacular view of the lake, the skyline of Downtown L.A. or Angeles Temple, the beautiful white gothic building with a dome top. I could see the reflection of the Angeles Temple reflecting from the lake, as I was walking down the stairs. It was as if God was displaying all the world's beauty just for me. From the bottom of the stairs to Jerry's Department Store on Sunset Boulevard was approximately 7 blocks away. This was the first time I walked to Santa Ynez Street to cross Glendale Boulevard into the park. I was not leaving anything to chance.

By the time I arrived at Jerry's Department Store, it was 4:00 PM. I tried on the tailored pants, and they fit like a glove. The salesperson put the pants and shirt on a wooden hanger—the tie inside one of the shoes a new pair of socks and underwear. Off I went. I still had to have my hair cut. I decided on Jonny's barber-shop on Temple Street; it was a straight line from Sunset Boulevard to Temple once I made it around the corner to Echo Park Ave.

The closer I got to the Echo Park playground, the more I was beginning to rethink getting my hair cut. I had to go through the tunnel that crossed under the Hollywood freeway. It was dark and smelly in there, and I did not want to get jumped by some street gang. It was still daylight out; I could see to the end of the tunnel onto the baseball field. I picked up the pace and made it through the tunnel in no time.

I crossed Temple Street, and Jonny was sitting in his barber chair, reading the afternoon paper. He did not like cutting my hair; he always complained that I waited too long in between haircuts. It took Jonny all of 30 minutes to cut my hair. Once he was done, I was out of his shop like a shot. I dislike cutting my hair at Jonny's. It was that walk up the steep hill on Temple Street to Belmont Avenue. It wasn't a long walk, but the hill was steep, and my legs felt as if they were going to give out once I topped the hill. I went back to the house with time to rest and take a shower.

It had to be around 6:00 PM when I started to get ready for my performance. Mrs. Cobb wanted all the performers to show up 45 minutes early. I made it on time. Mrs. Cobb said I look like a new ten-dollar gold piece, shiny and impressive. She had the chorus and the orchestra set up, and I rehearsed some of the numbers. Mrs. Cobb gave me one last tip before the show began.

"Ruben, make sure that you turn the pages of the music sheets, that way you keep up with the chorus and the orchestra."

I stood on stage in the auditorium on a wood box right in front of the seated orchestra. Behind the orchestra was the chorus behind the curtain.

I was feeling unstoppable. There I was, standing 10 feet tall. The auditorium was beginning to fill up with parents and some of my classmates. I could hear the sound of leather shoes hitting the wooden floor of the auditorium. I turned around to see if the hall was full. I could see right out the door on to the street, and the sun had gone, giving way to darkness.

There I was, looking out the door in the middle of the auditorium. I felt as if I was frozen, looking out into the darkness. I remembered what my father once said, "There is nothing worse than being in a room full of people and feeling alone." There was not a soul in that room with me from my past. I am alone!

243

Mrs. Kurt, the school custodian, dressed to the nines, came to see me lead the orchestra. She walked over to me, sensing something was wrong. She asked me if I was okay.

"Mrs. Kurt, if someone I know is not here on earth, do they hear the music in Heaven?"

"Son, I do not think they can. I know they can hear the music. Ruben, are your parents here?"

"No, I am looking for Linda and Tom, but I do not see them."

Just then, Mrs. Cobb tapped on the music stand. That was her cue to signal to the performers and audience that the show would start in 3 minutes.

I turned back around, facing the orchestra. The lights were dimmed. I was standing up straight, almost as if I was at attention. I picked up the baton with my right hand. Mrs. Cobb let the audience know that one of her pupils would be leading the orchestra. She struck the music stand one more time, and I began to conduct the show.

The feeling of all that power coming out from the instruments. It was as if the heavens were going to open up. Next, the chorus chimed in, as if Angels themselves were singing. The sounds of the orchestra and chorus were right on cue with my baton. I was not just some kid waving a stick, up and down or sideways and crossways, I was keeping the violins, cellos, trumpets, and saxophones in tune with each other.

This went on song after song, and each time one song ended, and another began, there was applause, that feeling of appreciation for all our hard work. To hear the song Silent Night Holy Night, I knew that if the audience was pleased, so were the Angels in Heaven. By nine o'clock the concert had ended. Mrs. Cobb had introduced me to the parents as I was turning to take my last bow.

I walked out of the auditorium past Mrs. Barnum's office and out onto the school stairs. Looking up, I could see the American flag fluttering in the night breeze as the moonlight shone on it. Causing the flag to light up the night sky in its colors of Red, White, and Blue.

As I was standing at the top of the stairs to the right of the door, I expected to see a chauffeur-driven limousine coming to retrieve me and deliver me safely home. I just stood there looking up Rosemont Avenue. I could hear someone calling out a name. I did not pay attention to what name they were calling; I just knew it was not Jack or John. I milled around the stairs waiting for my limo driver when I heard a car door slam, and someone was taking me by the hand, yelling, "Let's go. Damn it, let's go!" It finally dawned on me that it was Mary calling me. "Ruben, come on. Let's go."

By the time she took my hand, Mrs. Kurt had said to Mrs. Barnum, "You know there may be some truth to what Ruben is saying, that Mary is his babysitter."

As I was walking down the stairs, I saw Tom and Linda drive by. Mary still had me by the hand, pulling me into the blue panel truck. Mary climbed into the panel truck first, grabbing and pulling me around her and pushing me to the back. "Next time I call you, come. Do you hear me!"

"I did not hear you calling me. I was not looking for you. I was looking for Richard. He was in the school choir singing. How could I hear you?"

We made it to the house, and Mary was still upset. It was a surprise to see Tom and Linda waiting for me when we arrived. The moment Tom noticed that Mary was angry, he and Linda said what a good job I did and left. There was one more day of school left, and I did not want to miss it. I went into the house and into my bedroom, hung up my pants and shirt, and went to bed.

The next morning, I was up at my usual time at 6:00 AM. I made myself two eggs for breakfast and finished up my homework. Turning in my homework was one of the conditions that Mrs. Cobb made with all the show's participants. All homework assignments have to be turned in on time.

I left the house on time and walked the seven blocks to school, leaving me enough time not to be late. I arrived at school on time. I was on the ground; this Japanese kid came over to me.

"Hey, you think your hot stuff now?"

"I guess after last night's little performance, I am. Look! Leave me alone. I don't want to know you."

"I don't want to know you either." Like all kids before this one, I told them to get lost. Wouldn't you know it, he did not like the way I said get lost, and fists started flying.

The next thing I knew, Mrs. Lopez had us both by the shirt collar walking us to the principal's office.

"Ruben, you would think after last night's performance, I would expect you to walk away from a fight. You, David, what are you going to tell your parents? I expect this kind of thing out of Ruben, but you?"

I said, "What, Mrs. Lopez? I am not the one who started the fight. David did." Mrs. Lopez stopped and looked at David. "Did you start the fight?"

David answered, "Yes, Mrs. Lopez. I started the fight."

"David, I am going to let you off with a warning. Next time you're going to the principal's office."

I said, "Mrs. Lopez, do I get an apology?"

David looked at me and said, "Ruben, I'm sorry, and I won't do it again."

I wasn't satisfied. "Mrs. Lopez, I don't want an apology from him. I want one from you."

"Ruben, if you did not start the fight this time, you will next time."

"Mrs. Lopez, you are just one of life's lessons on what not to do to children. You and your kind are why I respect a child more than an adult."

David and I walked away, leaving Mrs. Lopez with a stunned look on her face. The rest of the school day was uneventful.

It was not until Vivian, Maryann, and I were walking to the house that things started to heat up.

Katherine and Kenneth were walking past when Kathy asked me, "Ruben, why are you walking with those Mexican girls?"

"Kathy, you know this is no way to start out Christmas vacation. So give it a rest."

Katherine and her brother Kenneth decided to cross Temple Street and walk on the other side of the street. Vivian began bitching as Kathy and Kenneth crossed the street.

"Ruben, this is why I don't like walking with you. We are always getting some kind of static from people for you."

"Look, Vivian, all I am doing is trying to enjoy the next two weeks, and if I have to spend it by myself, that works for me. So go on ahead of me if you like. I am not asking you to walk with me."

"Hey Ruben, does that go for the rest of us?" Maryann asked.

"No, but why is it we cannot make it two blocks without something happening?"

We made it down one more block, crossing Mountain View Ave, then crossing Westlake Ave around the corner to Bonnie Brae Street. The neighborhood retirees were sitting on the front porch. I looked over, and the woman spits out this black tar substance. At the top of my lungs, I shouted out, "Did you see that! Did you see that? I have never in my life seen anything like that before."

I took off running and never looked back; I was sure that she had some kind of sickness, and I did not want it. The only thing I feared for the next three days was I was going to catch what the woman had. I had taken a bath twice a day out of fear of getting sick.

Christmas Eve was finally here, and Tom and Linda came by; they dropped off a big bowl of banana pudding. They did not stay too long. Rodolfo and Emily Sanchez came by and left me a gift for Christmas and told me not to open it until Christmas Day. This was a far cry from the Christmases that I had with my parents, but it had to do.

In this household, there was no such thing as peace on earth. The gift that Sanchez gave me, I had to hide it out of fear that someone would break it just like they have destroyed everything else that belongs to me. I hid the present in the closet behind some trunks that Mary had some of her lifelong belongings in. I knew that it would be safe there, tucked away in the back of the dark closet.

Christmas morning was finally here; it was like any other day in the Gonzales household. The one present I was enthusiastic about was the one the Sanchez's gave me.

The box reminded me of being back with my parents. It was professionally wrapped with green paper with a thick red ribbon going across the four sides of the box with a red bow in the middle of the gift. It was heavy and loaded with loose items inside. I could feel and hear that it was a box inside a box. I carried the box to the front where Mary, Paul, Danny, Yolanda, Vivian, Maryann, and Sally were sitting waiting for me to open my Christmas gift. I sat on the floor to open it. I was careful about opening the gift. I wanted to savor the memory of my parents.

I guess I was taking too long because Danny reached over and ripped the box open. He did not pull the box all the way open; I had to finish the job.

I opened up the box and pulled out this wooden shoeshine box. All the contents of the wooden box spilled onto the floor. There were black and brown shoe polish, black and brown washcloths, and two wooden shoe chain brushes.

Everyone started laughing when they saw what spilled out on the floor.

Paul made an odd comment. "Ruben, now you have a way of supporting yourself."

I had no clue what Paul meant by his comment; I certainly had no objections to making money. I spent Christmas day watching Mary prepare Christmas dinner. Mary cooked a 20-pound turkey, stuffing, and mashed potatoes. She did not allow or ask her daughter Yolanda to help out in the kitchen. Danny did most of the chopping of the vegetables that went into the stuffing.

I was beginning to distinguish what kind of person Mary was. I recalled my mother and fraternal aunts always had to do something for Christmas dinner. That was the law of the land in Grandma Rose's house.

Here was Mary not preparing her daughter for life; the only thing she wanted Yolanda to do was to wash the dishes. I knew that someday I would want to make a Christmas dinner for my own family, so I knew watching Mary and staying out of her way was going to help achieve that goal.

Of course, there was the occasional dinner out with my parents. Still, the best dinners were when my mother cooked for my father and I. The joys of being in the kitchen with my parents were memorable.

Now witnessing what Mary was doing to her own daughter, what did I expect from her? Mary was always crying about how she baked cakes and pies for the holidays up until that one Thanksgiving Day that Charlie had told her he knocked up Chita. That was a lot of hogwash; the only thing I ever saw Mary make from scratch was flour tortillas, and that was when she wanted flour tortillas.

Christmas Day ended like any other day. People coming and going; it was the usual Gonzales family gathering. The day ended well, only because there was no alcohol invited to dinner.

Christmas Day became the day I started a new year for me. It always brought me a year closer to leaving this inferno that my stepmother Jacqueline and Aristotle Onassis had placed me in. I was beginning to understand that this was where my paternal grandmother and aunts and uncles wanted me to be. New Year's Eve was just the end of 1966, and the beginning of 1967 would bring me closer to the Blessed Day that I would leave.

# SECRET MEETING

**1967 STARTED OUT BEING** a problem first thing Monday morning. How was I going to make it to school? I had two options: walk down Bellevue Avenue or take Westlake Ave; Bonnie Brae was undoubtedly out of the question. I was not going to walk past Mrs. Jenkins's house and catch whatever she had. I have never in my life seen another woman besides Mrs. Jenkins spit that color before, and I do not want to see it again.

I had to think this through. Bellevue was a cul-de-sac, and I would have to take a chance of walking down the dirt hill and falling and hurting myself. I would have to hold on to the chain-link fence as I walked down the dirt hill and still risk falling or walk down over the bridge to Westlake. If I walked Westlake, Mrs. Jenkins lived one house behind the other. I definitely could not choose Westlake. I am going to take Bellevue to Rosemont and walk across the bridge. Whatever Mrs. Jenkins had, I definitely did not want.

I made it to school and onto the playground, where my classmates gathered, playing, and chatting. It was the same old routine. Poindexter's on one side and cool kids on the other. I had always moved at ease between the two groups, but this time the class came together as one.

I could not believe it; I was in a circle surrounded by both groups of kids. They were all greeting me at the same time. I was experiencing what my teachers had wanted me to from my classmates. Given the right tools and with my ability, I was a peacemaker. I guess it was the baton that I was holding at the Christmas concert that brought us together on the playground.

Mrs. Phermint, our teacher, came onto the playground and gathered us up for our monthly assembly meeting. Like soldiers, we walked to our assigned area. This time, I was at the front of the line walking to the middle of the playground yard.

I was face to face with Mrs. Barnum.

For the first time, we were in the place of honor. Our classroom was usually in the far back row. The whole school gathered on the first Monday of the month, and this was the first Monday of the year.

The class stood in the place of honor!

I kept asking myself, *What did we do to deserve this place of honor? Is this just another one of Mrs. Barnum's ways of scolding the entire class? If scolding us did not work, what makes her believe she can shame us into behaving?*

The assembly started with the Pledge of Allegiance. I placed my right hand over my heart and began to recite the pledge. I tried staying focused on the flag, but I kept thinking, *What does this wretch Mrs. Barnum have in store for us?* I was so fixated on the flag that I did not realize we had moved on to singing the Star-Spangled Banner. Still fixated on the flag, I could see what the composer of the Star-Spangled Banner was seeing as he was composing the song. He was witnessing his world being destroyed all around him, but the flag was still there. Never have I ever experienced this before.

I was aware that reading a book could take you to exotic and exciting places, but least of all, not a song. Especially the Star-Spangled Banner. It had taken me. Still fixated on the lyrics that I heard as the sound faded away, there the flag was, waving in the wind.

Mrs. Barnum was calling out someone's name to come up to the podium where she was standing. She called out the name, time, and again. I was curious as to why the person whose name she was calling did not go up to the podium and join her.

I looked around the yard to see who would walk up to the podium. Still, no one stepped up to join her. She called out the name one more time, this time, Mrs. Phermint came around from the left side of Maritza and grabbed me by the arm.

"Ruben! Mrs. Barnum is calling you. Join her at the podium."

"Mrs. Phermint, I did not do anything wrong."

"Ruben, I know that. Join Mrs. Barnum at the podium."

As I walked up to the podium, I had to think of a way to get myself out of whatever she was going to accuse me of doing. Here I was, standing next to my nemesis Mrs. Barnum; my back was still facing the crowd.

Looking up at the purple-headed dragon lady, Mrs. Barnum, I turned around facing the crowd.

Mrs. Barnum said, "Ruben, we would like to thank you for the great courage and performance that you showed and gave the parents and faculty of Rosemont Elementary School. I waited for the New Year to show the faculty's and the students' appreciation for your leadership, courage, and performance."

The teachers and faculty applauded first, and the students joined in next. I was overwhelmed with emotion. I thought of my mother and father; I wish they were here with me so that they could take part in my accomplishment. What would they say if they were here?

Next, I was receiving recognition from my peers. With all that was going on around me now, did I accomplish this?

I guess my dad, President John Fitzgerald Kennedy, was right; I am a survivor!

The applause had died down. Mrs. Barnum asked me to say a few words.

"Mrs. Cobb, I thank you for the opportunity that you have given me and the trust that you had to let me lead the orchestra. Thank you.

"Mrs. Phermint, I thank you for your patience and under-standing when you said music and arithmetic go hand in hand. Thank you.

"To the members of the choir and orchestra, I give you my thanks. I know there were times that some of you felt that I did not belong in the orchestra. Thank you too. Thank You!"

The students and teachers began to applaud again as I walked away back into the line from where I emerged. The line of students that stood face to face with Mrs. Barnum was the line that broke up the assembly. It was the protocol that Mrs. Barnum walk behind us into the school building.

It was the same mundane thing in the classroom. Recess and lunch were taking a turn for the worst. I was able to get along with my peer group, but Vivian and Maryann had a difficult time dealing with theirs. What was it that adults refused to believe? The kids in school begin to understand, Vivian and Maryann were not related to me in any way?

When Vivian dealt with confrontation, she used racial slurs. Maryann would use profanity when she had a problem. Maryann was quick with the four-letter word, and for some reason, she did not care who she was talking to. When the three of us met on the playground, my friends would ask me, "What are you doing with them? You are too different; you do not look alike."

"What's going on with you, Ruben?"

"Why is it when we call your name Ruben you do not answer us most of the time?"

It was becoming so frequent that most of my classmates referred to Vivian and Maryann as 'them.'

Katherine Brown was a good friend of mine. For some reason, Vivian and Maryann did not like seeing me socializing with Katherine.

I avoided Vivian and Maryann while we were in school. The racial name-calling that Vivian aligned herself with I wanted no part of, and I did not understand it. What does the color of somebody's skin have to do with whom they are? I do not know. Katherine was a friend, and that was fine with me.

I had my own share of problems with Mrs. Barnum, Maryann, and Vivian's problems to compound them. This Monday was not going to end without me being called down to the principal's office. It turned out while Vivian was on lunch break, she called some kid of Mexican descent a racial slur over a ball game.

Mrs. Barnum called me into her office about 2:00 PM. There sitting were Vivian, Maryann, and this kid named José. It turned out, José preferred to be called Joe. I was not sure why I was there, but wherever trouble was, it seemed to find me.

"Ruben, did you hear what happened between your sister Vivian and Joe during lunch this afternoon?"

"Mrs. Barnum, first, Vivian is not my sister, and second, I was not there. Vivian was on one side of the playground, and I was on the other side of the playground."

"Vivian made derogatory remarks about Joe."

"Mrs. Barnum, that is the way that Vivian speaks. Just what does this have to do with me? I was not brought up to speak that way. I know the meaning of derogatory, but I do not look at a person's origins, only their attitude."

"Ruben, are you taught racial hatred in your household?"

"Mrs. Barnum, Vivian speaks in the same fashion that her mother Mary speaks. If you want any more information, call Mary. Still, my advice to you is to find another way to solve this problem if you do not wish to receive an ear full from Mary."

I guess Mrs. Barnum is a glutton for punishment; Vivian had to stay in the principal's office until she got a hold of Mary. Sitting in the principal's office was one of the things I disliked. I never knew what the principal's office was used for until I lived in the Gonzales household! When I was with my parents, this kind of thing never happened. Sending someone to get me, being sent to the principal's office, it was unheard of. This office was not a place to frequent, but here I am.

Mrs. Barnum finally talked to Mary; I do not know what was said between the two. When Mrs. Barnum opened the door and came out of her office, I could see the steam coming out of the ends of her purple hair. That is how upset she was. "You three can go back to class" was more like "Get the hell out of here." She had the revenge of a devil when she asked the three of us to leave the office.

It was 2:30 PM when I returned back to the classroom: 30 minutes until school was out. It is not much you can do in 30 minutes. The end of the day was here, how I dreaded the walk back to the house. I was still frightened of running into Mrs. Jenkins. The moment the bell rang, I knew that I was going to take Temple Street to Westlake Ave; that way, I did not have to see Mrs. Jenkins.

It never fails, Vivian and Katherine were going at it again, name-calling between the two of them. I was able to see and hear what Vivian, Maryann, and Katherine were saying. I was determined not to get involved in their argument. I told Katherine's brother Kenneth, "Let's stay out of their argument." I had had enough of Vivian and Maryann's foul mouths.

Kenneth and I arrived at Westlake and Temple Street.

"Hey, Ruben, why are you going up Westlake?"

"Kenneth, I am not going to pass Mrs. Jenkins's house; she has something wrong with her, and I don't want it."

Here was this tall slinky African American kid Kenneth standing with the small white kid standing on the corner discussing Mrs. Jenkins. What she may or may not have. The store owner of the clearance store right in front of us came outside.

"Just what are you two kids discussing? You are blocking the entrance to my establishment. Would the two of you please move on and stop blocking the access?"

"Kenneth, I'm going to leave. See you."

I continued on my way to the house. I made it all the way to the top of the hill on Burlington Ave. Larry Garcia came out onto the little porch of his house, shouting, "Hey Ruben! Hey Ruben! What did you get for Christmas?"

"A shoeshine box and everything that goes inside a shoeshine box."

"It sounds like you have everything you need."

"Yes, I guess you're right, Larry. Everything, for what, Larry?"

"Just saying that's all you need. Why don't you bring it by later so I can check it out?"

"Look, Larry, why do you want to see a shoeshine box? No, Larry, you want something else with the shoeshine box."

"Maybe, Ruben, but bring it by anyhow."

I walked away. Larry's interest in the shoeshine box piqued my curiosity. Why did he want to see my shoeshine box? I was the one person in the neighborhood that Larry did not like. No, this jerk had an ulterior motive, and I was going to find out what it is.

The one generic thing about this household was that they all walked in the front door and through the living room, passing the bedrooms and bathrooms, right to the refrigerator — opening the door. It was always the same disappointing look on their faces. Two things could happen: the light will turn on, or the light will be off. Well, at least the electricity bill and the telephone were paid. Gone were the days when my parents made sure that there was some order to life.

I closed the refrigerator door and walked over to the oblong green pantry that Mary had filled with random vegetable cans. I found a can of corn. Things were beginning to look up! Can of corn in hand, I walked over to the cabinets where Mary had the dry goods. I took flour, cornmeal, and baking soda and placed it all on the counter.

I started reading the back of the cornmeal box. As I was reading, I felt like I could do this. I measured out the cornmeal, flour, and a dash of baking soda and placed it all in a bowl. There was no milk, so I opened the can of corn and dumped it into the bowl with the liquid. I combined all the ingredients, mixing it thoroughly, and placed it in a baking dish and into the oven. The recipe on the back of the cornmeal box instructions calls for 30 minutes of cooking time. I periodically checked the dough for doneness. The tip of the knife was clean, so I pulled the cake out of the oven and placed it on the kitchen counter.

I stared at my creation; there was no way on earth I was going to eat this. The cake had cooled down, Charlie came into the kitchen. He went right for the refrigerator; he opened and closed the door. I could not help but think, *Here's my guinea pig*. I'll let him try it out. Charlie cut a piece of the cake to taste it. Looking at me, he asked, "Did you make this?"

"Yes, I did. How is it?"

"You have not had a chance to taste it? Not bad at all; you need honey to go with the cornbread."

Charlie walked out of the kitchen, eating a more significant piece of the cornbread, as he called it than the previous slice.

I had to try the cornbread for myself. If Charlie did not go into compulsions of cardiac arrest, I could take the plunge myself. I took a small piece, and he was right; it was not bad, but I may have used too much baking soda. The taste of the baking soda came through.

There was still the nagging problem; how was I going to make it to and from school without walking in front of Mrs. Jenkins's house? I couldn't walk down Temple Street with Vivian or Maryann; there was the fighting going on between Katherine and Vivian. 1967 was not turning out to be the blissful peace that I had longed for. How was I going to find any peace or tranquility in my daily life?

Los Angeles does not have season changes like New York City or Hyannis Port. It was around the middle of March when I began to let my guard down. This obsession that I had with Mrs. Jenkins was subsiding, and this racial thing between Vivian and Katherine was diminishing as well. I guess that is what the end of winter and the beginning of spring is like in Los Angeles, California. Things just work out okay.

During lunch, I met with some friends in the school playground. We decided to meet after school. Frank, Luciano, Bogart, Larry, and Tommy agreed we would all walk home together. It was friends being friends. The bell rang at the end of the school day, and we met on the corner of Rosemont Avenue and Temple Street.

I had known these guys for the last three years. Frank had to be my best friend; he reminded me of my little brother. He had dirty-blonde hair, green eyes, and freckles on his face. Here we were, all walking down the street; it was as if God himself was smiling down on us. I did not have a care in the world.

Bogart and Larry made a left on Alvarado; Frank, Luciano, Tommy, and I continued walking down Temple Street. We were pushing and shoving each other as we were walking. I was totally at ease as we were walking. We made it around the corner and up to where there was a group of adults standing and talking.

I was walking sideways, talking to Frank, when someone screamed, "Grab him!" I heard another voice say, "Which him?"

The woman's voice said, "The one with the red curly hair, the white child." The man had a tight grip on my arm and pulled me into the front yard. I started shaking and turning red with fear. The man who had my arm handed me over to Mrs. Jenkins. By this time, the whole gang of friends stopped in their tracks. By now, Mrs. Jenkins had me by both my arms. She was not hurting me, but she did not have a kind, loving look on her face either.

"Boy! I want to tell you something. You see that gentleman standing there? He is a retired Los Angeles judge; this gentleman is a retired policeman. This gentleman still works for the Los Angeles Board of Education, and I am a retired meter maid. We have all paid our dues to society. We have contributed to the well-being of the City of Los Angeles. Boy! Just who do you think you are, running off out of here the way you did? What, you have never seen an African-American before?"

"No! Mrs. Jenkins, no!" I started shaking and pulling away, but Mrs. Jenkins was hell-bent on getting her answer.

"Boy, I want to know what's your problem?"

Just as she said that Mrs. Jenkins turned her head to the right and spit out this big brown wad. It landed in a can of some sort.

I started shouting, "Let me go! Let me go! Please let me go!"

"Boy, what's wrong with you? Why are you so terrified of me?"

"If I tell you, will you let me go?"

"Why yes, boy."

There it came again, she let go another, right into the can.

"Mrs. Jenkins, what is that you spit out? All that brown stuff. I don't want to catch what you have, that's it."

No sooner did I say that the group of adults let out a roar of laughter. One of the gentlemen said, "Let him go before he faints on the spot!"

"Son that snuff is chewing tobacco. You've never seen anyone chew tobacco?" Once she said that I was sure Mrs. Jenkins was going to strike me, but instead, she pulled out this little round can out of her overall pocket.

"Son, this is snuff. You place it between your cheek and gums. That way, I do not have to smoke cigarettes."

"Mrs. Jenkins, I am sorry, but I have never seen a woman dipping snuff before. This is the first time. If I offended you in any way, I am sorry."

"Son, your mother raised a fine young man. You had me believing that you were afraid of something else."

"Mrs. Jenkins, I do not understand what you mean by something else."

"I know, son, I can read the expression on your face and hear the sincerity in your voice." Mrs. Jenkins gently let my arm go. I walked away. I could sense that it was going to be a long California spring and wondered what the summer would bring.

The gang of us continued to the house. Vivian, with her usual valor, started criticizing and ridiculing me.

"Ruben, why would you think that a person who is black spit black? You have to be really fuckin' stupid to think something like that."

I came to a complete stop, looking at Vivian from head to toe, and asked, "Why me, Lord? Why me? What have I done to deserve this kind of cruel, vulgar treatment?"

I had no idea what the profanity meant, only that I was not intelligent enough to figure out what type of sickness Mrs. Jenkins had, if any, at all. Looking past Vivian, I noticed the Hollywood sign in the far-off distance. That was the only thing keeping me from crying. I could feel my eyes start to well up and a lump in my throat.

After living with Vivian and her family for the last four years, I learned to reach deep inside my soul to overcome their brutality and move on. Today would be no exception. I continued walking across the bridge, leaving Vivian talking to herself.

Clipper looked at me with his green eyes. "Ruben, sometimes I think your name is not Ruben. Vivian is not related to you."

"Clipper, I cannot argue with the truth!" Clipper turned to the left to his home, and I turned to the right to my house.

The next day on our way to school, Vivian and Kathy were at it again. The name-calling and the fact that I was a honky and

Vivian was a Mexican seemed to bother Kathy. I had no understanding of why Vivian and Kathy's disagreement was so caustic.

Kathy told Vivian, "I'll see you after school." I did not give Kathy's statement a second thought.

Recess came around, and Kenneth, Katherine's brother, came up to me, "Ruben, do you know that Katherine means what she said? She is going to beat the shit out of Vivian."

"Kenneth, Kathy is right. Vivian is not my sister. How do I fight with the truth?"

"Ruben, if Vivian is not your sister, why don't you stop her from calling you her brother?"

"Kenneth, I have told everyone and anyone that Vivian is not a thing to me, but they do not want to hear it. So what can I tell you?"

"Ruben, if you tell Kathy what I am telling you, I'll beat your ass."

"Kenneth, we have been down that route, and that just is not going to happen." As I was standing there talking to Kenneth, I was looking out of the corner of my eye.

Kathy and Vivian were glaring and snarling at each other in the far-off distance.

"Ruben, you never answered my question. Why is Vivian calling you her brother?"

"Kenneth, maybe someone is paying her to say she is my sister, I don't know!"

Recess ended, and Kenneth and Kathy returned to our classroom. All had been forgotten.

Lunchtime came, and Kenneth, Kathy, and I were walking down Temple Street to get lunch. Vivian walked up behind us and started to talk as if everything were fine. The four of us parted ways on the corner of Temple Street and Bonnie Brae Street. Kathy and Kenneth made it across the street when Vivian and Kathy started arguing again; it was the same old racial remarks. I being white, Vivian being Mexican, and Kathy being colored, and I am not Vivian's brother. As we were walking, Vivian asked me, "Why don't you say something to Kathy?"

"Vivian, you are well aware that I am not your brother, and I did not ask to be here with you people. Katherine and Kenneth are my friends, and she is telling you the truth. I'm not your brother, and you saying I'm your brother does not make me your brother."

We finally made it to the house. As usual, we came home to an empty house. The refrigerator was just as empty as the house. The one noticeable thing was the light in the fridge did not come on; this was just another day in the household of the Gonzales family.

Vivian called the shop, but Mary was nowhere around. Here it was, 12:15 noon, and Mary still had not made it to Gonzales & Sons, her and Paul's place of business. I could hear Paul with his heavy accent telling Vivian, "Your mother is not here now."

"Dad, tell Mom that the electricity is off."

Paul lost it. "What the hell does your mother do with the money!"

It's funny how Vivian calls Paul every kind of son of a Bitch when he is not around, but when she calls him, it's 'Dad.'

"I'm calling to let you know that the electricity is off." Vivian hung up the phone. I could see she was upset by the expression on her face.

"Why the hell did we come here for lunch when I know damn well there is nothing to eat?"

"Vivian, it's called hope. We arrive here with confidence that things will change, but just as much as we hope, it remains the same. Let's go back to school."

This was not the first time I left this house without nourishment, and it would not be the last. At this stage, I was begging to understand the Communist culture. You keep someone hungry, and that's all they think about is the pain of hunger. Today I would have to rely on the California weather to ease through going without having lunch. Vivian and I made it back to school in no time, with five minutes to spare.

Lunch was over, and I was back in the classroom with hunger pangs the entire afternoon. The next break would be at two PM, which was ninety minutes away. Luckily, Clipper had not eaten all his lunch, and his mother told him to never discard it. The afternoon break did not come soon enough.

"Hey, Clipper, do you have any of your lunch leftovers?"

"Yes, I do!"

"Let me have it."

"Okay, but you have to eat it. Take it with you when we leave the classroom."

"Will do."

The bell rang, and the class lined up to exit the room and go to the playground. Like the friend that he is, Clipper came out with a brown paper bag; he looked like something out of a Norman Rockwell painting. "Here, but you better eat it."

"Clipper, what's in the sandwich? The way you say 'you better eat it' scares me!"

"Your afternoon snack is in the bag, Ruben."

We walked over to the bench and sat down with lunch in tow. I opened the bag and pulled out the nicely wrapped sandwich. It brought tears to my eyes. "Clipper, this sandwich was made with tender loving care. This is the way my mother made my school lunch, and yes, the napkin was still in the bag. How many napkins does your mother put in your lunch bag?"

"She places three, one for recess, one for lunch, and one for the afternoon break."

I placed the napkin on my lap, opening the sandwich onto the napkin. I turned the sandwich with the two sharp corners facing each other. It was a sandwich wrapped in perfect form.

Now that I have eaten, I was able to think clearly.

The last forty-five minutes of class was always devoted to the homework assignment. Today was going to be math, and who does not like math? Not that I was good at math or that it came easy for me, but if you know how to count, you can make changes. Math helped me with my business adventures.

The clock struck 3:00 PM, and the classroom kids all lined up to head out the door with the teacher. The last one out the door was the teacher. She would lock the door behind her.

There was always one teacher for the school who was assigned guard duty on the corner of Rosemont Ave. and Temple Street to keep us from running across the street. I had a habit of crossing the street to see how fast I could make it to the house, but it happened that today Vivian, Maryann, and I met at the same time on the same corner.

We made it two blocks when Vivian and Kathy started arguing. There were several racial slurs hurled back and forth. Vivian was yelling out at Kathy to mind her own damn business.

Kathy, hollering back, "Ruben, why are you walking with those people? I'm going to tell your mother that you are associating with the wrong crowd."

"Kathy, you do not know who my mother is or where she lives."

"I can follow you home and wait there until she comes out of the house and let her know."

Vivian yelled at Kathy, "What do you think is going to happen to you if your kind comes across the bridge?"

Kathy yelled back. "You don't see that Ruben has red curly hair, sparkling brown eyes, with freckles on his face? That boy is a honky, white boy. So Vivian, when you get to your house, look in the mirror and have the honky Ruben stand next to you."

What came next was a racial slur that I did not understand, and no American person of color likes to hear. Vivian yelled it out at the top of her lungs at Kathy. All the time, Vivian, Maryann, and I were on one side of Temple Street, and Kathy and her brother Kenneth were on the other side of the street.

Kathy came back at Vivian with, "Who are you calling that word when you are just as black as I am, bitch! So bring your black ass across the street so I can put some blue on it!"

In the heat of the moment, Kenneth hollered, "Vivian, don't come across the street. Kathy means what she says!"

I turned to Vivian. "Did you hear what Kenneth said?"

Kenneth shouted again, "I've seen Kathy fight, and she is going to tear you apart. Stay on that side of the street."

Vivian, being Vivian, was already walking across the street.

"Ruben, are you going to help me if Kenneth jumps in the fight?"

"Vivian, how do you want me to defend a lie? I am not your brother, and that is what this is all about. You are asking me to participate in a crime, and I'm not going to get involved. You are on your own if you cross the street."

Kathy yelled, "Hey, Vivian! I'll take the three of you on if you like, and I'll still whip your asses with one hand tied behind my back."

Kenneth yelled out one more time. "Vivian, she can do it. Don't come across the street."

Vivian yelled back at Kathy, "Keep your ass on your side of the street where you belong."

She replied, "Vivian, don't use the road between us as an excuse to not come across the street. Just admit that you are afraid!"

We were in between Westlake Ave and Bonnie Brae Ave when Vivian dashed across Temple Street.

Kenneth let out one enormous yell. "Ruben, stay on the other side of the street. Kathy will beat your ass like it's never been beat before!"

By this time, Maryann and I made our way across the street where Vivian and Kathy were pushing each other. We all were on the corner of Bonnie Brae and Temple Street right in front of the Krispy Cone Factory. Where there happen to be a glass door, and the employees could see what was happening on the street.

Kenneth warned me one more time to stay out of the fight. Kathy came at Vivian with a cross to the jaw and with an uppercut to the chin. Kathy's arm's length had to be a good 40 inches, and her legs even longer. Vivian did not have the arm length that Kathy had; it was apparent that Vivian should have stayed her ass across Temple Street.

Kathy landed one blow to the right side of Vivian's head and down went Vivian, flat on her back. As she was falling, she was screaming, "Ruben, help me!" as she was bouncing off the cement.

Kenneth, Maryann, and I were standing over Kathy and Vivian when Kenneth turned, looking at me, "Do not jump in! Kathy beats the hell out of Leonard, and he is in junior high school."

"Kenneth, Why would I jump in the fight when Kathy is right? Vivian and I are not brother and sister; she is not related to me at all, in no way. Do you understand that, Kenneth?"

Kathy was still on top of Vivian pounding the hell out of her. When two adult men came out of the factory. They tried to pull

Kathy off Vivian, Kathy was still holding on, punching Vivian, and these two guys could not get Kathy off her. By this time, a third man comes out to help get Kathy off Vivian, and still, the three of them could not get Kathy to let Vivian go. The one-man had Kathy by the legs, the other man had one arm, and she was still putting up one hell of a battle. They had Kathy mid-air. One of the guys that had her right leg let go. As he let go, Kathy landed on Vivian. All I could hear was a big gasp for air coming from Vivian.

By this time, there were now five grown men trying to stop the fight. Kathy was slugging Vivian non-stop. The five factory workers grabbed Kathy, each taking their part of her. One had the right arm; the other had the left arm. The same went for Kathy's legs. They were trying to pull Kathy off Vivian. Finally, the fifth man grabbed Kathy's waist and started to pull her off.

Maryann looked at me. "Ruben, why don't you help Vivian?"

"Maryann, I am not going to support Vivian if you keep saying I am your brother!"

I could see that these five guys were making some headway. Kathy started coming up in the air; however, they could not hold on to her. Kathy was like a crab out of the water, reaching for any part of Vivian she was able to. Kathy was punching and kicking as they were pulling her ever so high. She was off of Vivian and standing firm and tall.

"Vivian, if I ever hear you call Ruben your brother again, I'll give you some more of what I just did. Like I said before, take a look in the mirror next time you start with that word that you like to call people of color when you are just as dark as me and our kind."

"Ruben, you are lucky I do not do the same to you just for hanging around with these people."

At this point, Vivian, Maryann, and I went north on Bonnie Brae. Kathy and Kenneth took off south on Bonnie Brae. Vivian was moaning and groaning for the next three blocks.

"Ruben, why didn't you help me?"

"Why? Vivian, from the time that you arrived here, you have made it very clear that you were not going to help me to get back to my parents. How do you expect me to help you with that attitude?

Every chance you people get, you tell me the same thing. 'I am not going to help you get back to where you came from,' so Vivian, don't ask me to help you if all of your so-called family is going to keep me here against my will. This is what you have to put up with: my indifference towards you people."

"I'm going to tell my mom that you would not help me."

"Vivian, you tell anyone you want, and I mean it."

"I hate when you say 'I mean it,' Ruben!"

The three of us finally made it to the house.

I did not care if Vivian was hurt or if she needed help. I took my shoeshine box and went over to Larry's house.

I sat on the back stairs and waited for Larry to come out. The wait was not long. I had to sit no longer than thirty minutes. Larry came out of the back door of the small bungalow that he shared with his parents and sister. Larry and I were about the same age, but he's a lot bigger than me.

The first thing he said was, "I hear Vivian got her backside handed to her."

"Yes, if that is what you want to call it."

"Ruben, did you bring the shoeshine box?"

"Yes, I did; it's right here. Larry, are you going to tell me what you want with it?"

"I'm going to show you how to make money with this box, but first I have to build a shoeshine box for myself." Larry took the measurements of the shoeshine box and jotted the results down on the note pad.

He became frustrated at the way that his drawing of the shoeshine box was turning out.

"Ruben, this is not working out the way that my father and I had planned it. So let me keep the box overnight, and I'll give it back to you tomorrow after school."

"Larry, you know I can't do that! I cannot leave it here; one of the kids will tell Mary, and there will be cane to pay."

"Look, Ruben. Did anyone see you coming here with it?"

"No, but I live right across the street, Larry. You can see right into the living room from here."

"Well, do you see anyone in your living room from here?"

"No!"

"Well, then, we are fine. I will not tell anyone what we are going to do."

"Larry, how can I trust you?"

"Ruben, my dad will not let me go to shine shoes without you. I've been discussing this with my father, and if you don't go with me, I cannot go."

"Larry, there comes a time when I am going to have to trust someone, so I guess it's going to be you! If you tell anyone in the neighborhood what we are planning, it will surely get back to Mary, and it will be my, or should I say our, backside that will pay the price. It is getting late, take the box inside, and I'll see you tomorrow after school, Larry."

I was dreading walking across the street into that dungeon of a house. If it was not one crisis, it was another, but this time the crises are of my doing. I made it no further than the vestibule of the house. To the right of the door, I could see Vivian, Maryann, Sally, and Yolanda sitting on the sofa waiting for me. All at once, the four of them yelled, "Boy, are you going to get it! Vivian and Maryann called Mom and Dad. Boy, you are going to get it!"

"You mean your mom and dad, right?"

Yolanda stood up and started yelling at me, "Why didn't you help Vivian?"

I answered, "Why! Yolanda, I am here because you keep telling people I am your brother, and I am not. The problem here is you are well aware that this entire family is involved in a crime. I've heard every one of you saying 'if I am going you are going' and where are you going? To jail. I am not going to be a part of this crime, nor will I join you or help you.

"Kathy is just one person who will not go along with your offense, so why blame it on me? If you told people the truth, I would not have to hear how much you hate me. Vivian got a beating for her lies, so do not expect me to participate in your family's crime, Yolanda.

"Keep mindful that I do not want to stay here with you people, and I mean it!"

In an hour or two, Mary and Paul would be here, and I was going to have answers to their questions. I'd be better off if I start doing my homework to keep my mind off this afternoon's event and what was in store for me when they arrived here.

As always, my homework was not in the boys' room where I left it. If I ask the girls what happened to it, all I would hear is, "I do not know," so it was better not to ask.

Lucky for me, it is history homework, and the book is here, minus the missing questions. The teacher had written ten questions on the blackboard, and I copied them down. I knew that I had folded the paper and placed it in the book before school let out. I made sure I had it. I'll read the chapter twice and write down the essential information, names, dates, and places. This way, if the teacher asks me any questions, I'll be able to answer the question correctly.

I spent the next few hours doing my homework. When I heard the blue panel truck stop in the driveway, a dead silence came over the house. That feeling you get when the room is full of people, but you can hear a pin drop.

Mary walked into the house, fists clutching two bags of groceries, one in each arm, and Paul was still parking the truck. He came in and went right into his bedroom. Mary prepared dinner for her and Paul. What was leftover was for us to eat. I could still hear that dead silence reverberating throughout the house. No one said a word.

It was not unusual for me to forgo dinner if I did not see what Mary put in the food. It's not the evil that I witness that I am afraid of; it is what I've seen Mary put in the food and give to her own family that I fear. Yolanda, Vivian, Maryann, and Sally finished up their dinner, and it was left up to them to pick up the dishes and clean up the kitchen. There was no way on God's green earth that I was going to clean up after these people. I did not ask to be here, and I was not going to help out. Sally was the lucky one; she was the last one that Mary had added to the crime. Not that Sally was young; just she was eager to please my captors.

I was still in the boys' room when Sally came in.

"Ruben, Mom and Dad want you."

"Well, Sally, I guess it's time to dance to the music." This is one dance I could do without. I walked out of the bedroom that was off of the kitchen, where Yolanda and Maryann were still cleaning up. As I passed Yolanda, she commented on how I was going to get my ass beat like a stepchild.

I look at her, "You think so!"

I walked past the girls' room. Vivian was lying in bed on the front porch that they turned into a bedroom. There she was, lying in pain. I could not comprehend why Vivian insisted on calling me her brother.

I have heard a conversation that Vivian was to receive 1,000,000.00 dollars, but was it worth it? Why could she not realize the Kennedy's and Onassis have now become a criminal organization just by saying she is my sister and fighting for it? I've seen tens of thousands of dollars change hands to keep my identity from the public, but was it worth it to Vivian to go through this? I had to ponder, *Why would she not open her eyes and mind to her plight?*

I walked into Mary and Paul's bedroom, where they were sitting. Mary was sitting in one recliner and Paul in the other. Mary was smoking a Salam Cigarette and Paul a pipe with some cheap drug store tobacco; they filled the room with cigarette and tobacco smoke. Mary was sitting there, flipping her cigarette ashes out the window. "What is this, I hear? That you did not help Vivian with this Kathy girl?" It would be nice if that was the way Mary called Kathy, but I am not going to stoop to Mary's level. First, what does Kathy's race have to do with this when all she was looking for was the truth?

"Vivian is not my sister, and you are not my parents. I am not going to lie for you. Why should I? Just because Vivian, Maryann, and Sally are willing to call the two of you their parents in public, I am not. If what you want me to do is call you Mom and Dad in this house, it is your house, but out in public and to my friends, you are my babysitter, and Paul is not a thing to me. Remember, I did not ask to be here! I want to go home; this is not my home."

The startled look on Mary and Paul's faces surprised me; they were speechless. It was as if I brought them back to reality. I knew there were going to be repercussions for my inaction not to help

Vivian. All the torture and evil that Mary had to do to me did not work. I still did not forget my parents, President John F. Kennedy and Marilyn Monroe.

Mary was looking at me, "Mijo, go to bed."

"My mother never called me mijo! I do not like you calling me mijo! I am not your mijo!"

The dead silence had broken in the house. By no means were their marching bands. I walked out of their bedroom into the boys' room and closed the door.

The next day, I was off to school without any fanfare. I followed my usual route to school. I met up with Kathy and Kenneth; we made light of the fight of the previous day.

"Where is Vivian?"

"Kathy, you know that she is unable to walk; she barely made it to the house yesterday.

"You are correct; Vivian is not my sister, and I cannot stop her from calling me her brother. What I can do is go along with her in private but not in public."

"Ruben, what do you mean by that, public?"

"Katherine, we are walking to school together out here in society for all eyes to see. You are part of that public, as well as your brother Kenneth. I've been in places in this country that would not allow us to walk side by side down the street."

I hoped that Kathy understood that all I was trying to do was survive.

"Ruben, this is why I know that Vivian is not your sister. It is not that you do not resemble her; it is also the way you speak to her. I hear the teachers' comments on your use of the English language; they believe that you come from different social status."

"Kathy, please do not take this the wrong way. I consider you a friend, and the teachers are correct in their assumption."

"The teacher said that your parents are divorced and that they left you with your babysitter."

"No, Kathy. My parents were never divorced, and they never met Mary. My stepmother and her Sanchos handpicked Mary as my babysitter. My parents would never have chosen a beast like Mary to care for me."

"Ruben, the only thing I want you to do is to keep them damn Mexicans away from me."

"Kathy, let's dispense with the name-calling, please. I'll tell Vivian and Maryann not to agitate you anymore; hopefully, they'll heed to the advice. Kathy, you stay on your side of the street, and I'll try and keep them on their side of the street. Just walk on your side of the street, Kathy; that is all I am asking.

"Kathy, we are going to be called into the principal's office sometime today."

"I know. What are you going to say, Ruben?"

"I'll tell the truth. Vivian is not my sister, and she should not have walked across the street. She is the one who started the fight. Kathy, it seems as if I am in the principal's office at least once a week, and sometimes I am just in the wrong place at the wrong time, and this is one of those times, Kathy!"

Rosemont Ave. came up quickly. I dreaded entering the school this morning. The worst part was that I was innocent in all this, but Mrs. Barnum was going to hold me responsible for the fight. This was not going to be good at all!

Kathy, Kenneth, and I walked onto the school playground with a group of our classmates in tow. There was a tell-tale sign that something had happened on the way to school this morning or yesterday afternoon when we left school. Either way, Mr. Martins was going to find out what was going on. He was the school teacher assigned guard duty that month.

"Kathy, Mr. Martins is coming over. Keep it down. I don't want him to know what we are discussing."

Mr. Martins came up to us. "Why are you kids all huddled together? What are you up to? You kids are always rebelling against something." I turned to face Mr. Martins.

"Oh! It's you, Ruben. I should have known. What is going on?"

"We were talking about how beautiful the San Gabriela Mountains look this morning; did you notice the snow on them on your way in, Mr. Martins?"

"Do you want me to believe that you kids are admiring the weather this morning? Something is going on."

This time was the first time I was saved by the school bell ringing, but then again, fate has a way of stepping in.

"Kids, line up in your appropriate area and wait for Mrs. Lee."

We formed the same two lines as always, boys on one side and girls on the other. Kathy lined up to the right of Kenneth and me so that we could continue our conversation. Kathy and I were whispering. I made sure that Kenneth was in front of me so that the teacher would not see Kathy and I talking.

"Kathy, old purple-hair Barnum is going to call us into her office before 10:00 AM, so be ready; that way, we are in and out of her office by recess. Mrs. Barnum is not going to interrupt her break time for us, or me for that matter, so be prepared to pay the piper, Kathy."

Recess came and went. We still did not hear from the principal's office. It was going on lunch, and the clock was still ticking away. While we were in class just before lunch, I wanted to send Kathy a note. Luck would have it, the teacher asked if there were any volunteers to gather up the books; I raised my hand to say yes. The only problem was I was three rows of seats away from Kathy's row.

I gathered up the first and second rows' books and placed them on the bookshelves, and I casually walked back to retrieve the books that were sitting on the front desk in the third row. As I walked past Kathy's desk, I placed a note on her desk without the teacher noticing what the motive behind me being so helpful was. I finished up putting the books in the bookcase and went back to my seat. Kathy read the note. She looked over in my direction, nodding her head ever so slightly, not letting the teacher know we were up to something.

Kathy followed the instructions on the note to meet me outside the main school building. This way, we could talk on our way to lunch. The lunch bell rang, and the class let out for lunch.

"Kathy, did you bring the note with you? Let's get across the street. Kathy, one of the men who came out of the Krispy Cone factory, wrote down our names and said he was going to call the school. What do you think happened? Do you think he called?"

"I don't know, but I am not going to worry about it."

"Kathy, I am worried about this fight. Knowing my family the way that I do, there will be retribution. It's not the beating or the pain that you inflicted on Vivian. It's that you defended me and that they will not tolerate it. My grandmother is the matriarch of the family; she had contempt for my father, and I always knew that she felt the same for me."

"Ruben, what the hell are you talking about? Ruben? What does contempt mean?"

"It means not to like someone, that's a careful definition of the word. People who live comfortably do not hate. They use words like dislike or antipathy. Kathy, if we are not called into Mrs. Barnum's office by the end of the day, something is wrong. I have to go."

"See you later."

I left Kathy at the corner and walked up the hill to the house. Vivian was still lying in bed, nursing her wounds. She asked me again why I did not defend her.

"Vivian, this is a place I do not want to be. Why you don't understand that I'll never know. If the fight had been for any other reason, I would have gladly helped you, but you are asking me to fight against the truth and that I can't do. Vivian, the only time anyone in this family is friendly or concerned about me, is if they want someone to believe that we are related. Otherwise, you take my kindness for weakness, and you people have become the kind of people to keep your kids from. When you tell me 'never look for me to help you' to 'go back to where you came from,' I don't doubt that you mean what you say. I have to get back to school, bye."

I walked back to school, eating a slice of bread with sugar on it. I made it back to school before the lunch bell rang. I tried taking my mind off of when Mrs. Barnum was going to summon us to her office. The anticipation was killing me. The more the afternoon wore on, the more agitated I became. I did not know what the consequence was going to be for not stopping the fight or at least helping Vivian. There was no word over the loudspeaker, and no one came looking for us from the office. Perhaps I am not out of the woods yet. I still have to wait until 3' o clock, and I would be home free. I'll be out of here. The long hand on the clock finally hit 12, and the bell rang. I was safe from being accused of instigating the fight between Kathy and Vivian.

After the bell rang, I decided to get out of Dodge as fast as I could. I was walking at a fast pace, hoping that some teacher does not grab me and escort me to the office. I was walking past the principal's office; Old Purple-Hair Barnum was not sitting in her office. I was getting this uneasy feeling. It was unorthodox for Mrs. Barnum to let me slide for any mischief or mayhem I may have caused, and my unwillingness to get involved or stop the fight did not help. I scurried past the office and onto the street on down to the corner and crossed Rosemont Ave; there was no way I was going to let Mr. Martins stop me and take me to Mrs. Barnum.

Once I made it across the street, I was home free and on my way. Before I knew it, I was at the house; I was the first one to make it to the house. The days were gone when I had to change out of my school clothes and into my play clothes. That cheerful, gleeful sound that I was used to hearing was gone; all that was there was this vast, hollow sound of nothingness. I could feel and hear the tears on the walls of the house, hitting the floor before I drowned. In all that, I stayed outside and sat on the front porch.

I sat down, looking across the street, just over the horizon of the palm tree. I stood fixated on the top of the palm tree. I did not want the eerie feeling of being alone to creep up on me. I sat on the porch until Larry came out of his back door and waved at me to come over to his house.

Larry had one hand on the screen door holding it open, and the other was holding the shoeshine box that I had received as a gift from the Sanchez's for Christmas.

"Larry, where is the shoeshine box that you built?"

"Take yours, and I'll bring mine out."

Larry had never invited anyone into his house, and today was no exception. He came back with the shoeshine box in hand.

"Look, here it is. How do you like the way it came out?"

"It's sweet. You and your father built this last night?"

"Yes, we did, in one night. He wanted me to return your shoeshine box A.S.A.P. Ruben. I want you to take both shoeshine boxes with you. Tomorrow, bring them with you to the bus stop in front of the B.C.D Market. I'll meet you there around 3:30 PM, and we'll go downtown to the Central Market and shine shoes for money."

"What do you mean, Larry?"

"Ruben, we are going to make money shining shoes."

"Larry, I do not shine shoes for money; that is what the household help does."

"Ruben, what the Sam Hell are you talking about? Where did you come from? What, you think you are better than me? Look, we are kids, and this is what kids do to make money, you moron."

"Larry, if you think I do not know the definition of a moron, you are mistaken. I just never believed that President John F. Kennedy's and Marilyn Monroe's son would be shining shoes, that's all, so blame it on my upbringing. I never believed that President John F. Kennedy's and Marilyn's son would be going through the trash. Looking for empty bottles, cleaning up after his classmates after school, and shining shoes!"

I continued, "And Larry, I am not accustomed to being called names. If you ever call me a rude name again, I will not talk to you anymore, and I mean it. Name-calling is unnecessary; it is a clear sign of a lack of good breeding."

"Ruben, this is why the people in the neighborhood do not like you. The way you walk and talk differently from us."

"Larry, if you like, you can go by yourself."

"Ruben, no! Please no! My dad said if you do not go with me, I could not go at all. He does not want me to travel downtown by myself."

"Larry, you're three times my size; you're just a coward. Your father did not tell you not to go alone! Grow up and admit that you're afraid to travel alone downtown; the place is too large and scary for you!"

"Ruben, are you going with me or not?"

"Larry, you are such a baby. You have that same vulnerable look on your face as my cousins Joe and Katie. If I were to walk into a room, Joe pisses his pants, and Katie would fall down on her ass crying. Don't worry; I am not going to burst your balloon. I'm going with you."

"Okay, take the shoeshine boxes with you and meet me in front of B.C.D. Market at the bus stop at 3:45 PM. We have to take the 42-bus downtown; it will leave us in front of the Central Market. The ride should only take 15 minutes. Giving us enough time to pick the right spot to shine shoes."

With the two shoes shine boxes in tow, I walked across the street around the right side of the house and in the back door. I did not want any of the nosy Gonzales's in my business. The more I hid my goings-on from the Gonzales family, the better off I was.

I came out of the bedroom, and Vivian was lying on the sofa, still nursing her wounds. She was giving Yolanda, Maryann, and Sally a recap of the fight with Kathy. How I just stood there and let Kathy beat the crap out of her. *What was going to happen to me because I did not stop the fight?* I stood between the front room and the kitchen leaning against the door railing. Like all hens, the girls stopped talking when they noticed I had entered the room.

Yolanda was the first who spoke.

"Why didn't you help Vivian? I want to know." It was not that I did not have an answer for her; all I was thinking was that today is Thursday, tomorrow is Friday, and the next day is Saturday. I'll be safe, but what about Sunday?

"Yolanda, you either have a short memory, or you think all that voodoo you people practice is working on me. You know full well I am not related to you people and why I am here. Vivian is not my sister!"

"You could have stopped the fight."

"Yolanda, you refuse to believe that I do not want to be here. I would be better off in a boys' home than with you, God-forsaken people.

"Yolanda, the whole neighborhood knows that I was kidnapped, but they choose to turn a blind eye to what is happening here. I cannot walk past anyone in this neighborhood without hearing whispers. 'There he goes' 'do you know who he is? He's

President Kennedy's and Marilyn Monroe's son". I try to get along with you, but I will not go along with your crime. Yolanda, there has not been one week that the police have not been here for one reason or another. Why doesn't the neighborhood inform the police of what is going on here? Because they do not want to get involved? Oh, how lucky am I, or should I say how lucky are you."

The next day, it was the same routine, but now I had to meet Larry at the bus stop. I made it to the house from school in record time. I dropped off my schoolbooks, picked up the shoeshine boxes, and ran out the front door as fast as I could. I made it to the bus stop without any of the other kids seeing me. I walked as quickly as my little legs would carry me with the two shoeshine boxes, one in each hand.

I made it around the corner of Union and Temple Street. I looked down the street; the bus was two blocks away. I darted across Temple Street in front of Taylor Drug Store and across the street to the bus stop. I made it in the nick of time as the bus came to a complete stop. Larry stuck his head out the back-window, shouting, "Ruben get on the bus."

I was on the bus in no time. The shoeshine boxes were too heavy and bulky for me to reach into my pocket and pull out the fare for the ride. I placed the shoeshine boxes on the floor and pulled the fare out of the right pocket that held the money.

"Hey Mister, don't take off until I get to the back of the bus; I do not want to end up rolling to the back of the bus."

I managed to make it to the back of the bus without causing a scene.

"Larry, these shoeshines boxes are heavy. One is bad enough, but two is the worst. Let this be the only time I do this for you. Next time, you take your shoeshine box to school with you or pick it up at your place. This is just too much work for me to do. Running from school to the house and from the house here to meet you because you are too cheap to pay for the bus twice is ridiculous, Larry! It's just plain ridiculous! By the way, where is your homework?"

"Ruben, I did it at school."

"Larry, you do not even have your schoolbooks, where are they?"

"They are in my school locker."

"Your school locker! You guys in junior high and high school have everything."

Larry and I made small talk until the bus turned onto Hill Street in downtown.

Once the bus driver turned onto Hill Street, I could see the Central Market on the left side of us, and on the right side was Bunker Hill. There were still Victorian homes that lined the top of the hill. The bus finally came to a stop in front of the Central Market. I looked over to where the Angels Flight Railway was going up the hill.

Larry looked over at me, "What is wrong with you? We get off here. This is our stop!"

"Larry, I had forgotten Lena lives just atop Angels Flight at the top of Bunker Hill in one of those Victorian rooming homes. If she sees me, my goose is cooked. She may tell Mary that I am here in the Grand Central Market shining shoes."

"Ruben, we'll be on the other side of the market on Broadway. The chances of that happening are slim to none."

"Okay! Let us get off the bus and get out of here!"

This is not the first time I had been in the Grand Central Market, but it was the first time I have seen it at 4:00. The Hill Street entrance had less action going on as I walked through the market. Things started to come to life the further we walked into the market.

We walked down the middle of the market as if Larry and I were the owners. The market was bustling with activities by the sellers and buyers; the colors of the different fruits and vegetables made me feel as if I was a king among kings. We made our way to the Broadway side of the market. Right in the middle of the market was a lunch counter one step from the busy street of Broadway.

I noticed that there were other boys my age shining shoes. I watched what Larry was doing and decided I would have to mimic him if I was to make any money at all.

I would have to muster up some courage to walk up to someone and ask if they would like a shine. "Hey, Mister! Would you like a shoeshine?" The first person I asked did, and it did not go so well.

"Son, you look like you just rolled out of your diapers. I don't think you know what you are doing."

I tried it again. "Miss, would you like a shine?"

"Child, does your mother know what you are up to?"

"Madam, my mother is no longer with us. I'm just here to support myself."

"Son, I did not need a shoeshine." She opened her purse, took out a dollar bill, and handed it to me.

"Madam, I can't take your money. I have not worked for it."

"Son, as I said, I do not need shoeshine, but please take this. Just the jester that you asked me if I would like a shine tells me that you have a proper upbringing. This place is not a place for a child like you." She bent over and placed the dollar bill in my shirt pocket, and walked away. It looked as if I was going back to the house without making money.

Luck would have it, another guy finally said yes. I rolled up his pants so that I would not get the shine on his pants.

I sat down on the ground and opened the lid to the shoeshine kit and pulled out the black color polish, brush, and cloth to remove the polish. The first step was to brush off the dust from the shoes, keeping the bristle from the brush from dragging against his sock. I wrapped a white cloth around the third and fourth fingers of my right hand as tight as I could. I placed my two fingers that were covered with the white cloth into the black polish, taking just enough to do one shoe. I rubbed the polish ever so lightly in a circular monition, making sure not to make a mess. I tapped the sole of his shoe with the bottom of my hand to indicate that I finished one shoe, and it was time to start on the other.

I repeated that same action on the left shoe; now, it was time to remove the polish from both the shoes. I pulled a clean, soft white cloth out of the shine kit. I turned the smooth side of the fabric down, holding it tight across the shoes in a horizontal motion. I was removing the excess polish and bringing the shoes to a high-gloss shine.

That is what should happen, but in my case, that is not what happened. I finished up, and I could see the gentleman's face; he was not too happy. "Son, let me give you some advice. If you are pursuing a career in the shoeshine business, you need more practice on non-paying customers."

"Sir, I'll take your advice and put it to good use."

"Son, I'll pay you for the shine, but no tip."

"Sir, I can't argue with that, and I thank you."

Larry had finished up his fifth client and came over to me.

"Ruben, how much money have you made?"

"Ten cents."

"Ten cents! That's all?"

"Yes, that's all, Larry.

"Larry, you see those women over there? They both told me that I do not belong here and I should go home to my mother. Another woman gave me a dollar and said I should go home to my mother. Maybe I do not look raggedy enough or needy; who knows? Let's go back."

We walked back to Hill Street and waited for the bus back to our own neighborhood.

"Ruben, we'll come back tomorrow, but early in the morning. Tomorrow is Saturday, so we should make some real money tomorrow."

Larry and I sat in silence on the way back. I sat thinking about what was going to take place over the next two days. Saturday was beautiful, but what about Sunday? What did it hold in store for me? That is when the Gonzales and Gomez family would hold their family meeting on what I have done or what I have failed to do. I still had the fight between Vivian and Kathy in the back of my mind, and Mary being silent on the matter was making things worse. The emotional turmoil that I was going through was causing me to forget to eat.

"Larry, I have to get off this bus to eat something before I get sick."

"Ruben, wait until the bus stop is in front of Big Top Liquor Store. We can go into Poncho's Bakery and buy some sweet bread and milk."

"Larry, why do Mexicans call it sweet bread when the bread is not sweet?"

"Ruben, there are two kinds of Mexican bread, one made with sugar, and the other made with salt. It is called sweet bread, or Pan Dulce, which is the same thing."

The next morning, it was the same thing. Mary prepared breakfast for her and Paul and left of us to fend for ourselves. Thank God I was learning how to cook. I did not require the care that these two people had to offer.

Mary and Paul left early on Saturday morning. It was one of the busiest days of the week at Gonzales & Sons Television and Radio Repair Shop. If not for Mary's mismanaging Gonzales & Son's bookkeeping and Paul's alcoholism, they would move up into the middle class in no time, but they were going nowhere fast. I made myself two fried eggs and had two pieces of dry bread, and I was out the door.

Even though Larry lives across the street from me, it was easier for us to meet on the footbridge. There were just too many eyes on my goings and comings. I waited for Larry in the middle of the bridge. As he came in a clear view, I noticed that his shoeshine box was bouncing off the left side of his leg. I shouted out to him, "Let's go! I have been waiting here for the last fifteen minutes. What took you so long to get here? You live less than two blocks away.

"Larry, let this be the first and only time that you are late. I wait for no one, you understand that? 10 o'clock is 10 o'clock, not 10:10, but at 10 o'clock. You're lucky I'm here waiting for you. I know how to get to Grand Central Market by myself. I don't need you."

"Ruben, I am only 10 minutes late."

"Larry, I could already have walked to Belmont High School in that 10 minutes. No, instead, I'm waiting for you! Let's go!

I see you made some improvements to your shine box."

"Yes, I did. I painted it and added a strap to it. How do you like it?"

"It's an improvement. Where did you get the strap from?"

"My dad. He cut the end off one of his old belts."

"Larry, I hope it is the one he uses on you."

"Ruben, that's not even funny to say."

"Larry, I've seen your father whip your backside, and I did not say that to be funny. Larry, my parents never hit me with their hands or a belt. What they did was talk to me. Boy, could they both talk with words that went to the heart. Whatever I was doing, or when they wanted me to change my attitude, I did."

"What are you talking about? I've seen Mary take a raze strap to your ass, Ruben."

"Yes, you have, but she is not my mother. I'm talking about my parents, not Mary." We continued on our way.

"Let's go this way to the central market," I said.

"Which way?"

We walked down Beverly.

"No, that is the long way. By the time we arrive, we'll be so tired that we will not be able to shine shoes. Let's walk down to Glendale and make the right turn into the tunnel. It will lead us next to the market on Hill."

"No!"

"Larry, I walk this route all the time, and this is the fastest way to go. We'll be at the central market in no time."

"Ruben, you walk too fast. I'm going to go along with you but slow down."

"Larry, your legs are longer, and you're bigger. Why is it you want me to slow down?"

"Ruben, you are a runt compared to me; it's your small size that makes you faster and quicker."

We made it to Grand Central Market in 45 minutes. Fast walking causes me to feel better.

I had my first client within the first 5 minutes of my arrival. This time, I was more relaxed, and any apprehension or self-doubt had evaporated into thin air. I was shining shoes like a pro. Larry was not doing too bad himself. It occurred to me that this was not the first time he was shining shoes to make money. He had the shoe drill down pat. Out of curiosity, I wanted to find out if my suspicion was right.

"Larry, have you done this before?"

"Yes, I have. My dad would take me to Lincoln Park, and I would shine shoes there on Sundays."

Larry was taking one client after another; I had a slower pace. To the right side of me was an older gentleman working fast. He would make his shoeshine rag sing as he was removing the polish. The rag would make a popping sound, and he would hum to the pop.

I was making 25 cents to his dollar.

"Excuse me, sir. Why is it that I am making 25 cents to your dollar? That's just not fair."

"Boy, it's like this, I put a shine on the man's shoe *and* entertain him while shining his shoes. You just shine shoes. Son, by the way, what is a rich white boy like you doing down here shining shoes? Did you get in some kind of trouble, and your dad wants to teach you a lesson? If that's so, this is the right medicine to cure the pain. If you do not learn from this, you never will."

"Sir, I'm here to trying to earn my way in this world." Boy, it seemed as if my words have fallen on deaf ears.

"Sir, my name is John, but my parents called me Jack. For now, you can call me Ruben. I don't need the grief that will go over the wire if you don't."

"Hell, boy, you don't look like a Ruben to me! Jack fits you better. Say, do you know who you remind me of? You look like President Kennedy." Like I said, my words fall on deaf ears.

"Sir, it's lunchtime, and I need some nourishment."

"Son, I'm Joe, nice to meet you."

"Joe! Nourishment!"

"Jack, all I need is to hear you speak to know that you are on the wrong side of the tracks!

"Jack, you need to get you a little stool to sit on while you shine shoes. The dust and dirt you have on your pants will not come out."

"Joe, I will see you later."

"Not if I see you first, Jack!"

I walked around the other side of the open-air restaurant. Larry was sitting on the floor, shining shoes, he had two pairs of shoes, a black pair, and a tan pair. He had already finished up one, and he was working on the tan pair. I stood there looking at him, going to town on the last shoe. He had his hand in the shoe with a brush in the other. He was bushing the tan shoe to a high-gloss finish. There he was, tilting his head back and forth, admiring his work as the shines were coming to a mirror finish.

"Hey Larry, I'm hungry! Where are we going to eat?"

Larry was in shoeshine-boy mode, still going to town with the shoe brushing it back and forth with his head bent down, oblivious to the world around him.

"LARRY! Snap out of it!" He glanced up at me with that same glossed-over look on his face. He looked at me as if I brought him back to reality!

"Ruben to Larry, Ruben to Larry, are you there?"

"What do you want?"

"It's about time you landed, Larry. I'm hungry, where are we going to eat?"

"Let me give this guy his shoes back, and we will go to lunch." Larry got up off the cold cement floor, took the shoes, and handed them to the guy behind the counter.

Larry got his money, and we turned and walked away. "Larry, here it is midday, and this place is bustling with activity. People are buying and selling. Larry, I've been here in this market early in the morning when people are delivering fruits and vegetables, vendors running back and forth, but I needed to see it like this. It is like something out of a movie."

"No, Ruben, you are wrong. This is real life! Let's walk around to the other side of the market."

"There is another side?"

"Yes, it's where the deliveries are made during the day." We walked out onto Broadway, passing the open-air liquor store that is noticeable from the street. For the first time, I took a good look at this side of Grand Central Market from the Broadway side.

The liquor store looked like a display that you might find in an elegant Los Angeles Museum. There were rows of different classes of wines from all over the world.

"Larry, we are going to eat there. Where they sell fried shrimp and French fries?"

"Yes, here. Look, you get two dozen shrimp and French fries for a $1.25."

"Larry, I need more to eat than that!"

"Ruben, there are plenty of places to eat here. All I want is the shrimp and fries."

"Yes, but the line is too long, there are too many people trying for the same thing."

"The line will move fast, so let's get in it." Sure enough, in no time, the lady behind the deep fryer was handing me a small brown bag full of shrimp and another with fries.

"Ruben, try this red sauce."

"Is it hot with chili?"

"No! Just try it. All it is is red vinegar with pepper."

"No, it's a little more, not just pepper and vinegar."

"Try it."

"Okay. This meal is not bad for $1.25." We finished up our lunch and then it was back to work shining shoes. By 3:30 to 4:00 PM, our customer base was dwindling, and it was time to go.

As in all business adventures, there is the problem of transportation. How would we transport ourselves from one place to another? We decided to take the scenic route, which meant we would have to walk, no bus or taxis for us. Larry, being the frugal one between the two of us, made the decision to walk back to the house.

On the long walk back to the house, I stayed silent. All I could think of was what was going to happen tomorrow when the Gonzales's and the Gomez's have their weekly meeting. Who was going to show up and ask why I didn't help Vivian? The explanation I give to Mary and Paul should be enough, but for these people, it never is. We finally made it to Temple Street and Glendale.

"Larry, I'm walking to the wooden stairs. I can't make it up the Hill of Temple Street." The incline was just too steep. We continued under the overpass of the Hollywood Freeway. We finally made it back to our own neighborhood. I rounded the corner, looking out past the palms that stood out as if it were welcoming me back. The sky was bursting with colors, reds, yellows, and ambers.

As I walked past Carmen's little house, I began to say to myself, "Why me, Lord, why me!" I knew that I would have to endure this ordeal that I was going through, but why me! What chaos would these people ambush me with as I entered this household? Luck would have it that I arrived in an empty house. It is turning out to be a pleasurable, peaceful, and tranquil end to a productive day. No one was going to be any wiser to the day that I had.

I bathed and decided to go to John Francis Rudley's house. John was one of the neighbors that lived atop Belleview, not even a half-block away. He was locked in the 1920s, the kind of guy that would give me a cup of coffee, maybe two but never three.

I walked up the stairs to his house and turned around to admire the magnificent skyline of Downtown Los Angeles. I was taken in by the Hall of Records and the Los Angeles City Hall Building. When the sun hit the city hall just right, it became the only building that was intriguing to me. It reminded me of the obelisk protruding off the desert of Egypt.

Old Man John was not your typical neighbor; he did not like walking from the back of his house to the front door to answer the door. It was customary for his visitors to walk to the back door of his home.

I turned back around and started taking the path from the front to the back door. The door was always unlocked, but still, I knocked on the door. It was John's style to holler 'come in' unless he was answering the front door.

It was not unusual to find Yolanda, Vivian, Maryann, and Sally sitting around his kitchen table having coffee and pastries. There were times when I've even walked in on them and heard them discussing me, and this time would be no different. I felt like an unwanted guest in his home as if someone paid him to watch me.

This evening, Old Man John was pumping Vivian and Maryann for information about the fight with Kathy. It was becoming a habit for Gomez's and Gonzales's and their criminal counterparts to stop discussing me when I entered the conversation. I did not make it to the table when John started questioning me about the fight that Kathy and Vivian had had. John, with his thick Polish accent, asked me why I did not help Vivian.

"John, Vivian is not my sister, and why should I get involved in a fight to cover up a crime? I do not want to be here with these people. Kathy was only alluding to the truth: Vivian is not related to me."

"Ruben! I'm going to tell Mary what you are saying that Vivian is not your sister."

"John, I notice that you do not mean you are going to tell my mother, you are leaving yourself wide open. You even agree with me that Vivian is not my sister. You old bastard, I can see I am not wanted here, so I am leaving."

I walked out of his house with knots in my stomach. It was as if the whole world was against me, and Sunday was not even here yet. This fight that I was not a part of was somehow my fault. Just what was I going to do when the Gonzales and Gomez family came together to discuss this past week's event? It was only last summer at a Gonzales/Gomez family and friends' barbeque that I overheard Mary telling her guests that I believed that she was my mother.

*All of Mary's guests were standing around talking in the back yard. I overheard their conversation on how Mary had me believing she was my mother to Tony, Cleo, Dooley, and his wife, Marjorie. Dooley, looking over at Mary, "Mary, I do not believe that Little Kennedy believes you are his mom at all. I'm sure he is pulling one over on you. There is no way in hell that the boy feels he is your son."*

"Dooley! My word to God, he believes that I am his mother."

"Mary, I don't care what you tell me. Now, are you going to convince me that Little Kennedy thinks that you are his mother? How is he going to forget that President John F. Kennedy and Marilyn Monroe are his parents when he is older, and he lived with them?"

"Dooley, my right hand to God. Ruben believes I am his mother."

*Seated (left to right): Gilbert, Unknown, Richard (Dickey Mary's eldest son), Unknown, Tony Stack, Unknown, Unknown*
*Standing (left to right): Dooley, Daniel (Danny Mary's last son), Unknown, Robert (a.k.a. Bobby), Charlie (Mary's first son from Paul)*

"Mary, he calls you 'mother' out of simulation, not that he thinks you are his mother. Who is going to forget that President Kennedy and Marilyn Monroe are your parents? When they are always in the tabloids together or on the news?"

Mary called her daughter-in-law Chita over for back up. "Chita, have you heard Little Kennedy call me mother?"

"Yes, I have!"

"Mary, him calling you mother and him believing it are two different things."

"Dooley, I'm going to prove it to you."

Mary called for her grandson Raymond. "I want you to go into the house and call Ruben 'Uncle Ruben.'"

I turned away from the window and began to tiptoe away. There was not a soul that had any idea that I overheard their conversation. I tiptoed past the bathroom. I could hear everyone coming in the back door into the kitchen. I looked out of the bedroom window when I saw Raymond running by it. I made it to the middle of the living room when Raymond was in front of me. I tried to get around Raymond, but by this time, Chita, Charlie, Tony, and Cleo were coming in the door. Everyone who was in the back yard was either in the kitchen or the front room. There was no way for me to escape out of the house. I did not tiptoe fast enough. Raymond's little legs were faster than mine. There he was, Raymond, eager to please Mary. Standing right in front of me, I felt my blood run cold through my veins and my ears turning red with anger.

Raymond called out, "Uncle! Uncle Ruben!" He did not get to finish the third 'uncle' when I grabbed him by the throat and began to choke him.

"Raymond! You people have taken everything from me! You are not going to take that too! If you ever call me Uncle again, I'll rip your tongue right out of your mouth! Do you hear me! I asked you a question. Do you hear me!

"You are not going to carry this crime on to another generation. I'll not be a part of it, Raymond, and no one is going to make me. Do you understand what I just said? Do you?" By this time, I had my hands on Raymond's shoulders. I was in the zone of no return.

I began to hear this faint scream in the background as I was holding Raymond. "He is going to kill him; he is going to kill him." It was Chita's voice that I heard crying out!

"Stop him! Stop him!" No one came to Raymond's defense. Mary and her guests were all in a state of shock! The anger that I had displayed for Mary and her guests had witnessed rendered them utterly useless!

"Raymond, it is not in me to hurt a child, but if you call me your uncle or refer to me as your uncle again, I'll hurt you. Do you understand me? I will not be a part of this crime, do I make myself clear!"

I was slowly beginning to regain my composure and sense of awareness. I let Raymond go and slowly walked out.

Dooly was the first voice I heard as I was walking out. "Mary, I told you Ruben did not believe you were his mother! It's just a word for him. He uses it the same way I call you Mary. There is no way that he doesn't remember that President Kennedy and Marilyn

Monroe are his parents. You have every one of us believing that this is a perfect crime!"

I was not going to stick around for the aftermath of my action or their delayed reaction.

There was no place that I could retreat to except my sanctuary. Still feeling angry and sad, I strolled down to Echo Park. When were these criminals going to understand that I want to go back to where I came from? What was this all about? Why did Grandma Rose, Uncle Robert, and Uncle Edward leave me here with these beasts? Why? My mother worked for my brother and me, why am I here?

I walked to the lake where I could clear my mind, body, and soul. I was torn by what I had done to Raymond. The saddest part about this afternoon's event is that I have more care and respect for children than these adults. Now, these criminals have taken that away from me too. These reprobates have taken my innocence, my childhood. Now they want to destroy life itself. I would apologize to Raymond, but he, Mary, and the rest of these criminals will only see it as a sign of weakness.

Why is this all coming back to haunt me now? What does this have anything to do with the fight that Vivian and Kathy had? When I said, How do you fight the truth, Vivian is not my sister? Thank God it was Saturday, and I did not have to deal with this until tomorrow.

I found myself sitting on John's front stairs of his house, wishing to be any place but here. I did not get comfortable when the Gonzales Clan was coming down the stairs. Mary was the more vocal, and the vulgar one spoke up first.

"Hey, Ruben! What that hell are you doing sitting there all alone?"

"Waiting for you people. Let's go home."

We walked across the street and around the corner. The only sound that I heard was the whistling of the wind passing by my ears. I dreaded the weight on my shoulders; it was more than anyone should have to handle. Just what was tomorrow going to bring? It was going to be Sunday, and the usual crowd would be gathering at Mary's house. Just how was I going to explain why I did not help Vivian fight off Kathy? What words would it take to make the Gonzales and Gomez clan understand that I do not want to be here with them?

Sunday morning was here, and I did the usual Sunday ritual. Sundays, I enjoyed attending Mass. It was a six-block walk to Our Lady of Loretto Parish Church. It was the one place that I found peace and solitude. Where I was welcome and at home. It was the one thing that no one could take from me, and that was to be a Roman Catholic American. It was the old establishment bending with the new. This was how I was going to endure. The morning would take care of itself, but what would the afternoon bring? The answer was in the hands of my captors.

It was late afternoon when I saw someone walking across the footbridge; he was yelling.

"Ruben, where are you! Ruben, where are you!" We met in the middle of the bridge. He looked at me, "Did you hear me calling you! Did you hear me call you?"

"No, I have no idea who you are calling for."

"Get your ass home; they want to talk to you."

"Oh, it's you, Danny! Who are they, Danny?"

"Don't be a smart ass, Ruben."

Danny and I walked back to the house. There are three things about living on a cul-de-sac. The police drive right by it as if it does not have an exit, parking is readily available. It's an excellent place to hide President John F. Kennedy's and Marilyn Monroe's son in plain sight for the world to see.

The moment I entered the house, everyone stopped talking. Richard, Mary's oldest son, asked me the first question.

"Where have you been?"

I hesitated to answer out of my lack of respect for him. I knew that someday I would lure this fish in. I could not let show the disdain that I harbor for him. The adults call him Richard. The adolescents called him Dickey. He had a reputation of being some kind of badass Cholo from East L.A. Rumor had it; he was no more than a coward. That is putting it lightly! To me, he was just a fly on the table; anyone could swat him away.

"Dickey, I went to church this morning, and the priest asked me to stay and sing in the afternoon choir. Mass ended less than thirty minutes ago, and now I am here. Danny mentioned you wanted to talk to me. What is it you wanted?"

"Oh, never mind."

His little brother Robert asked me the same question, "Where have you been?"

Robert was called Bobby. Bobby was not a Cholo in any sense of the word, but he acted as if he could take on the world. I heard Bobby could hold his own when it came to defending himself. He reminded me of my Uncle Bobby Kennedy; they both were small in stature, but what they lacked in size they made up for in attitude. It was apparent that both Dickey and Bobby were willing to take on someone small in stature but never anyone their size or more significant than them. I was relieved; the anxiety that I was having over the past week was dissipating.

The one person that I did not expect to question me about the fight was Chita. I had no idea the extent of Chita's involvement in this crime as to ask me why I did not help Vivian. It was last summer when I went ballistic on her son Raymond for agreeing with his grandmother Mary to calling me, Uncle Ruben. Chita had to be a moron to question me.

"I want to know why you did not defend Vivian?"

"Chita! I am well aware that you do not answer a question with a question, but who are you to question me?" I began to tense up. The tips of my ears felt as if they were turning red hot. I kept asking myself, just who is Chita to question me? Who did she think she was? It would be detrimental to my health if I answered her rudely. There were just too many adults between me and the door.

"Chita, I have a sister and a brother, and they are both younger than I am. You people are trying to make Vivian my older sister. Why should I defend a lie? Vivian is not my sister; I do not understand what is going on here." Just at that moment, I glanced out of the corner of my eye to see Mary signaling Chita to stop.

"Ruben, I just wanted to know why you did not help Vivian."

"Chita, why is it okay for you to admit to each other that President John F. Kennedy and Marilyn Monroe are my parents? But when I mention it, it's taboo. Why is that?

"How many times have you told me you were going to tell Mary what I was saying? When I tell people, Mary is not my mother, there is nothing I have to be ashamed of.

"Mary is not my mother, and I am not going to let you people take my mother away from me. I am talking about my real mother, Marilyn Monroe, when I say, my mother! Do you understand that!

"My mother!" I shouted, turning to Mary, and pointing at her. "Not her, do you know that! NOT HER!"

The rage I felt was bouncing off the walls around me. Now, did Chita have the nerve to question me? I would say no more! I turned and walked out of the house.

I walked to the only place that I could find peace and solitude, my sanctuary. I needed to calm down and regain my composure. Just the thought of what I had just said to Chita was going to bring even more havoc into my life. The only thing I could do to calm down was to sit here in the park, watching the ducks floating on the lake. Take in my surroundings—the boathouse where families were renting boats to cruise around the lake and children playing.

I finally calmed down and walked back to the house. I do not recall staying this upset for this length of time. It was a real feeling that this was going to be my life forever, and there was no way to stop it. When I arrived back at Mary's house, her lunch party was over.

# SOLITUDE

**THINGS FELL BACK INTO** place after the Sunday afternoon lunch party. I was growing accustomed to living in California. I seemed to have lost my sense of time. One season rounded right into another. It was not like living on the east coast where there was a change of seasons, and I was able to place time to an event.

The time was here. I would have to call Mary 'mother' instead of her first name. I did not like calling Mary her name, Mary, either. Sometimes when I could get away with it, I called her Mrs. Gonzales or Mrs. Gomez. She would become irate and answer, "I never married your son of a bitch father!" Before she could finish her sentence, I was in the wind.

I was walking along Echo Park Avenue, taking in the scenery. The boathouse was just ahead of me. Off to the right was the reflection of the boathouse shimmering off the water in the lake. The boathouse seemed as though it was coming right out of the water and floated away into the sky. I was passing the boathouse when I heard someone calling out, "Jack." I stopped in my tracks. It was Linda!

"Oh, how are you, Linda? What are you doing here?"

"I'm fine, and you, Jack? How is your mother?"

"You mean my mother or Mary? Which one?"

"Jack, I wanted to know if you still remember your parents at all. I am still trying to convince Tom to adopt you."

"By the way, Linda, where is Tom? Oh, I see him."

"He is over there playing pinochle. What are you doing here by yourself?"

"I'm looking for bottles to sell."

"Does Mary know what you are doing?"

"No, she does not. Please, Linda, I would like to keep it that way."

"Do not worry, Jack; you have my confidence."

Tom was a heavyset man, but he could scoot as he put it. It was not but a moment later, he was standing behind me.

"Tom, how did you come upon us so quickly? A moment ago, you were sitting down there on the bench playing cards, and now you're here. That was fast!" Tom ordered Linda to get in the car.

"Ruben, what were you and Linda talking about? Did you tell her anything?"

"Tell anything about what Tom?"

"Anything!"

"No, I did not!"

"I am going to tell your mother you are down here."

"Tom, that is going to be hard to do, you know that. If you are going to tell Mrs. Gonzales, that's fine with me. Tell her what you want."

Tom did not strike me as someone who would tell anyone anything. I know that he would not fink on us to Mary that Linda and I had spoken.

"Tom, Linda, I'll see you later."

It was too early to go back to the house, and it was a beautiful afternoon, so I continued on my quest for bottles. In no time, I had walked past the swimming pool and into the overpass of the Hollywood Freeway. I came out of the other side on to the baseball diamond. There were these two gentlemen dressed in baseball uniforms thumbtacking paper to a bulletin board advertising the upcoming baseball league, and over to the right was the tennis courts. With my bottle in hand, it was an easy decision to make. I walked over to the gentlemen in baseball uniforms. I asked them, "What are you pinning to the bulletin board?"

"Son, the park is going to start up a baseball league for kids. You look like a capable young boy. Would you like to join up?"

"Yes, I would!"

"Come back on Friday. I'll be here with all the information you'll need to join. By the way, my name is Leo. I am the team manager; this is John. What is your name?"

"Ruben, sir."

"Ok, Ruben. Be back here Friday after school at 4:00 PM."

I was on my way back to the house when I was getting this unsettling feeling as if I was going to have a life-altering experience. When I felt this way, it was hard for me to rid myself of it. It was as if my body was fighting with my spirit and soul. There was no unity between the three.

I went back to the house and Mary was there. It was unusual for her to be here at this time. My foot had not entered the house when she started. "Where in the hell have you been? You look like you have seen a ghost!"

I feel as if I did.

"Well, I am not going to take you to the doctor."

"No, I do not need a doctor; I feel different."

"What the hell do you mean different?"

"Just what I said, different! I need to lie down."

"This is not a rest home or a hospital. Help clean up around here."

"Why should I? Who's coming over that you want to impress? You have four other people here that can help you clean up this dump, ask one of them."

Danny had always blamed me for his mother weighing 350 lbs. But I thank God for that one. There was no way she could come after me for talking back to her. How does this reprobate Mary always seem to snap me out of whatever I'm feeling? And this time was no different.

As I was standing in the living room, the news came over the TV. That my Uncle Robert F. Kennedy, Senator from New York State, has decided to run for President of the United States. Mary was looking at me.

"What do you think of that, SABIO!"

Mary had always said I was the best Voodoo person that she has ever come across. Mary referred to me as Adivino or Sabio when she wanted advice on a matter or wanted to know the outcome of any given situation. This time she wanted to know if my Uncle Bobby was going to be our next President.

"So, Adivino, is he going to win?"

"Are you asking me, or did my Uncle Bobby ask you to ask me? Go back and tell him the question should be not is he going to be the next President of the United States, but will he make it to the end? That part is totally up to him and what he does when the time comes."

When Mary called me Sabio, I knew the meaning of the word. Sometimes my Grandmother Rose referred to me as Adivino. A priest once called me Adivino. Both words have the same general definition.

Mary's ruse did not fool me. She was here to ask me if my Uncle Robert F. Kennedy was going to be the next president and for no other reason.

Friday was here in no time, and I forgot about the little league. I was with Clipper, and we were walking to his house from school. Clipper was the friend that I had decided that I wanted to keep as a lifelong friend. He reminded me of my little brother JonJon.

We walked up Clinton Ave. It was the steepest hill in the neighborhood, and Clipper lived at the top of the hill. Today was one of those days that we should have taken the dirt path to his house.

Clipper's house was by far the cleanest in the neighborhood. On our way home from school, he asked me if I would like to join the little league with him. "Clipper, I have forgotten that today is the day to sign up for the little league. I was planning on joining the little league."

"My mother is not home, so wait for me out here in the alley behind my house while I change my clothes."

It took Clipper five minutes to change. He came out with two baseball gloves and a ball. It was a beautiful California day; the sky was blue for as far as the eye could see. I felt as if I found a brother in a friend. Clipper handed me a glove as he came out of the wooden gate behind his house. We started to play catch with the baseball as we were walking down the alley.

I did not make it five hundred yards when I noticed a big dark navy blue chauffeur-driven four-door Imperial Chrysler automobile going by. It was moving at a snail's pace. I had a birds-eye view of who was in the back seat of the car. As the vehicle was rolling past, Clipper shouted, "Throw the ball, Ruben! Hey! You look as if you saw a ghost."

I froze at the moment! I did not know what to do, in which direction to go! There were bushes to the right and a wooden gate to the left of me. Clipper was in between the bushes, and I was to the left. The only way out was through the wooden gate. I was totally in a panic mode. I could feel the blood running cold to my feet. So I dashed to the wooden gate. I could see the red taillights come on and the dark navy blue Imperial backing up.

It stopped in the middle of the alleyway blocking the alleyway entrance. The back door popped open, and I heard a voice calling out.

"JACK, COME HERE! JACK, COME HERE!" I recognize the raspy voice!

"Jack! Come here." I waited for the other shoe to drop, and here it was. Why of all days did it have to happen today? Why!

"Jack, did you hear me calling you?"

"Yes, I heard you."

Clipper was in awe! He was white as a sheet. "Ruben, do you know who that is?"

"Yes, I do, Clipper. Yes, I do."

"Why is she calling you, Jack?"

"My name is John, but my family calls me Jack."

"But do you know who they are?"

"Yes, I do."

"Ruben, that is the President's mother, Rose Kennedy and his wife Jacqueline, the First Lady of the United States."

"Yes, it is. I am Rose Kennedy's grandson, and Jacqueline is my stepmother."

My grandmother's voice said, "Junior, come here. I do not have all afternoon to wait for you. I want to talk to you."

I was reluctant to talk to her. Whatever my Grandma Rose had to say was not going to be pleasant to hear. I slowly walked up to the back door of the car. My grandmother yanked me into the back seat of the vehicle. She had me in between her and my stepmother. "What I have to tell you I want you to understand and keep in mind. I had to come all this way because you cannot or refuse to get along with the Gonzales's."

"Grandmother, what do you mean?"

"Jack, stop right there. I am not here to debate the situation with you. I am here to let you know what's going to happen.

"Mary called me and informed me that you do not know how to get along with others. Mary's daughter Vivian had a fight with a girl by the name Kathy Brown, and you stood idly by and did nothing. I'm here to tell you, this is where you are going to stay."

"Grandmother, this is not what you promised my parents. This is not at all what you promised!"

"Jack, this is where you are going to stay, do you understand me?"

"But this not what you promised!"

As my grandmother and I were arguing, Jacqueline was preoccupied with her purse. She pulled out a bottle of pills and took a few.

"Jack! Your parents are no longer here, and I do not have to keep my promise."

"Grandmother, you promised them and me that you would take care of me!"

"Jack, this is where you are, and you are going to stay." Looking at my stepmother Jacqueline, "You see what you did? You know what you did!

"She would not be doing this to me if not for you kidnapping me from my mother. I lay all of this at your doorstep! You did this to me. However, Grandma Rosie, I hold you responsible for all past and future destruction that you have bestowed upon the family and me."

Glancing over at my grandmother, "I do not want to stay here with these people! You have to take me from here; Find another place for me to stay, just not here. Please, Grandmother! Please!"

"Jack, this is where you are going to stay. Never look for one Kennedy to help you because no Kennedy is going to help you to return to where you came from, do I make myself clear on that! I mean, no one!"

"Grandmother Rose F. Kennedy, you are leaving President John F. Kennedy's and Marilyn Monroe's son, your grandson, with despicable people. The Gonzales family has done unspeakable things to me at night while I am sleeping."

*"Jack, if what you are saying is true. You are soiled, and there is no way I can bring you home now."*

"Grandmother, my parents put money in a bank account for me, so did Grandpa Joe. Use the funds to pay for my care. I'm only asking you for what is mine."

Jackie was still fumbling around in her purse as my grandmother and I talked. She pulled out a bottle of pills, opened it up, and dumped out two pills. *She downed the pills without water.* I placed my right hand on Jackie's right hand and my left hand on my Grandmother Rose F. Kennedy's leg.

"Before I leave, I want both of you to understand: I forgive you for what you have done to me and for what you are going to do me. When you are on your deathbed, you do not have to ask for forgiveness. You'll both have the solitude of knowing I forgive you."

This time, instead of being pulled in by my right arm, I was being tossed out by the left arm.

*"Grandmother, by no means is this over! You do what you have to do, and I'll do what I have to do!"*

*"Jack, by the time that happens, I will be dead."*

"No Grandmother, God doesn't want you, and the devil doesn't need you. Stepmother, your time is coming sooner than hers." With that said, my grandmother abruptly removed me from the car.

I stood frozen inside myself. I tried to move, but I was overwhelmed with despair. *The only part that seemed to move is my head to watch the car drive away—the contempt and outright unadulterated hate that my Grandmother Rose F. Kennedy had for her son, my father, President John F. Kennedy, had just sealed my fate.* Standing there, I finally realized that I was alone. I turned to Clipper, "Let's go. We are going to be late."

That was all I could do or say to keep my tears back; it was all too commonplace for me to cry in silence.

Clipper and I began to walk the five blocks to the baseball field. All the way there, we tossed the baseball back and forth to each other, between the silent tears and tossing of the baseball back and forth. I was praying, asking the Lord, our God, to defend and protect my brother JonJon and friend Clipper from the evil, harm, or ill will that my family may bring upon us. "Please, God, I implore you to deliver us from evil as you delivered your Son Jesus Crist from evil."

We made our way to the park; the baseball manager was standing with one hand on the fence, holding himself up.

"Hi, John!"

"Ruben, you're back, and this time you brought your little brother with you."

"No! Sir, this is my friend Clipper; we came to join the little league baseball team."

"Ruben, you do not look too happy today, anything wrong?"

"No! I just received some bad news, that's all, sir. I have to leave!"

The pain that I was suffering in silence was more than I could bear. I left the field without saying goodbye to Clipper or the baseball manager. I strolled across the baseball field into the tunnel under the Hollywood Freeway to the playground side of Echo Park. I found myself crossing the street, walking along the lakeside of the park.

The trees were to the left of me and the lake to the right. I was still hearing the echo of my grandmother's words ringing in my ears. *Never look for one Kennedy because no Kennedy will ever you help to get back where you come from!* I continued onward, finally reaching my sanctuary, the place that I felt safe and at peace with the world around me.

I sat on my favorite bench and looked out on to the lake. I would not allow myself to cry. I did not want to shed a tear; instead, I was better to suffer in silence. I knew that I could not just sit here and wallow in self-pity, but what was I to do if my grandma Rose was not going to keep her promise that she made to my parents and me long ago?

# DEVISING A PLAN

**AFTER TWO HOURS OF** self-pity, it became apparent that this self-indulgence was something I could not afford and refused to take part in any longer. I rose from the park bench and walked around the lake.

I decided to devise a survival plan. The best that I could hope for was that Clipper was able to play the position on the little league team that he tried out for. This way, he may be overjoyed with his accomplishment, and he would not recall meeting my grandmother or my stepmother. The one thing that concerned me was JonJon, my little brother. What was I going to do about him?

The best thing I could do about JonJon was to not talk about him. My mother said it best when someone asks about him. She would calmly reply, "He is in your eyes." I recall her saying that on many occasions.

The less I speak about what I remember about my past life, the more Mary and her immediate family will believe that we are family. I was well aware that my very survival depended on Clipper, so I would not talk about what my grandmother said to him. The only way I was going to pull this off was to stay away from Clipper for a while.

Before I knew it, the sun was going down, and I had walked around the lake three times. I did not want to run into Clipper on the way back to the house. I ran up the big stairs. It was ten stories high. By the time most people made it to the top, they were out of breath. I, on the other hand, had no problem.

I stood at the top of the stairs, looked down over the lake, and panned over to Downtown Los Angeles and knew I was going to make it. To my surprise, I had made it to the top just in time to see the LA skyline light up. I had an overwhelming feeling of renewal as I stood there, taking in the scenery.

I had spent the weekend avoiding Clipper; it was not until Monday on the school playground that I had seen him. I gave out a big holler.

"Hey, Clipper! What position on the little league are you playing?"

"I wanted pitcher, but I'm playing shortstop." Clipper and I never spoke about my Grandmother Rose F. Kennedy, nor did we talk about my stepmother Jacqueline B. Kennedy either. I wanted to put some distance between me and my Grandmother Rose F. Kennedy. Besides, Mary was all the evil I could handle at this point in my life.

1967 was turning out to be a pivotal time in my young life. I had already come to terms with my kidnapping, my parents' demise, and now Grandmother Rose F. Kennedy's decision to leave me in Mary's clutches. How was I going to navigate between the classes of life, or are they one and the same?

Time had passed, and in one aspect, my Grandmother Rose was right. I was going to have to go along to get along with the Gonzales's. Meaning if I am going to survive, I would have to find a way to get along with the Gonzales family. I knew that if Mary ever found out that my grandmother and I talked, she would use it to her advantage against me. What Mary does not know will not hurt me, and that is a good thing.

The summer of '67 ended uneventfully. It was not until I returned to school that things started to heat up. Mary and Paul's marriage seemed to be falling apart, and everyone was growing up. I never cared for Paul very much; he was a man that had a dark side to him.

It was evening. Paul, Mary, and Danny were sitting in the main bedroom in the house, talking. I had just come out of the kitchen and walked into the doorway of the bedroom to tell Danny that he left the refrigerator open. Paul glared at me.

"Why don't you close the damn door!"

"I did not open the door, so why should I close it?"

I had seen that same look on Paul's face before. He was not going to brutalize me the way he did Vivian.

Mary had told Paul, "Vivian did not attend school for twenty consecutive days." There was no way on God's green earth that he was going to lay a hand on me!

Paul was up and out of his recliner in no time, and I was out the door. I was running so fast that I could feel the wind streaking through my hair. I made it to the top of the hill and around the corner in full view of the neighbors. I looked to my left, and there was Martha and her sisters. They were shouting, "Run, Ruben! Run, Ruben! Run!"

As I was passing Martha's house. I took one more glance over my shoulder. Paul was gaining on me. I looked back one more time.

"Paul! Do not run after me! You are not going to catch me!" I did not get the word 'catch' out when I heard *lop!* I looked down. Paul was sliding on his belly on the gravel. I heard the gravel tearing into his skin. I did not bother to stop. I was still barefoot and running as fast as I could while Paul was lying on the ground.

I did not stop running until I made it to the park. It was dark, and I could see the streetlights reflecting off the lake. I sat down and began to calm down. It seemed that I always ended up in the same place after a crisis. The only thing I could do was roll up into a fetal position and stare out onto my scenery.

I believe that fate sometimes steps in, and on this night, it did. The night did not seem so dark to me. In fact, I could see the beauty of the night. It felt as if Mother Nature herself was putting on a show just for me. There was no grey in the night, only dancing lights and the music of the traffic in the background. I stayed balled up for two or three hours in the same place, gazing onto the lake.

I finally came back to reality and knew that I had to return to the house. I walked to Charlie's and Chita's apartment. I could see the light on in Raymond's bedroom from the alleyway. I knocked on the door of their residence, to no avail.

I walked back to the house; I could hear voices. It was Mary, Charlie, and Chita talking. Mary was informing them about what had transpired earlier that evening. As I was entering the house, Mary called out, "Ruben, if that is you, come in here now!"

There they were, the three of them sitting Mary, Charlie, and Chita. Charlie opened his mouth first.

"Ruben, why did you not take your punishment if you were going to run your mouth?"

"Charlie, first and foremost, Paul is not my father, and second, I did not ask to be here. How many times do I have to repeat that! All that you need to do is inform my grandmother that you do not want me here."

"There is no way in hell your grandmother is going to take you from here."

"Charlie, I can only tell you what my grandmother said to your mother."

Mary looked at me, "Mijo, come here."

"My mother never called me mijo, but what do you want?"

"Just come here. I am happy that you did not let Paul hit you, but you started a lot of trouble here tonight. Did you see what you did to Paul? He was pretty bad off. His face and stomach were cut up and full of blood. Are you hurt? By the way, where are your shoes?"

I looked down at my feet, and to my surprise, I did not have any shoes on!

"Mijo, how did you manage to walk without shoes?"

I left the room without giving Mary an answer. I had to check for blood on my feet. They were both in good shape— no cuts or bruises on them. Paul did not return to the house for the next three weeks. Tom and Linda came by to see Mary in the middle of the week.

They were in Mary's bedroom, talking. What they were discussing in her bedroom would echo in my room next to hers. It was as if she wanted me to hear what the conversation was about. Mary and Tom were discussing what had happened between Paul and me. Tom was asking Mary if it was safe for me to be living in the house with her and Paul.

"Tom, I guarantee you Paul will not harm Jack."

"Mary, we cannot risk this kind of behavior. You know damn well given a chance Jack will call the police on us. We have to look out for his wellbeing. Remember, Ruben is the son of President John F. Kennedy and Marilyn Monroe."

Linda excused herself from the room. As she passed my bedroom, she motioned for me to follow her into the kitchen. Linda placed one finger over her lips. She was signaling me to be quiet and to follow her.

I tiptoed into the kitchen, where Linda was waiting to enter into the restroom. She asked me where the light was in the bathroom hall. She was on one side of the doorway; I was on the other side. This way, no one would notice us talking. Linda bent forward to whisper in my ear. "Would you like to come live with Tom and me?"

I nodded my head, yes.

"I would like you to meet me in the park on the lakeside in your favorite place in two days. This house is no place for you to grow up. I would like it if you came to live with Tom and me. Tom and I have already talked about it, and we would be happy to have you with us."

I left back into my bedroom, and Linda stayed in the restroom.

Linda and I met just as she instructed me. It was around 9:00 PM; it was dark out, and the rush hour had ended. Glendale at Belleview is the main throughway, and the lakeside of Echo Park was a good a place as any to meet. The trees, bushes, and shrubbery would shield us from passersby and vehicles.

"Linda, you do not look well."

"Jack, I am fine!"

"Linda, the bench over there will shield us from any busybody. Let's sit there."

"What bench?"

"Linda, there are benches built in the wall that runs along this side of the park. Right there around the corner is a bench. Let's sit there."

"You do not respond to the name Ruben very well, if at all. I should call you, Jack." She continued. "Tom and I were talking; I want to make it clear, would you mind if we adopt you?"

"No! Linda, Tom has kids of his own. I remember them."

"Yes, his ex-wife Lois cares for them."

"Linda, I can tell there is something different about you. Your voice does not have that same confidence in it."

"Jack, if someone does not get you out of the hands of the Kennedy's, they will destroy your life along with Mary's help. I want you to have the life you were born to have."

"Linda, any place is better than having to live in the Gonzales household. They are not good people.

"Linda, I am fearful for the both of us. If my family finds out what you want to do for me, they will try and stop you."

"Jack, this is no way for a child of your innocence to live. I want you to be patient and give me time to work with Tom so that we can help you."

"Linda, how am I going to contact you? Mary and Tom don't like it when there is a third party listening in on their conversations. Mary goes as far as hanging up the phone on Tom; they are cautious."

"Jack, I going to talk to Tom and let you know what we decide."

"Linda, how did you get here?"

"A friend from my church group drove me here. I'll walk out with you."

"That's ok."

I walked away and turned back to see Linda getting into the car. The oncoming car traffic blinded me. I could see the silhouette of the driver, but I could not make out if the driver was male or female. The stoplight finally turned green, and Linda was out of sight.

I crossed the street in no time and up the wooden stairs to the house. I did not give much thought to what Linda and I discussed. The thing that worried me the most was, what would the Kennedy clan do if they found out what Linda was willing to do for me? How was this going to affect Linda's life?

# 1968 APPARITION AND DEATH

**67 WAS ENDING ALMOST** as it had started, except for possibly leaving the Gonzales's. I was hopeful that Linda would come through and convince Tom to adopt me and get me out of there. Looking back at the fight between Vivian and Kathy changed all parties concerned. Gonzales's started keeping a closer eye on me.

The meeting I had with my grandmother and stepmother made me determined to survive. What my grandmother said was between me, her, and the lamp post. I knew that Jacqueline would never mention the conversation to anyone, much less Mary.

The Gonzales household was becoming increasingly chaotic. There was not a corner that I was able to turn that I did not run into a Gonzales or one of their relatives. I felt like a bird trapped in a cage with all eyes on me.

After Paul had taken a cruise on his belly, he finally began to understand that I did not like being in the Gonzales household. He used to stay away from the house two to three days a week. Now he stays gone for weeks at a time. No one seemed to mind that Paul was not around. Mary was supposedly working in the shop when Paul was on one of his frequent excursions.

Things came to a head when one morning, Paul had gotten out of bed about 10 AM. He started arguing with his oldest daughter Yolanda.

Yolanda had asked Paul where he had been for the last three weeks. "Why can't you support your own family?" she said.

"Yolanda, just what the hell are you saying? I support all you hounds."

Yolanda yelled for her little sister Maryann to come to the kitchen. All hell was about to break loose. I could see the expression on Yolanda's face. Her neck started turning red, which earned her the nickname the Rooster. By the time Maryann came into the kitchen, the Rooster was in full bloom. "Maryann, didn't you have to give our mother $65.00 to pay the rent this month?"

"Yes, I did, Yolanda. I was saving it for my birthday."

Paul was standing in front of the stove at the time. He had one hand on the hot coffee pot, and the other hand had a cup for the coffee.

I stood in the kitchen behind the table, watching what Paul was going to do next. I was thinking, When was Mary going to step in and stop Paul? Paul picked up the pot with his right hand as it finished percolating. I could see this look of indecisiveness on his face. Do I throw this hot pot of coffee into Yolanda's face to shut her mouth? It was in that instant that Mary finally shouted out, "You are not going to throw that pot of coffee at her, Paul! It's okay with me that you beat the hell out of the boys, but you are not going to hit the girls! I want you to get the hell out of this house, Paul! Leave now!"

Paul put the coffee pot down and turned and walked away. Looking over at Yolanda, I could see the fighting look on her face. That look of sheer fear at what had just taken place. I asked myself just what was I doing in a situation like this? This family discord was only another display of how Mary manipulated her family members into doing her dirty work.

Mary had walked from the kitchen to the living room following Paul all the while.

"Paul, you are not going to treat my daughter that way! Get the hell out of here now." Mary repeated the same words, "You can beat the hell out of the boys if you like, but the girls are another matter altogether! Paul, I want you to leave this house right now."

Mary did not have to repeat herself; Paul was fully dressed and out the front door. Mary turned to me. "Ruben, do you think he's coming back?"

"Why are you asking me?"

"Just answer the question."

"Mary, the question is, do you want him to come back? We both know that I don't care if he returns or not. He is not my father; he is Yolanda's father, according to you."

"God damn you! Someday that smart mouth of yours is going to get you into a world of trouble."

"I don't know why! All I'm doing is telling the truth. He's not my father."

I don't know whom Mrs. Gonzales thinks she is fooling, but she instigated the show this morning. She was going to use the morning's events to her advantage. I did not believe that she asked Paul to leave for the sake of Yolanda or the rest of the girls. Mary always had an alternative motive for her actions. I knew I was going to find out what it was.

Seventy-two hours had not gone since Paul left the house. I left school to have lunch. When I opened the door to the house, Tony Degtano was coming out of Mary's bedroom. Mary's vulgar language came into play. Vivian asked Tony, "What are you doing here?"

Before Tony could answer her, Mary responded for him. "Why don't you worry about me having something to eat and not what I put in my ass." I had no idea what Mary was saying; however, when she did get vulgar, it was to change the narrative of the conversation. I knew that someday I would be out of here, and I would not have to hear this kind of vulgarity anymore.

This afternoon lunch would be no different from any other day of the week. It never failed; I would walk into the kitchen up to the refrigerator and open the door, and the light came on. The only thing I found was a jar of mustard and a jar of mayonnaise. So, I had to go to my old standby. Sprinkling sugar on a slice of bread and that made for a sweet lunch.

As I was leaving to return to school, I looked at Tony and asked for Cleo. "Ruby, in all marriages, husbands and wives have problems, and she is probably at work."

"Tony, it's bad enough that I have to put up with the name Ruben, now you want to call me Ruby too? It is bad enough that the elderly lady and gentleman down the street call me Ruby, but what is your excuse?" The neighbors say I never answer them when they call me Ruben, but when they call me Ruby, I turn and smile.

"Please do not call me Ruby to make yourself feel better. You are well aware of what my real name is. Tony, you can call me John or Jack, either one, but there is no good reason for you to call me Ruby." I walked out the front door and returned to school.

It was two to three days later when I saw Mrs. Gonzales again, and for that matter, Paul was not around either, which was not a bad thing. The Gonzales's and I seemed to get along in a more civilized manner when Mrs. Gonzales was not around. It was by no means peaceful or a place of tranquility. Just that Mary's destructive, evil ways were not around to influence or manipulate her children. Mary left us on our own for a week at a time. When she did return, I felt it was not my place to ask her where she had been. Did I even care where she was?

Yolanda was the oldest of the five of us adolescents; Yolanda did the unthinkable. Yolanda asked her mother Mary or should say, Mrs. Gonzales, where she had been. Mary's answer was quick and precise. "I had to stay at the shop working for the last 72 hours while your father Paul was out on one of his drunken stupors."

By this time, I was old enough to know that Mary was not one of the most truthful people that I've met so far. Of course, not being the smartest cookie in the package, Yolanda bought into Mary's answers. The only thing I ever witnessed Mary doing at the shop was to answer the phones and collect the money and do the bookkeeping. She never arrived at the shop before 2:00 PM or stayed after 7:00 PM. Just who was she trying to convince?

It was Sunday morning around 8:00 AM the next time I saw Paul; he was coming out of his bedroom. Once again, Paul was here to play the adoring family patriarch. Still, he was just as vicious as his counterpart Mary.

As I sat at the table writing, I looked up to see Paul looking at me. How could God give us such a beautiful day with such a disgusting scene? There Paul was, coming out of his bedroom through the living room on his way to the restroom. Shirtless, pants unbuckled, and barefoot. It was a moment in time that etched in my memory.

It was more of a feeling that I missed my dad. My dad never walked around like that.

Paul, looking at me, asked, "Just what the hell are you looking at!"

"Nothing, nothing!"

"Don't give me that. The way you were looking at me as if I am nothing."

I was becoming more encouraged by my answers. In a way, I *was* looking at nothing. Paul continued on his way into the bathroom. He came out shaved and showered, looking like a new man. He went on into his bedroom and finished getting dressed without saying another word.

Paul looked like a man with a plan. He came back into the kitchen to have his coffee, bacon, eggs, and fried potatoes. He finished up his coffee and headed out the front door. As Paul was leaving, Mary asked him, "Where are you going?"

"To the shop, and I do not want you to come down there, you understand me? I'll be back later. We have to talk."

Mary is fifteen years Paul's senior. Paul's last words to Mary told me he had no intention of coming back. She did her usual routine, and by 1:00 PM, she called a cab and was out the door.

It was around 5:00 PM. Paul called the house, asking for Mary. Yolanda told him she left at 1:00 PM.

That evening, all was peaceful and blissful, until Mary decided to eavesdrop on Yolanda and Vivian's conversation. They were talking about boys. Mary, not being one to mix her words, started lecturing Yolanda and Vivian about the facts of life.

Mary was in between the kitchen door and the bedroom, leaned over to one side to prop herself up. "Let me tell you girls something. When you get married, you are going to get your ass screwed one night, and twice on Sunday!"

I had no idea just what she was talking about. And being well aware of my surroundings, I did not bother to ask. Yolanda's eyes started to well up; she did everything she could to keep her mother from knowing just how much she hurt her feelings.

"If you girls bring any boys home from school, I don't want you bringing them into your bedroom and closing the damn door."

I had no real understanding of Mary's words. I could see Yolanda turning as red as a rooster. Sally overheard what Mary had said. She was looking at Mary, bewildered.

"You and Tony were behind closed doors. Why can't Yolanda and her boyfriend be behind closed doors?"

Sally was asking out loud what I was thinking in silence. Just what does a closed door have to do with anything?

The next morning, I could not wait to get to school. I wanted to know why Yolanda's face had turned so red. I asked my teacher why girls should never take a boy into her bedroom and close the door.

"Ruben, you have older brothers. Ask one of them. When you are in Junior High School, you'll be better able to answer that question yourself. The one thing that is not lost on you is innocence.

"Ruben, I want you to write down these two words and look up the definition: vulgar and profanity. You can be vulgar without using profanity; you are too innocent to understand the difference."

I did what Mrs. Lee instructed me to do. During the afternoon vocabulary lesson, I looked up the words 'vulgar' and 'profanity.' Mrs. Lee was right; you can be vulgar without using profanity, but it is all relevant to one's upbringing. I never believed that Mrs. Lee would ask me if I looked up the words that I had asked her earlier that day! She took me by surprise. Mrs. Lee had me stand up at my desk and asked me to give my definition of vulgar and profanity; all I could feel was the blood escaping my veins.

"Mrs. Lee and classmates, my best interpretation of vulgar and profanity brings to mind something that my mother said. 'If words fail, pick up a thesaurus. That is always a more profound and everlasting way to express yourself without being vulgar or using profanity. You want your words to have meaning and an everlasting effect. Therefore, choose your words wisely.'"

"Ruben, I have met your mother, and she does not strike me as someone who speaks that way."

"Mrs. Lee, you met my babysitter, not my mother. Please save me the lecture. I am not ashamed of Mary either. I am telling you

Mary is not my mother, and you never met one of my parents. What is wrong with people like you?"

"Ruben, that is a derogatory remark, and I want you to go to the principal's office."

"Mrs. Lee, I said nothing derogatory. All I am doing is stating a fact. What is wrong with people like you? Mary is not my mother, and you turn it into a whole other issue." Mrs. Lee handed me the hall pass. As I was walking out the door, I could not get a handle on what just took place and why Mrs. Lee was so upset. One thing was for sure, Mrs. Barnum was going to set me straight.

It was a Friday, and it was becoming a habit that I was in the principal's office. I still see that little boy standing at the counter peering into Mrs. Barnum's office, asking himself, What have I done to deserve this trip to the principal's office? Mrs. Barnum took one look at me. "You, again?

"Ruben, you are one student that I have their parents' telephone number attached to my memory."

I did not have my right foot in Mrs. Barnum's office when she had someone on the telephone tell her that Mary was not in her office. It was Friday, and Mary was not there; I knew Mary would not be there at the shop. She was usually having her hair done next door at Cleo's beauty shop. Thursday, Friday, and Saturday were three of the busiest days of the week; Mary was not in the shop! There was indeed something wrong in paradise.

"Ruben, your mother is not at her place of business, so return to class. I'll take care of you on Monday."

I was up and out of Mrs. Barnum's office. That feeling of safety was short-lived. I made it back to the classroom. Mrs. Lee sent me to the back of the room and told me to stand in the corner with my face to the wall. I stood for the last fifteen minutes of class in the corner with my nose pressed against the corner of the walls. It was time to line up to leave school. Mrs. Lee pulled me to the side.

"Ruben, I want you to think about what you said."

"Mrs. Lee, I have no idea what you are referring to. I did not say anything wrong."

"Ruben, the term 'you people,' is a derogatory remark. It is the way that you emphasize 'you people'. I am Afro American, and some people may interpret that as a racial remark."

"Mrs. Lee, if I have offended you in any way, that was surely not my intention. What I meant by my statement is, what would it take to make people understand that Mary is not my mother. When I have overheard, you say I do not resemble Mary, Vivian, Maryann, and Sally, nor do I speak like them. So if I have offended you in my inability to make you understand these people are not my relatives, well, you are surely wrong. Again, I am sorry if I offended you. That is not the way my parents raised me. For me, to use a person's race in a derogatory manner would mean that my parents' teaching was in vain.

"My parents taught me that we are all in this world together and that we should respect one another. When we respect one another, it makes for a better understanding of the races. Now, will you let go of my arm?"

She walked me to the head of the line and walked us all out onto the street. She watched me walk across the street.

I waited with Mark Bartholomew, a classmate. He was a good friend of Richard. They were both at the top of the class academically. I wanted to align myself with them to achieve my goals. Mark was the older of his two brothers. Not only was he the oldest, but he was at the head of our class. If I had difficulty understanding the homework, he would help me out. Mark was born in Hawaii, and his parents were some of the most helpful people I have met in the neighborhood. Mark and I walked to his house to study. I was surprised to hear before I could come onto his property, I had to meet his parents.

When we arrived at the back of Mark's house, I had to wait in the back alleyway for his mother's okay to enter into the backyard.

"Ruben, don't worry; my parents have to meet all my friends before they can come onto our property. They want to know that we get along and if your parents know of your whereabouts."

"Mark, this reminds me of something my parents would do."

"Ruben, you said that as if your parents are deceased."

"They are, but I remember them. Mark, your mother wants to know if I would make a suitable friend."

We walked through the backyard up to the back door. Mark had me wait on the back porch to let his mother know he and his brother made it home safe. She came out back where I was and opened the screen door to get a good look at me.

I tilted my head forward.

"Good afternoon, Mrs. Bartholomew; it is a pleasure to meet you. I am Jack, no, Ruben. Pleased to meet you."

"Ruben, are you from the neighborhood?"

"Yes, Mrs. Bartholomew. I live about three blocks from here at the top of the hill and to the right. The third house on the left side of the street."

"Do your parents know you are here?"

"Mrs. Bartholomew, my parents are deceased. Mary is my babysitter, or governess for a better word, but yes."

"Ruben, Mark's father has one rule before Mark can play after school. He and his brother have to do the homework, and if his brother needs help, it is Mark's responsibility to help him. So if you want to stay and do your schoolwork, that is fine with me."

This was the first time I felt like I was in a real home since the death of my mother. The peace and tranquility to be surrounded by a genuine and loving family was something I had forgotten.

Mark's backyard was half a block with a park-like feel to it. Mark, his brother, and I sat on the picnic bench, doing our homework. It was the first time I buzzed through my homework just as fast as Mark did. It was history, math, and writing; each subject took no more than 20 minutes to complete.

It was the first time in a long time that I let my guard down and was engulfed in the learning process. There was no Gonzales, Gomez, or Rodriguez's around to distract me from my studies. It was indeed a unique experience to get rid of the chaos that I had become accustomed to since the death of my parents.

We finished up our homework and played football in the backyard. The sun was turning the California sky a gold color, signaling me it was time to leave. Besides, Mark's father would be home soon, and I did not want to wear out my welcome.

"Mark, it is time for me to go. I want to thank you and your family for their hospitality. Mark, thanks for the help with the homework."

Mrs. Bartholomew asked me to leave out of the front gate, but I preferred going out the back way. I found it interesting how two of my school friends separated by an alleyway, did not know each other. Mark lived on the Bellevue Avenue hillside, and Frank lived on the Clinton Ave. hillside. Here I am, walking down the alley on my way back to the dungeon.

I took my time getting back to the dungeon. I strolled, enjoying the spectacular show that the sky was putting on. It all came to an abrupt end when I put my foot in the front door of the house. Mary shouted vulgarity.

"Just where the hell have you been?" Her language did not surprise me; it was the fact that she was even here at 5:30 in the afternoon. In an instant, I was startled back into the reality of where I was.

"Why do you speak to me that way when you know I am not one of your kids! Why! How many times do I have to correct you, Mrs. Gonzales?"

Once I said that the living room became eerily silent. It was more of a deafening silence that came to my ears that had a bee ringing in it. It took me a few seconds to realize that Mary and I were not alone. Linda and Tom Proctor were sitting on the couch, and Tony was sitting adjacent to them. Linda, with an expression of total surprise, said, "Mary, I did not know that he spoke to you that way."

Mary replied, "Linda, I told you that these kids have no respect for their elders."

"Mary, that is not what I mean; he knows you are not his mother, but yet you still are holding him here!"

My heart sank to my feet; I could feel my face and ears turning red as if I was going to explode. I glanced over out of the corner of my eye, and I could still see that look on Mary's face. I knew that I had to do something because there would be consequences. I ran over to Mary, hugged her, kissed on the cheek, and left the room. As I was leaving, I felt I could cut the tension in the room with a knife.

The girls were in the back bedroom, whispering to each other. I had no interest in knowing what they were conversing about, so I turned around and walked out the door. Tony, Linda, and Tom went from the living room into Mary's bedroom to talk in private. I tossed my schoolbooks on my bed and placed my homework between the mattress and box springs for safekeeping for Monday morning.

Most of the time, there was an adult conversation going on in Mary's bedroom, it was meaningless, and this time was no exception. Not to say that I like to eavesdrop, but as my grandfather Joseph P. Kennedy would say, the bedroom is nowhere to have a private conversation.

The only thing that was coming out of the conversation that I could hear was, "How are you going to tell him?" As I was lying there, I was beginning to think to myself, who is him? This him person is sure important to the four of them. I could not understand for the life of me, who was him? This 'him' person piqued my interest. I wanted to meet this 'him' person. The rest of their conversation was meaningless to me.

Mary was making a big deal out of how she was going to tell him. "After what had happened to him."

Sally walked past my bedroom. I guess Mary had waved at Sally as she passed her bedroom. I could hear Mary tell Sally to go get him. The next thing I knew, Sally was in my room with a message: they want you.

"Who are 'they,' Sally?" Of course, I knew who they were. I just did not want Sally to know that I overheard what was being discussed in the next room.

*"Mom wants you!"*

*"Sally, she may be your mom, but she is not mine. So who wants me?"*

*"Oh! I'm telling what you said. Ruben, I'm telling."*

"So? Go ahead, tell. See if I care." I darted out of the bedroom before Sally could run and inform Mary what I had just said. I did not need Sally adding fuel to the fire that I had started before I walked in the door.

"Mother, you want me?"

"Yes, mijo!"

Without haste, I casually walked over and sat down next to Mary, taking and holding her hand as I was sitting on the bed where she was sitting. I sometimes wondered who the better actor was, my mother Marilyn or me? But either way, everyone in that room bought into the act except for Linda.

"Yes, mother?"

"I have something to tell you, and I don't want you to take it too hard — Paul threw me out of the shop." I sat there in silence, not knowing how to respond. It was not that I cared, but what did this have to do with me? I did not ask to be here! Mary knew how to manipulate my silence and use it to her advantage. How was she going to seize on this opportunity?

Speaking to Linda, Tom, and Tony, she said, "I told you, out of all the kids, Ruben was going to take it the hardest." From past experience, I knew that it was in my own best interest that I let Mary chalk this up as one for her. Besides, it's like Linda said, I better leave well enough alone.

However, I still did not understand why Paul was not letting Mary into the shop and what it had to do with me. I am not going to ask! I got up and walked out. There is something said for remaining silent when people believe that your world is falling apart.

The only one in that room that understood that I genuinely did not care was Linda. I don't know if it was her nursing skills that helped her to see my true feelings, or what I had said during one of our meetings. Either way, her facial expressions, and body language told me she was on my side. I was more afraid of what may happen to her and less concerned with my own well-being. I was passing through the frame of the door when Linda asked Sally and me if we had eaten.

"Oh! Linda, I have not. I don't know if Sally has."

"Well, Tom and I brought groceries for you."

"Thank you, Linda. I guess I'll have something later."

Linda and Tom had left, and it could not have been more than fifteen minutes later that Mary and Tony had gone too. I still had no clue what was going on. For that matter, it was none of my business or my concern. The one thing that upset me the most was when people think that I care when I do not. The only thing I cared about was me, myself, and I. If I wanted to know about JonJon or Caroline, all I had to do was watch the news on TV or read the newspaper. Why should I care that Paul wouldn't let Mary through the door of the shop? Unless it was a part of the ransom payment? *Oh well, Mary has gone. Let me see what there is to eat.*

I walked past the girls' bedroom. I noticed that they were still whispering to one another. The girls had a secret, and they were not going to share it with me. As I have done in the past, I ignored their whispering. I knew sooner or later they would let me in on it. The one good thing about these four was they never had an interesting thought or idea to add to a conversation. If I wanted to intrude on their whispering, I could play the concerned brother.

I made it to the refrigerator to see what there was to eat. I opened the refrigerator door, and the light came on, but all I could see was the back of the refrigerator. It was that same old sight, nothing but emptiness. What happened to the groceries Linda and Tom dropped off?

I tried to do what I've seen Charlie do: make a mustard and mayonnaise sandwich. But the mayonnaise made me gag, so that was totally out of the question. I closed the refrigerator door and walked a few yards into the girls' room and asked, "What happened to the food that Linda and Tom had brought?"

Yolanda was the spokesperson for the four of them.

"I guess while you were not looking, Tony and my mother cleaned out the refrigerator. It seems as if you are the only one who has not eaten."

"Well, Yolanda, it does take a humongous amount of food for your mother to maintain her 350-pound figure now, doesn't it?"

Yolanda was turning as red as a rooster, and it was time for this bird to hit the road. I was out the door like a bolt of lightning; there was no way she was going to scratch me with her fingernails the way I have seen her do to Danny. Oh no, not me.

I was out the door and decided to head down to the playground. It was Friday, and the gym was still open. I had raced down the three blocks to the gym. It was closing up as I was arriving; that was just my luck. I asked the head coach, "Why are you closing the gym early?"

"I have some personal business to attend to, so you are out of luck." Wouldn't you know it?

Like any kid, Friday went right into Monday. The only unusual thing that took place that weekend was Mary and Paul were nowhere to be found. Not that I was looking for them, but it would be nice to have some adult supervision. Little did I know that this was going to become the new norm!

Monday was the first time I saw Mary since last Friday evening. I did not understand how she could leave her daughter Yolanda all by herself. I realize that Mary is my caregiver, but the Rooster is her daughter. The other three girls were as on their own as I was. The more that the weeks rolled by, the less I saw of Mary and food was becoming scarcer. There were some peach trees in the next-door neighbor's backyard. I resorted to picking the fruit and eating them.

Things became so bleak that Mrs. Barnum called Vivian, Maryann, and I into her office to find out why we were coming to school hungry. It was the first and only time anyone in the school showed any compassion for us. Mrs. Barnum took us into her office and began to question us.

"Why are you coming to school without having breakfast?"

"Mrs. Barnum, I understand your question. What I do not understand is why the concern now? Is it because there are three of us missing too many days of school? And it is affecting the teachers' pay? Or perhaps your salary? Why now?"

"Your parents own their own business, and it is my understanding that it is doing quite well."

"Mrs. Barnum, how many times do I have to tell you? These people are not my parents!"

"Young man, at this point, I'm not interested in what you have to say." Maryann shook her head and smiled as Vivian leaped forward and said, "Paul had thrown Mary out of the shop, and they are in the process of getting a divorce."

"Why is it that this is the first I hear of this Vivian? Vivian, you should have notified your teacher the day that you learned of your parents' situation. Vivian that still doesn't tell me why you are not attending school regularly and why you are coming to school without breakfast and lunch money. I'll have to get in contact with your mother."

Mrs. Barnum had Mrs. Richards place our names on the free lunch program for the next two weeks. Now you can return to class. As we were leaving, I turned to Vivian, "You know we are going to get into trouble when we get to the house."

"Ruben, why are you so negative about everything?"

"Mrs. Barnum is going to call your mother and ask if she is divorcing Paul. Just because they told you they were getting a divorce doesn't mean it's true. So, that is what you girls were whispering about in your room? Your mother and father getting a divorce?"

"Why do you care?"

"I don't. I'm just asking, Vivian."

I returned to class; I did not bother to read the note Mrs. Barnum gave me to give to my teacher Mrs. Lee. I handed Mrs. Lee the note and returned to my seat. Just before lunch, she called me up to the front of the class. My stomach tied in a knot. "Mrs. Lee, what I have done now?"

"Ruben, I want to talk to you out in the hallway."

This is worse than I expected. I should have read the note. Mrs. Lee waited for me to walk through the door first, and she closed it behind her. I could not help but feel like this is going to be one heck of a big deal.

"Ruben, I understand that your parents are getting a divorce."

"What?"

"I understand your parents are getting a divorce."

"No! Not my parents. You mean my babysitter and her husband."

"Ruben, don't take it so hard."

"Mrs. Lee, as I told you before, Mary and Paul are not my parents. What is it going to take to make you understand that John F. Kennedy and Marilyn Monroe are my parents! Just what is it going to take? Can you tell me, and maybe I can get it through to you! I couldn't care less if Paul and Mary divorce! Why won't you listen to me? You people are all the same!"

"Ruben, return to the class."

"Mrs. Lee, the only good thing that is going to happen for me today is I'll have a free lunch; that's it."

I turned and opened the classroom door, leaving Mrs. Lee to ponder my questions. I spent the rest of the day thinking, *How long would I have to live my life in survival mode?*

Things went from bad to worse. There was no way I was going to walk back to the house without Vivian and Maryann. The two of them would have to enter the house before me to make sure everything was fine.

The closer I got to the front door of the house, the more I could hear their mother Mary screaming. "Why the hell did you S. of B. tell Mrs. Barnum I was getting a divorce? Just why the hell did you do that? Now I have to go to see her! She is threatening to have all of you removed from the house. Is that what you God damn people want?" There was no way I was risking walking through that door and having Mary speak to me that way. Not me!

"Where the hell is Ruben?"

I hightailed it out of there. I was going to the playgrounds to get away from all this chaos.

I was in the park playing carroms when Vivian and Yolanda came to get me. "Has your mother cooled down yet?" I asked them.

"Yes! She wants you to come home with us."

"Home! You mean the dungeon, don't you?"

"Look, let's go!"

"Okay, I'm going, but let's take a long way back."

Vivian looked at me, "I'm not the one in trouble here, you are. You should have stayed and taken your medicine the way I did."

"What medicine? I didn't know they were getting a divorce. You're the one who opened your mouth, not me."

"Anyway, the playground is closing. Let's go."

"Vivian, how lucky are we that your mother was home today of all days to answer the phone when Mrs. Barnum called?"

I walked into the door of the house; the first thing out of Mary's mouth was, "I don't want to be bothered with you, Ruben."

She went into her bedroom with Tony and closed the door. I could hear them talking. Mary had received a phone call. I don't know who the caller was. She and Tony were listening to every word the person on the other end of the line said. Mary hung up the phone and opened the door.

For the first time in two or three months, Mary went into the kitchen and prepared dinner. She finished making dinner and called us all to the kitchen for dinner. This was the first time all of us had sat down for dinner since Paul had thrown Mary out of the shop. I couldn't help but wonder why Mary was giving us dinner. *What is her alternative motive?* Mary was totally out of character, and it scared me. The feeling became even more frightful when she started seating us. There was no way on God's green earth that I was eating what she put in front of me! I'll starve first!

Tony said to Mary, "Mary, I did not know that he does not like to take food from your hands."

I said, "No! Tony, it's not that. She works too hard for us. So why should she have to serve me? Sally and Maryann are the youngest ones. They need her help; I don't. I am capable of serving myself."

I served myself dinner and sat down at the table. I always had an uncomfortable feeling when I sat down to dinner with the Gonzales's, especially with the adults. I never understood how these people wanted me to sit down and have dinner with them. For me, it was always an unnatural feeling. To be sitting across from them, and the change of cuisine was hard to get used to. I often asked myself, Why am I here? Who is the beneficiary of me being here? Why!

It was one of those times that I could not pretend that everything was fine. I got up from the table, taking my dish and fork with me, and washed them.

I turned to walk away from the kitchen sink. Mary told me to do the rest of the dishes.

"Me! Do the dishes? Me! Look, you have your daughter Yolanda and three other girls to do the dishes. If you want someone to do the dishes, tell them to do it or do it yourself. I'm not here to clean up after you people!"

I walked out of the kitchen. Yolanda came after me, "Just who do you think you are?"

"Exactly who I am, why? I'm not asking to be here. Remember that if you do not like it, you can always call my grandmother and tell her to come to pick me up."

"Ruben, I hate you!"

"Yolanda, at one time or another, I have heard those same words from everyone in this house. So what's new? When you have something important to say to me, ask for my permission first. Then and only then may you speak to me."

I never understood why Yolanda and her siblings liked to confront me when they were well aware that they were no match for me. I was beginning to think that I was the only one that understood what Mary was doing. How was she going to use this dinner to her advantage? The only way to know is to let this scenario play out.

The next morning, Mary was upset and extremely nervous. She made Vivian, Maryann, and I breakfast. Now I had to watch her closer. Mary never cared if we had eaten before going to school, why now? As they say, there's something rotten in Denmark.

We sat down for breakfast, and Mary started getting dressed. She called a taxi. The four of us got into the cab, and Mary told the driver Rosemont Elementary School. It was already 9:30 AM, of course, so we were late. Mary was never on time for anything. We pulled in front of the school and walked into the main office where Mrs. Barnum, the school principal, was waiting for us.

We went into Mrs. Barnum's office. We exchanged pleasantries, which I had never done before with Mrs. Barnum. I turned on the charm, being as polite as I could. Mrs. Barnum went so far as to mention how courteous I was. I was able to impress Mrs. Barnum with my pleasantries; Mary far surpassed me.

Mrs. Barnum started the conversation by asking Mary if she was getting a divorce and how she was coping.

"Mrs. Barnum, I gave Paul 25 years of my life and 10 kids. 22 years out of the 25 I spent building the TV and radio repair shop, Gonzales and Sons. Now I am not even able to enter into my own business that I helped create, where I spent the last 22 years working and slaving, trying to keep a roof over my kids' heads. I was lucky if Paul let me buy food for my kids, much less purchase a pair of decent shoes. Just look at how he has left me. Without a source of income or any way to feed my children."

By this time, Mary was crying. I could see the tears rolling down her cheeks; she was clutching her chest and sobbing. Wow! Mary had manipulated Mrs. Barnum to her side.

I could see that Mary had spun her web and had Mrs. Barnum wrapped around her little finger. Mrs. Barnum had bought into Mary's malarkey. I had to bite my bottom lip to keep from laughing. I wanted to let Mrs. Barnum in on Mary's secret. If you worked out the numbers, and believe me I have, Mary did not have the shop for 22 years.

Paul opened up the shop after my kidnapping, and if you add in the year 1955, it does not add up to 22 years in business.

"Mrs. Gonzales, how are you supporting your children and paying your bills?"

"I saved some money over the years, but that is about to run out."

Mary started sobbing heavier and gasping for air as if she was having a heart attack.

"Is the children's father giving you any support at all?"

"No, Mrs. Barnum, he is not. I do not know how I am going to feed my kids, much less where their next meal is coming from."

"If you have time, Mary, I would like you to return here next week. I am going to call a social worker for you; they'll help you sort out what benefits you may be entitled to. If you don't mind,

I would also like to call in the school district psychologist. I want to help you with Vivian, Ruben, and Maryann to cope with this divorce before they start getting into trouble. I want you to know I'm going to do everything I can so that you stay together as a family unit." By this time, there was not a dry eye in the office. Mary even had me feeling sorry for her.

Mrs. Barnum had Mrs. Hilton call a taxi for Mary. "Mary, I want you to come back here next week at the same time at 9:30 AM."

I looked out the window of the office. I could see the yellow cab pulling up in front of the school. By this time, Mary was clutching my hand as if I was her savior. I tried pulling away, but Mary held on.

Mary started pulling me out the door of Mrs. Barnum's office. Vivian and Maryann followed right behind us. As Mary was pulling me, her back to Mrs. Barnum, I noticed that same satisfied look on Mary's face. That look that she always had when she pulled something over on the police, judges, doctors, and lawyers. I even witnessed her pulling one over on the Federal Bureau of Investigation. Mary knew that she had gotten away with manipulating Mrs. Barnum into doing what she wanted.

We walked with Mary to the cab. I turned to walk back into the school. I could hear Mary's laughter as she entered the cab. Out of the three of us, Maryann was furious with Mary's action.

"Ruben, how could Mrs. Barnum be so stupid?"

"Maryann, as long as you keep going along with this charade that I am your brother, Mrs. Gonzales is always going to get away with her nonsense. I have been trying to let people know what is going on with us, but all you do is say, 'I don't know.' The only reason why your mother gets away with what she does is because of the simple fact that you back her up. You could have told Mrs. Barnum that Mary is not your mother. Instead, you and Vivian sat in Mrs. Barnum's office in silence."

I asked Vivian, "Vivian, what is a social worker? And what do they do? How is she going to help your mother?"

"Hell, I don't know!"

"I was asking a question you don't have to be rude."

I walked to class and gave Mrs. Lee the note that Mrs. Barnum had given me for being tardy for class. I spent the rest of the morning, thinking about where Mary came up with all the malarkey she was feeding Mrs. Barnum. It had to come from either my Uncle Robert F. Kennedy or my Uncle Sen. Edward Kennedy. That's what was being discussed on the telephone yesterday when Mary and Tony were in her bedroom. That was why she closed the door and told us not to make any noise. The rest of the school day was pretty much uneventful, and I never did find out what a social worker did.

I did not see Mary until the following week. She was having a meeting with Mrs. Barnum and a social worker in the school office.

Mrs. Barnum introduced us to the social worker; her name was Mrs. Starr. She was from the welfare office.

Mary's face was turning pale white! "What do you mean she is from the Los Angeles County Welfare office? I disapprove of people who receive welfare. I have worked for the past 22 years in my own business, and now you people want me to go on welfare." Mary started turning on the tears.

Mrs. Starr began to console Mary.

"I am here to help you in any way I can. Mrs. Gonzales, how do you intend to support your children if Paul is not around and refuses to support them? These programs are in place to help people in society to return to full employment again. There is no shame with the government helping you do that. If you do not accept government assistance, how are you planning on supporting yourself and children?"

"I don't know, Mrs. Starr. If Paul has it his way, he'll leave me without a home for my children and me. My attorney has just informed me that Paul wants the business and our house. The home that I worked for the past 22 years. The problem is we were in a common-law marriage."

I could see the look on Mrs. Starr's face; she was in shock. Mary was playing the innocent victim to a T, and Mrs. Starr was taking it all in. Just like the rest of the officials that Mary came across. Vivian, Maryann, and I sat in silence watching Mary spin her web the way a mother tarantula would do, and she's going in for the kill.

"Mary, may I ask your children a question or two?"

"Go ahead, Mrs. Starr."

Before Mrs. Starr could utter a word, Mrs. Barnum glared and snarled at us.

"I want you children to be polite with your answers, do you understand me?"

I spoke up first. "Mrs. Barnum, my mother raised me to be courteous and respectful, but respect is earned, not given. For me to be polite depends on the question."

Mrs. Starr said to Mrs. Barnum, "How do you want these children to be polite when their father is leaving their home?"

Maryann spoke next, "Paul is not my father, Mrs. Starr; I do not care if he goes or stays. The man is a pig!"

It was Vivian's turn. "That man is not my father."

Just then, Mrs. Barnum looked directly at me and told me not to say a word.

I answered anyway. "Mrs. Barnum, I have for the past three years said to you that Paul is not a thing to me."

"Ruben, that is quite enough."

"Mrs. Barnum, Mrs. Starr is here to get to know and interview us, and your opinion does not count! Do you understand me?"

Mrs. Barnum said, "Mrs. Starr, I informed you that these children are undisciplined and ill-mannered."

I said, "Mrs. Barnum, the three of us have told you the truth, and all you have done is degrade us. That purple hair dye has seeped into your brain."

Mrs. Starr came to my defense before Mrs. Barnum could utter another word. "Mrs. Barnum, these children are going through enough without you adding to it."

She turned to the three of us. "What did the three of you have for dinner last night?"

Vivian answered, "I had a balogna and cheese sandwich."

"Did you have milk with your dinner, Vivian?"

"No, I did not."

"Did you have breakfast this morning before arriving here?"

"No, I did not."

"Maryann, what did you have for dinner last night?" She wasn't paying attention. Mrs. Starr asked again, "Maryann, what did you have for dinner last night?"

Maryann had no respect for authority, and I cannot say I blame her; one has to be careful when questioning her.

"I don't know where Vivian got the bologna and cheese from, but it did not come from our refrigerator." Mrs. Starr was startled by Maryann's answer.

"Maryann, you mean to tell me you did not have dinner last night!"

"No, I had peanut butter and jelly sandwich on old stale bread."

"Ruben, what did you have for dinner?"

"Mrs. Starr, I do not recall if I had dinner last night."

"So, it's pretty rough on you since your father left."

"No, since they killed him. He did look for me and almost found me."

Mrs. Barnum became infuriated. "Ruben, this is not the time to talk about this. Answer her questions!"

Maryann chimed in, "When are you people going to listen to him!"

Mrs. Starr said, "Mrs. Barnum, this family is going through a life-changing experience; I understand Maryann's attitude. This family is in crisis, and Mrs. Gonzales is too ashamed to accept public assistance."

She turned to me. "Ruben, I am going to ask you one more question. Did you have breakfast this morning?"

"Mrs. Starr, this morning was no different from any other morning in the Gonzales household. No, I did not have breakfast this morning or any other morning."

"Mrs. Gonzales, I would like to have the school psychologist see your children if that is fine with you."

"Mrs. Barnum, I never married Paul. I prefer to be called Mrs. Gomez."

"Mrs. Gomez, would you sign this slip giving the school psychologist the right to speak with your children?"

Mary leaned over the desk that was separating us from Mrs. Barnum and signed the permission slip.

Mrs. Starr said to Mary, "Mrs. Gomez, for me to help you and your children, I need you to sign these forms."

"Mrs. Starr, what are these forms going to be used for?"

"These forms are to start the process to receive public assistance for you and your children. I am going to give you an appointment for next week; here is a list of things that you'll need to bring with you. You require immediate assistance. Whatever documents you do not have, we'll discuss that during your next interview. Here is my card. The telephone number and address are on it. Try to keep the appointment time and date." I still had no clue what social service is or does.

The recess bell started ringing as Vivian, Maryann, and I came out of the main office. There was no way we would make it to class. We decided the best thing to do was make our way to the cafeteria. To say Maryann was flustered was a mild way of putting it. She was pissed off.

"Ruben, why is it no one listens to us? Every time you try to tell somebody what's going on, they all take my mother's side, and that pisses me off."

"Maryann, I understand that you are upset, but do you have to be so vulgar? And now you bring Mrs. Barnum and Mrs. Starr's race into it. Maryann, all they are trying to do is help you."

"Ruben, if it was not for you, I would not be here."

"Maryann, I am not the one that is telling you to say you are my sister. On more than one occasion, I've told you not to say we are relatives in any way, shape, or form. So don't blame me for what you're paid to say.

"Just tell the truth and stop taking the money that my family is giving you to say you are my sister." We made it to the school cafeteria. I pick up a piece of cinnamon toast and a small carton of milk. The cashier asked me for 15 cents.

"Mrs. Barnum said that she added my name to the lunch list."

"She said she did. But your name is not here. 15 cents, please."
Wouldn't you know it, a classmate was standing right behind me.
Bogart!

"Ruben, you don't know you have to pay for your snack at recess? Lunch is free; how did you manage that?"

"Bogart, I let you have it once don't make me have to do it twice."

"Here's 15 cents, you cheapskate."

"Thanks, Bogart!"

"Ruben, wait up, we'll sit together. So Mr. Rockefeller, what happened? No money?"

"Look, Bogart, you lent me two bits; that doesn't entitle you to question me."

"I hear your parents are divorcing."

"What of it, and what's it to you, Bogey? Bogart, we have 10 minutes to eat, so let's eat and drink our milk."

"Ok, white bread, let's eat."

"Bogart, you and Kathy Brown have to come to some kind of consensus. She calls me honky, and you call me white bread. What's up with that?"

"Ruben, you're lucky there are no crackers on the table, so white bread has to do for now."

"Bogart, just what is that supposed to mean?"

"Ruben, sometimes I wonder just where you come from. What la-la-land did you live in?"

"Bogart, let's get back to class before recess ends, and we are late."

Bogart and I finished up our snack and hurried out of the cafeteria onto the schoolyard. Mrs. Lee came out onto the yard to escort the class into the building and into our classroom.

She closed the door behind her as she always did. Mrs. Lee looked around the room, taking her usual headcount of how many children may or may not be late returning from recess. I felt as if I was always singled out by whatever authority was around.

"Ruben! Where were you this morning, and why were you an hour and a half late getting to school?"

"Mrs. Lee, I was in Mrs. Barnum's office this morning. I was not late."

"Where is your permission slip?"

"It's on your desk, right where it's supposed to be."

"I don't see it."

"Maybe because you didn't look!" The skinny tyrant picked up the permission slip and read it and did not attempt to apologize. If this morning was any indication of what the rest of the day or week was going to be like. I didn't need it!

Wednesday came. It was after lunch, so it had to be about 1:00 PM when a hall monitor entered the classroom with a note. He did not get out of the classroom when Mrs. Lee called me up to her desk. It never ceases to amaze me that when the hall monitors from the main office came into the classroom, it was for me. Mrs. Lee stood up in front of the class.

"Ruben, take this hall pass and go to the main office." I looked down at my desk in dismay. I pushed my chair back and returned the chair to its rightful place. I walked up to the front of the class and took the note.

"Mrs. Lee, you could have been just a little more discrete. You could have called me up to your desk. Did you have to stand up? Are you aware that 90% of the time, the accusation I'm accused of doing I did not do? Do you have to humiliate me this way? You act as if you are employed by the Gestapo." Wouldn't you know it, Mrs. Lee jotted down my comment on the note and sent me out the door!

As I was walking to the office, I could feel my stomach knotting up. It was getting tighter. What am I being accused of now? I entered the main office doorway. To my surprise, Vivian and Maryann were sitting in the office with blank looks on their faces.

"Ruben, what did you do now?"

"Why me? Vivian, I did not do anything!" I walked up to the counter and placed my hall pass in the basket. The school secretary informed me that Mrs. Barnum would be with us momentarily, so have a seat. The only place to sit was between Vivian and Maryann.

"Ruben, why are we here?"

"Vivian, what makes you believe I have all the answers to your questions? I have no idea why we are here, but one of us has done something."

Mrs. Barnum's office door opened, and out came Mrs. Barnum. "I would like you three to go into my office and have a seat."

I was the first of the three of us to enter into Mrs. Burnum's office. Vivian and Maryann followed in after me.

"Maryann, please close the door behind you."

I asked her, "Mrs. Barnum, why are we here?"

"First, I'd like to ask the three of you, how are you coping with your parents' divorce? I do not want the three of you to speak all at once. Ruben, you go first."

"Mrs. Barnum, are we going to go through this again? I have explained to you in the past that Mary and Paul are not my parents. Pres. Kennedy and Marilyn Monroe are my parents. Why do you think I care what happens to Mary and Paul?"

"Vivian, what do you think about your parents' divorce?"

"Mrs. Barnum, I do not care if they divorce or not."

Maryann's turn to answer. "Mrs. Barnum, I have a question for you. Why is it you buy into Mary's B.S.? Why? Do your children have a habit of lying to you? Let me tell you something, Ruben is telling you the truth. Mary and Paul are not our parents!"

"I see that you children are under a great deal of pressure. I want you to go to the nurse's office."

We got up out of our chairs and virtually walked right into the nurse's office. The school nurse and this other woman were waiting for us. Mrs. Barnum decided to join us.

"Hello, children. I'm from the Board of Education. I'm a psychologist. Mrs. Barnum invited me here because she was concerned about your well-being.

"I'm here to find out how I can help you cope with your parents' divorce. I want to ask you, Vivian, how are you dealing with your parents' divorce?"

"They're not my parents, so why should I care if they divorce or not."

"Ruben, what about you?"

"Look! These people are not my parents. I wish people would take the time to listen to me. President John F. Kennedy and Marilyn Monroe are my parents."

"Maryann, you are the youngest of the three by two years. Am I correct?"

"Yes, you are."

"Vivian was born in 1954, Ruben in 1955, and you in 1956."

"Yes!"

Maryann had issues with authority. Questioning her was not the best way to deal with her.

"Since you are the youngest, how do you feel about your parents' divorce?"

She replied, "Look, Missy! What's up with all the questions? If I answer you, are you going to do something about it?"

Mrs. Barnum took one long step forward and ended up right in Maryann's face. Maryann stepped up, leaning forward right back at Mrs. Barnum. I stepped back out of Maryann's way. I knew what was coming next!

"Look you purple-haired bitch! Get out of my face!"

The psychologist tried to intervene. "Mrs. Barnum, this is a normal reaction that children display when their parents are getting a divorce."

Maryann shouted at the therapist. "What! Look, Ruben has told the truth from the first moment he saw you. Mary put a fake birth certificate on the counter in the main office the first time Ruben started school here." Mrs. Barnum refused to believe what she was hearing. Maryann continued, "What is it going to take for you people to understand that he is not Mary's son?"

Maryann's actions were as rude as her words. She hopped off the doctor's couch and shouted, "You fuckin' people make me sick! I'll see you later. I'm going back to class."

Vivian and I rushed after her. All I heard from that point was, "Mrs. Barnum, that is the kind of reaction I was expecting. Do not be alarmed." Maryann was down the hallway, and Vivian and I were five steps behind her. The girl was gone.

Thank God it was the end of the school day. Three o'clock arrived in the nick of time. It made no sense to return to class. The moment I opened the door, the bell rang.

"Ruben, take your seat."

"Mrs. Lee, after the humiliation and embarrassment that I just went through, I'm leaving!"

"Ruben, you are leaving the same time your classmates are leaving."

"Mrs. Lee, the profanities and expletives that Maryann used to express herself was embarrassing, were not warranted, and I'm ashamed for her. Her facts, although true, don't justify name-calling."

For the first time, I saw a genuine display of concern for me on Mrs. Lee's face.

I continued. "Mrs. Lee, the way that Maryann carried on, all I want to do is get out of here. I have enough problems without Maryann adding to them."

Mrs. Lee walked us out of the school building and out on to the sidewalk. "Ruben, I'd like to talk to you. What Maryann did has no bearing on you; it is her way of coping with the instability at home."

"Mrs. Lee, I wish that were true, but the fact of the matter is that is just Maryann's attitude. Mrs. Lee, I'll see you later."

I dreaded walking back to the house. The closer I got to the house, the heavier my feet were becoming, and my legs did not want to move. What kind of backlash was Maryann going to bring me? What kind of retribution is Maryann's mother going to bestow upon me for not stopping Maryann's vulgar mouth? There is going to be cane to pay for not stopping her!

Why me, Lord! Why me! I know darn well if I would ever get a police officer, lawyer, or a judge to hear what I have to say, they would tell me that I partook in this crime. It was not that I condone what these people were doing; it was just that I had to survive — it was all about survival, that's all! I had to go along to get along. The closer I got to the front door of the house, the clearer Mrs. Gonzales's yelling was becoming. She was calling Maryann everything but a child of God.

"I want to know just what the hell you were thinking; you told the school psychologist who he is! Just what the hell are you planning to do if the police come knocking on the door! Maryann, do you know if the cops ever do something about this, we'll all go to jail! Do you understand me! I hope a car hits you. Not just hurts you but kills you! Maryann, you could have ruined everything with your big mouth. If you don't learn to keep your mouth shut, you don't know how I'm going to leave you!"

Should I go in the door or take off to the park? Either way, sooner or later, I would have to hear Mrs. Gonzales's big mouth.

I mustered up the courage to walk in the door. The first thing I heard out of Mrs. Gonzales's mouth was, "Where the hell have you been? What took you so long to get home?"

Mrs. Gonzales had never been one to display any self-respect; it would have been nice if she did. However, she preferred to use vulgar and demeaning language to get her point across.

I answered, "Look, you are nothing to me, so don't talk to me that way! Do you understand me, Mrs. Gonzalez! I am not one of your kids to have to put up with your foul mouth. You talk to your kids that way, not me, and I mean it."

"I want to know why you did not come to my defense when Maryann was talking about me."

"How do you want me to defend you when it goes against the truth? The only thing she did was clarify the reality of the situation that I am not your son! If you can't control Maryann, what makes you believe I can or even want to! I am not asking to be here, nor do I want to be here, so what's your problem? If you're going to keep me here, it's like my Grandmother Rose said, do it on your own accord! Do not turn to me for help!"

This voice came out nowhere. "Mary, I did not know he spoke to you that way!"

"Tony, where did you come from out of nowhere?"

"I was sitting on the couch the whole time."

"Oh! I was not even aware that you were there, not that it would have made a difference."

"Yes, Ruby, you were on a roll."

Mrs. Gonzales said to Tony, "He is in one of his moods. Let's go. I don't like to be around him when he is in a bad mood."

Tony and Mary were out the door, and I left right after they did. Whenever I tried setting the record straight, there was always a repercussion. I decided to take a walk around the lake to clear my head and figure out what Mary's next move would be. She was not going to let me get away with not defending her, and the school psychologist was no help. Talking to the psychologist solidified Mary's stronghold on my kidnapping and assured her that this was a *perfect crime*.

I was walking around the lake, taking in the sights and sounds. I thought, *If this is the beginning of 1968, what will the end have in store for me?* I still had the hope that Linda and Tom would take me away from this chaos. If Tom's kids were in Dallas, Texas, and Linda is from the same place, maybe that's where I'll end up. When hopes and foresight come into play, forethought wins out. The future did look promising right now. Just what am I going to do until Linda makes her decision?

Mary and Paul's divorce court date had finally arrived, and there was still no decision made about where I would be staying. Vivian, Maryann, and I, along with Mary, took a cab to the Los Angeles Superior Court. I had not seen Paul in six months, not that I was missing much.

Mary's attorney John Mikus was there also. He was a tall, bald-headed man with a potbelly. He dressed in a cheap gray suit without a white T-shirt under his white shirt. He was not a very impressive man, not one that I would picture to fit the mold of an attorney. He reminded me of some of my hobo acquaintances who could not make it back into the mainstream of society after the 1929 stock market crash. Mr. Mikus at least could have had his suit pressed or a shoeshine, but this man didn't even do that. How could he stand in front of the judge looking this way? His white shirt looks as if he had spilled his breakfast on it.

I overheard Paul's lawyer and Mary's lawyer John Mikus discussing Yolanda and Danny, his older son and daughter. Paul felt that Danny and Yolanda were too old, and he should not have to support them. He suggested Danny work to support himself while attending school, and Mary should support Yolanda. The consensus was that Danny and Yolanda would stay with their mother.

Vivian, Maryann, and I would have to take the stand and answer some questions the judge was going to ask us. Sally's fate had already been settled; she was only eight years old and should stay with Mary.

Being in a courtroom had become old hat to me. Mary's four older sons were either in jail or juvenile hall. They had a hard time keeping their hands off other people's property. So I was able to witness firsthand that you do not speak to a Judge unless he asked you a direct question. It was like being in my grandmother Rose Kennedy's house: you converse with an adult on your own accord only if they speak to you first.

It is a standard procedure that all parties involved in the case have to be in court by nine o'clock. The two attorneys notified the court clerk that all parties were present. The court clerk did his usual thing, All rise! Court is now in session. The judge sized up the courtroom, and the court clerk called the first case: Gonzales v Gomez. Mary and Paul, accompanied by the lawyers, went through the two swinging gates, Mary on the right side and Paul on the left of the entrance. Vivian, Maryann, and I were told to wait outside the courtroom in the hall.

One by one, we were called into the courtroom. Vivian went in; first, the door closed behind her. I peered through the crack in the door. She was asked to take the witness stand, which she did. I could barely hear what the judge was asking her. He asked her a few questions, and she had this terrified look on her face. He asked her which parent she would like to live with.

"Your Honor, I don't know."

"Well, young lady, do your parents treat you well?"

"No, your Honor, it's not that."

"Well, if that is not the reason, what is it?"

"Your Honor, Paul and Mary are not my parents, so how can I choose which parent to live with?"

Before I heard the answer, the Marshall was at the door. He pushed open the door, "Son, I want you to stop eavesdropping.

You'll have your turn on the witness stand." He went back inside with Maryann.

I could see Vivian was still on the stand, and she was still scared! Maryann was next on the witness stand. I walked to the water fountain to get a drink of water. When I came back, I took a peek into the courtroom, and Maryann was in the witness chair. I did not try to eavesdrop again; I was too afraid of the Marshall coming out and scolding me. The Marshall did not give me time to take my seat on the bench when he came out to get me.

I was instructed to take my turn on the witness stand. I was told to raise my right hand and swear to tell the truth, nothing but the truth, and the whole truth so help me God.

"Counselors, whose child is this? Which one is the parent?"

"Your Honor, they are Ruben's parents."

The judge turned and asked me which parent I preferred to live with.

"Your Honor, these people are not my parents! I want to go home if I may."

"Son, I know that it is hard for a son to choose between his mother and his father, but again I have to ask you which parent do you want to live with?"

"Your Honor, these people are not my parents; how many times do I have to repeat myself? I just told you the truth and nothing but the truth. I am not their son. These people are not my parents!" At that moment, Mary's attorney John Mikus stood up and said, "Your Honor, I would like a recess."

I continued. "But, your Honor, I was taken from my mother by force."

Mary's attorney interrupted again. "Your Honor, again, I ask you for a recess."

"Counselor, I could understand one child saying that these people are not their parents. But three? There is something wrong here. I'm going to grant you the recess."

Mikus rushed us out of the courtroom and down the hall away from the courtroom. We were face to face. I was looking up at him, and he down at me.

343

"Just what do you mean they forcibly have taken you from your mother?"

"Just what I said, I was kidnapped by force from my mother."

"If that is the case, just who are your parents?"

"President John F. Kennedy and Marilyn Monroe are my mother and father."

He turned to Mary. "Mary, these kids do not resemble you or Paul in the slightest. Ruben looks Caucasian. Look at his red hair and freckled face and light skin. Look at his arms. They have freckled from his short-sleeve shirt right down to his fingers and knuckles. Just look at him for God's sake!

"Cleo tried to tell me what was going on with this child and you, but I thought it was a petty rivalry, nothing more. I am going to ask the Judge for a continuance, you and Paul figure out what you are going to do."

We left the courthouse and got into a taxi. Mary gave the driver the address and did not say another word. The cab driver took Temple Street to Burlington Street; he made a right turn onto Burlington.

"Mrs., there is no 510; you have to be on the other side of Wilshire Boulevard."

"Yes, there is an address 510 N. Burlington Street; most people can't find it. Drive around the bend and up the hill. Take a right at the next corner. At the end of the street, make a right; the next block is Burlington."

We pulled in front of the house. I was not aware that Mary could move as fast as she did. By the time Vivian, Maryann, and I were in the house, Mary was frantically making phone calls. One call after another until finally, someone answered her.

"I want all you kids to get the hell out of my room and close the door behind you."

I can only assume that she had talked to one of my relatives. I don't know which one. When she finally opened the door, she emerged from her room. Mary was in a foul mood, and her language was just as offensive.

"Why did you godforsaken S.O.B'S tell the judge that you were not my kids? Why! The three of you want to see me in jail! Is that what you want? To see me go to jail? Vivian, you're the oldest here. You know darn well, Paul is not your father. You were supposed to tell the judge that you want to stay here with me! Maryann, that goes for you too! Richard, Robert, Charlie, and Gilbert, including Danny, all know what to do and say when they get in front of a judge, but not you two, why?"

It never fails; the first words out of Vivian's mouth were, "What about him?"

I said, "Vivian, what about me?"

"Ruben, you said the same thing to the judge."

"That's true, but I do not want to be here; you do! I could never figure out what I have to do with these people. What is it going to take to make them understand that I'm not going to go along with their crime?"

Vivian asked her mother, "What about Ruben? He told the judge that you guys were not his mother and father! What about him?"

"Damn you, if I go to jail, I'm taking you with me, do you understand me, Vivian? I'm taking all you sons of bitches with me. I told you before, no one is going to believe who he is if we all stick together, but no, you and Maryann have to open your big mouth. Just what the hell is wrong with the two of you?"

"I don't know!"

"You are going against our plans when we do not stick together. Who is going to believe that we have President Kennedy and Marilyn Monroe's son in this dump! Who! I want to know! You godforsaken people make me sick!" Vivian was stunned and speechless.

Maryann, on the other hand, said, "You're lucky I did not do worse. If you think I'm going to let you get away with talking to me that way, you are out of your mind. I want you to know when the time comes, I'm telling the truth! For now, Ruben is holding on to your apron strings, but I can't say that about tomorrow. Remember, you still have not given me what you promised, and I want it!"

I chimed in. "Mrs. Gonzales, I have seen my stepmother Jacqueline, Aristotle Onassis, my grandmother Rose Kennedy, and two of my uncles giving you money not to talk about who my parents are. You are getting pennies for trying to make people believe I am your son. Maryann is truthful that she is involved in this for money. Maryann, you are paid pennies for your involvement. That million dollars that you are waiting for is never going to come. I know my grandmother; all you have to do is take a look around you. If she can do this to me, just what do you think she is going to do to you?

"You people disgust me; I'm out of here."

I walked over to Mark's house to find out what the school home-work assignment was for the day. As I was walking to his house, someone walked up behind me and tapped me on the shoulder.

"Hey Ruben, didn't you hear me calling you?"

"No, I did not, Anthony."

"Where are you going?"

"I'm on my way to a friend's house to get the homework assignment for school."

Anthony was a kid in the neighborhood that was persona non-grata. I did not associate with him, and I did not want to.

"What friend are you going to see?" he asked.

"Anthony, what are you doing, writing a book?"

"Yes, I am," he replied sarcastically.

"Well, leave this chapter out!" I turned back around and started back on my journey to Mark's house. I walked up the flight of stairs and knocked on the door, but there was no answer. I cannot say that I was disappointed that he was not home. So much for a study partner. This is the third time I've been here, and he has not answered the door.

As I was walking back to the Gonzales dungeon, Anthony was working on his father's white four-door Ford station wagon.

"Hey, Ruben! How about giving me a hand?"

"Anthony, you know in life there is no such thing as a free ride. What is in it for me?"

"I'll provide you with lunch."

"Lunch! More like money works better for me, Anthony, that way I'll be able to pick and choose what I want to have for lunch."

"Ok, give me a hand."

"Anthony, you are a Gonzales family friend. Why don't you ask Danny to help you?"

"Well, I just thought since you're here now, you might help me."

"Look, Anthony, if you are going to pay me, I'll work with you, but helping you is definitely out of the question. I am not your friend." Anthony's father came out from under the car.

"Hey, Dad, why did you come up here?"

"I had to meet the person you are talking to. Oh, you're talking to this smart-aleck kid."

"Excuse me, sir; I'll have you know I am not a smart-alecky kid. I'm a kid that is smart enough to know that I do not want to engage in the tyranny of slave labor. The American Revolutionary war brought those days to an end in 1783. What is at hand is the almighty dollar. You know, In God We Trust, that's what I'm fighting to gain."

"You're not just a smart-aleck but a smart one too! Give me a hand, and I'll teach you a trade that you can use for the rest of your life."

"Instead of giving me a piece of fish to eat for a day, you're going to teach me to fish so that I could eat for the rest of my life? Is that what you are saying?"

"Yes, exactly!"

Thus began my fourth career: learning the mechanics of an automobile.

I stayed around until the sun went down, and Carl was true to his word. He had spicy Italian ham on hero bread with lettuce, tomato, onion, and provolone cheese. It was the first time in an exceedingly long time that I have had spicy Italian ham. It brought back memories of being in New York with my mother and father.

As I was eating my sandwich, I could feel my eyes start to well up. It was one of those moments that I allowed myself the luxury of remembering my parents. I looked out at the reddish-golden sun setting on the horizon, thinking, *Where would I be if they were here with me?* I turned to look at Anthony and his father. It was time to go.

"Bye, Ruben! Come back to help us tomorrow."

"All right. After school, I'll be here."

I arrived back at the house, and it was the same routine. This time, the refrigerator light did not come on when I opened the refrigerator door. The electric company turned off the electricity. I walked into my bedroom, gathered up my history book, walked to the corner, and sat down under the streetlight to try and memorize the chapter.

As I finished up the school assignment, I glanced up to see Yolanda, Vivian, Maryann, and Sally coming down the stairs from old man John's house. When the cabinets and fridge were bare, that is where the Gonzales went for a free meal. On occasion, I have been to visit there myself, but I always ran errands for him in return for eats, as old man John called it.

Old man John portrayed himself as someone who was stuck back in the '20s, how he made $.15 an hour waiting tables in Chicago and San Francisco. The façade that he was displaying did not fool me. I knew that he came from the past, and someday I would expose him for what he was. In no time, the Gonzales kids were all around me.

"What are you doing sitting here all by your lonesome, freckles?"

"Well, it looks like your mother forgot to pay the light bill again. Sally, you can dispense with the name-calling. So, what did old man John give you? A cup of coffee and beans with mush to pick you up?

"When are you people going to learn that that man is a miserable human being! Who is he to watch me for my family? You never noticed from his front porch window you could look right down into the house. Do you think that is a coincidence, or did my family send him? Is it your lack of intelligence or your willingness to play into his charade that keeps you people talking to him?"

"Ruben, you think everybody in the neighborhood is trying to make your life miserable."

"Yolanda, I call it the way it is. I'm telling you John gave up his family to be here to watch me. In time, his own family is going to say to him all they want is his money and not him. If you choose to believe me, that is fine with me, but if you don't, shame on you."

The girls walked off when the light went off in their brains.

"Ruben, come with us; all the lights are off in the house."

"I'm not ready to go yet!"

"Yes, but come with us, we are afraid to go inside."

"Oh! You are scared of the dark. And how is that my problem? You girls are not decent people, and now you need me?

"Wow! That's interesting! And I guess you think I should get up and go with you inside. Here's a newsflash, bring yourselves up here and sit down because I'm not going in the house without electricity, so cop yourself a piece of sidewalk."

We stayed sitting under the streetlight until it was time for bed, and besides, these people had suffered long enough.

Mary was spending more and more time with Tony, leaving us alone without any adult supervision, leaving us to fend for ourselves. The one thing I had in my favor was that I enjoyed rising at the crack of dawn. I was never late for school and was old enough to take care of myself.

I spent that spring attending school and learning to work on cars whenever Anthony and Carl needed a hand. Anthony and I were becoming known as the backyard mechanics of the neighborhood. We did the occasional tune-up, brake job, and oil change. We split the labor cost in half, which was not a bad deal for an after-school job.

To my surprise, Tom showed up before I left for school.

"Jack, I want you to get in the car."

"Tom, where are we going?"

"Jack, get in the car. I am going to take you to meet some people."

"What people?"

"Jack, get in the car."

"Okay, I'm going."

He drove us to the Farmers Market on Third Avenue and Fairfax Avenue. He stopped at Du-pairs restaurant to have breakfast. I noticed that Tom was continually checking his watch for the time.

"Tom, where are we going?"

"I'm taking you to meet some of your mother and father's friends."

"Really! Which ones?"

"Jack, you'll see when we arrive at our destination." We finished up our breakfast and walked around the Farmers Market. It was around 10:00 when Tom said it was time to go. We got into Tom's Green Ford Galaxy and headed down Fairfax and made a right hand turn onto Wilshire Boulevard. We made it all the way to the Beverly Hills golf course. He made a right-hand turn and came to a stop at the gate.

"My name is Thomas Richard Proctor, and I have to meet with Frank Sinatra and Dean Martin. I have a scheduled appointment with them to leave Jack here."

"Thomas, I am sorry, but Mr. Sinatra and Mr. Martin have not arrived as of yet. Since you are not a member, I cannot let you in. If you would like to come back later, I'll be glad to let you in when they arrive."

"I see my name on the roster, so why can't we wait here?"

"Your name is listed here, but the only way I can let you in is if your parties are here. Since they are not, I suggest you come back when they are."

I could see that Tom was flustered and extremely upset. He was hesitant to turn the car around and drive off. I asked him, "Tom, will you be bringing me back here again?"

"Jack, I do not know! They were supposed to be waiting for you. They knew that I was coming; I made the arrangements with both of them."

"Tom, maybe you have the time of day wrong or the wrong day?"

"No! This is not a meeting they should have missed or arrived late to."

The man at the gate said, "Sir, you're going to have to back up. Turn around and come back later, please."

It was the first time that someone was not intimidated by Tom and did not let him do what he wanted. Tom backed up and drove off.

"Jack, it's too late for me to drop you off at school, so I'm going to leave you back at Mary's place. I want you to keep this to yourself. I am going to see what I can do for you later. I do not want you to mention this to anyone that I brought you here."

"Tom, I do not have anyone to tell. Mary tells people that she has me by her apron strings, but in fact, all I am doing is trying to survive. I only let Mary know what I think she should know, and that's usually nothing of importance. Besides, I haven't seen her in about three weeks; she's busy babysitting Tony, not that it's any of my business what she does or what she doesn't do."

Tom drove to the other side of Echo Park Lake, where he dropped me off.

"Why are you leaving me here?"

"Jack, do you have any idea how many people are paid to watch you? Do you believe that old man John Rudley is your friend?"

"No! I know he is not my friend, and I know what's going on. You would have to be a blind man not to see what's going on in the neighborhood."

"I've always told Mary you're not stupid." Tom turned on Laguna Ave from Echo Park, made a quick U-turn, and let me out behind the church.

"I want you to walk Laguna up, and I'm going to play pinochle in the park."

I did what Tom told me to do. It was not a long walk, just awkward. I hated walking down that steep alley; I was always afraid of falling and rolling into the middle of Echo Park Ave. into oncoming traffic. I had to think about how I was going to get over the fear of walking down this alley. My dad said to think about the weather if all else fails you.

The downside to living in California, especially Los Angeles, was that there was no seasonal change. I never knew if it was summer or winter or spring; the seasons rolled into one.

I made it down the alley and back to the house. It was the same feeling of emptiness as I entered the house; it never felt like home. I always thought that I was an unwanted stranger when I came into this house, and today was no exception.

The telephone was ringing as I walked into the house. I answered it. Anthony was on the other end; he asked me if I would come over and help him work on a car.

"Anthony, I expect to be paid for my work, am I making myself clear? I want half of the labor, exactly half. Is that understood?"

"Yes! I do!"

"Okay. I have to change my clothes. Give me 15 minutes, and I'll be there."

One of the neighbors had an old '59 black Ford four-door Mercury. It was running rough and burning the usual amount of gas. Anthony had already driven the car and figured out what repairs were needed. The only thing I had to do was make a checklist for parts and cost.

I took a pad and started jotting down the make and model of the car and how many cylinders it was. We went to the parts house on Glendale Boulevard. We purchased spark plugs, points, condenser, distributor cap, wires, oil, and a filter; I wrote *major tune-up* at the top of the list.

We arrived back to the alley behind Anthony's house. I took the eight spark plugs out of their boxes. I took the Motor manual repair book and started reading how to gap the spark plugs. It was easy enough. In the meantime, Anthony was removing the spark plugs from the engine. I began to think, He could do all of this himself why does he need me?

He was having trouble with two spark plugs, one in the far back right side of the engine and one on the left side. He gave me a ratchet with an extension and told me to remove the spark plugs from the back closer to the firewall. Then it hit me. His father's and his hands were too clumsy and big to get into tight spaces.

It took us all of three hours to do the tune-up and change the oil. We finished before the sun went down. Anthony wrote out the work order for what we had done to the car. My concern was the labor cost. He charged $35 for our labor. I looked at that and asked him, "What are you doing? Anthony, don't you think it would be easier if you made it for $34 or $36 for labor? That way, you don't cheat me out of my $.50. It is easier to divide. Remember, I want to be there when you get the money, that way I get my half."

The older man came down the stairs from the apartment on the corner. He paid Anthony the $35.00 for labor. I was in total shock because $17.50 was my part of the labor cost, and that is what Anthony gave me. I had one problem: where do I put the money? If I take it back to the Gonzalez household, someone is going to go through my pants like they do everything else and take it. The only thing these people know how to do is steal, lie, and cheat. Just have to find a place to hide it. I took my proceeds and headed back to the dungeon. What is that old saying? The devil never sleeps. When I got there, Mary was there waiting for me.

"Where the heck have you been!"

It would be nice if that were the exact words she used, but I am going to dispense with the other two. "Please don't talk to me like that; I don't like it. I'm not one of your kids for you to speak to me that way."

Mary left it at that.

For the next week or two, Mary was here in the house when I went to school and returned from school, and even when I came back from playing. I guess she was trying to be a decent human being to her daughter Yolanda, but for me, I had no use for Mary. She was just there taking up space.

It was Sunday when Mary started to badger me, causing me to leave, making me feel like my presence was annoying her when I was around. One afternoon, when I arrived back at the house from school, Tony and Mary were there. I walked into the house, and Mary told me, "I want to talk to you."

I don't know what set her off, but she wasn't too happy.

"I hear you are telling the neighbors that I am not your mother."

So what is new!

"I'm going to tell you something, young man. You see this birth certificate? I am not going to let you leave this house until you reach the age of 21, according to the date on this certificate and not the age that you have. Do I make myself clear?"

"It's funny, but this is not the first time you're telling me this, and what happened to me in school and the courtroom, you think I don't know that already! Are you finished, Mrs. Gonzales? Or is it Gomez?

"You know that was a rhetorical question, Mrs. Gonzales. Oh! Maybe you don't know the meaning of rhetorical, sorry. I know how to eat with some of the most famous and high-class people in the world. I didn't ask you if you knew what fork to use with your salad, what I asked was do you know the definition of rhetorical. I'll see you later."

I took off to old man John's place. John offered me a cup of coffee, rice, and beans.

"John, why do you prepare black beans and rice in the same pot?"

"Ruben, just one less dish to do."

I hung out there for two hours, waiting for Mary to leave the house. To my surprise, she was still at the house when I got back. She had told the girls about the argument earlier in the afternoon, and of course, Tony backed her up. Yolanda was the only one of the four girls that spoke up.

"Ruben, if you don't stop talking to my mother the way that you do, you're going to have to leave."

"Yolanda, that is fine with me. I'm not asking to be here in the first place." I turned and walked away and went into my room. It was not like Mary to be here; there had to be another reason why she was still here.

I closed the door and went to bed. It was easy for me to fall asleep, and then if I did fall asleep, I would sleep for four or five hours at the most.

The next morning, I got up and was getting ready for school. It was totally out of Mary's character, but she was preparing breakfast for us before leaving for school. She always did for Paul but never for us kids.

This morning, she was extra nice. I figured maybe she was turning over a new leaf. I left for school. When I returned from school, she started badgering me and telling me to go out and play. This badgering went on for three days. On the third day, she asked me, "Why the heck are you not at the park playing?"

I could not have been there for 10 minutes when the phone rang. Mary began to insult me, so I figured she was just in a bad mood. I high tailed it out of there, and I went to Echo Park to play.

It takes about five minutes to walk to the park. It was just another beautiful California midafternoon. I walked down Bellevue Avenue through the walkway. As I was walking, taking in the scenery, I noticed two big houses, one to the right of me and one to the left of me. How beautiful a day it was; warm sunshine, everything was looking fresh.

I walked into the playground and started playing carroms with one of the kids from the neighborhood. I won the first game. "Look, boys! Mother Nature is calling and have to answer the call; I'm going to the boys' room."

I walked to the park and turned to the right to go into the rec center when I noticed there was a car parked just behind the stop sign on Echo Park Avenue.

I stood there looking and staring, and my blood ran cold. I could not believe what I saw. In a moment, I started running to the corner and shouting, "Uncle Bobby, Aunt Ethel, Kathy! It's me, Jack."

Just then, the car started rolling towards the stop sign. "Uncle Bobby! It's me, Jack." I knew that I was moving, but it felt as if I was standing still or stuck in slow motion. Again, I shouted, "Uncle Bobby, Aunt Ethel! It's me, Jack." The car stopped. I could hear Kathy shouting from the backseat, "It's Jack, that's Jack, stop! It's Jack!"

I made it to the corner, and my Uncle Robert F. Kennedy and my Aunt Ethel were speeding away going north on the Hollywood Freeway. As they were passing me, Kathy and I locked eyes. She was screaming, "Jack!" We were simultaneously shouting each other's names. Kathy! Jack! Kathy! Jack!

I cried, "Kathy! Kathy! Kathy! Make him stop! Please make my uncle stop. Make him stop, Kathy. I want to go home!" Everything happened in an instant, not a moment, but an instant. I watched them going up the Hollywood Freeway.

I walked back to the rec center; the game room door was open. The director and his assistant were standing there. He was about 6'2, blonde hair, blue eyes, with a shaggy hair cut. He was wearing a white T-shirt, gym shorts, and white tube socks. He was leaning against a built-in storage case with his arms folded across his chest. Standing tall as he looked down at me, I felt defenseless.

If not for my curly hair standing up, I would not have been any higher than the middle of his chest.

"So you're the one that the Kennedy's come to see. I would not have believed it if I did not see it with my own eyes! You're the one!" He reached for the comb that I had turned in as collateral to play carroms. When you check something out to play with, you have to leave something of value. It is returned to you when you give the item back.

"Here, take this and leave the playground. If you continue to come here and socialize around the other children, you can get one of them killed. The way that Sen. Robert F. Kennedy went through that stop sign is proof that there's something wrong here.

"Please, before you get an innocent bystander killed, don't come back! If I see you around here again, I'm going to throw you out."

"If you believe that, why don't you call the police? Tell them what you saw here today, see what they tell you!"

"The police are going to tell you to leave it alone. I don't want you here, and I don't want to see you here again." It seemed the only people that I ever met had a yellow streak running down their back. When will it all end? My family has taken everything from me, and now they have taken this from me, too, my sanctuary. The place that I come to forget my troubles. The place I find true sportsmanship, where the playing field is level, has been taken away from me too. What am I going to do now! I grabbed my comb from his hand and headed out the same way I came in.

I stood in the doorway, looking out at the lake across the street, thinking, *What do I do now?* I looked to the left, I looked to the right, I looked straight ahead, and asked myself again, *What do I do now?* If I went back to the house, Mary was going to question me, and I don't want her to take pleasure in my suffering.

I started moving, but I didn't feel as if I was controlling my movements. It was best if I walked across the street and sat staring at the water. I could not believe what had taken place moments ago!

As I was sitting in my favorite spot, gazing out on the water, I began to think. *How much more is my family going to take from me? When are they going to leave me alone?* I sat in silence, taking in the atmosphere, thinking, *I have to come up with some plan to get the hell out of here.* I sat there for a good two hours trying to think of some way to get out, but it just didn't come. It was getting late, and I decided it was time to go. I took my time walking back to the house, Lo and behold, Mary was there.

Screaming and yelling started the moment I walked in the door.

"Where the hell have you been?"

"I did what you told me to do. I went to the park."

"Oh yeah, I forgot that I sent you out to play. So did you see anyone interesting, or did you do anything exciting?"

"No, I just played a couple of games of carroms and strolled around the park a bit; that was it."

"Mijo, are you sure you didn't see anybody?"

"Oh yes, the criminals that you and Richard associate with, that's whom I saw."

"What do you mean by that?"

"You said that Dicky used to bring his criminal friends over here, and you would entertain them. So, you know what criminal element I'm referring to."

She laughed! "You know, mijo. You're right. I know."

Mary started preparing dinner, and no sooner than she finished, Tony came over. She called me for dinner around 8:30. The whole gang was at the table; Yolanda, Vivian, Maryann, and Sally. One by one, they asked me what I was doing in the park if I met any interesting people.

"No! I didn't meet anybody of any substance; just a bunch of gangsters I encountered, that's all."

Tony asked me a strange question.

"Ruby, why don't you eat what's in front of you? You refused to eat in the seat that you are assigned to eat at."

"Tony, I have my reasons. I don't like to eat off the same plate or use the same fork or knife more than twice on the same day. I prefer not to eat because you never know what one might put in your food. So, it is better to be safe instead of sorry."

As I was sitting at the table, that same feeling started to come over me. Just what the heck was I doing sitting here with these people! From the moment that I arrived here, I knew that these people and this place was not for me.

"I'm exhausted; I'm going to my room."

"Mijo, you have not finished your dinner!"

Since when did she care if I had dinner? Much less finish it!

"I'm exhausted; I'll finish in the morning."

I got up from the table. I could barely make it from the kitchen to the bedroom. I flopped down on the bed and laid there motionless. My body was not able to move or reluctant to move. I tried to fall asleep, but I could hear Tony and Mary talking in the next bedroom. It was almost as if I was in the room with them.

I could feel myself falling in and out of sleep. I was in a state of hypnagogic. I was aware of my surroundings, but unable to move. I knew that my body was lying on the bed, but I could see myself moving from my room to Mary's room.

A sense of peace and tranquility came over me, and my room filled with white light. A light that I have not seen since my mother had died. The white light engulfed the room; it was even spewing out into the next room. I was standing there looking down at my body and could hear Mary tell Tony that I left the light on in my room and had fallen asleep.

The room became brighter, and it filled with the fragrance of fresh white roses. The kind of scent that comes after a spring rain. I could feel a faint burst of air. Here I was, standing between my body that was lying on the bed. And this lovely, soft-spoken lady wearing a long white dress with a veil over her head and a rosary in her hands. The hum of her voice put me at ease.

"Don't worry, son; everything is going to be okay. I am not here to do harm, and no harm will come to you; everything is going to be fine. You have a long journey ahead of you; it will become difficult and trying, but you will make it to the end. I am here to give you the blessing of God, the Father. In the name of the Father, the Son, and the Holy Spirit, may God be upon you. Don't be afraid, my son."

I fell asleep, but this was a peaceful sleep. All I could see were beautiful, colorful hills as far as the eye could see. There were flowers on both sides of me; I ran through them without a care in the world.

I was free of any torment or hardship; it was a peace that I never felt before. I could see a tall man off in the field. The closer I came to him, the more familiar he became. He was wearing a dark navy blue suit with a powder blue shirt with a blue, red, and white tie. The closer we were getting to each other, the clearer his image became.

"Dad is that you!" He put out his hands, picking me up.

"Son, it's you! It's you!

"Son, I want you to help your Uncle Robert. Someone is going to kill him tonight."

"I know, Dad. The Virgin of Fatima told me. She said not to worry, that everything would be okay."

"Son, I need your help."

"Dad, I am little and unable to help him. I already told Mary that he'd win the election, but he would not make it to the end of the race.

"I am genuinely sorry, but I am unable to help you."

"Son, you are the only one whom I can come to for help. I'm sorry for what my brothers and sisters are doing to you, but I need your help."

I was still feeling hypnagogia. I felt the moonlight gently caressing my face. The keen awareness of my surroundings, but again, I was not able to move. I was able to hear Mary and Tony still talking in Mary's bedroom. "We have to tell him what is going on." I could hear and feel the chaos that was going on. I heard the sound of ambulances and police cars racing up and down the street in the far distance. Mary and Tony still saying, "We have to tell him, we have to tell him."

I had my face to the window when I heard a voice in the next room saying, "I'm going to tell Jack now."

My back was to the bedroom door when someone pushed it open, and all the noise and lights and chaos came rushing in. I turned to look at who it was standing in the doorway. I could see the figure. It was Paul. "They just killed your Uncle Robert F. Kennedy! He's dead!"

"Paul, I already know. Let me go back to sleep! You did not have to wake me up to tell me that." I turned back towards the window, looking up for a moment, and fell fast asleep. Waking the next morning was just another day in paradise.

Until I tried putting on my pants. It seemed that overnight, I grew two feet. I went from a boy to a man. I could barely button my pants button. I couldn't wear shorts to school because it wasn't allowed. Just what was I going to do? The pants legs were right in the middle of my shin bones of both legs. I tried on a long-sleeved shirt, but it came to the center of my arms. Things were going from bad to worse; even my underwear was too tight. I looked for a clean pair of socks, pulled my pants as high as they would go, and decided it was just better to carry on with the day. There was nothing I could do about it.

When I walked into the kitchen, Mary looked at me. "What the hell happened to you last night? You went to bed one person and woke up another. How did you get so tall overnight?"

I did not want to throw fuel on the fire, so I said it was Santa Clause's elves who did it.

"I got up out of bed, and my pants and shirt would not fit anymore. I have to go to school." I opened the front door and could still feel chaos in the air, but all in all, it was a beautiful morning. Especially the fact that I had grown about two feet overnight.

I was feeling sentimental about my father. I recalled my father once saying, "There is light at the end of the tunnel. We just can't see it, but it's there." I had that one bastion of hope left: that Linda and Tom were going to somehow take me from this mystery that surrounded me.

I did the usual thing, I went back and forth to school, still scrounging around for my next meal. Selling bottles, newspapers, shining shoes, and now learning to work on cars seemed like a means to an end. My grandpa Joe Kennedy was right; the old bear was right. It was easy to make money; the trick is how to hold on to it. This 'easy come easy go' was not working for me, but for now, it's all I had.

It's funny, but I did not understand what my uncle's death had to do with the Gonzales's, Gomez's, or Rodriguez's, but everybody disappeared. I didn't know if I was hiding from all of them, or they were hiding from me. It seemed like I was alone, or maybe I didn't care. I didn't see Mary anymore until one day, Anthony told me, "Your mother's looking for you."

"Anthony, that is the most impossible thing that could happen! My mother is no longer on this Earth. If you are referring to Mary as my mother, I have to inform you that she is not my mother. I would prefer that you say 'Mrs. Gonzales is looking for you,' and not my mother."

It happened that Anthony and I were on our way to the auto parts house and saw Tom, Tony, and Mary driving by us in Tom's car. Anthony decided to follow them to see where they were going. "Anthony, this is not a good idea. Leave Mary to her own business, and let's go on with our own."

They pulled in front of Bearagons Restaurant on Sunset Boulevard and got out of the car and went inside. We parked and followed them inside. I could see the expression on Mary's face; she was not too pleased. "What are you two doing following us?" I laughed it off.

"Me following you? Someone has to keep an eye on you. I never know when you're going to strike, so it is better to prepare for it."

Tom asked Anthony for a favor. "Would you help me with Linda? I want to borrow your car to follow her."

"Sure, Tom, why not."

Mary had a big grin on her face. "I told you Anthony was your man! He'll help you, don't worry, and he'll keep his mouth shut. I want you two to go home and wait for us." We left the restaurant, went on to the Part house to purchase what we needed, and left. Anthony was eager to please Tom.

Anthony gave Tom his car. Tom and I went to the California hospital in Downtown L.A. to pick Linda up. I didn't know that Tom and Linda were having marital problems. I got in the back of the car, and Linda sat in the front seat. The first thing she asked Tom was, "When did you get this car?"

"I bought it. Linda, you know the IRS is looking for you?"

"What do you mean, Tom? You're supposed to take care of our taxes. I have given you my paycheck from the moment we were married. That is the agreement that you made with my parents and me. I would give you my check, and you would take care of the taxes."

"No, Linda. I take care of my taxes, and you take care of yours." Tom drove to Melrose and Harbor Ave. and dropped Linda off in front of her apartment. I watched her walk up the stairs as Tom was driving away. I had no clue that Tom and Linda's marriage was in that much trouble. I heard whispers in the house. This was the first time I had seen the severity of their problems. This had Mary written all over it. I could sense where this was going. I knew that I had to do something about it, but what, I didn't know.

# THE TABLOID

**AFTER LINDA'S UNTIMELY DEMISE,** I was once again alone. Now indeed, left alone. Mary had moved in with Tony, leaving the girls and me to fend for ourselves. I had heard my mother Marilyn say how our past comes back to haunt us. I figured that I was too young to have a history. I should have followed her advice and looked up that old cliché: your past will haunt you.

The summer was winding down; there was a wedding to attend. Josephina asked Yolanda and Savani to be a bridesmaid at her upcoming nuptials.

I happened to stop by Savani's house, where Yolanda and Josephina were visiting. They were talking girl-talk about who's what, I don't know. Josephine preferred to be called my her nickname Josie. I always felt that Josie fit her fondness for her. She She was just a charming girl. She was still that same girl that I met in the shop that Paul and Mary owned. I walked into Savani's dining room, and there Josie was, just as cute as pie!

"Hey, Josie, how have you been? Long time no see. I hear you're going to marry Henry?"

"Yes, I am. Ruben, if you help out with the wedding, I'll give you an invite."

"That sounds good to me. I'll have to work to dance at your nuptials."

"I need you to stop by my mother's house and help with some chairs and take them to the Columbus Hall on Olympic."

"Fine, where does your mother live?"

"I'll come and get you."

"Okay."

Josie had a strange look on her face. "Hey! You guys know Thomas Richard Proctor? Is he the same guy that killed his wife, Linda?"

"Yes, Josie, he is. How did you find out he killed his wife, Josie?"

"It was on the Channel 7 Eyewitness News at 11:00 PM. Ruben, how did you get the news?"

"Mary told me, so she thinks."

"You mean your mother."

"Not you too, Josie! Not you, too! Josie, I'm surprised that you did not remember Tom. He and his ex-wife Lois lived behind the shop at about the same time as your family did."

"Yes, but I did not know him back then."

"Josie, I met you before I met Rodriguez's family. I cannot believe that you would forget me so soon. Josie, I have to go now. Let me know what time you want me to help you. Just don't be late! I'm a stickler for punctuality. I'll see you later."

Josie returned around 2:30 PM. She drove us down the Hollywood Freeway and got off at the Melrose exit and made that same left turn onto Melrose. I did not give it very much thought at the time, but looking back, Linda and Josie's mother lived no further than three blocks from each other. Josie made a left turn off of Melrose and made a left turn into a driveway. I got out of the car and started loading chairs from the garage into a truck.

As we were finishing up, I heard this woman's voice coming from behind the back side window of the house. She was screaming, "Get that son of a bitch out of here now! I do not want him in my house!

Josie, why the hell did you bring him here!"

Josie answered, "Why don't you want him to help?"

"Because he knows damn well about who his parents are and he is not doing a thing about it. I want him the hell out of my house."

"Mother, it is not his fault; he's only a child, and you don't have the right to treat him that way!"

"Remember where he comes from!"

"I'll get him out of here, but I invited him to my wedding, and he is going. I am not going to uninvite him just to please you; besides, I need his help."

I turned to Josie, "Josie, that is what I go through when you insisted on calling Mary, my mother. You and your mother know that President Kennedy and Marilyn Monroe are my parents. So please refrain yourself from referring to Mrs. Gonzales as my mother."

I finished loading up the chairs in the back of the pick-up truck. We were out of there like a flash of light. Josie drove to Columbus Hall in Downtown LA.

We pulled in front of the hall and parked and started unloading the chairs. This area is considered a bad part of town. WOW! I had some insight to its reputation. Mary's oldest son Dicky was always getting his backside handed to him in this neighborhood. To hear him tell it, it took three guys to put a knife in his back, but for some reason, I knew he was talking horse manure. With Richard, it was always three guys knocking him around, even when Minta, his wife, left him with a black eye on more than one occasion. I could see the handmade marks on his face of a small woman who punched his lights out.

I just had to check this area out to see what I was in for. I wanted to see if my instincts were correct. There was no surprise here; Dicky's a plucky and should have never socialized down here. No wonder those cholos sent Dicky packing every time he came down here. These guys are stand-up guys, my kind of people. They demanded respect, and Dicky's lack of the code did not suit the neighborhood. As in every community, there are good and bad people; this neighborhood is no different.

The moment Josie came to a full stop, I was out of the car and unloading chairs. It was one flight of stairs up, and we finished unloading the chairs in no time. I had a look around. The place had more of a night club atmosphere compared to a dining hall, but still, it felt comfortable here. I noticed that there was no pretentiousness in this group of people that were helping out. They seemed to know one another and worked together as a community to help Josie and Henry's wedding go off without a hitch. I knew that I was witnessing a family of true unity. The anticipation I was feeling was overwhelming with excitement. I was going to attend my first real wedding on my own. I just knew it was going to be a blast!

I arrived back to my stomping ground and immediately started to prepare for the wedding. I took my white plaid shirt and my black and gray trousers from the closet and set up the iron and ironing board. I took a towel and moistened it, and proceeded to iron a straight line into my trousers and white shirt. I retrieved my shoeshine box and put a high-gloss shine on black dress shoes. The shine had such a high gloss that I could see my pearly white teeth reflecting from the shoe.

There was one more thing to do, and that was to get a haircut without the shave. Believe it or not, I would have got a shave on this day if I would have needed one. Today, I made up my mind. I was going to make my chin stand out just as my father does on the half-dollar piece.

I took a page out of my mother, Marilyn Monroe's playbook. I put some man's Brut Cologne in the bathwater in case I pass gas at the wedding. I even made sure that I washed twice behind the ears before disembarking from the bathtub. I dried off and went to work on my hair.

I had the hairstylist give me a hair trim and style. I did not want him to take out the curls in my hair. I left my hair with a little moisture in it so that the curls would not lay flat when I applied the Yardley English Lavender Brilliantine hair pomade to my hair. I shook my hair, gentle enough to remove some of the dampness, and spread a small amount of Yardley between my fingers and ran them through my hair. I was careful not to add too much Yardley to my hair, leaving the curls intact. Trying to keep the Yardley and Brut fragrance from overwhelming each other. I had enough insight into the world of style, thanks to the President of the United States. And a movie star to prepare for a night on the town. I figured, why not use it to my advantage!

I continued dressing, putting on new undergarments, right down to my silk black knee-high socks. I pulled on my trousers, put a black belt through loops of the pants, and put on the white shirt. I had lined the inseam of my trousers on both sides of the legs so that the pleat crease came out perfect, right on up to the ironed black and red tie.

I was ready for the 10-minute ride to Immaculate Conception Parish Church, where Josie and Henry were getting married. On the way to the church, I began to ponder the predicament that I was in. What are the odds that Josie would end up in the Rodriguez family? Susana (Chita's sister) was married to Henry's older brother Xavier, and Chita married Charlie, Mary's son, from Paul. Is this divine province, or is this what happens when you are involved in a crime? Either way, I'm not supposed to be here, but I'm here, and I'll have to hope for the best outcome. I pulled around the corner from the Church and parked.

I waited in the car for an extra 10 minutes to make sure the church was full of onlookers. Now was my moment to enter that church. I had had my legs flat to the floorboard so as not to wrinkle my pants and shirt. I walked around the corner up the stairs to the main church doors. I placed my left hand on the left door handle, my right hand on the right handle, taking a firm grip of both doors handles. I took one step back and used my weight to sling open the two doors simultaneously, making sure that both doors would swing wide open.

As I opened the door. I heard the guests in the church gasp as I stood there for a minute or two, letting the sunlight deluge the church with a ray of colors; everyone turned to look to see who was entering the church. All eyes were on me. I walked in one foot in front of the other, stopping in the middle of the church while all eyes were still on me. I took my seat. I heard whispering. "Who is that?" Of course, I am the 'that' causing all the whispering. I sat in the pew, feeling a bit awkward as if I did something wrong. Without thinking, I had broken church protocol. There are only two times that someone is to enter the church through the main doors, and this afternoon was not my time.

Henry took his place at the front of the church. I was trying to get settled. I looked up at him; I felt as if his eyes were piercing me.

The wedding march started playing, and Josie came walking down the aisle, looking as beautiful as ever.

The wedding ceremony went off without a hitch. Someone in the wedding party handed me some rice before I could make it out the door. I was standing outside the church when the bride and groom came out of the main center doors. I threw the rice high in the air, making sure the rice did not hit the happy couple in the face. I was standing there asking myself, just what was I doing here? In this place, that does not want me here. Feeling out of place, I walked to the car and drove to Knights of Columbus Hall on Washington Blvd.

Again, I had second thoughts about what I was doing here; *am I doing the right thing by being here?* I got out of the car, took a few steps, and leaned against the front fender of the vehicle. As I was leaning against the car, I began weighing my options. Do I go inside to the party or leave? I was feeling totally out of my element as if I did not belong here and was not wanted here as well, but what would be the consequences if I leave? Every time I go against the prevailing winds, I am either told I think I am too good to socialize with the group or who do I think I am. Heck! I am going inside. I am too hung up on my thoughts.

As I was trying to enter the hall, two bouncers stopped me. "Hey, wedo, what are you doing here?"

The other one said, "You don't look like you belong here!"

These were not the kind of guys you gave any lip service to.

"I know Josie. She invited me here."

"Wedo, you think I believe you? Where is your invitation?"

"I did not receive one."

"Ay Wedo, do you know what happens to white boys like you when they try to crash a wedding party in this neighborhood?"

That was not a question!

Just as I was turning to leave, Josie waved to the bouncers to let me in.

Once I was inside the hall, the dilemma arose: where was I to be seated? The bride had a problem with the seating arrangement; she was not sure which age group I fit in. Does she seat me with the adults or the children? The age that I had been before arriving into the evil clutches of Mary or the one that God himself allowed me the privilege of having?

"Jack, have a seat where you feel most comfortable."

She turned and walked away.

I decided on my own accord that I would best be served if I mingle with the guests. I did what came naturally to me from the moment of my kidnapping. I had lost all trust in people offering me something to eat or drink. Staying at Mary's taught me two things: sleep with one eye open and do not eat what is placed in front of you.

I settled on sitting at the young adults' table; they are finicky eaters. I'm sure that I'll find someone to trade meals with me, ensuring it is voodoo free. The meal was nothing to write home and tell mom about, but on the other hand, the Rum Cake was outstanding.

One of the guests at the table started engaging me in conversation. "You're the one that came through the front door of the church."

"Yes, I am."

"What made you enter through the front of the church?"

"I just did it!"

"You did it, without giving any thought to your actions."

"Yes! That happens to be what I did!"

"Are you aware of how upset the bride's mother was when you did that?"

"Did what?"

"Entered through the middle doors of the church."

"Is there some significance behind coming through the main doors before or after a wedding ceremony that I should be aware of? If I have done anything to offend anyone, I do apologize for my actions. I assure you, it was unintentional."

"What, you are not a Roman Catholic, Jack?"

"Yes, I am. It keeps me from walking in Cain's sandals. How would you like to dance? This is a wedding, after all."

I was lucky that she accepted my offer to dance. We danced around the floor as if I knew what I was doing.

"Jack, did Yolanda teach you to dance?"

"No! It was my parents that taught me to dance, but mostly my mother. My dad had a back problem from World War II and was unable to dance for any long duration of time; however, he did his best to teach me a step or two." The music came to an end; I thanked her for the dance as we were walking back to the table.

"Jack, most boys leave me on the dance floor, but you brought me back to the table. Why?"

"This one you have to blame on my father. He said never to leave a lady standing in the middle of the dance floor. It's proper etiquette to return her to her seat when the music stops if you ever want to dance with her again."

I just thought to myself, I'll walk her back to our table; thank her for the dance, and say 'it was nice meeting you, Grace.' I did not believe she would notice a difference.

I headed to the men's room, where I encountered more static about my race.

"Hey, Wedo! How was your dance with one of our women out on the dance floor? What's up with that? Who do you think you are! Who invited you to our party?"

"Gentlemen, I am here at the invitation of Josie and Harry Carillo, the bride and groom. Yolanda is a bridesmaid at the wedding."

"That's right. She is your sister."

"No, she is the girl that has a childhood crush on Josie's brother Larry."

"That may be, but you're her brother."

"No, her mother took care of me after my parents died."

Just about the time I was going to get my backside handed to me, the bridegroom walked in, saving me from a fight. "Jack, what's going on?"

"I was just leaving Henry. Congratulations, again."

"Little Kennedy, thank you for coming to the wedding. Josie and I want you to know that you are our special guest here tonight. I'm surprised that you enjoyed yourself the way that you have here tonight. I hope that we can have you over to our home sometime in the future for dinner."

"Henry, thank you for inviting me here today, and I am looking forward to seeing you before your departure to Vietnam. Later, dude."

I was out of there like a flash and on my way back to my own neighborhood. There was no need to stay around the wedding reception if I wanted to make it back in one piece. I never understood why people were offended by reddish blackish hair, flushed red freckled cheeks, and white skin.

I was back at Mary's house. As I was walking up the walkway, I noticed that the living room light was on. I opened the front door; no one was there. After Paul's departure, that was becoming commonplace. The one thing out of place is this pigsty was a few old and current tabloids lying on the coffee table. They were laying out as if someone wanted me to pick one up and read it, or at least look over the front pages. The only time I would waste my time reading one of these tabloid newspapers is if I was in line at the grocery store, and that's because it's free to read. Without giving it a second thought, I made it to my bedroom and crashed.

I woke up a few hours later, still dressed to the nines. My legs were hanging off the bed, and my shoes were still on my feet. I started undressing and hung up my shirt and pants. As I removed them, I tucked my socks into my shoes, making sure that there were no garments lying on the floor. It's what my mother instilled in me, making sure there is nothing on the floor that would cause me to trip and fall. It was too early in the morning to be up, and I was still too exhausted to function to top things off. Feeling a bit incoherent, it would be better if I get more shut-eye.

I laid back down, falling into a semiconscious sleep; the next thing I knew, it was daylight out. I could feel the warm morning sun radiating from my face. This was one of the few days in my young life that I allowed myself the luxury of sleeping past 6:00 AM; on the other hand, 7:00 AM is not overindulgent either.

It was turning out to be one of those days that I missed having someone who did everything for me. It was helpful to dance the night away when your parents are footing the bill, but when you have to do it, you are on your own. I rolled out of bed, tidied up my side of the room, and had an early bath before anyone else was up. Living in a three-bedroom with one bathroom and seventeen other people teaches you to utilize your restroom time wisely. Be the first one in and the first one out. I'm wasting time. It will be cut down to zero if I don't get going.

Sunday morning was like any other day in the Gonzales household. If you did not do something for yourself, no one was going to do it for you, whatever that may be. By this time, things came together for Mary; she was receiving all the benefits that Social Welfare Services had to offer. Still, somehow, she managed to squander the money and food stamps away, leaving us no better off than without having welfare. This situation led me to become even more self-sufficient.

Today is Sunday. Why should I have to think about this now? I'm going to Mass! I was dressed and out of the house. I walked the six blocks to Our Lady of Loretto Roman Catholic Church. Just my luck, I made it in time to find seating in the balcony. It means I'll have to join in with the church choir, oh well.

For the first time, I realized and accepted that I was on my own. I am sitting here in church all by myself in Mass, the first time I made an adult decision. One that was going to help me to make the right sound decisions. As I was listening to the sermon, I felt at peace, and that is something that I could take away from Mass. I was alone, but not by myself; there were three rows of people sitting in front of me that I did not know, and still, I did not feel lonely.

When Mass ended, I hurried out of the pew; I did not want the chorus leader to invite me to next Sunday's Mass. He would expect me to join in the chorus every Sunday, which was not a bad thing, but I never knew what was going to happen from one day to the next, much less what I'll be doing next Sunday.

I took my time to get back to Mary's place. I came around the corner and noticed Tony's car parked in front of the house. It was already 1:30 PM, that is kind of early for Mary to be here. Something was going on. As I was getting closer to the door, I could hear the conversation die down. The whole Gonzales gang, including Tony, looked like the cat that swallowed the canary.

I looked around the room. As I entered, I was getting an uneasy feeling, as if Gonzales gang were all expecting some negative response. The same three tabloids were laid neatly on the coffee table from the night before. As long as I have been staying in this house, nothing stays in one place. These people wanted me to comment on the tabloids on the table. My parents and Uncle Senator Robert F. Kennedy were on the front cover of all three tabloids. This is what I would call a triple play if I were a baseball player or a trifecta in horse racing. Well! I am surely not going to play these people's games. If they want my opinion on something, they have to ask me a directly.

"Hey, what is going on now? What are all you beautiful people doing this afternoon?" I wanted to break the ice in the room by asking a question.

Mary spoke up. "First, we are going to have a barbeque today. Your big brother and Minta are coming over today."

"I did not know that I have a big brother!"

"Yes, you do."

"Well, if you say so, but it does not make it so."

"Dicky wants to see you."

"Oh! For what! You know full well I do not care for him and his wife. Why should I wait around for them? Give me one good reason; all I ask for is for one good reason! I'm letting you know now, someday Dicky is going to push me off the deep end, and I'm going to send him to the promised land if he gives me a chance, and I mean what I say."

Just then, Tony added his two cents in.

"I did not know that you did not like Richard and Minta, Ruby. I don't know if you are aware of the circumstances in which they met and married, Ruby."

"Surely, it is none of my business; nevertheless, you do not pull someone out of jail and marry them to knowingly get involved in a crime as Minta has done."

"Ruby, what does that have to do with you?"

"Tony, I am the crime. You think I wanted to be here? Just take a look around you before you answer that question." I left the room so as not to upset anyone.

I learned from experience never to stay around the Gonzales household when there are more than three of them together. Forget about it when alcohol was involved. Someone was going to start a fight. Why it was that I was the one who had to be in the middle of their mayhem, I'll never know. I've survived by making it a point to leave when the Gonzales and Gomez family socialize together. What made Dickey start a family, knowing that I was kidnapped, is beyond me. There has not been a week that has gone by that I did not hear, "If I go you go, remember that."

There was only so much I was willing to listen to, and I would have to leave. I finally made it to my room and laid down.

I was still at rest when Dicky and Minta arrived at 3:00 PM. I heard their voices and was on my feet. My disdain for Dickey and Minta was ever-increasing. *Before I do something rash, let me keep my cool and leave.* These two know full well that Mary provoked Tom into killing Linda to keep me here so that they can maintain their lifestyle.

The first thing Dicky and Minta did was sit Mary down and tell her whom she should or should not give money to in her family. Who knew my kidnapping was going to maintain five families? Especially when you have the Kennedy's of Massachusetts bank-rolling the whole operation. I could tell just by the way that Dicky came marching into the house it was going to be about money.

Just as I was leaving, I heard Dicky say, "Where are you going?"

"Oh! Are you talking to me?"

"Yes."

"I'm going out."

"I can see that, but where are you going out to?" I made it out the door without having to answer his question. I did not return until I was sure Dicky and Minta were both gone.

I did not see Dicky's green GTO parked anywhere on the street. Walking back into the house, the first thing I hear is:

"Mijo, where have you been?"

"My mother never called me mijo, why do you do it? She called me sugar, son, or Jack but never mijo! I am not your mijo, do you understand me! Do you really believe that I do not know what you are doing when you call me mijo! You want people to think that you are a loving, caring mother as if I was your own son.

"You tell that to them, but you hate even your own kids, including Richard, or do you prefer I call him Dickey like I do."

"Ruben, someday he is going to beat the living hell out of you and don't expect me to stop him when that day comes."

"How should I wait? Standing up or sitting down? No, I think I will sit down. You are going to make sure the day is a long way off that you can take to the bank. So long as you keep calling me mijo, I am going to make sure people understand I am not your mijo! Just try and call me 'son' and you'll see what I am going to do; that is a line I'm not going to let you cross, do you understand me! Now, I'm going to my room, and I don't want to be disturbed, understood?"

Sundays marked a new start for me, brought on by Monday. It's not just another day of the week, but a whole new beginning. It's time for me to start standing up for myself. If I'm going to make it out of the hell that my kidnappers Jacqueline and Onassis placed me in, I have to keep my wits about me. I'll think about what I have to do in the morning.

It was a new day, and I was feeling good this morning. As I rounded the corner of the living room, I noticed the tabloids were still lying on the coffee table, in the same order and neatness as they had been for the last four days.

Mary was sitting in her recliner, having morning coffee, which was way out in left field. "Aren't you supposed to be babysitting?"

"No, the mother stayed home. Sit down and have yourself a cup of coffee." I could do one of two things here. Indulge her by having a cup of coffee. Or come right out and ask her, "What do you want to know?" I figured that it was better to have coffee with her, just to find out what she was up to. I walked back into the kitchen, poured myself a cup of coffee, and returned to the living room. Mary had one of the tabloids in her hands, reading it.

She was holding the tabloid with both hands; the headlines read *Marilyn Monroe gave birth to a baby boy in 1959*. I took a seat to the left of her on the sofa. "Ruben, I've never seen you read a newspaper, book, or magazine."

"That's true."

"Why don't you pick up one of the papers on the table, take a look inside, and tell me what you think?"

"Why would you want to know my opinion on the trash that's written in a tabloid?"

"Oh! Just wondering."

" 'Just wondering' are your famous last words when you want information without asking a direct question, Mrs. Gonzales."

"Mrs. Gonzales, you are too funny! I'm here. Why would I want to read a pack of lies? I do ponder whose benefit the tabloids are serving. If the tabloids were to write the truth, I would not be sitting here with you now. It's almost as if someone is out to destroy the deceased. The legacy of my parents, or perhaps their love for someone that is still here on this earth."

"Mijo, do you think Marilyn Monroe had a child in 1959? I was just wondering." That was the motivation behind Mary, offering me a cup of coffee. I had to literally bite my tongue to keep from falling down laughing. If I talk about my parents Marilyn Monroe and President John F. Kennedy on my own accord, I get my backside handed to me, but when a Gonzales or Gomez does it, that's fine. How do I reply to Mary's question?

"Why do you want to know if Marilyn had a baby in 1959?"

"I was just wondering. Ruben, you think there is any truth to the matter?"

"Well, it doesn't matter to me, but if she did have a son in '59, I'm not saying she did, just that he is being cared for, but for how long I do not know. Now you can go back and tell my stepmother what I said."

Knowing Mary, she was going to twist my words to suit her own needs. It was our own flesh and blood that was letting my stepmother Jackie and Onassis destroy our life. Just what would they do to my brother if they knew that their evil plan did not work on me? Once Mary asked about my brother, I knew I was going to keep his identity from anyone and everybody.

I finished up the cup of coffee, took the cup back into the kitchen, washed it out, and placed it on the rack to dry, leaving the house through the living room.

"Mrs. Gonzales, I'll see you later." Just how much later was totally up to her.

As I was walking around the neighborhood, I was pondering Mary's question. If Marilyn had a son born in 1959, we would both be better served if I elude answering that question for as long as possible. I don't need his death on my conscience. I just hope that my little brother JonJon understands when the time comes to explain what happened. That our mother left him with our father until she set up and secured a home for us. She had never entertained the idea that she would leave him with our dad for good!

Now I have the same worry that I had with Linda; how long would it be before someone decides it's time for JonJon to go? 1968 is turning out to be a tumultuous year thus far. Just what the remainder of the year was going to bring me was anyone's guess.

I continued scouring the neighborhood for retirees who needed help doing household work or gardening; however, my efforts were turning out to be futile. As I rounded the curb, there came Frank, Bogart, Timmy, and Larry. Frank and I had been friends for about three years, the kind of guy I want my brother to emulate. Bogart had that Humphrey Bogart tough guy image going on. If I were in a brawl, I would want him on my side. Timmy was another friend of mine. His brother Tommy was in my class at school. Larry was just a little bit unreliable. I did not care for Larry during school. Why would I trust him out of school? He was with Frank, and that was good enough for me.

We all decided to take a walk down to the lake. As we were walking, we filled our pockets with stones to skip across the water of the lake. We finally made it across Glendale Boulevard on to the lakeside of Echo Park. Stone skipping is something I enjoyed with my parents, so this was old hat for me. The object here was to see who can make the stone skip the furthest. We each took our turn, skipping the rocks across the lake. There was no clear winner once we started flicking the rocks at each other.

We decided to have a race from Santa Ynez Street to the other end of the lake where the boathouse was to see who would make it to the finish line first. We started running when the traffic light turned green. But of course, Frank and Timmy, having big brothers, weren't going to wait for the light to change colors. They were off and running. Larry took off right after them. Bogart and I waited for the green light, and we were off and running.

In no time, we were all running neck and neck. Just as I was gaining momentum, Frank ran off course up a small grassy embankment, and the rest of us followed him. He made it to the top of the mound of the embankment. Frank dropped onto the green grass and started rounding down the mound as fast as he could. As Frank was rounding down the slope of the hill, the other three followed. I stood on the mound, looking down at them. Instinct kicked in, I was off and running as if a bolt of lightning hit me; I was going to be the winner in this race one way or another.

By the time the four of them came to rest at the bottom of the mound. I was standing there with a grin on my face. I had won. I thought of my little brother. There was no way I was going to let them win. I would never hear the end of it. "Hey, you guys. Let's get out of here! I don't like the way those three guys are watching us.

"I know one of them. He is a Carbahall. I fought with him about six months ago on the other side of the park. He's a badass, and he thinks we are in his territory. Not only that, he wants payback!" I said.

"Ruben, who died and named you boss?"

"Larry, you come from the Flats around Rampart Police Station. We live here; this is our territory. I'm telling you, let's get out of here. You don't want to mess with those guys."

"Ruben, what are you, chicken?"

"Larry, you need to take a step back!" About that time, one of Carbahall's homeboys was standing behind me.

"Hey, wedo, didn't Richard teach you to keep your backside in your own neighborhood, or do I have to?"

I said, "Ay, dude, I have no beef with you. And yes, I am a white boy. So you can dispense with 'wedo.' I am aware that 'wedo' means a white boy. You know full well I don't have anything to do with the Gomez's or the Gonzales's. So what is your problem?"

He walked up on me while Larry was giving Carbahall's boys attitude. "Oh yeah! What about you?"

I said to Carbahall, "Look, homeboy, you can take it down a notch. I don't need this from you, and I am not Richard's brother."

"Oh! You're the one!"

"Yes, I'm the one, and we both know Richard is not my brother!"

"Well, what are you doing in our park? Gonzales and Gomez are not allowed to use the park."

"Well, we both know that I am not one of them, so leave me out."

"Hey, you're a smartass!"

"I was not speaking to you with vulgar language; I would appreciate respect here for yourself and me."

"Now I know why people say you think you are better than them. Ruben, I'm going to have to teach you some respect."

"I'd take you up on your offer, but your boys here are going to end up helping you out, and three against one is not working out too well for me."

"I'll tell you what the three of us against the five of you."

"I'm not looking for a fight."

"You say Richard is not your brother, but it seems to me like some of his cowardice rubbed off on you."

"Look, I'm not looking for a throw down with you."

"Why don't you talk it over with your homies. They don't look willing."

"Frank, Bogart, what do you think?"

"Ruben, I've never known you to walk away from a fight."

"Frank, these are some bad dudes. You don't want to tangle with them. One on one I can handle but the other two here together, I'll get my backside handed to me."

"Ruben, I'll tell you what, how about the three of us against the five of you? That way, it will be an even ass-kicking."

"I am willing to go a couple of rounds with you, but I can't speak for my boys here."

One of Carbahall's friends said, "What, Ruben, is your crew chicken shit?"

"Ay Carbahall, tell your boys I don't need the lip service!"

"Ruben, you and your boys have a powwow?" The first one to speak up was Larry.

"Let's do this!"

I turned to him. "No, Larry." I said to the rest of the guys, "I'm telling you guys, Larry is a wimp; he is going to back down!"

"Ruben, who are you calling a wimp!"

"You, Larry, you!"

"Ruben, you're afraid!"

"Larry, you are the only one among the five of us that I have not seen defend themselves in school."

"Ruben, you're the one that's full of it."

"Larry, I'm telling you if you wimp out, I'm going to jack you up myself! Frank, Bogart, tell him I'll fuck him up if he chickens out. I mean what I say, Larry! I'll tear you up, man!

"Frank, I'm going to tackle the one giving us the lip service. The other two the three of you should be able to take down. Frank, whatever you do, don't go down, and for God's sake, do not kick the guy when he's on the ground. If you do that, it's all over for us. Keep the fight fair."

All eight of us were back on the top of the mound; how we got up there, I'll never know. "Well, if we are going to do this, does anyone have any weapons on them? Let's check. Empty your pockets; everyone lift up your shirts and turn around. Are we all good? Yes, we are!"

I tried tackling the ringleader, but he would not go down. He was holding his ground until we lost our footing on the grass. As we were going down the hill, I could feel his knuckle streak across the tip of my nose. That was when I lost it! As we were rolling down the mound, I gave this guy a right uppercut to his jaw and a left to his right cheek.

We came to a rest at the bottom of the mound, and we were still going at it. I got to my feet when he yelled, "Stop, stop. I've had enough!"

How the eight of us ended up at the bottom of the mound is anyone's guess, but we did. Frank, Bogart, and Timmy held their own ground. Larry indeed wimped out. He just stood there watching the whole thing go down. It would have been comical to the seven, but we were too battered and bruised. The fight lasted all but five minutes. We came to rest at the bottom of the mound. We sat on the grass with our legs tucked up under our chins and chest with our hands holding our heads.

All except Larry. Who was standing five feet away from us at a safe distance. Frank and I were both looking at him. "Frank, you know I am going to have to take care of him."

"I know Ruben. I know."

The guy that had instigated the fight looked over at me.

"Hey, I was a hundred percent sure you were a coward. I was going to make you man up, but you fight like a junkyard dog!"

"My dad instilled in me if someone challenges you to a fight, you fight like the dickens, in other words, like hell. He would say, Jack, if you back down from a fight, your challenger is going to keep trying to provoke you until they succeed.'"

"I thought I was thorough when I enquired about having weapons. I should have also asked if any of you had any self-defense training."

"Yes, we have. The three of us take karate self-defense classes."

"Frank, Bogart, Timmy, it is time to go! Both Frank and Bogart simultaneously asked me, "Ruben, what are you going to do?" as we were walking towards Larry.

"Hey, Larry, what happened to you? It was your idea to fight those guys. You just stood there doing nothing. Why didn't you help Bogart and Timmy?"

"Look, I thought those guys were going to win, and I did not want to get hurt."

"Oh, really!"

Larry's answer enraged me! By this time, we were face to face. I placed my left foot behind me and cold-cocked him with a right to the jaw and a left to the head; I gave him that old one-two punch, and he went down. He was lying flat on his back.

Frank, Bogart, and Timmy were standing there in shock.

"Ruben, Larry is supposed to be your friend."

"No, Frank, he is your friend. I told you before I don't trust him."

"Ruben, my brother Tommy told me not to mess with you; now I see why!"

Bogart looked down at Larry in awe at what he had just witnessed.

"Larry, you had that coming. I can't believe it! Ruben took you down with a one-two combination punch."

"Larry, you do not start a throw-down and back down at the last second. You could get someone killed doing that, and there is no way that I'm going to let someone get away with that. You guys get him out of my sight before I kick him in the lake and drown his ass. If one of you thinks about giving Larry a helping hand up, I'll give you the same thing I gave him. Let him crawl on his hands and knees like the coward that he is to that water spigot to help himself up."

"Ruben, I'm going to tell my father what you did to me."

"Larry, go right ahead, tell your father. I'm sure he'll want to know what kind of son he has. You coward!

"Timmy, take him back to his mom. Tell her to call the police on me. I'll be waiting to hear from them or your father, Larry. Frank, Timmy, take this bastard coward home to his mother."

Bogart and I walked inside the park while Frank, Timmy, and Larry walked on the sidewalk. There were twenty feet of grass between us. "Hey Frank, you guys, take the left side at Santa Ynez. I'll walk on the right of the street."

We all made it to the corner of Bonnie Brae and Santa Ynez; this is where we parted ways. Bogart and I continued on our way to Bogart's house.

We walked the four blocks arriving at Bogart's pad. As we rounded the corner, I could music blasting from his pad.

"WOW! Bogart, the only difference between the haves and have nots is money; this party is rocking.

"Who has a party in the middle of the week! Damn! Bogart, you left this happening to hang with Frank and me? Why!"

"Ruben, my mom has a party two to three times a week. I get tired of people coming and going in our house."

"Bogart, this is so cool to see this; it takes me back to my parents."

"Ruben, my mother says the same thing about you. She thinks I could learn a thing or two from you. How you call her 'Mrs. Gomez' when you see her, and you offer your seat to a lady when they enter the room. How well your mother brought you up. You are well-mannered for someone your age, and you have a broad vocabulary. Ruben, she believes most people are intimidated by you. She also thinks your parents are hiding out from the mafia or the police."

"No, Bogart, it's nothing like that. My stepmother and her soon-to-be husband took me from my mother and left me here."

We entered the house, and the party was in full swing; it was happening. People were dancing, conversing, eating, and drinking, enjoying themselves. Bogart's mother came up to us.

"You boys look like you have been in a brawl. Ruben, you have grown about two feet from that the last time you were here! Bogart, who won the fight?"

"Mom, Ruben came through, but Larry chickened out on the onset."

"Bogart, I told you Ruben would come through in a tight spot. Get cleaned up and have something to eat and enjoy yourselves."

"Thank you, Mrs. Gomez, for the invitation."

I turned to Bogart. "Bogart, I cannot stay long; I don't want Mary to send out the cavalry looking for me."

I stayed for ninety minutes; I thanked Mrs. Gomez for having me. "Ruben, if you like, you are welcome to stay longer."

"No, Mrs. Gomez, I have to get back to my place, but thank you for the offer. I enjoyed myself."

"Bogart, walk your friend to the corner."

I said to Bogart, "Bogart, you have some beautiful sisters."

"Hey, not you too, Ruben!"

"Yes, me too. I'm going up the dirt hill and stopping off by Frank's place. I want to make sure he does not get into trouble for fighting. His mother will have his brother knock some sense into him. See you later!"

As I was crossing Alvarado Street, I hoped the Gonzales's didn't destroy my friendship with Bogart as they did with Bobby Faulkner and Luciano. I have to find a way to keep my friendships a secret from them.

I was climbing up the hill preoccupied with my thoughts and had gone past the alley. I had forgotten about this incline. By the time I made it to Frank's place, my legs were giving out. I finally made it to Frank's house. Out of breath, my legs were hurting from the steep grades that I climbed to get here.

I was just about to holler out when Frank's mother yelled out, "Ruben, don't you dare call me 'Mrs.' You make me feel like an old lady! You call me Tilley. You have been Frank and Roy's friend for going on 5 years. Frank's at his grandmother's."

I walked across the alley to Frank's grandmother's; I could hear someone doing the dishes. I walked up to the window.

"Oh, Miss Garcia. Is Frank here?"

"Yes, he's in the front yard with Roy."

"Don't mind my daughter. Call her Tilley, and you'll do fine! I'm going to tell Frank to open the gate and let you in."

I walked to the gate door to the back yard. Frank gently opened the gate. Tilley called out, "Frank, don't go too far; dinner will be ready in 10 minutes."

"Shush! Ruben, my grandfather is sleeping."

His grandfather shouted, "Frank close the gate at once! What are you boys up to?"

"Oh! Grandpa, I did not want to wake you."

I said, "Mr. Garcia, how are you this afternoon?"

"I'm fine. Frank, the way that your mom and grandmother talk across the way, how can I take an afternoon nap?"

Frank nodded his head, indicating 'let's scram'. We took off running to the front of the yard.

"Hey, did your mother notice you were in a fight?"

"No."

"Bogart's mother took one look at us and asked who won the fight."

"What did you tell her?"

"I told her it was not a fight; it was a draw between the five of us and the three other guys. Frank, I came by to see how you were doing."

"I feel as if someone hit me with a baseball bat."

"Me too, I'll see you later."

I could barely make it to the house. My aches and pains have aches and pains! I made it to the house. The first thing I did was clean out the bathtub and run a hot tub of water for a bath.

For the next three days, I stayed around the house nursing my bruises. By the middle of the week, I was tired of being taken advantage of by the girls. I was cleaning and picking up after four girls and myself. I asked Vivian, Maryann, Yolanda, and Sally when they were going to give me a hand cleaning up. They sat there looking at me as if I was talking to the wall. "I'm talking to the four of you! Someone answer me, please."

"Ruben, if you want this place cleaned up, do it yourself!"

"Vivian, you and Yolanda are the oldest, and when I return, I want the dishes done and this place clean."

"What are you going to do if it's not clean?"

"Yolanda, you don't want to know. Just know this, I mean what I say! You'll be sorry if the house is not clean when I return, and I mean what I said."

I returned to the house a few hours later; the living room was still a mess. Most homes have a wastepaper basket but not this house. I had to look for a brown paper bag. My mom's rule was to start cleaning from the top down; what falls on to the floor, you do not have to pick up twice.

I looked over at Vivian. "I don't smoke. Why should I have to be the one to empty the ashtray? This ashtray has been full since Friday. Here it is Wednesday, and no one has emptied it."

"Ruben, that is what you are here for!"

"Vivian, you're right. This ashtray is full. Take a look at it. There has to be about four packs of cigarettes in this big ass ashtray! I am going to ask you girls one more time, are you going to help me clean this dump up?

"No answer? Fine! So you people think this is funny! I'll show you funny."

I picked up the ashtray. Bent over the sofa and turned the ashtray upside down out the window; I placed the ashtray back from where I retrieved it right in the middle of the living room coffee table.

"Ruben, what'd you do that for? You have a bag in your hand that you could have put the ashes in!"

"Hey, if you don't like the way I do things, start cleaning up after yourselves! Look, these tabloid newspapers have been lying on this coffee table for a week and a half. All you people do is sit around smoking and do not take the time to clean up after yourselves."

I finished up the living room and moved on to the kitchen. There were still three days of dirty dishes sitting in the sink. I started stacking dishes to the left of the sink on the kitchen counter. There were enough cups, glasses, and plates to serve a small army. I looked over the task at hand. Thank God this is a double sink! One side of the sink, I filled with soapy water. The other side of the sink I filled with rinse water.

While I was preparing to tackle this chore, I could hear the girls laughing and giggling in the living room. I did not let their silly laughter annoy me; I was going to get this job done. I was sure of one thing; this was going to be the last time these witches sat on their backsides while I do the dishes!

I turned around, took two steps, and opened up the back-kitchen door as wide as it would open. I took another two steps to open the screen door that opened up into the backyard. I had a clear path to the backyard; it was all systems go. I walked back into the living room. "Okay, ladies, are you going to do the dishes, or do I have to?"

In unison, they give me their answer, "If you want the dishes done, you do it."

"Okay, if you want it that way!" I walked back to the kitchen sink and started tackling the job at hand. I washed and rinsed the first dish clean. I turned to hurl the plate that I washed out the door into the backyard, never to use it again. That's one less dish I'll never have to wash again.

I was on a roll, hurling the dishes out the back door until I hit the kitchen wall with a glass that made a crashing sound. It brought music to my ears. One more glass that I do not have to deal with anymore. My hurling streak was over. Another dish crashed into the wall.

I paused for a moment, trying to hear if there was laugher still coming from the living room; it seemed to have calmed down. I continued with my work. The next dish hit the wall with a crashing sound that reverberated out of the house! Yolanda, Vivian, and Maryann came running into the kitchen.

"What are you doing!"

"I'm doing household chores, Yolanda."

"I can see that, but the dishes go into the dish rack to dry, not on the floor. Ruben, why are the dishes in the backyard! Why!"

"It's simple. No one wants to do the dishes, and I was tired of seeing them stacked up. So I decided to take matters into my own hands and toss the dishes out into the backyard. This way, the dishes that break will not have to be cleaned."

"Get out of the way. I'll finish up the dishes."

"Yolanda, are you sure? I don't want you to have to trouble yourself with menial housework."

"Ruben, I'm going to tell Mom on you."

"Yolanda, you can tell your mother anything you like! Just make this the last time I have to do the dishes. If there is a next time, I'll toss all the dishes in a trash can. I mean what I say, is that clear?"

"Ruben, just who do you think you are?"

"The same person that went to bed last night and got out of bed this morning, that's who!" I backed away from the sink, and Yolanda took over. What a triumph! I got these girls' attention and off their duffs.

I walked out of the kitchen into the living room when I heard the telephone ringing.

"Hey, Anthony, what's up."

"Ruben, can you come over and give me a hand?"

"Just what is it you want a hand with Anthony?"

"I'll let you know when you get here."

"Okay, bye, I'll be over in a few!"

As I was talking on the phone, I kept a watchful eye on the kitchen, waiting for the girls to come after me for all the broken dishes. There were more dishes on the kitchen floor and backyard than there were left to wash. "Bye, I'll see you people later!"

I could not put the phone down fast enough!

I walked over to Anthony's to find out what Anthony wanted, which put two blocks in between the girls and me. I could see Anthony and his father from the alley-way working on a car. He was working on a '57 Chevy; it looked like it was in excellent condition from my vantage point.

"Hey, Carl and Anthony, what's up."

"Help me tune-up, change the oil, and replace the brakes on my car, in exchange I'll finish teaching you to drive."

"That sounds like a plan to me, Anthony!"

"The first order is to make sure the car brake is set and place a brick behind each rear tire and roll the car against the brick. This way, the tire is locked in place against the brick and should not move."

We jacked-up the front end of the vehicle and placed a jack-stand and a milk crate under the frame of the car and did the same to the left side. Anthony worked on one side of the car and me on the other side.

I removed the tire and placed it under the front axle, just in the event the jack-stand gives way. Walking to the other side of the car., I watched as Anthony demonstrated how to remove the brake drum from the front axle. It was my turn to remove the drum from the axle; it was relatively easy to do. It was a terrific feeling of achievement every time a part had been removed; there was a unique tool for it. However, we were backyard mechanics, and with a craftsman's screwdriver and pliers, we could fix almost any vehicle.

The one important thing to remember is to not mix the right working parts with left working parts of the brakes. I made sure to place the left side parts on the left side of the trunk of the car. This way, if I did not come back to help out, Anthony would not have a problem with which parts belong on which side of the car.

It was getting dark out, time to close up shop. I did not dare leave without Carl taking a once-over of our work. Carl was a heck of a father figure. Still, if we left any of his tools lying on the ground, he'd give us the third degree. 'Your livelihood is on the ground.' 'How do you expect to earn money without your tools?' 'Do you know that I was working in a coal mine at your age?' Carl came out and did his once over. "You boys did an excellent job; I made dinner. Go get cleaned up and come to have supper."

We had dinner, and I headed back to the dungeon for a night of rest. Stopping at the top of the cul-de-sac and admiring the skyline of Downtown Los Angeles never ceases to amaze me. I could see the city hall, Hall of Records, and the Occidental Building lighting up the night skyline.

It was best to look for the silver lining of life before entering Mary's house. The one good thing about being in this dungeon was no one was here. I was all alone, but I did not feel lonely. There had to be something better out there in the world for me. I needed to learn to be more patient and seize the moment when it comes.

The next morning, I was up at 6:30 AM, ready to start work at 7:30 AM. Anthony arrived at about 7:45 AM in his father's 1959 white Ford Station Wagon with a manual transmission. Anthony told me to take the driver's side. "It's time for you to start learning how to drive."

Anthony was not the best driving instructor I've had, but then again, if he was willing to teach me to operate a manual motor vehicle, that was fine with me. He would call me all the foul mouth words he could come up with, but if I was going to learn to repair cars and drive, I would have to tolerate his nonsense.

I drove down to Winchell's Donut Shop; I couldn't believe I made it without running a stop sign or grinding the gears. We ordered two coffees and two donuts to go and headed for the auto parts store. We dropped off the two front drums to have them ground down. This way, the brake shoes would fit the arch inside the brake drum.

In the meantime, Anthony and I returned to his place with oil, an oil filter, and a tune-up kit. Anthony got under the car to remove the oil filter and drain the oil. I opened the tune-up kit and counted eight spark plugs, distributer points, and one condenser. I opened up the motor manual and looked up the make, model, and year of the car and also the engine type. I gapped the spark plugs to the specification that I read in the motor manual. I placed the spark plugs on the fender of the car, four on each fender, in the box they came in. This way, if they fell on the gravel, they would remain clean.

Anthony came out from under the car. He asked me to hand him the spark plug gauge, which I did. Anthony rechecked my work. He checked the gap in the spark plug and asked, "Since when did they teach Mexicans to read, Ruben?"

"What! Anthony, all I did was gap the spark plugs; I did not damage any in doing so. What is your problem with all the name-calling? First, you know that Mary and Paul are not my parents, and second, I could do you one better about your heritage. Being Italian American doesn't give you the right to insult someone. Christopher Columbus may have discovered America, but he did it with Queen Isabella of Spain's money. Next time you insult someone take a look back at history. I'm leaving!"

I rose from the milk crate that I was sitting on and left.

"Ruben, please don't go!"

"Anthony, I've had it with your insults. It is better that I leave instead of kicking your backside."

"You have to stay here. Suppose the car falls on me or I get hurt. Who is going to help me?"

"Why should I care if you get injured or need help! You have your older brother who should be out here watching you, not me!"

"Please stay! Carl Allen and I do not get along. Please stay!"

"Anthony, I'll stay, but if you insult me one more time, I'll drop this car on you and make it look like an accident, and I mean it!"

It would have been a foolish mistake to leave while I was receiving free education in auto mechanics and driving lessons as well. That didn't mean that I would not drop this car on him while he was under it. I'd do it in a heartbeat. What I learn here today is going to last me a lifetime; this is something I would have to reconsider.

We got back to work replacing the old spark plugs with the new ones, making sure every spark wire went in the correct cylinder. I watched as Anthony removed the distributor cap and removed the points from the distributor itself. Carl had told Anthony not to set the points at the top dead center. That is when the points open at its highest point, sending the spark to the spark plug, igniting the gas in the cylinder.

As all sons do, he did not heed to his father's advice. Anthony set the points at its highest point, which ignited the gas in the cylinder before the top dead center, and the engine did not run at peak performance. After three tries of setting the points, Anthony finally had the engine idling correctly. Carl came out into the yard to give his final approval.

"The two of you working on this car should have finished two hours ago. If you plan to open up an auto repair shop, you need to learn that time is money."

"Carl, that's my grandfather's favorite cliché. Carl, for me, this is a learning experience. I may or may not work in the auto repair business, but I'll know when an auto-mechanic tries to pull one over on me."

"Now, I'm going to make sure you two did everything to exact specifications." Carl had Anthony start up the car and let it idle. He took a dime out of his pocket. He stood the dime on its edge on the hood of the vehicle. "If this coin stays balanced, that means a job well done. If it falls over, the points or spark plugs were not gapped to the correct gauge setting."

I've heard stories about how all one needed to repair a model T-Ford back in the day was a pair of pliers and a screwdriver, but this takes the cake! He let the dime go, and there it stood on its edge. The motor was purring like a cat; the points and spark plugs were both gapped correctly. The dime did not fall over or move.

It was time to head back to Cargo's Auto Supply to pick up the drums. The service person asked us if this was the first time we replaced shoe brakes on a car.

"Yes, it is."

"I've marked both pairs of shoe brakes, one left and one right. Make sure that is the way you put them back on the axle according to their markings."

We were in and out of Cargo's in a matter of twenty minutes, and we were back putting on the brakes. The hardest part of working on brakes for a car was to reassemble the brake shoes to the axle. In this job, it was still true. One only needed a pair of pliers and a screwdriver. It would be easy if you had the right tool for the job, but in our case, we made do with what we had.

Placing the pins, washers, and self-adjuster brake assembly took no effort at all. The two spring is what brings the whole braking system together; it holds the braking system and the axles in place. Once all these nonmoving parts were in place. It was time to slide on the drum to the axles, greasing the bearings but not over-greasing them and tightening the central bolt just enough so the drum turns freely but does not come off.

The next thing to do was adjust the brake self-adjusting assembly. It's a two-step process, turn the drum and listen to hear if the brake shoes are dragging against the drum. If the drum spins too freely, the self-adjusting will not kick in and self-adjust. Once the work is done on both front axles, spin the drum, leaving a slight drag on the drum. The final step is to get under the car and spin both tires simultaneously. If they come to a stop at the same time, you're done. It enables the self-adjusting brake assembly to adjust the brakes, preventing the car from pulling left or right when applying the brakes to slow down the vehicle or coming to a complete stop.

It was time to road-test the car. Anthony drove the '57 Chevy back and forth a couple of times to make sure the vehicle would stop.

"Hey Ruben, get in. Let's take a spin around the block a couple of times."

"Oh no, not me. You go ahead, I'll stay here and wait for you to return."

Anthony pulled out of the driveway, turned left, and came to a complete stop at the end of the alley. He backed up to where I was standing and came to an abrupt halt.

"Now that you can see, the car stops get in."

"Where are we going to test drive the car on our way to the grocery store?"

I sat in the front seat of the car without saying a word. Carl never let on at any time that he worked as a mechanic at a Ford dealer. He had to road-test the car before he gave the final say on the finished job. Had I known that, I would not have been so apprehensive about taking a test drive! I could not even look at Anthony when he was talking to me.

What was I going to do if we have an accident? If the wheel that I worked on falls off? When we made it the six blocks to Safeway Market and came to a complete stop, I felt somewhat relieved. Anthony bought what he needed to make hamburgers. It was back in the '57 Chevy for the road-test back.

"Anthony, why didn't you tell me I would have to be in the car with you for the test drive?"

"Why?"

"This ride is giving me the heebie-jeebies, dude! I can't wait to get the heck out of this car!"

"Ruben, are you afraid of your own work?"

"Yes, I am."

"That is why you have to road-test your work. This way, if something happens, it happens to you. It also helps you to have confidence in your work."

"Where are we going?"

"We are on our way to your house."

"My house? I don't have a house. Let's go to yours."

"I mean the Gonzales house!"

"Why there?"

"I'm going to prepare the hamburgers there."

"Anthony, how many times do I have to tell you; I do not like to socialize with the Gonzales's; they are no good! Someday you are going to see what I mean about these people. I just hope it is not too late when you learn how no-good they are."

"Look, Ruben, I'll prepare the burgers, and one of the girls can clean up when I finish cooking."

"Anthony, this I have to see!"

"Ruben, what are you laughing at?"

"You, my boy. You!"

By the time we arrived in front of the Gonzales house, all my fear of the car not stopping or one or both tires and drums heading south had sub-sided. All-in-all, Carl made the right decision in not informing me that I had to road-test my work.

Anthony had become a welcome visitor in the Gonzales home. Whereas I was made to feel like an unwanted stepchild, here but not wanted, which was fine with me. By this time, I had learned never to be in the Gonzales home when there is more than three Gonzales's at once. It was for my own survival. Mary had already had Chita and her sisters drive a wedge of hate, jealousness, and contempt between the girls and me. The only way I could deal with their feelings for me was with kindness.

I did not want to enter into the Gonzales household today. There were just too many of them here, and something was bound to happen. Anthony got out of the car, grabbed both bags of groceries, and walked up the walkway right into the house. I could hear the girls' voices.

"What did you bring with you, Anthony?" one of the girls asked.

"Oh! I want to make burgers for all of us. Carl gave me $25.00 for Ruben for two days' work."

Vivian asked, "What kind of work does he know how to do?"

"He worked on my car with me. Carl likes his work and believes that he would make a good automobile mechanic."

"Ruben? Make a good mechanic? Don't make me laugh, Anthony! He can't even get out of bed before 11:00 AM if not noon, and he is going to make a good mechanic. He'll be lucky if he can wash dishes for someone!"

"HA! HA! Well, Carl wants us to open our own garage together."

"Anthony, let your father Carl know he is wasting his time and money on him."

I could hear and see the envy in Vivian's words and body language.

"Hey, Anthony, let me know when the burgers are ready."

I left the kitchen where all the girls had gathered before they could all go on a rampage against me. Anthony was still carrying on how his father always wanted to find someone reliable like me.

I recall I had asked Anthony why he called his parents by their given name. His answer was that when he was a child, his parents' friend called them Carl and Mona, why couldn't he? I could never imagine me calling my parents by their given names. Who does that, and why do his parents allow it to continue? I finally washed all Vivian's negativity out of my thoughts and returned to the kitchen.

By this time, Anthony had a burger in one hand and the spatula in the other; he was cooking and eating at the same time. Vivian was sitting at the kitchen table adjacent to the kitchen stove. She had one burger in her hand, and a hamburger patty cut into tantalizing little bite-sized pieces lying on the plate in front of her.

I looked down at Vivian as she was eyeing me, then I looked at the bite-sized patty morsel.

"Ruben, don't you dare! If you take a piece of meat off my plate, I'm going to stab you, do you hear me!"

Anthony looked down at Vivian from where he was preparing the burger.

"Vivian, you would stab him over a piece of meat? Would you!"

"Anthony, let him try it and see what I do." I was in shock to hear Vivian repeat herself.

Would she have the gall to stab me over a piece of meat?

My subconscious was telling me that there was something that I needed to know, but my conscious was saying to me, she is going to stab you. The conflict between my subconscious and conscious was in a great battle. I needed to know the answer. Is she the one! Is she the one!

I looked down at Vivian one more time.

"Ruben, I'm telling you if you take a piece of meat from my plate, I'm going to stab you!"

Something compelled me to take the meat. *If you don't, you won't be prepared for the next time.*

Anthony repeated himself, "Vivian, would you stab your little brother over a piece of meat?"

Just then, I reached for the tantalizing morsel of meat.

All at once, Vivian plunged the fork into my forearm at full force. She pulled it out of my forearm; blood came gushing out. Again, she plunged the fork in between my forefinger and thumb. This time, Vivian had driven the fork clean through both layers of skin. I could hear the screeching of the fork as my hand was being dragged across the plate. She pulled the fork out of my hand. I fell into the chair that was just to the right of me.

Blood was everywhere.

I was overcome with anguish and began to cry. It was not the pain that I was feeling or the blood, but the fact that I had the answer to my question. Anthony looked at Vivian.

"I can't believe you did that! Vivian, I can't believe you stabbed him not once but twice! There is blood everywhere! Just look at how he is crying and the pain he is in."

"No, Anthony. It's not the pain that I'm in, not at all. It's that someday, she is going to try to kill me! Just as her brother Danny has tried to end my life. Now I have to worry about Vivian!"

I got up from the table and went into the bathroom, pulled off my shirt, and began to wash off the blood. I took my blood-soaked shirt and pants and placed them in cold water and took a bath to remove the blood from my chest and arm.

As I was bathing, I could hear the girls asking, "Vivian, what happened?"

Once my arm and hand stopped bleeding, I got out of the tub and went into my bedroom for some clean clothes. I dressed in a hurry and took off to Echo Park Lake, where I could find refuge and solitude and cogitate how I was going to deal with Vivian in the future.

I was going to remain the same kind-hearted person that I was but not be sympathetic to her well-being. I stayed in the park until the sun went down. I went back to an empty house; there was not a soul in sight.

A week or two later, Anthony called and asked me if I would like to earn some money working on Tony's car.

"Anthony, I have to think about it."

"What do you mean think about it, what is there to think about? It's about making money, Ruben."

"Anthony, I'm well aware of that, but here's the thing. If you did not give me the $25.00, the money that I earned, what makes you believe I'd work with you again?"

"Oh, help me out here, Ruben. How was I supposed to know that Vivian was going to stab you? You should not have taken the piece of meat from her plate."

"That's true, but then again, I would never know that someday she is going to try and kill me. Anthony, I know eventually she is going to try to kill me. I hope you're not there to witness it."

"Ruben, are you going to work with me or not?"

"Okay, I'll work with you. But I want to be paid, do you understand me, Anthony? Am I getting through to you?"

"Yes, Ruben, I'm going to pay you."

"Come pick me up; I'll be waiting for you. Do not come into the house. I'll go outside. If you come in unannounced, I will not work with you ever again; do I make myself clear!"

"Yes, but why don't you want me in the house?"

"Anthony, you don't get to ask me questions. That's just the way I want it. I'll meet you outside!"

Anthony pulled up in front of the house. As I was walking out the door, Vivian asked, "Where are you going?"

I stopped dead in my tracks and turned to stare her down.

"What's it to you where I'm going? Mind your own business!"

"I'm going to tell Mom on you."

"That's right, you tell your mom anything you want! Just stay out of my business!"

I turned to walk out the door. I could hear Vivian yell, "Close the door, were you born in a barn?"

"If you want the door closed, get off your ass and do it yourself. That is the way I found it: Open!"

I walked up to Anthony and opened the car door.

"Hey, it's time for the driving lesson; move over."

I put the car in reverse and backed up the hill. I brought the rear end of the vehicle around the right corner like a pro. Looking at the dashboard and dropping the car into drive, we were on our way. It finally dawned on me that I could see over the steering wheel. I did not have to adjust the seat or the rearview mirror.

Hell, this is turning out to be a great end of summer. I was driving down Sunset Blvd on my way to Tony's apartment. I was even able to parallel park the '63 two-door T-bird. I feel fantastic!

Tony's apartment was in a shady part of Sliver Lake off of Sunset Blvd and Vendome Street. His apartment was located on the first floor of a two-story building. Anthony knocked on the door, and Mary told us to come in. Anthony opened the door to Tony's studio apartment. Mary was sitting in an armchair, and Tony was lying on his bed. Mary rose to her feet.

"Oh! Mijo, I heard what Vivian did to you," she said as she started to cry, tears running down her face.

"I want to be there for you, but I have to take care of two kids at night." I have never heard of both parents working the night shift before. As I was standing there listening to Mary's drivel, I wondered if she believed that I was taken in by her nonsense. I had not seen her for most of the summer, and she wanted to convince me that she had been babysitting! Just what is behind this woman's logic, I'll never know.

"Mrs. Gonzales, would it bother you if I tell you I don't care what you do or don't do? I came here for Tony's car. Besides, Vivian would have never stabbed me if you did not already okay it; in fact, you put her up to it. These people never do a thing without the okay from you first!"

"Ruben, Tony forgot, he has a doctor's appointment this afternoon, and his arthritis is getting worse. By the way, Tom had his first court appearance."

"How do you know?"

"Tony and I went to his arraignment."

"How did he plead?"

"Oh, we arrived late, but we were able to talk to him."

"Oh, well! Anthony, let's go."

"Ruben, you should attend Tom's trial."

I paused for a few seconds before answering her. How foolish does this woman think I am? She believes she needs to manipulate me into attending Tom's trial?

"What makes you think I want to attend Tom's trial, Mrs. Gonzales? Repairing Tony's car was just a ruse to get me to talk to you. It would suit you better to tell me what you want next time. I'm leaving. See you people later."

As I was leaving the apartment, Anthony came after me.

"Wait, you can go back with me." I kept my back to Anthony as we were talking.

"No, Anthony. I think I'll walk back. It's not far."

I thought to myself, if I do the math, it's about the same distance between here to the house as walking from the house to downtown Central Market. I could be back in the house in 45 minutes.

How was I going to make Mary understand that I did not want to bother with her? Tony had a birds-eye view, standing in Mary's living room when I was going to pull Raymond's tongue out of his mouth for calling me, Uncle Ruben.

What point was Mary trying to prove?

How much longer do I have to endure this chaos? It gripped my childhood; now, it's taking ahold of my adulthood, too? The one thing I was beginning to understand: I would have to get along to move along.

I found myself at the front door of Mary's house. It's funny that I don't recall this door every needing a key to unlock it. I entered into the house; I felt this eerie feeling take hold of me. I was neither wanted here, nor did I belong here. It was as if the house itself had an opinion and was telling me to get out while I can.

It was funny to me, but I finally understood what my mother meant when she said to the real estate agent, "I'm looking for a home that my sons and I can feel safe in and has charm. The kind of home that welcomes you back each time you return." This house was speaking to me and was telling me to get out while the getting is good. What a laugh, or maybe I should listen to the house's ghostliness!

As I was standing in the living room, I could feel the warm sunlight caressing my face as it was beaming through the windows. I was alone, but then again, I did not feel lonely. As I glanced around the living room, I noticed the coffee table had the latest additions of all three tabloids. Mary and Tony had to have arrived here before I did. The girls would not waste their money on a newspaper, much less a tabloid. I turned and closed the door behind me; I was standing outside on the front porch. I was questioning myself, how was I going to make it out of here?

The end of summer was finally here, and Mary and I were not on speaking terms. It was like my Grandmother Rose F. Kennedy said, you do not socialize with the help. I was enjoying my new-found freedom of not having the Gonzales's watching me.

Two days before Tom was to go on trial for killing his wife, Linda, Mary stopped by the house. She wanted to make sure that I attended the hearing. Mary never let on why. She just said that she would go to any lengths to get me there. I had only one interrogative, was Tom going to tell the truth about why he killed Linda? That was the one burning question I had.

Anthony and I drove down to the Los Angeles Criminal Court House early. I wanted to be on time. I made it in time to hear the first witness called to the witness stand.

He was a small white man around 30 to 35 years old. He had light brown hair and brown eyes. I did not hear his name, only that he and his wife became friends with the Proctors from the moment they became members of their church.

He said that they were a lovely couple and that he could not imagine being here today under these circumstances.

The prosecutor asked him, "How long have you and the Proctors been friends?"

"We've been friends going on five years." I could see the strain and anxiety on his face from the back of the courtroom.

The prosecutor said, "Sir, I'm going to show you some photographs. Do you recognize the person in the picture?"

"Yes, I do."

By this time, I could see the tears running down the man's flushed-red face.

"Would you please tell the court who is in the picture?"

"It's Linda Proctor." Before he could say another word, he began to cry.

I could see the image the prosecutor placed on the stand in front of him. They were of Linda still dressed in her white blood-soaked nurse uniform with a bullet between her eyes. I guess Linda's friend and neighbor was only to identify Tom's wife, Linda, in the photographs.

The prosecutor excused the witness. As he was walking past Tom, he looked directly at him, saying "How could you? How could you!"

He kept on going with his head hanging down as he walked out the door.

"Anthony, I cannot hear or see any more. I'm leaving."

I was shocked to see the brutal way that Tom had ended Linda's life. Here was the man that put a gun to my mother's chest and told her, *'if you move, I'll kill your son.'* Memories that I tried to block out all came flooding back after seeing the picture of Linda.

I wanted to get out of the courtroom as quick as I could, but my body felt as if it was moving in slow motion. I finally made it out of the courtroom. I leaned on the cold marble wall to gain my composure.

I did not want Anthony to see me crying. I held my head down and cried in silence. I could not take the agony anymore and ran into the restroom. I made it into the restroom stall and began to vomit. I was worried about my future. Just what was going to happen to me now?

I heard a tap on the door. Before I opened it, I took some tissues and wiped tears off my cheeks and eyes, and my mouth from the vomit. It was a deputy marshall. "Come here, son."

He took me over to the sink, ran the water, and told me to cup my hands and drink from them. "Son, there is nothing worse than the dry heaves. You should be fine now. Go home; you have no business in a place like this."

He walked with me out of the restroom. Looking at Anthony, he said, "Is this your brother? You should have more sense than to bring him to a criminal courthouse. Take him home!"

"Ruben, are you going to come back here again?"

"Anthony, if I have to take the bus, walk, or if you drive me here, I'll be in that courtroom. I want to know if Tom is going to clean his conscience or take one for the team. If Tom does not tell the truth about why he killed Linda, I will. I don't care how long it takes me. The more that is done to keep me here, the more I'll have to write about in a book."

Anthony drove us to Mary's house, where everyone was waiting to hear what happened in court. There was Danny, Yolanda, Vivian, Maryann, Sally, and even Tony and Mary sitting around the kitchen table waiting for the news. Anthony went into the kitchen before I did.

"So Anthony, how did Ruben like the trial?"

"Mary, he did not say a word to me about it. But he's in the other room, ask him."

Mary repeatedly called out from the kitchen, "Ruben, come here; Ruben, come here. I want to talk to you."

I stayed in my room, acting as if I was oblivious to what was going on in the kitchen.

Of course, I was well aware of the conversation that Mary and her family were having, but I was not going to move until she sent someone in here to get me. That someone would be none other than Sally.

Sally came running into my bedroom.

"Ruben, Mom wants you. Didn't you hear her calling you?"

"Sally, I heard her calling for Ruben, but not me!"

"Well, she wants you in the kitchen."

"Tell her I will be there in a minute." I waited for Sally to make it into the kitchen to enter, so she could relay my message.

Mary said, "Why didn't you come when I called you?"

"You called me? I did not hear anyone calling me."

"How could you not hear me calling you when you are in the next room?"

"Well, I heard someone calling for Ruben but not me. Forgive me if I did not come running, but you should have given me a different name if you wanted me to come running, one that I can respond to. Now, what can I do for you?

"You are all sitting around this table like hens in a henhouse, that includes you two, Danny and Tony. Is the henhouse rooster around? Now, what is so crucial that you have to hear it from me?"

"How did you like the first day of Tom's trial?"

"Mrs. Gonzales, I was surprised not to see you and Tony there at the hearing."

"How many damn times do I have to tell you, I never married your father!"

"Mrs. Gonzales, you and I are well aware of that. So should I call you Mrs. Lopez, or is it Mrs. Gomez in your own words?"

"What kind of shady deal are you trying to pull off here today?"

When I was feeling my oaks, Mary would say I was on my high horse, and at this particular moment, I was feeling mighty high. "Mary, the only thing I want you to do is to understand that the longer you keep me here, the more I'm going to have to say. So keep on keeping on!"

I knew that I couldn't stay in the Gonzales house after my little outburst of disrespect for Mary. It was time for me to vacate the premises before all cane broke out. It was hard for me to walk out of the house with a straight face. I don't know what these people were expecting, but by the expression on their faces, they did not get it.

"Anthony, let's go to your place."

We were in the car, and we were out of there.

"Ruben, how could you talk to your mother that way?"

"Anthony, if she were my mother, I would not have any reason to. I adore and respect my mother. And I am talking about my real mother. She did everything she could to keep my little brother and me safe. Mary could not hold a candle to my mother!"

Since I was the one that was cash strapped, Anthony and I agreed that I would clean up the backyard at his place while he prepared for a barbecue.

It was like my mother has always said, "Never show up to a party empty-handed." The cool part about Anthony's parents' property was two rental units and the detached unit Anthony occupied.

On the outside were a chief style barbecue and a small but cozy place for a picnic area that Carl built himself. I was cleaning one small patch of the yard.

As I looked around, I felt as if I had been taken to another place. The backyard had a country feel to it as if I was in the middle of nowhere. There was a small willow tree in the middle of the yard and ivy-covered a chain-link fence. I felt at peace and that everything would be fine.

As I was finishing up the yard work, I could hear Grandpa Joe's advice on money matters.

*"Jack, what is wrong with this picture?"*

The thing about the Bear of Wall Street was his willingness to give you free financial advice only if he was able to participate in your financial success. I began to assess the situation.

*There are three viable living quarters here. One should be used for sheltering the family, and the other two should be set aside as income property; to do anything else is a waste of income.* The Bear of Wall Street would invest the money in the stock market or save it to invest in real estate. The tricky part is, do you hold on to it, or do you spend it?

> *"Remember, it is easy to make money; the difficult part is holding on to it."*

At that moment, Carl came out of the back door of the first house, carrying a platter of meat.

"Ruben, what are you doing?"

"I'm earning my next meal."

"Your next meal!"

"Yes. Anthony is going to barbecue, and I have to clean up."

"I wanted to barbecue this afternoon, too. Where is Anthony?"

"He is in the back house in the kitchen."

"I'm going to talk to him."

Carl came out to the backyard. "Ruben, you did an excellent job on the yard."

I finished gathering the foliage and placed it in its appropriate container. Carl was right; I did improve the scenery. The odd thing was, I've never once heard Carl give Anthony or his brother a 'that a boy,' not once!

Carl gently eased Anthony out of the way and took over the barbecuing. While Carl was doing the barbecuing, I went in to watch the News on television.

There was a news story that I caught the tail end of. It was something about my brother and sister Caroline and JonJon Kennedy.

The newscaster said something to the effect that they almost drowned off the coast of Acapulco, Mexico. I was not sure of what I was hearing, and I was surprised at the news. It was only a month or two ago I read an article in the newspaper. My stepmother Jacqueline Bouvier Kennedy had married Aristotle Onassis to keep JonJon and Caroline out of harm's way.

I did not want anyone to notice that I became solicitous over the news of my brother and sister. I played it off. I was still not sure of what I had heard. Maybe it was a mistake, but my instincts were telling me I needed to listen to the story from beginning to end.

The six o'clock news was beginning when Carl finished up barbecuing. Luck would have it that there was no room at the picnic table for me to eat. I asked Anthony's mother Mona if it was okay if I ate in the house.

"Of course, Ruben. Go right ahead, but be sure not to spill anything on the sofa or carpet."

I went back into the bungalow and sat on the sofa, attentively watching the news, while all the time, I made sure I did not spill anything.

The news came on. JonJon and Caroline Kennedy almost drowned off the coast of Acapulco, Mexico, while swimming off the motored boat that Jacqueline and Aristotle Onassis had chartered for the day. "If not for one of the crew jumping into the water to save them, we may be looking at a different outcome. The crew member said that the two children were yelling for help and that Onassis just sat there doing nothing."

As I was watching that segment of the news, my appetite was slowly drifting away. I did not want anyone to notice a change in my feeling except for being content with the meal. I went outside to help clean up after the barbecue was over.

"Please, Mona, let me take care of the dishes."

"Oh, no, Ruben. Carl does the dishes."

"Mona, Carl was gracious enough to barbecue, let me help out by cleaning up."

"Okay, son, if you want to give a hand, that is fine with me."

I gathered up all the dishes and went into the kitchen to start washing them.

Were Jacqueline and Onassis going to kill my brother and sister because JonJon was my mother's son, and Caroline called my father, Dad?

Why does all this evil persist in my life?

I have to come up with some way to keep them out of harm's way. I decided to take a cue from my mother. When her friend would ask her what she did with the baby that was born in 1959. Her answer was, "He's in your eyes." As far as my sister was concerned, I will only say good things about her.

I finished up the dishes and went into the living room and fell asleep watching television on the sofa.

It was 2:30 in the morning. I woke up, looking around and asking myself, where am I? I felt as if I was weeping in my sleep. It's best that I walk back to the house and leave for school in the morning from there.

No matter how dark the hour, there was always a glimmer of hope. The peace and solitude that surrounded me on the walk back to the house felt as if I was not alone.

The moon's rays were turning the night into a gleaming array of soft grays almost the color white. It made me feel as if everything was going to work out for the best. That sometime shortly, I would see my brother.

As I rounded the corner, the array of white light seemed to fill the warm night breeze with optimism. I entered the house. As I closed the door behind me, the white light was flowing through the door. I walked into my bedroom and laid on my bed and slept till morning.

Of course, it was off to school without breakfast, but then again, there was no adult supervision around either, so who was going to prepare breakfast for five people?

I made it to class on time, but there was the same question that I could not get a handle on. I never gave it much thought, why I was having so much trouble concentrating in school. For some reason, the teacher would ask if I had breakfast before leaving for school. It was hard for me to grasp just what breakfast had to do with my concentration. There was also the question of why I was the thinnest one in the family.

How did they know I was the thinnest one out of my brother and sister? "Do you know them? Did they attend school here?" I replied.

"I can tell by looking at them, you are the thinnest."

"Mrs. Lee, I'm sorry, you mean the Gonzales's. They are not my brother and sister. It would be impossible for you to know my brother and sister. My real brother and sister that is!"

"Ruben, make sure you have a snack at recess. You are incoherent. Now, take your seat."

I made it through the day without another incident. The one thing about living in L.A. was the weather. It was summertime all year round, making it a nice walk to the house. How many people who live here in Los Angeles ever give it a thought that they are living in the middle of the desert? If not for the aqueduct that was built in the year 1913, this city would be desolate by now. Now how does that make me a communist? All I did today in class was state facts, but somehow I'm a communist? So much for a history lesson on LA. I'll probably receive a failing grade on the paper. I should stick to what I know: politics. If I do that, someone will label me a Republican, which is not a bad thing in itself.

I finally made it to the house, and it was the same mundane thing. I entered the house without a soul in it. Walking directly to the kitchen, opening the refrigerator, standing there for a few seconds, looking all the way to the back of the fridge, and closing the door. Some habits are hard to break, and this is one of them.

I walked back into the living room. On the coffee table were the weekly tabloids. Of course, the number of tabloids dwindled down to one. In full view, the headlines read something about the drowning of Caroline and John off the coast of Mexico. Wow! Mrs. Gonzales must not have gotten into bed until after 2:00 AM this morning, just to be informed about her partners in crime. Besides, this is last week's news.

The phone rang. I answered it.

It was Anthony on the other end. "Hey Ruben, how about you come over and help me work on the neighbor's car?"

"Anthony, you have an older brother, ask him to help you."

"You know that we don't get along, Ruben."

"Look, Anthony, I want to get paid. This bartering does not cut it for me. Whatever profit you make, I want half of it, do you understand me?"

"Ruben, I have the tools, I get the customer, and I have the know-how, all you are doing is helping out."

"Anthony, I have one suggestion for you: get yourself another pigeon. I'm not slave labor."

"Okay, I'll give you half the money. I'll be there in 10 minutes."

Anthony was lucky the guy Bob next door asked him to work on his 1963 Dodge Dart. It was a white four-door V8. The fortunate part was that Anthony was using Bob's backyard as his work area. There was no major work that needed to be done to the car. It was a tune-up and an oil change.

"Anthony, I came over here for this? You could have done this work by yourself. What? We're going to split $25.00? That comes to $12.50 apiece. It's no wonder your father is always pissed at you."

"Ruben, I'll buy you dinner. With my own money!"

"No, thanks!"

"Dude! I'll give you half of the money."

"Anthony, you're not going to *give* me anything. I am going to work for it."

"Just stay and give me a hand."

"A hand doing what? This is a one-man job."

"Suppose I get hurt? Who is going to help me?"

"I forget you're accident-prone, and you cry like a little girl when you get cut. You do not like the sight of your own blood, Anthony!"

It took us all of 3 hours to tune up the car and change the oil and filter. Sure enough, Anthony cut himself on the undercarriage of the vehicle. He was screaming for Mona and running into the house. I could not believe my eyes. What a fuss Mona was making over her son's little cut. Actually, the cut required four stitches.

How funny is that! That is where the other hour and a half went: going to the doctor. I guess he was right to have someone with him in case someone was hurt. Bob paid Anthony, and I received half of the profits after the cost of the auto parts were subtracted, which came to an additional $15.00 minus the dinner that Anthony offered. I tried to leave before Carl arrived home, but he beat me to the punch.

I could hear the screen door to the first house slamming; only one person slams the back door that way. Carl!

He came rushing into Anthony's bungalow. "Just how on God's green earth did you cut yourself? That's the very reason I did not want you to work on cars. Why do you think I stopped working for Ford? It was dirty, and I was always getting hurt. I told you not to get in a hurry when you are working on cars. You either get cut, burned, or a damn car could fall on you, in which case you are dead. Look at Ruben; he's cleaned up and ready to go."

Oh, how I dislike when parents use me as an example. Sometimes, some things just do not let you forget where you come from.

Carl's words reminded me of when my Uncle Robert would tell Joe, my cousin, to man up. "The only thing you know how to do when Jack walks into a room is to fall, cry, or wet your pants!"

I could see Anthony's face turning red. The same way my cousin Joe did.

"Carl, Anthony, I'll see you later."

I left out the back door just as fast as I could. As I made my way down the alleyway, I could still hear Carl yelling at Anthony.

I hurried back to the house. As I came to the corner, I saw Tony's car was parked in front of the house. Things were going from bad to worse. I had not seen Mary and Tony in a month or two; I wonder what they're up to or want?

I paused at the top of the hill. Do I go into the house or turn around and go to John's house to have a cup of coffee and wait for them to leave? Just as I was making my getaway, I heard Sally scream, "Ruben is here!" To keep the peace between Mary and me, there was no alternative but to go into the house and play nice.

I walked into the house; the whole gang was there; all the girls, including Danny. Mary was sitting in the recliner, and Tony was to the right of her.

"Hey! What are you two doing here?"

"Just what do you mean by that? I'm your mother!"

"Oh, we are still playing that game?"

"Here I work all night trying to put food on the table for you kids, and this is the thanks I get."

There were just too many of Mary's kids in this room for me to mouth off. So I had to stand there and take her malarkey.

"Oh, I had forgotten that you babysit at night."

"Yes, I do."

I had to bite down hard on my bottom lip to keep from asking when I can meet the kids she babysits. The only kid she was babysitting was the one sitting next to her: Tony.

"So, what brings you two by?"

"I came by to see you."

"Me! Why me? Shouldn't you be worried about Sally? Why me?"

Yolanda steps in. "Ruben, why are you mouthing off?"

"I'm not mouthing off; I'm asking a question, that's all. Can't a person ask a question, Yolanda?"

Mary reached out and picked up one of the tabloids that were neatly laid on the coffee table. I thought to myself, Oh, we are going to play this game again. It was the same headlines about my brother and sister. The only thing Mary did not do was shove the paper in my face. I was not going to play her game. If Mary wanted to know my opinion about my brother and sister, she was going to have to ask me right out. I am not one of her children that she can manipulate into giving up information freely. We'll carry on this charade as long as she likes.

"I'll see you people later. I'm going to Old Man John's."

Mary and I carried on our charade over the next three weeks. By the third week, she was back at it again. This time, she was alone reading the same tabloid sitting in the same recliner.

"Mrs. Gonzales, how many times are you going to read that tabloid?"

"You know me, I always have a book to read in my hands."

"Yes, that's very accurate, but you know something? I've never seen you open it or read it. The tabloids you usually read from cover to cover. Why is that! Just whom do you think you are fooling? That was a rhetorical question. I'll see you later. I'm going to John's."

As I was leaving, I could see the steam shooting out of Mary's ears; I just had to laugh!

Foolish people do foolish things.

Saying I was going to Old Man John's place saved me from having to answer any question. If not for him, I would not be here. Most of the time, I would go to see him, but not this time.

It was the end of the school day, and Anthony was parked in front of the school. He waved for me to come over.

"Hey, what are you doing here?"

"I came to get you so that you'll help me build a bookcase."

"Anthony, how do you know that I'll help you?"

"Ruben, if there is one thing I've learned about you, it's that it is hard for you to let people down. You always say yes, but when it's no, it's no."

"Anthony, I hope you are not taking advantage of my good nature. I'll turn on you when you least expect it. I don't look too kindly on you showing up here unexpectedly. I'm going to help you out this time, but do not do this again."

I got into the car. Anthony took off. The next thing I knew, we were in front of the house.

"Aren't we going to your place, Anthony?"

"Yes, but you need to change your clothes."

"We are going to build a bookcase, not play in the mud."

"Ruben, there is going to be a lot of dust in the air."

"Okay, that makes sense."

"Meet me back at my place."

"Will do, Anthony."

I ran in the house and lo and behold, the whole gang was there, including Mary and Tony. The room when silent when I entered. I didn't know who was more surprised by my entering the house, them or me. Surprised is an understatement, I was irate! I was holding it all in. I tried not to let anyone in the room read my facial expression or my body language. "Tony, I did not see your car parked in front of the house."

"I'm having work done on it!"

"Oh."

I walked into my bedroom to change clothes.

"Mijo! Where are you going? I have something to ask you that we all want to know."

"Look, I have no time right now. Ask me later."

The only way I was going to answer any of her questions was if I had a clear shot out the door. There were just too many Gonzales's in this house for me to shoot off my mouth. I could hear them whispering, but I could not quite make out what they were saying.

"Mijo, come here!"

"Danny, your mother is calling you."

"No, you!"

"Why me? I'm not her mijo. My mother never called me mijo. Jack, Sugar, yes, but mijo never."

I made sure I was standing at the threshold of the front door.

"Mijo, what do you think about the president's kids almost drowning?" That's what I had been waiting for, this very question.

It was my moment to cut loose.

"Mrs. Gonzales, you go back and tell my stepmother Jacqueline Kennedy and Onassis if anything happens to JonJon or Caroline, I'll track her down. And kill her; do you understand me? Tell her for me: if anything happens to my brother or sister, I'll find her and kill her!

"Now, here is your problem that you have. I may start with you, and anyone else who gets in my way. Believe me, God will allow me to carry out my wishes. The crime has to end someplace! And I mean what I just said!"

"Ruben, that's good. Let all that animosity out."

"Mrs. Gonzales, I bet you don't know the definition of the word animosity. I'm trying to make it as clear as possible, I mean what I said! I'll see you people later."

I could tell by the still silence that was emanating from the living room that I drove my point home! I had to get out of there before everyone understood the meaning of my words. I moved just as fast as my legs would stretch out.

How did Grandmother Rose, Uncle Edward, Stepmother Jacqueline, Onassis, and the rest of the Kennedy Clan think I was going to give them an okay? To kill my brother JonJon and my sister Caroline?

What gives these people the idea that I was willing to walk in Cain and Abel's shoes for the rest of my life?

I was at the top of the hill. I could see off in the distance Anthony getting into his father's white '59 Ford Station Wagon. He met me at the bottom of the hill. "Come on, get in. We're going to buy some lumber for the bookcase."

"Anthony, do you even know what size bookcase you're going to build?"

"Yes. Here, open the magazine next to you with the directions in it. Study the layout of the bookcase, that way we measure twice and cut once."

This time, it was not about how much money I would make, but the experience of learning a new craft. I was eager to participate in this building of the bookcase. If I could do this, I will take woodshop in school next year.

Anthony purchased everything he needed to move forward with the building of the bookcase at the neighborhood hardware store. We loaded the lumber, nails, Phillips head screws, glue, wood putty, and the wood stain into the station wagon. We made it back to Anthony's place in under ten minutes. We unloaded the car, and Anthony parked in the very spot he took the car from.

We laid out all the material in the courtyard of his bungalow. Between Anthony's father and brother Carl Allen, they had every tool needed to repair automobiles or do home repairs.

We followed the magazine's instructions to the letter. We measured twice and cut once. The project went off without a hitch. We had sanded the wood and stained it when Carl came to see what was going on.

"Anthony, what is all the noise coming from out here?"

"I'm building a bookcase."

"Where did you get the money for all this wood?"

"The money I was making working on cars I gave to Mona to save for me. So that I would have the funds to build the bookcase."

I looked up at Carl and got this edgy feeling as he was looking at me.

"Anthony, how much money did you spend on all the stuff?"

"One hundred dollars of my own money." With that said, Carl turned and walked away.

"Anthony, why isn't your father or brother helping you with this project? I feel as if I'm interfering with your family."

"Ruben, I've never gotten along with Carl or Carl Allen. I sometimes feel like an outsider in my own home. My sister had to live with my aunt because Carl was too mean."

"Anthony, there is a difference between strict and mean."

"No, he was just mean and harsh! You're more of a friend than Carl Allen is a brother."

We spent the rest of the afternoon assembling and staining the bookcase. It was nightfall when we finished the bookcase; it came out better than we both expected it to.

"Anthony, I'm going to stay here tonight. I'm too tired to go back to the house."

"You can stay in the second bedroom."

After the episode with Mary and her children, I did not need to be told twice that I was not wanted there. It was time for me to start planning out my future, and just now, I wondered, was I going to survive?

# PLANNING OUT THE FUTURE

**I DID NOT SEE** much of Mary anymore. And I did not want to socialize with the rest of the Gonzales's. I kept them at a safe distance, in hopes that I would lose all contact with them. I felt that the further they were from me, the better off I'd be.

I was beginning to feel independent of the stronghold that the Kennedy clan had on me. I would sometimes see my grandmother, aunts, and uncles whisk past me in the neighborhood or downtown L.A... The one thing I was no longer a witness to was money exchanging hands between Mary and my family. With the killing of Linda, all that changed.

I did take woodshop in school, hoping to become a carpenter if need be. However, automobile repair was becoming more lucrative. I was at the point where all I had to do was open the hood of a car, diagnose the problem, and repair it on my own. If Anthony and I were going to open up an auto repair shop, we needed to find a way to price our labor.

Some of the shop owners around the neighborhood advised us to add 25 percent to the parts bill. Doing so would give us an average labor wage. It would work if we had a resale number. For now, we would have to settle for working out of Bob's backyard in exchange for doing gardening work in the front and backyard. It's okay for now, but I was not sure how long I wanted to be an auto mechanic. There just had to be something better out there in this world for me.

I was sitting in my Social Studies class, and the teacher wrote the words 'Affirmative Action' on the board. He asked the class if anyone had heard or knew the meaning of these two words. I've heard those words before, but where? Without thinking, I raised my hand. I could feel my blood run cold.

"Yes, Ruben, what do you think it means?"

"Affirmative Action is a word that my father used to ensure that minorities have an equal opportunity for housing, education, and employment."

"Ruben, I am sure your father did not come up with Affirmative Action. What you mean is you may have heard your father talk about Affirmative Action."

"Why is it people like you do not want to believe me? My father started Affirmative Action, but you want to give the credit to President Johnson!"

The teacher bent over his desk and wrote a note and handed it to me. "I want you to take this to Mr. Sharp's office."

"Why, what did I do? How is it my fault if I am telling the truth!"

"Young man, I am not going to have you disrupt the classroom."

"I am beginning to understand my grandmother; she was right when she said the classes should not mix; I'm out of here."

I was walking out of the classroom. Todd yelled across the room, "Ruben, you always thought you were better than everyone else!"

I made it to Mr. Sharp's office and knocked on the door. As he opened the door, he said, "Ruben, this is becoming a habit with you. What? You like being in the Boy's Vice Principal's office?"

"Mr. Sharp, there is nothing more that makes my day than to come in here to watch a coward do nothing."

"Let me have that note that's in your hand now! Go out into the waiting area. I'll call you when I'm ready."

I handed Mr. Sharp the note and walked out the door.

Mr. Sharp calls in the office monitor, which was another student that brown-nosed to get ahead.

"I want you to keep Ruben in this office while I step out. Now close the door while I make a call." The office monitor was not in my clique, but he had the arrogance to try and talk to me.

"Oh, you've pulled your nose out of Mr. Sharp's backside to breathe? Because I know you're not talking to me."

Just as I was getting up out of my chair, the door opened. Mr. Sharp came out of his office. "I'm going out. Don't let Ruben leave this office, is that understood!"

"Yes, Mr. Sharp."

By the tone of Mr. Sharp's voice, I knew I was in some big to-do. I waited for Mr. Sharp to come out of the principal's office across the hall.

"I have to go to the restroom. I'll be back."

"You know you're not supposed to leave this office."

"If you like, I can urinate in the corner of Mr. Sharp's office."

"Here, take this hall pass and go."

"Hey, you're just as much a peon as I am around here, so you know what you can do with your hall pass!"

I was out the door looking to see what direction Mr. Sharp had gone. I followed him to the same classroom that I left. I walked to the opposite side of the hallway and scurried down the stairs and back into the office. I had to see where he was going. I knew that he did not want to deal with Mary. He always found a way around calling her. I have seen some of the teachers whispering as I passed their class. It seemed that the Gonzales boys' reputation left one heck of a corrupt smell behind.

Mr. Sharp came back and went into his office. As he walked back into his office, he turned to me.

"You. Follow me into my office."

I got up out of my chair and took three steps into his office and left the door open. I stood in front of Mr. Sharp's desk, looking down at him.

"Ruben, who is the authority figure around your house? Take a seat! Ruben, what is the meaning of 'you people'? What kind of remark is that? I hope you have a good explanation for your comments!"

"Mr. Sharp, I am not here for my comments. I'm here for one reason: I said that my father was President John F. Kennedy. He started Affirmative Action and that you people want to believe it was President Johnson. When the fact of the matter is, my father, President Kennedy, left the ball in play, and Johnson made off with it. People like you do not give credit where credit is due. The problem you have is President Kennedy and Marilyn Monroe are my parents. So if you are not going to do something about that, what am I doing here?"

"No, I'll do better than that. Either I swat you, or I call your mother."

"No, Mr. Sharp, you mean Mary! I do not think I would be standing in front of you if my mother was here on this earth today. But you go right ahead and call Mrs. Gonzales or call the police. After all, it is your prerogative!"

"Leave my office and wait in the next office."

"Mr. Sharp, the tone of your voice oozes pride in your office! However, it is the size of a matchbox. So don't lean back too far or you'll fall out the window!"

I watched as Mr. Sharp made three calls, but no one answered him.

"Ruben, come in here. How can I reach Mary, and don't give me a smart-aleck answer, do you hear me?"

"Well, she babysits at night."

"What does she do during the day?"

"I don't know. I never met the kids; she says she babysits, so I don't know what she does or her whereabouts. What I can tell you is to let me go back to class."

"Oh, so you're afraid of your mother?"

"No, but Mary is trying to get in contact with you."

"You want me to believe that she is looking for me when I'm here five days a week, 8 hours a day!"

"Mary believes you are avoiding her calls."

"I am going to suspend you from school, and you're not going to return until she comes back with you. I want to see you and her in my office in that chair before I let you back in school."

"Mr. Sharp, that's not a good idea. I do not want to see the carnage that Mary is going to leave in this office. I am telling you to let me go back to class."

"Mr. Gonzales, this is not over, and it's 2:57. When the bell rings, you can leave."

I walked out of Mr. Sharp's office and kept going. I walked the mile from Vermont and First Street on more than one occasion, but this time, I was not in a hurry to arrive at the house. Not being one who wasted his time, I knew that I would have to come up with a plan until Mary reared her head. I spent the next three weeks going to the library, working on cars, and doing yard work.

I tried to spend four hours a day in the library, reading and writing. I could not get a grasp on the concept of third-person takes an s, sometimes, not all the time. I understood that it was a rule, but I could not get anyone to answer the question, what makes it a rule? There has to be an answer! On my quest for the third person, the librarian came over to me.

"Shouldn't you be in school? I have seen you here at the same time for the last three days."

"The VP expelled me from school."

"Where are your parents?"

"They are deceased."

"I'm sure you have relatives."

"I do, but they probably wish I were dead. That way, they would not have to keep an eye on me. The so-called doctors and specialists told my parents and relatives I would not live past eighteen years old, and somehow it has been changed to twenty-one years old."

"Son, you have to have a guardian."

"What is a guardian? Don't tell me, let me look it up in the dictionary."

I reached over and grabbed the dictionary. "I have not had a guardian since Nov. 22, 1963."

Looking back up at the librarian, I said, "the only guardian I have is the one God gave me, the rest are out for their financial gain."

"Son, I'm sorry to have to tell you this, but I cannot let you come in here before 3:00 PM. That is the rule of the library, not me."

"I would come back at 3:00 PM, but I don't want to destroy your life." I never believed that I would have to leave a place of learning.

By the third week, the phone rang at Mary's house. If there was one thing that I just refused to do, is answer the phone. It made me feel as if I was participating in a crime, but this time the phone would not stop ringing. I finally answered it.

"Is this the Gonzales residence?"

"Yes, it is."

"I would like to talk to Mrs. Gonzales."

"She is not here."

"I want to leave a message for her. Ruben has not been in school for three weeks."

"Yes, that's because Mr. Sharp suspended me."

"Suspended you!"

"Yes, Ma'am!"

"He did not tell me that. Ruben, is your mother working?"

"Well, she babysits at night, so she says, but I never met the kids."

"Well, would you happen to know if Mary is receiving welfare from the state?"

"Yes, she is, but you could not tell by the looks of the refrigerator!"

"This is what I want you to do. Come to school on time and go into the cafeteria, and have breakfast. Don't be late."

The next morning, I was up and out of bed by 6:30 AM. By 7:15 am, I was out the door. Wouldn't you know it, the devil never sleeps! Mary and Tony were pulling up in front of the house.

"Mijo, where are you going?"

"Oh, don't make me laugh. You're just too funny, Mrs. Gonzales!" I kept smiling as I passed her and Tony. Just who does she think she is fooling?

"So how is your babysitting gig going? That was a rhetorical question! I'm on my way to school."

"Let me check on the girls, and I'll take you."

"No, I prefer to walk! Since when do you care if I make it to school or not? I don't have time for your nonsense. Besides, this is not the first time I walked to school, and it probably won't be the last.

I made it to school in record time. Having helped out in the cafeteria in elementary school taught me one thing: Don't be the first one in line, or you'll end up with yesterday's leftovers. I had my breakfast, which happened to be free. Things are looking up. I finished up my breakfast and walked over to the attendance office. I explained to the lady in the office what was going on, and she said, "You're not supposed to be here."

As I was turning to walk away, the truant officer walked in with Mr. Sharp.

"Ruben, I want you to take this note and go to class."

I looked at Mr. Sharp with a grin on my face! I took off like a rocket. I was out of there and on my way to homeroom.

The homeroom teacher took one look at me. "Oh! It's nice to see you let us welcome you back, Mr. Kennedy."

"Think nothing of it, teach!"

"Take your seat!"

I made it to the fifth period without an incident. Wouldn't you know it, right in the middle of the fifth period, some hall monitor from Mr. Sharp's office came in. The next thing I knew, I was on my way to the Vice Principal's office. For the first time, I did not have to wait. I walked right into Mr. Sharp's office.

"Have a seat, Ruben. I'm going to call your mother."

"Mr. Sharp, I would prefer if you call Mary, my guardian, that way, we can get along. Mr. Sharp, before you make that call, I want to forewarn you. I am sure my uncle did not like the scenario the last time Mary sent me to wait for him. Undoubtedly you will not like yours here today either!"

"Ruben, it sounds to me like you are afraid of Mary."

"Whatever derives from you and Mrs. Gonzales's conversation, don't let it reflect on me. She has a vulgar way with words, and that is something my parents would have never tolerated. I suggest you let this disagreement that we have evaporate."

"Ruben, you are like the rest of the boys in this school; you are afraid of your mother."

I leaned back in my chair, "Mr. Sharp, have it your way. Call her, or do you want me to dial the number for you!"

What Mr. Sharp was not aware of was Mary's contempt for authority. I have been in the courtroom and witnessed her tearing the judge a new one. God only knows what Mary is going to do here; she has the upper hand in this case.

I could hear Mary saying, "Hello, who is it?"

"Mr. Sharp from Virgil Junior High School, the Boys' Vice-Principal. I'm calling about your son Ruben; I have him sitting in my office now."

"You're calling me about Ruben! Just who the hell are you kidding here? I have been trying to get a hold of you for the past three weeks, and you have not returned my calls! Now you're calling me about Ruben! What the hell is this! I entrust my daughters to your care, and you let the other boys in your school put their hands on my girls! Just what the hell is this! Now you are calling me for Ruben!

"Mr. Sharp, if you ever try to pull a stunt like this again, I'll have you up against the school board, do you understand me! Now, I want to know what you're going to do for my daughters!"

"Mrs. Gonzales, let me send Ruben back to his class."

I said, "Mr. Sharp, I told you she was looking for you and not to call her. I have no fear of Mary, but it's how she manipulates information to suit her needs."

"Take this and return to class."

I walked out of Mr. Sharp's office, feeling sorry and embarrassed for him at the same time. Mary never cared for her daughters. She used what had happened to them to suit her own needs once again!

I often wondered when all these educated people were going to open their minds to what Mary was doing.

I understand that my father, President John F. Kennedy, gave his life for his country, but he was my father first. What makes everyone turn a blind eye to what's going on around them?

I walked into the classroom; all I heard was, "Where is your hall pass?"

I handed the note to Mr. Cotto. "Now, take your seat." I was never one to hide in the back of the classroom out of fear that the teacher may call on me to answer a question. I always looked for the first row closest to the door in the fifth chair in case there was a fire. I wanted to make sure I was out of the classroom and out of the building without getting hurt.

Yes, that also lead to me being called on to participate in in-class activities. I was more of a willing participant in class activities than I wanted to let on. That is the one thing Mr. Cotto did not understand.

The last ten minutes of class were set aside for the homework assignment. Mr. Cotto wrote the assignment on the chalkboard for the classroom; he turned and looked directly at me.

"Ruben, you are going to write a two hundred word essay on what you mean by 'you people.' I want it on my desk with the rest of your homework, do you understand me? If you come into my classroom tomorrow without it, you're not coming back to my class."

"Mr. Cotto, you are a sore loser. If I were you, I would ignore my words. Someday I'll write a book about what took place in my life, and your name is going to be in it. Just keep that in mind. What happens here today will be read tomorrow!" The bell rang; it was time for afternoon recess.

What is he going to do with a two-page essay? On the meaning of what do I mean by 'you people'?

I had given much thought to what Mary had said to Mr. Sharp during recess. I was embarrassed by Mary's inability to command the English Language. How anyone could believe Mary was my mother is beyond me. But that's life, and I have to deal with it.

I cruised through the rest of the day without any fanfare. The one good thing about attending Virgil Junior High was the RTD bus was right outside the school door. I'll stop off at my locker, gather up the books, which I would need for my homework, and be out the door and on the bus in no time. The next stop would be the Echo Park Library.

Within twenty minutes, I was at the corner of Temple Street and Laveta Terrace. The library was at the end of the cul-de-sac. With a walkway under the Hollywood Freeway to Belleview, from there, it was just four blocks to the house. First things first, I needed some carbon paper. I walked into the library and asked the librarian if she had any carbon paper.

"Yes, I can sell you some for 25 cents per sheet. How many would you like?"

"Twenty-five cents! That's all I have, so let me have one sheet, please."

I found a vacant seat in the back of the library. I sat down and started writing the first thing that came to mind on the usage of 'you people.' It took me about ninety minutes to write the first draft. I proofread it and corrected the mistakes, which was another thirty minutes. I was into the essay for two hours, and I still had not finished the final draft. I checked the spelling and took the carbon paper, placed it between two pieces of paper, and started working on the final draft.

I was coming up on the finish line of the essay when I heard the library was going to close in 10 minutes. I placed the carbon copy in the front of my folder and the original in the back. This way, if one of the Gonzales finds the carbon copy and tears it up, I'll still have the original. I finished just before it was time for the library to close. I made the right turn to go into the underpass and quickly changed direction.

I remembered what Steven did, Mary's nephew. He and his homeboys were lying in wait for some innocent victim to come through the underpass so they could knife him. They wanted to witness their victim bleed out. Besides, sitting in the library for three hours did not help, the walk should be good for me. It was only one long block to the wooden stairs and another block or two to the house.

The next morning, I was up early for school. Hopefully, the attendance officer would do something about Mary's lack of super-vision, and she can find a suitable foster home for me. Anything is better than having to live with all this evil that is engulfing my life. I made it to school on time, which was a feat in itself. The home-room teacher was surprised to see me.

"Well, Mr. Gonzales, nice to see you grace us with your pres-ence; this makes two days in a row."

I had no idea he was addressing me.

"Ruben, when you enter a room, it is customary to say, 'good morning' or 'hello.' Since it is morning, 'good morning' would be most appropriate."

I continued walking to my seat and sat down. Then here comes the homeroom teacher stopping at my desk. I am still oblivious to what is going on. I look up, and the teacher was glaring at me, like a bull ready to charge the matador.

"Ruben, I was talking to you, and you refused to acknowledge me!"

"I had no clue that you were speaking to me."

"I find that hard to believe; I spoke to you twice. I called you by your first and last name. Just who do you think you are?"

"The problem is not with me but with my name. My parents called me Jack, John, and when I was extra sweet, my mother would call me Sugar. Which, by the way, was almost all of the time. So if you insist on calling me Ruben, I may or may not answer! So, until you get the authorities involved, you'll just have to deal with it, and that is totally and utterly up to you. What you intend to do about it is on you!"

He walked away from my desk, leaving me upset. If this was the beginning of my day, what was the end going to have in store for me? I made it through the first period without ruffling the teacher's feathers. I didn't pass the threshold of Mr. Cotto's classroom, where he was waiting to pounce on me like a duck on a June bug. "Ruben, before you enter this class, I want to see your homework. The other essay I told you to write, I want you to place it right here in my hand."

"Sure, do you mind if I go to my desk and pull it out first?"

"No, do it right here on my desk now!" That little mischief mouse has it in for me today. Do I hand Mr. Cotto the essay, or do I fumble through the folder? I'm going to be the bigger man here today and give him the essay.

"Oh, by the way, Mr. Cotto, good morning to you too."

"Ruben, take your seat!"

Oh, God!

He is leaving himself open for a good comeback, but I'll have to let it go. But oh! How I would like to ask him just where he would like me to take my seat too! Things seemed to die down between Mr. Cotto and me.

By this time, I was rolling through the day. It was not until I saw my old flame Maritza standing in the outside pavilion buying lunch did things really start looking up. She still had that gleaming in her eyes when she looked at me. I could never find the right words to say to Maritza. Before I could talk to Maritza, Palma walked up to me. "Ruben, guess who's back!"

"Palma, I can see her, it's Maritza."

"Oh, you still have a crush on her?"

"Pam, is it that obvious?"

"Yes, it is, Ruben."

"Pam, the entire grade school knew that I liked Maritza. I never made it a secret. Let me go before she leaves."

"Oh, you sick puppy."

I stuck my hands in my pockets to make sure they were not all sweaty in case Maritza and I shook hands. I walked up to her and said, "Hello Maritza. It's nice to see you; I heard that you moved out of your old neighborhood. What brings you to Virgil? I heard you were attending Brendon Junior High."

"Yes, my parents bought a house on New Hampshire Ave. the next block over from Vermont."

"Oh, you literally live around the corner."

"Yes, I am."

"Maritza, I have to get lunch. Would you like anything?"

"No, thank you."

"If your books get too heavy, I'll carry them for you."

As I was walking away, Pam said to Maritza, "Isn't Ruben sweet!"

She replied, "He was always lovely, but I don't know about sweet. He was outright mean sometimes."

I felt as if I just hit the Irish sweepstakes. Maritza was back! I got back in the lunch line after talking to Maritza. I happened to get behind Larry and Bogart.

"Hey, you two are not going to ride me about Maritza; you understand me?"

"We'd never think of doing that."

"Oh no, not you two. That's all the two of you did in Rosemont Elementary School was make fun of me and the one that got away."

"Yeah, Ruben, Maritza is still cute, and you still have no chance in hell of going out with her."

"It's like my dad said, 'action is what separates the men from the boys.'"

"Ruben, both of us could take you on."

"Larry, after you whined like a girl in the park, you have no room to talk, and by the way, I'm still not satisfied with the ass-beating I gave you. Let's take our place with the other ninth-graders; maybe we'll find Frank there."

"Yeah, Ruben, you can tell him Maritza is back and still not your girlfriend."

Bogart, Larry, and I walked over to the designated area for ninth graders.

It was a makeshift fence to keep the seventh and eighth graders out and some flunky guards. As I was walking through the gate, the same flunky that was in Mr. Sharp's office was now trying to stop us from entering the holy ground.

"Dude, you need to take a step back and get out of my way."

"Bogart, step in, please. You do not want to get Ruben started. He's pretty rowdy."

"I'm going to report you to Mr. Sharp."

"To each his own, now, get out of my way."

"Ruben, is there a day that you are not in Mr. Sharp's office?"

"Yes, the day that some dodo like you does not mess with me."

"Ms. Baxks, you startled me, and how are you doing today? I had no idea you were behind me."

"Yes, Ruben, all the while. Are you giving Vincent a hard time?"

"No, he knows that I am in the ninth grade, and he's trying to stop me from enjoying one of the perks of being a ninth-grader. Besides, Ms. Baxks, most of these jerks have no idea that this is a form of control. How bogus can the powers get Ms. Baxks?"

"Ruben, you are in my fifth-period class, so you'll be front and center in the classroom to explain what you mean by bogus."

I walked in and mingled with my other classmates. Frank was sitting on a bench, and Mark was sitting behind him, with a tree separating them. These guys lived across the alley from one another. They still do not talk to each other.

Mark is Hawaiian, and Frank is Caucasian; what makes these two so close but so far away from each other? The one common denominator is me trying to bring these two together so that we can become friends. There was Pamela, Jeanie, and Maria getting along without any reservation; however, my male friends are a world far apart, separated by a bench and a tree between them.

Somehow, I always found a way to mingle between each clique of friends. There were the kids like Rolando, who thought of me as an arrogant backside. Who did not want to believe my explanation of why I would not answer to the name Ruben or Ruben Gonzales. Rolando did not want to think that someone with a last name like Gonzales could not roll the R in Rolando. It comes out El Ganzo.

I came, I saw, and now it was time for me to leave. I could not take all this politicking between my peers. I was going to the bleachers in the main yard where all the cool ninth graders hung out. Maybe El Ganzo is right; I'm arrogant in my own way.

"Larry, Bogart, Frank, Mark, I'll see you later. I'm going to the yard where we all share the shade from the trees."

I walked from a stifling sound of silence into the sounds of kids enjoying life. They were running, playing basketball, and talking. I walked across the yard to the bleachers, where the cool kids were sitting. Palma's twin brother Mike stood up.

"Hey, Ruben, did you get kicked out of the ninth-grade hell hole? Or what, you came over here to join us, peon?"

"Mike, the suite you have going on here looks better from afar."

"Now that you're here, you think you can join us little people? Is that it, Ruben?"

"Mike, you're lucky I can take a joke." The bell rang, and it was time for fifth period in the main building on the second floor.

I tried to arrive at class before Ms. Baxks but no luck.

"Ruben, you're the first one here. How nice of you to arrive on time. What did you think, by entering before me, I would forgive your comment on the yard?"

"Ms. Baxks, you don't miss a trick, do you?"

"Ruben, take your seat." The class filled up with all 30 students.

Ms. Baxks stood in front of the classroom and expanded on what I had said earlier in the ninth-grade courtyard. "I am not sending Ruben to the boys' Vice Principal's office for the reason he believes, but for his off-color remarks to Vicente. Now explain to your peers why you think that the ninth grade courtyard is bogus. Come to the front of the class."

I took two steps, and I was front and center.

"If all of you would turn around, you'll see Vicente seated in the second row in the second to last seat. We are in the same class-room, which indicates that we are in the same grade. So when I was entering into the ninth grade court, he had no reason to stop me. Other than to abuse his authority. So it left it open to my inter-pretation of what was going on at the time. I referred to him as a dodo head. Yes, I genuinely believe that the courtyard is bogus.

"It is discrimination on school property; only ninth graders may enter, others need not apply. There is Herbert in the back of the classroom. Most of us in this classroom have known him since grammar school. I have not seen one of you in this room go out of your way to say hello to him. There is not one among my peers that have not asked me why I was socializing with Herbert. I have given you the same answer.

"I believe that there is no discrimination of people in death, so you practice in the here and now!

"Every student sitting in this school has heard of President John F. Kennedy and the Civil Rights Leader Martin Luther King. Both of the men believed in equal rights for every person in this building and across this nation. So who are we to deny anyone the right to the ninth grade courtyard? Especially when there is taxpayers' money involved. So I believe, and I hope that some of you in this classroom agree with me. That to deny anyone the right to enter the ninth grade courtyard solely based on grade level is in itself a form of discrimination."

Ms. Baxks asked the class to vote on the ninth grade courtyard. Two-thirds of the class voted in my favor.

"Ruben, take your seat. That was a well-thought-out defense, and you are up on current events."

I went back to my seat, and the only thing I could think was, one more class to go. I was on my way to my next class when I ran into Maryann. She was cussing and fussing with Danny Virtuous's mother. Mrs. Vircuous was trying to stop Maryann from going home.

"Ruben, come here. Maryann is leaving the school without proper permission."

I said to her, "Mrs. Vircuous, Maryann beats to her own drum. There is nothing I can do or say that's going to make her stay."

"Yes, but she should not let the other girls in gym class upset her." Mr. Sharp came out of his office, took one look at Maryann and me, and went right back inside his office.

"Mrs. Vircuous, let Maryann go home. We will both be better off."

Here comes Mrs. Miskawinski out of the girls' VP office. She asked Maryann to go inside. That was the wrong thing to do. Maryann's colorful language took over. This was when I took off to my next class.

The last period of the day was my business class. It was by far my best subject, and Maritza was in my class, minus her boyfriend Jack.

Maritza and I would talk in class. Once Jack was out of sight, I asked her if she was afraid of him. She answered, not really. I told her, "Jack is a football player, but I'm bigger than Jack is. So if you need some help, let me know. Maritza, I know you are the oldest in your family, and you don't have any brothers, so don't hesitate to ask, and I'll walk you home."

"Ruben, I was with you in the guidance counselor's office the other day. What are you going to take in high school?"

"I was looking into a military career. The R.O.T.C. seemed like a good idea at the time. The counselor told me, 'I don't think you have the temperament for a military career.' The one downside to all that is my uncle Edward is a United States Senator, and the hatred that he has for my father spilled over into my life. He would probably have me shot by someone in my unit. So why make it easy to get rid of me?"

"Ruben, you have always been charming, but sometimes you have a mean streak. Why would you think your family wants to get rid of you?"

"Maritza, it's about money with my family. They are jealous and envious of my brother and me. My Uncle Robert's oldest son and daughter would start crying the moment I walked into a room. My cousin Joseph would fall onto the floor and wet his pants whenever he would see me. Between the two of them, I was always the one who instigated their whining. It was always 'Jack, what did you do now!' When, in fact, my cousins are weak and cowards! My aunts and uncles did not like the reaction my cousins had when we interacted."

"Your name is Ruben, not Jack. Are you trying to be funny?"

"Maritza, it's a long story, one that my loving Grandmother Rose Kennedy and my aunts and uncles would not like to hear."

Business class began. The one thing about this class is it should be called bookkeeping class. All I was learning was how to take care of someone else's money. I took this class thinking I would learn how to invest in the stock market. To become a Bear like Grandpa Joe, one would have to have money to invest and be willing to lose it.

I was doing reasonably well in most of my classes, and I tried like the devil to attend class. Somehow, I knew that I would pay for Maryann's outburst in the hallway. This time I would genuinely be guilty by association.

I was sitting in the school auditorium a week before graduation day. I was told to go to Mr. Sharp's office. I was taking my time walking to his office. Just what have I done now to be summoned to the vice principal's office? My backside did not hit the seat when Mr. Sharp came out of his office.

"Ruben, have a seat in my office, please." I knew this was not going to be good!

I made sure to carry myself as the gentleman that my mother Marilyn would be proud of. I had both shoes planted firmly on the ground and was sitting up straight in my chair, looking directly at Mr. Sharp.

"Ruben, the faculty here at Virgil Junior High, feel that you have not earned the right to graduate across the auditorium stage here at this school."

"No, Mr. Sharp, there is not a teacher in this school who has not told me that I have improved over the last two years. You are upset that I have belittled your authority and made your opinion insignificant. I can see your face turn red with anger. Don't blame your narrowmindedness on me. I have been in this office when the school psychologist told you to keep an open mind. So do not blame me for who my parents are. For the last time, I'm telling you, President John F. Kennedy and Marilyn Monroe are my mother and father. If you fail to call the appropriate authorities, that is on you, not me."

"Ruben, here is your report card for the school year. You'll be attending Belmont High School in the fall. You are required to come to school until the last day of school."

"Mr. Sharp, if you think I'm going to come back here after this afternoon, you are wrong. I refuse to stay in a place that I'm not wanted."

"Ruben, you are the first student that has tried to reason with me."

"Mr. Sharp, you have no clue just how insignificant you are. You hold me accountable for what my father has done. He may not live up to your expectations as to what you believe a president of the United States should be, but that is your fault, not his or mine. So I'll see you in the funny papers, Mr. Sharp." With my report card in hand, I walked out of his office and through the front doors of Virgil Junior High. I could hear him say, "Come back here, come back here!"

# PAUL'S ADMISSION

**THE SUMMER WAS LOOKING** promising. I did not have to witness Mary or the rest of the Gomez's, Gonzales's, or Rodriguez's meetings with the Kennedy's. The one thing that I was trying to do was keep away from the Gonzales family. It had been about three years since I had contact with Mary's ex-husband or her son Bobby. The rest of the Gonzales clan would come to look for me if they did not see me for a month or two at a time.

With the first one hundred dollars I saved, Anthony, Vivian, and I planned a camping trip to Yosemite National Park. Anthony drove the five hundred miles from Los Angeles to Yosemite; it took us about 5 hours to arrive at the entrance of the park. It was about noon when we finally arrived at our designated camp area. We popped the tent, which happened to sleep six people. I had not felt this peaceful since both my parents and I were alone, just the three of us, in Miami Beach, Florida. No one had a clue who they were, for all anyone knew, we were just another family on the beach.

The sky was so clear. The moon was shining through the blue sky as if it was the middle of the night. I was even bedazzled by the fragrance that was permeating from the surrounding beauty of the forest. It had been eight years since I have felt at one with Mother Nature. I had almost forgotten just what it felt like to feel free.

I was feeling the loss of my parents. If they were here with me now, would they feel what I feel? Why were they taken from me at such a young age? I did not want Anthony or Vivian to see me cry or ask me what I was thinking, so I cried in silence. I continued to set up camp while all the time keeping my head down. The camp was finally set up, and it was time for lunch.

We had lunch and decided that it was time for a swim in Mirror Lake. The lake was a ten-minute drive from our campground. Once we arrived, we had to find a place to park, which would have been fine, but there was a half-mile walk to the lake.

Looking across the pond, I understood why it was named Mirror Lake. The reflection from the surrounding area was reflecting off the lake. It was as if the surrounding mountains and trees were put on display before going out to the grand ballroom dance. I could see the mirror image of Half Dome Mountain. When I tilted my head, the reflection would change. The splendor of it all was the same as looking up. Mirror Lake should be one of the wonders of the world.

I walked to the edge of the lake. Looking down, I could see my reflection staring back at me. There was a vast boulder protruding from the water in the middle of the lake. It was as if Mother Nature herself was daring me to swim out to it. The distance between the edge of the lake to the rock was not the problem. It was the icy cold water that I had put my feet in that was the game-changer. There was that inner voice in my head that was saying, "Go for it!"

I put my right foot into the water, feeling around to find out how shallow the water was. I did not see any rock at the bottom of the lake. I bent my knees, and off the rocks and into the water I went. It was a clean dive into the icy cold water. Once I was in the water, I started swimming with long, even strokes. The water was becoming chillier, but I knew if I kept swimming, I'd make it to the boulder.

I looked up at the boulder. I imagined that I could see my fingertips on it. The more I swam, the closer the boulder became. I finally made it. Before I could give it a second thought, I was out of the frigid, freezing water and on top of the boulder. I was shivering, and my teeth were chattering, but I made it.

I was on top of the mountain — me all alone in the middle of Mirror Lake, what a feeling! If the world could see Yosemite

National Park from where I stood at that moment, it would have to admit, there is a caring and loving God! What a spectacular view from this vantage point. It looked as if I walked across the reflection of Half Dome Mountain and never got my feet wet! The sun is, indeed, a poor man's blanket. I laid on the rock. To my surprise, it was warm. I wanted to stay lying on the rock for as long as possible; however, if the clouds blocked the sun rays, the water would become increasingly colder.

As I was soaking up the sun's rays, I felt a cool breeze flowing across my shirtless chest and bare legs. It was Mother Nature's way of letting me know it was time to dive back into the icy water. I took a step to the edge of the rock and dove into the water and started swimming as fast as I could. The chilly water gave me the incentive to keep on moving as quickly as I could. To slow down or stop swimming, the consequence would be too grave.

The distance between the lakeshore and the boulder was about the length of two Olympic-size swimming pools. I could swim that without a problem, but that was in a heated pool. Here I was, faced with getting back into an icy lake; if I made it out to the middle, I was surely going to make it back to the shore. I was out of the water, before I realized it, standing on my own two feet!

Vivian, Anthony, and I started walking back to the car. We were chatting and strolling along, shirts and shorts dry. I was surprised that Anthony was right, we did not need towels to dry off. There is something to be said about a seasoned camper.

Once the sun started to go down in Yosemite Valley, it disappeared quickly behind the mountains to the west. The valley became pitch black, and that was when the stars and the moonlight shone their brightest. It seemed that everyone in the campground had a flashlight. It was a throwback in time. I don't know if the first settlers of California came through this valley, but I would like to think they did. If they did, what would their campground have looked like? It was time to rise from that camp floor and enter into the tent and into my sleeping bag for the first night!

I was awakened the next morning by the soft-spoken voice of the camper next to us. The campers were in a hurry to start their day early. It seems that the early bird does get the worm! It was 6:00 in the morning when I stuck my head out of the tent. There was a line already forming at the restroom and shower. There was no time to waste; I gathered up my toiletries and headed for the restroom. Having to live in a house with seventeen people and one bathroom taught me to be the first one in, first one out.

As I was making my way back to the camping area, I saw that Vivian was up! For the first time since I had known her, she was out of bed before 10:00 AM on Saturday, which is not a school day. The one noticeable thing that a campground has that is lacking in the city is the feeling of community. The neighbor says 'good morning' to be neighborly, but the camper says 'good morning' because he or she means it!

Breakfast was going to be potatoes, eggs, and bacon. I piled, cut, and placed the potatoes in boiling water. By boiling the potatoes first, I reduced the frying time in half. I let the potatoes simmer no more than ten minutes tops. I drained the water from the potatoes and let any excess water evaporate. I placed them in a hot skillet. The sizzling noise that the potatoes made when they hit the skillet meant that the potatoes were going to cook to perfection. They would come out golden brown on both sides once I turned them over in the skillet.

Here I was, cooking in the middle of the forest, trees all around me. What a feeling! I placed another skillet on the fire to heat up. I set the bacon into the skillet. Again, the sizzling noise, but this time the aroma of the bacon came rising off the skillet. Giving me a sense of, this is what life is all about, just pure, clean living — being out in the open the way the human race was supposed to live. Lost in my thoughts, Vivian and Anthony simultaneously asked.

"What are you thinking?"

I looked around, and I became aware that I was sharing the campground with other human beings.

I made it a rule never to tell anyone my most profound thoughts!

"Oh! Not a thing. Standing here cooking."

Just as I answered, a neighbor from the next campsite came over. "I've been watching you. What were you thinking or better yet what were you imagining?"

"I was one with Mother Nature and all her splendor. It's been almost nine years since I have indulged in such tranquility."

"Son, you are too young to have those kinds of thoughts."

"Yes, I am, but I lost my parents not too long ago, and I am trying to survive."

"I could not tell by the way you look now. If you haven't noticed, most of the campers are watching you enjoying preparing breakfast. Thank you for taking the time to answer my questions and enjoy your day."

The stranger walked back to his campsite, and I continued preparing breakfast. The stranger was correct; I was enjoying the open air and my surroundings. We had our breakfast and spent the rest of the day hiking and sightseeing.

I broke the first rule of camping; I wandered off. I wanted to be by myself. I did not want to share the feeling of content with anyone. The cool breeze was caressing my face as I gently tilted my face to the sky. Looking at the top of the trees as they swayed in the breeze. The crackle of twigs and leaves as I walked in the woods was soothing to my soul. I did not want to stray too far off course. I turned around and headed back to the campsite.

At the end of the day, Anthony and Vivian had just about all they could take of Yosemite. They wanted to leave one day earlier than our scheduled departing date. Anthony decided we would take a journey to San Francisco. It just so happened that his aunt lived in Berkeley.

Anthony and Vivian wandered into the little town to call Mona, Anthony's mother, to have Mona call his aunt in Berkeley to let her know that the three of us would be staying with her for one day. I enjoyed the idea of being alone in the campground but dreaded the thought of going to Frisco. There was nothing more mind-clearing as being alone in Yosemite.

As I was lying on the ground, gazing up at the stars, I began to think about my plight and how it was going to end. The first thing I had to do was come up with a plan. How to get Mary and Paul to admit that I am not their son. This way, if I ever have to stand in front of a judge, I can say Mary and Paul finally admitted that they are not my parents. Just as I thought about what to do, I could see the headlights from the Thunderbird pull up. Anthony walked over to me.

"Ruben, what are you doing lying out here?"

"Oh! Nothing, thinking about life. Where will I be when I turn twenty-one, according to Mary's birth certificate."

"What are you talking about, Ruben?"

"Oh, never mind, Anthony. If you don't know by now, you never will. I'm going in and going to bed."

We were up and having breakfast by 7:00 AM. At 8:30, the tent was down, and the sleeping bags were in the car. It is camping etiquette to leave your camp area just as clean as you found it or cleaner. I had enjoyed the camping experience immensely. I cleaned up the area next to us as well. The Forest Ranger told us the first day we entered the Park, "A good camper does not leave his footprint behind. That way, no one would know you were there."

We were off and on our way to San Francisco. The first four hours of the drive to Yosemite National Park did not bother me as the last two did to Frisco. The closer we got to Frisco, the more anxious I became. Anthony and Vivian wanted to see Frisco before going to Anthony's aunt's place.

As Anthony was driving off the freeway, I wanted to jump out of the car. San Francisco was a city that I could live the rest of my life without visiting. It wasn't that I disliked the place, it was just a place that brought back unpleasant memories. The only thing I wanted was to eat and get the hell out of San Francisco! Anthony wanted to have lunch on Fisherman's Wharf.

"Look, Anthony, I'm not going to debate with you where to have lunch. I am not going to Fisherman's Wharf for lunch. If you and Vivian want to have lunch there, that's fine with me. But I'm not going to that place! Chinatown is up the street; I'll eat there. You and Vivian have lunch at the Wharf. I'm going to get out of here and find my way to Chinatown to have lunch and take the bus back to L.A. But I'm not going to eat at Fisherman's Wharf; do you understand me?

"Anthony! Do you?"

"Yes, Ruben, but your cheap ass is the one with the money."

"Don't make this about money! I feel awful, dreadful in this city. Here is where my whole world started crumbling for my mother and me."

"Ruben, have it your way. I'll have lunch in Chinatown."

Vivian turned her body and placed her left arm on the seat to face me.

"Ruben, why don't you want to eat at Fisherman's Wharf?"

"Vivian, what are you going to do? If I answer your question, you're going to tell your mother what I answered, and she is going to have one of you do her dirty work. So let's just have lunch here in Chinatown!"

We had our lunch. As soon as we finished, Anthony drove to his aunt's home in Berkeley. It was a lovely single-level house on the top of a hill. Anthony pulled into the driveway and parked under the carport. His aunt greeted us at the door. As we entered, I noticed a view of San Francisco in the far-off distance. She had us place our things in the guest bedroom. Vivian got the bed, Anthony and I had to sleep on the floor in our sleeping bags.

The next morning, we were up early. As we were having coffee with Anthony's aunt, she asked if Vivian and I were husband and wife.

Vivian spontaneously answered, "No! We are sister and brother."

I was stunned by the question! The only thing I could think to say was, "Yes, we are brother and sister for now!"

"I would never take you for brother and sister. You do not look alike. There is no resemblance at all, but you would make a cute couple."

Anthony, looking at me, said, "Ruben, please don't say anything."

Anthony and I loaded our things in the car and went back into the house. I thanked his aunt for her hospitality and for letting us stay in her home.

As we were walking to the door, she asked Anthony if Vivian and I were really sister and brother. "Anthony, they neither look alike nor do they speak the same. Ruben has an excellent vocabulary compared to Vivian's. I don't think they are brother and sister, Anthony!"

Again, I thanked his aunt and got in the back seat of the car; next stop, Fisherman's Wharf.

It was still early enough that we were able to find parking at the wharf. We sat in the open-air restaurant. As I was looking across the bay, I was thinking of my parents and the many times we came here to enjoy ourselves. As my father so often did, I had the White New England clam chowder for breakfast with sourdough bread. As he would often say, "I'll take White New England chowder over oatmeal any day of the week."

I was lost in the memory of my parents when Vivian said, "I'll give you a penny for your thoughts." I slowly drifted back into the here and now.

"What did you say? Did someone say something?"

"Ruben, what were you thinking?"

"Oh me?"

"Yes, you. Who else?"

"Oh, I was taking in the view. It is magnificent!"

"Ruben, who are you trying to impress? Anthony's aunt is not around anymore."

"Vivian, sometimes I forget whom I am speaking to; it all has to do with class."

"What do you mean by that?"

"By what Vivian?

"As I said, it all has to do with class. That's what I mean. Vivian, I am following my social class; that is what I mean. We do not have the same parents, and we come from different social types. That is what Anthony's aunt was trying to say. Just now, you don't like the way I speak. She noticed the differences in our vocabulary; we don't speak the same. As I have said in the past, I say now. If you don't like the way I command the English language, do not converse with me."

"Ruben, you make me sick! You think you're better than everyone else."

"No! Vivian, those are your thoughts, not mine. I'm going to the car; I'll wait for the two of you there."

As I was walking away from the table, I heard Vivian tell Anthony, "You do know that when he said he would take the bus back to Los Angeles, he meant it?"

"Yes, but we got him to buy breakfast."

"Anthony, there is a good chance he still may take the bus back."

I strolled along the wharf with the memories of my parents. How we walked down the sidewalk hand in hand. It was just the three of us. To hear the passers whisper to one another, what a beautiful family.

"Yes, but did you notice how tiny she is and how tall he is?" Memories. They never leave you. They come back in the least expected place and time.

I finally made it to the car. I leaned up against the front fender. Looking out across the bay, lost in my memories. I heard a faint voice saying, "What are you thinking?" The sound was drawing me out of my memories and back to my present-day plight. I turned to see who was speaking. I had this overwhelming feeling to say 'none of your business. I'm not sharing my very own memories with you, and you are not welcome to them.'

"Oh! It's you, Vivian. You startled me."

We got in the car, leaving San Francisco behind us.

Anthony decided that we would take Highway One down along the Pacific Coast Highway of California. The mountains on the left side and the Pacific Ocean to the right of us.

Anthony and Vivian wanted to pick up a hitchhiker, which was not uncommon to do. "Look, you two, I'm in the back seat, and there is barely enough room for me, now you want to pick up a hiker? That's not cool at all." Anthony sees a girl on the roadside with her thumb out and pulls over.

She runs up to the car, and Anthony asked, "How far are you going?"

"I'm going down to Carmel." She gets in the car behind Anthony, and he drives off. We made small talk, the usual thing.

Where do you come from? What do you do for a living? That sort of thing. Thank God she was only going to be with us for an hour or so. Anthony stops off at Santa Cruz, where Hannah picked up seashells on the beach.

Hannah placed the seashells in the trunk of the car, and we drive off. Hannah told us she was an artist, and she was visiting friends in San Francisco. They had given her a ride as far as their job was, and she would continue walking until someone stopped and gave her a lift to Carmel. Hannah seemed to be a nice enough person, but then again, who is not when they are in need? We made it just south of Carmel, where Hannah asked us to pull over and let her out. It was picturesque where she asked us to stop. Anthony looked in the rearview mirror at Hannah.

"I can drive you to your home if you'd like."

"No, this is fine. I live just on top of the hill in a small cottage surrounded by trees and flowers." This place was something out of a painting. The highway was in between the rolling hills with trees lining the right side of the road. To the left side were trees; between them, I could see the Pacific Ocean.

Anthony got out of the car to let Hannah out. They both walked around to the trunk of the car. Anthony was handing Hannah her bag when her seashells fell on the ground. The girl turned into the Wicked Witch of the West.

"These seashells are for my artwork! Now, look at what you have done! They are all over the place, you imbecile!"

I immediately got out of the car!

"Anthony, do not say a thing; she may have a switchblade on her! Get back in the car and let's get out of here!"

Anthony shouted out some expletives at Hannah that are commonly used among ordinary people. If it were up to me, I would have just said, 'have a nice day!'

We continued down the scenic highway US 1, only stopping for gas and to eat. We were finally able to see the city of Santa Barbara. We stayed in Santa Barbara to have dinner. The long 8-hour drive from Carmel to Santa Barbara took a toll on Anthony.

His fatigue was apparent when he was trying to get out of the car and walk into the restaurant. We had our dinner and coffee.

"Ruben, I'm too tired to drive. You are going to have to take the wheel the remainder of the way."

"Anthony, this is rush hour, and I am not used to driving in heavy traffic. I am willing to drive, but let's wait until the traffic dies down. Let's go and sit on the beach, and I'll buy another cup of coffee to go."

It was about 7:30 PM when we started driving to Los Angeles. The one part of the drive that was the coolest for me was the Grapevine. I always believed that Ford Motors built this '63 T-Bird to take on this stretch of highway. Man, there was a 390 Engine with a four-barrel carburetor under the hood.

I pulled all the way over to the left lane. There were no '65 miles an hour' for me. I was going to open this baby all the way. This Bird was flying with ease; my right foot was barely resting on the throttle, and she was talking to me. As if to say, *I have more to give.*

I topped 70 miles an hour, and she was eating up the highway. I had to keep my eye on the gauges to make sure the T-Bird did not overheat. My eyes were moving from the left side mirror to the rearview mirror as I held the throttle going up to 80 miles an hour and watching out for the California Highway Patrol. I was passing tractor-trailers, and those Sunday drivers to the left of me were taking their lovely time to make it up this mountain.

As I was approaching the top of the Grapevine, the T-Bird was ready to be airborne. I was at the top of the mountain, heading down. It was like an E-Ride ticket at Disneyland. What a ride into the San Fernando Valley of Los Angeles County. As I headed down the other side of the Grapevine, Anthony said, "Pull over. I've had enough rest." I eased up on the accelerator as I started descending down the mountain and pulled over into the next right-hand lane. I did not pull all the way over until I made it to the bottom of the Grapevine. Once I was at the bottom, I pulled to the far-right shoulder and let Anthony back behind the wheel.

"Anthony, you were afraid to drive the drive up the Grapevine. Does that make me your pigeon or a more capable driver? Which one would you have it be?"

"Neither, I was just tired of driving." It was another forty-five-minute drive to Anthony's house. We pulled up into the alley behind Anthony's bungalow, unloaded the car, and hung up the sleeping bags to air out. It was too late to do anything but shower and get ready for school.

The next morning, Vivian ran to her house to get ready for school. I was still asleep on the sofa when she left. As she was closing the kitchen door, I woke up. I sat up and had to think for a moment or two where I was. I scurried around, looking for my knapsack. I finally located it and took off out the back door. I ran to the house to bathe. I was ready for school in 10 minutes. I was heading out the front door when Vivian called out, "Wait up. I'll walk with you to school."

"If you don't hurry it up, we'll be late."

"Aw! Hold your horses. Wait 5 minutes!"

"Okay, but if you are not done in 5, I'm out of here."

Vivian and I did not make it to the footbridge when she started setting me up. "Look, Vivian, what is up with you? I told you three weeks ago to ask Dicky, Bobby, Charlie, or Anthony to take you to see your father."

"Ruben, you're here."

"Yes, but Paul is not my father, and I don't care if I ever lay eyes on him again. Now, stop asking me to take you to see him, and I mean it."

We made it to school. I managed to make it to homeroom on time. Some of the same friends I had in elementary school were in my homeroom class.

It made me feel as if I was in a rut, and I was never going to find a way out of here. My life was becoming routine. I ran into Vivian and her friend Dolores that happened to be the sister of a friend of mine named Rick Silva. Today was turning out to be a beaut. How could it get any more poetic than this?

"Dolores, how's Rick? I have not seen him for a long while."

"He is with his father."

"Oh!"

"Why the strange look on your face?"

"Sometimes I'm a bit naïve, that's all. I do not always put two and two together, and it comes out with four."

Vivian said, "Dolores, I've been asking Ruben to take me to see our father, but he does not want to go."

"Vivian, you're not going to go there again. Ruben, why won't you go and visit your father?"

"Dolores, I've known you and Rick since grammar school. How many times do I have to tell you? Paul is not my father, and I don't like the man."

"Ruben, I talk to Rick's father. Why don't you speak to Vivian's?"

"Someday, I'll answer that question."

"Ruben, you should take Vivian to see her father."

"Dolores, it's all in the wording. I'll think about it."

"By the way, how are those rushing fingers and roaming hands of yours, Ruben?"

"I hope you did not tell Rick!"

"I did!"

"Oh, God, you didn't."

"Yes, I did."

"What was Rick's reaction?"

"Well, the only thing he said was, Why, Ruben?"

"Dolores, I am going to prove to you that I am not a heel somehow. I'll see you around."

It had never dawned on me that Rick and Dolores had different fathers but the same mother. That why Rick's last name is Silva, and Dolores's last name was Olivera. Go figure. Two and two finally make four; I just had to laugh at myself as I was walking to class! The school day ended just like clockwork at 3:00 PM.

I waited for Vivian at the corner of Union and Beverley. To my surprise, Dolores was with her. The three of us walked to the house together. "Dolores, you live five long blocks from us, just up the hill from where we attended grammar school together. That's an awkward walk to your house."

"Yes, it is, but I'll call my sister. She'll come and get me." It was looking promising! As we were walking, another of Vivian's friend's name Wilber met up with us and decided to walk along with us. Wilber lived on the other side of the Hollywood freeway. The freeway happened to be the racial divide. Some African Americans lived on the same street with us, but they were an old adult couple.

As the four of us were walking across the footbridge, I found myself looking at Dolores. She was this nice, pleasant, soft-spoken girl with long black hair. She sometimes would work with her mother's housekeeping in some big hotel downtown. There had to be a way for me to beguile her. To show her I am a stand-up guy. That if she were to date me, I'd be there for her. I had to do more than carry her books for her. I had to come up with something before she called her sister for that ride home.

I walked with Dolores to the house and left the moment she was comfortable.

"Dolores, don't leave until I get back, please. I'll return in 5 or 10 minutes. So please wait."

I took off running as fast as my legs could move, which was pretty damn fast. It took me about 3 minutes to run the three blocks to Anthony's house. I came to the alley, and Anthony's T-Bird was parked in the back of his bungalow. I could see it when I rounded the corner of the alley. I was flying at this time. I pushed open the gate and went right into his bungalow.

"Anthony, I need a favor. Let me borrow your car."

"Ruben, where are you going?"

"Anthony, just let me have the keys. I don't have time! This is an emergency."

"Where do you want to go in my car?"

"Anthony, I need this favor. I'm not going into a song and dance over this. Just let me have the keys."

"Wait until I get out of the shower, and I'll take you."

"Anthony, if you don't let me borrow your car, I'll never do a damn thing for you again, and I mean it!"

"Ruben, the keys are on my dresser drawers.

"I'll be back in one and a half hours with your car."

I was out of that house like a flash of light. The next thing I knew, I was in front of the house. I pulled into the driveway and stopped the car; I took a couple of deep breaths to calm down. I walked into the house and told Vivian, "Let's go."

I hurried back to the car. I pulled the car out of the driveway. I parked in front of the house and opened the door for Dolores to make sure she sat next to me in the front seat. Vivian sat in the back seat with Wilber. I got in the car as fast as I could. I did not want Vivian to ask Dolores to ride in the back seat with her. I was going to make sure that Vivian got the hint that this was not about her.

Dolores looked at me with her big brown eyes and a surprising look on her face. "Ruben! I had no idea that you knew how to drive."

I looked right into her big eyes and said, "Dolores, I've been driving for some time now."

"Wow! I had no idea!"

"Don't worry; I've taken drivers-ed in school!"

"By the way, where are we going?"

"You'll see. Sit back and enjoy the ride." Dolores turned and started chatting with Vivian and Wilber while I drove. I made my way down Bonnie Brae Street to 6th Street and made that left turn on 6th Street and continued to Union Ave. and onto Pico Blvd. where I made another left and stopped at 1552 West Pico Blvd.

It just so happened that the Gonzales and Sons TV & Radio Repair Shop was open for business. I got out of the car to open the car door for Dolores. After all, it was all in for me at this juncture. The four of us walked into the shop. I let Vivian go before the three of us; she stopped at the counter where her mother once sat. There was a clear view where I was standing to where Paul was positioned in the back of the shop. He could see us arriving in the T-bird.

I could read his facial expression, he did not like seeing me.

He looked over towards Vivian, "Mija, how are you!"

"Dad, I'm fine, and you?"

"And what the hell are you doing here, Ruben! You know I'm not your father!"

"Paul, you're not telling me anything I do not already know! *It's nice you finally admit it.* Vivian has been asking me to bring her here to see you. I don't care if I never see you again in my life. Any man who has done to their father's last name what you have done to yours, I want nothing to do with. I have never referred to you as my father, much less called you my father. I'm well aware of who my parents are. If not for the crime that you and your ex-wife Mary committed, I would not know you.

"Remember, you have this business, and Mary has her home for a crime, not that you achieved this through work. Paul, it took me seven years to get you to admit that I am not a damn thing to you. Your ex-wife said she was going to confess her sins to me in 1980. Paul, there is one down and one to go.

Paul, thank you. Vivian, I'll wait for you in the car. Dolores, I thank you for your words of wisdom."

I walked out the door and into the Thunderbird. I could not believe that this day finally arrived! Oh, what joy! To have two unwilling participants, Dolores and Wilber, hear Paul say he is not my father.

Oh, joy!

Vivian, Dolores, and Wilber came out of the shop about ten minutes after I did. As they were walking out the door of the shop, I got out of the door of the car. I opened the door for Dolores and pulled back the bucket seat and told Vivian to get in. Wilber walked around to the driver's side and got in the back seat. As I closed the door, I looked down at Dolores's big eyes with a grin from ear to ear and kissed her on her cheek. I turned and got into the car. I looked over to see Paul leaning against the door frame of his shop. I looked up at Paul from behind the steering wheel, nodding to say goodbye.

There was dead silence in the car as I drove off. I had to bite my lip to keep from expressing any joy. I didn't want Dolores to feel sorry for me; however, this genuinely worked out to my advantage. I looked over at Dolores and tried to keep a solemn expression on my face.

"Dolores, I'm sorry that you had to witness and hear Paul's upheaval."

"Ruben, I do not blame you for not wanting to see him again in your life."

"I'll not be seeing him anytime soon."

I had one hand on the steering wheel and the other hand resting on the console. I glanced down. I realized that Dolores was caressing my hand.

"Ruben, I've heard rumors that you are ashamed of your parents, but after witnessing and hearing Paul's admission, I don't know what to believe."

"Dolores, I'm not here because my parents placed me here. I'm here because my parents trusted my grandmother, aunts, and uncles. Why would you believe I'm ashamed of my parents? Never! What?"

"Mary is not your mother. You look like an American White Boy, but you and Vivian do not have the same father. Ruben, your last name is Gonzales. Why?"

"Dolores, Gonzales is the name on the fake birth certificate that Mary and Paul used to make the authorities believe that I am their son. Dolores, it is detrimental to our health to discuss the matter at hand any further." I changed the subject. "Hey! Why are the two of you so quiet back there?"

It didn't work. "Ruben, you're not upset with what Dad said to you back there?"

"Vivian, why should I be angry when all Paul did was tell the truth? I'm not his son, or were you expecting something different?"

I dropped Wilber at his place first. I made a left on Beverly Blvd and a quick right into the alley between Westlake Ave and Bonnie Brae Street. Wilber was getting out of the car when he said, "Ruben, you knew Paul was not your father?"

"Yes, I knew. Why? The three of you seem to be more upset with Paul's outburst than I am, and I'm the one he confuses too, Wilber."

Anthony's father was usually shooting the breeze with his friends down the street from Wilber's place at this time of day. I did not want Carl to see me driving Anthony's car without him. So I decided to take Court Street to Alvarado. The bad thing about Alvarado and Court Street was that Court Street was a steep hill, and cars sometimes rollback at the top of the hill. I do not need an accident while trying to impress Dolores.

I finally made it across Alvarado and on down to Rose Lake Ave. I made a left on Temple and a quick right up Rosemont

Ave. across the Hollywood Freeway. The first house on the right was where Dolores lived. From here, it was just a few blocks to Anthony's place.

I returned the car to Anthony without a scratch on it. I was in the bungalow, handing Anthony the keys to his car when Carl crept up behind me.

"Ruben, was that you driving Anthony's car?"

"Yes, it was me. I was driving Dolores home."

"You made it back here in one piece and without a police escort, but don't let me catch you driving without a driver's license again."

"No, sir!" Carl was the kind of father that would do what needs to be done to help his sons become successful. Anthony and his brother Carl Allen did not appreciate their father. I was intimidated by Carl. He had that 'I'll beat the hell out of you if you don't heed to my advice' look on his face, and his attitude backed it up. I had to get out of there before my legs buckled underneath me.

Things were working out well between Dolores and me. Every chance I had, I would talk to her in school, or if she would come to the house to see Vivian, I was Johnny on the spot! One of the things I noticed was that Dolores did not care for Anthony. She believed that he was a bad influence on the entire Gonzales clan. I never argued the point with her. Probably because it's true, and I have a crush on her.

Vivian and Wilber were talking to Dolores about one of the weekend drives that we went on with Anthony. It was Saturday night, and Anthony decided that we should all take a ride up to Mount Wilson. It was a trip that I had made on many occasions. I learned how to drive going up and down Mount Wilson mountains. It was approximately an hour or two, depending on traffic to get to the top of Mount Wilson. On a clear night, I was able to see in the Los Angeles basin. This particular Saturday happened to be one of those nights.

The four of us piled into the Thunderbird and headed to Mount Wilson. It was around 9:00 PM when we left Los Angeles. We did not realize how cold and chilly it was going to be once we made it to the top of Mount Wilson. After all, it was up the hill from the City of Pasadena, depending on which road we took. Once we were at the top of Mount Wilson, Anthony pulled over and parked.

We all got out of the car. The cold chilly night air came rolling across my face. The Los Angeles basin was lit up like a million stars in the sky. I turned around, my back was facing the L.A. basin, and the moonlight was lighting up the passages through the mountain. It was a sight to see. The night sky was gray in color. Cars driving on the road in the far distance were twisting and winding with the roadway. I got back in the car while Anthony, Vivian, and Wilber talked. They began to feel the cold and came running to the car.

As we were headed back down the mountain, Anthony pulled out a marijuana joint. He held it up so that I could see it. I had seen a joint rolled before, but this one was rolled to perfection. Look at the perfectional job. The person who rolled this joint had to be the work of Gilbert; it was symmetrically perfect and tantalizing, calling me to partake in its enjoyment. I was quite surprised by its magnificence. The way that Anthony was rolling the joint in his fingertips and the reflection in the rearview mirror was begging me to try it.

"Anthony, you should know better! I have no interest in doing drugs! Tonight, it's pot. What will it be tomorrow? Not that I want to find out. I do not want to do drugs."

"Ruben, pot is not a drug." Vivian and Wilber happened to agree with Anthony.

"Vivian, you of all people should know not to smoke that. Remember when your mother gave us those red sleeping pills, and Charlie found out? He asked his mother if she gave them to us. She asked, why did we tell him where the reds came from? Charlie told his mother that if she ever gives us kids any illegal drugs again, he will call the police on her. Charlie is not here to stop you from harm; this one is totally up to you! The only thing that I ask is to pull over and smoke that thing outside the car."

Anthony turned and looked at me and said, "Okay, you win. I'll pull over, and you drive us home."

"Okay, that is fine with me, but you have to leave the windows open while I'm driving."

"No, open the windbreakers and crack the windows."

"Okay, Anthony, are you sure I'm not going to feel the effects of the smoke?" Vivian and Wilber busted out in laughter as if I said something funny, but I was dead serious! The three of them assured me that I would be fine.

I got behind the wheel and headed down the mountain while Anthony fired up the joint. The three of them handed the joint back and forth like old pros. They began laughing and turning up the radio as loud as it would go. I made it out of the mountains and on to the highway. It was smooth sailing from here; I was safe. I don't know what happened, but when I came to the bright lights on Foothill Blvd., I had come to a complete stop at the stoplight. I became light-headed, and the scenery started spinning. I could no longer control the car as I was driving.

"Anthony, something is wrong; I have to pull over." I could feel the car going from one lane to the other. Vivian and Wilber began to panic, shouting, "Ruben, pull over! Ruben, pull over!" I made it over to the right shoulder and got out of the car. I was in a full panic, but moreover, I was irate. I was on the roadway shouting, "How could you people do this to me! How could you do this! You said that I would be fine and I trusted you! I trusted you!"

"Ruben, please get in the car. If the police see us, we'll all go to jail!"

"No, I'll say what happened. I never took a drag of marijuana. Why should I have to join you in prison?"

"Just get in the car; let's get out of here." We made it to the house in one piece, but I was still pissed off!

The following Monday, Dolores asked me what happened over the weekend. "Dolores, I have no intention of talking to Anthony, Vivian, or Wilber for about six months after that incident. They gave me their word that they would never put me in that kind of situation again. I am going to hold them to it. I have no intention of ever trying or doing drugs, not even prescribed drugs. Dolores, are you coming over this Sunday?"

"No, that is the only day my mother is off work. She works six days a week, so Sunday is the only chance I have to spend time with her."

Sunday came around, and Mary was going to hold some big powwow with her immediate family members only. It seemed that there was trouble in Shangri-La that Mary had created. Charlie's and Chita's, as well as Richard's and Minta's marriage, were on the rocks. Charlie had never wanted to marry Chita in the first place. Richard was Minta's last hope of ever finding a husband. These four people always made me feel that I was the glue that held their marriage together.

Mary spared no expense. She prepared Richard's favorite meal: roast beef, baked potatoes, and carrots. This dish happened to be one of Mary's signature dishes. She called Lee at B.C.D. Market Sunday morning and asked for USDA Prime Choice cut beef.

"I need 23 lbs, Lee. Lee, I do not care what the price of the beef is going to be. I need it to be the best cut you have in your store and have it here by 11:00 AM. I'll pay double the price for the meat plus a big tip for your trouble." I was not one to stay around, but I wanted to know how Mary was going to manipulate her sons into staying with their wives.

At 11 o'clock on the dot, Lee was walking up the front walkway bringing the package right into the kitchen and placed it on the table. Mary handed him a wad of twenty-dollar bills and two books full of food stamps, and right back out the door, Lee went with a smile on his face from ear to ear! I watched as the meat came rolling out of the pink butcher paper. It was the size of a 6-month-old baby.

Before Mary told me to get the hell out of the kitchen, I left! Mary was not one to teach anyone anything that would be useful to them. I was savvy enough to read the labels on the products that she used to marinate the meal. So there was nothing to learn here.

By 3:30, in rolls Charlie, Chita, and Raymond. Dicky and Minta pulled up around 4:30. Dicky and Minta rarely brought their daughter Dede to the house, and today was no exception. The five of them went into the bedroom. Mary's bedroom had two recliners in it. One right at the door as you enter and the other was at the window where she would flick her cigarette ashes out.

Mary took her seat in her usual place. While Dicky sat to the right of her in the recliner by the door. Charlie sat at the foot of the bed, and Chita was on the right, and Minta was on the left side sitting. We knew better not to disturb Mary when she was having a parley as most criminals have.

The bedroom that I slept in was an echo chamber to the debate in Mary's bedroom. It seemed that Chita and Minta were upset that my stepmother Jackie and Onassis had abandoned them. They were arguing with Mary about how they were going to get the million dollars that they had promised them to help Mary keep me under wraps. The moment I heard the topic of their discussion, I left my bedroom.

I walked into the living room and told Raymond to come with me; we were going to the playground. I walked past Mary's window and shouted, "I am taking Raymond to the park. I'll be back in an hour or two!"

Chita shouted, "Bring him back in time for dinner!"

Raymond and I stood in the park for about ninety minutes. I pushed him on the swing for kids and checked out a ball from the recreation center. I made sure Raymond was exhausted before returning to the house. I wanted to keep Raymond occupied, and no one would be the wiser that I knew what they had discussed.

I could not believe that Tom killing Linda drove such a wedge in between my family and Mary. That is why I have not seen the Kennedy Clan around anymore.

What an afternoon! I better take Raymond back to the house before Charlie, or one of the other kids come looking for us.

As I was walking in the door, I saw Charlie, Chita, Minta, and Dicky were sitting around the kitchen table waiting to have dinner. Chita asked me, "Is Raymond back safe and sound?"

Mary had let the roast cook long enough for the meat to be tender. Dicky liked his meat cooked rare, and that is just the way Mary prepared it.

"Mijo, come sit down with your big brother to eat."

"Danny and Bobby are not here, and whom are you calling mijo?"

"Ruben, will you stop being a clown and come eat with your big brother?"

"No, thank you. I've already eaten. I'm going outside."

My contempt for Dicky and his wife Minta had come to the point that I did not want to eat at the same table with them! I could understand why Dicky would buy into his mother's manipulation, not unlike the rest of her family. These people were all cut with the same scissors. It was hard for me to grasp how these people sat down at the table and ate with each other.

Monday came, and for me, it always signaled a new beginning. Was Dolores going to follow me out of this place? All I had to do was convince her that I was not the S.O.B. that the Gonzales clan say I am.

It was a beautiful California spring day. The kind of day that the rest of the world wishes they had. I don't know what Vivian had said to Dolores, but she left the house never to return. I tried talking to her at school, but she went out of her way to avoid me. I would catch her glimpsing at me from afar, but she would never talk to me again after realizing that Dolores did not want to bother with me. I felt it was better that I start looking for someone who had never met any of the Gonzales' or my relatives.

I was not afraid of work, and I knew that I wanted to get married right out of high school. I felt as if life itself was passing me by. I was tired of living amidst all of the chaos among the Gonzales'. I could not see myself staying here for the rest of my life! There has to be a way out of this place!

Friday came around, and I was drowning in desperation. The fear that I would be stuck with the Gonzales's was overwhelming. I did not want to return to the Gonzales household. I took the bus to Downtown Los Angeles and got on a bus to San Francisco, the city I hate to love.

I got off the bus and found a cheap room in a hotel on Market Street within walking distance of the bus station. It was the first time I felt that no one was watching me. I was really on my own; there was no one around. I could live on my own. In a way, I had been from the moment that they kidnapped me from my mother's arms.

San Francisco gave me a welcoming feel, but there were those locked-up feels nagging at me. When I visited here, however: the people here were just as friendly as I remembered them.

I felt as if the city itself was talking to me. Telling me that this is the place that I was going to find what I was longing for: a wife. It was going to come from this very city.

I don't know why I rented a room, but I did. I only stayed in it for a few hours. I recall getting up early and having breakfast at an all-night diner. I walked back to the bus station and got on a bus back to L.A. I arrived back in L.A. late in the evening. The one thing about landing in Skid Row in L.A is there is a lot of action going on, but I would always find a place to eat for under $2.25 with tip.

I no sooner got back to the house when Sally handed me the telephone. It was Anthony wanting me to work on one of the neighbor's cars.

"Anthony!"

"I'll be there in the morning."

"I'm sure that we will not find a reliable prat house open at this hour. I need some sleep, so be here at 7:00 AM."

Anthony was at the house at 6:58 AM the next morning, and I was ready to go. Anthony was already a seasoned veteran of Winchell's Donut and Coffee House. Anthony was unable to function without his morning coffee. I had no problem going without coffee.

We drove back to Anthony's place and parked in the alley right behind the bungalow. A '58 Ford Mercury was parked in the backyard of Bob's home. I got into the Mercury and started it up. Dark black smoke came billowing out of the tailpipe. Which meant only one thing: the carburetor needs to be rebuilt.

"Anthony, today is Sunday, and you could have taken care of this yourself. Why am I here?"

"Well, it requires a brake job also, and you are faster with brakes."

I was getting ready to lose my cool; this older gentleman walked up with a hat on, chewing on a cigar. I looked at him. "Anthony, who is this guy?"

"He's the owner of the car we're going to repair."

The man said, "Hey little boy blue, I'm the mayor of the alley-way. I live right up there at the top of those stairs. I've seen you and Tall Boy working on cars out here all the time, sometimes right into the night. My car is giving me trouble, so I decided to ask Tall Boy here to take a look at it."

"Well, sir, it's nice to meet you, but it would help to know your last name, Mr. Mayor. I would not want to confuse you with the Mayor of Los Angeles, Sam Yorty."

"Little Boy Blue, you can call me Charles Rundy." Charles was a big man about 6"1 with blue eyes from Arkansas. "So, you boys think you can repair my vehicle?"

I replied, "Yes, we can. When we're finished, you should be able to get another three years out of this old girl."

"Tall Boy, your helper here says I should be able to get three more years out of my vehicle, is that true?"

"Mr. Mayor, hold the phone! I'm not Anthony's helper. We are partners in this endeavor we have going on here. It's a 50/50 percent we have here; if not, I'm out of here, is that understood, Charles? And that goes for you too, Anthony."

"Little Boy Blue, you do get to the point."

"Yes, Mr. Mayor, I do. Now let us get down to business, Anthony. Are we going to do the work or what?"

Charles, looking at Anthony, said, "The two of you look capable enough, so go ahead and do the needed repairs."

Anthony pulled the car into the garage, and we went to work. I started on the front brakes; Anthony went to work on the carburetor. By 10:30 AM, I had to remove the drums and brake shoes. I pulled the carburetor off the manifold. The brake shoes and brumes would not be ready until the next morning. The carburetor was an easy exchange, but it still had to be adjusted to the correct flow of fuel to air once the carburetor was back on the manifold.

We were back at the garage. Anthony was tinkering with the carburetor when Frank drove up.

"Hey, Ruben, what's up? Do you know where Anthony is?"

"He is in here at the workbench working on a carburetor."

Frank walked over to the workbench, where Anthony was. "Hey Anthony, I need a hand working on my car."

It was the one thing I did not want to hear or witness: Anthony and Frank becoming friends. It is strange now, the neighborhood piranha is now the boy wonder.

"Anthony, you think you can give me a hand working on my car?"

"I would, but I don't have time right now. Ruben can help; ask him."

He turned to me, "Ruben, you know how to work on cars? The last time I saw you, you were cutting grass."

"Yes, I made $35.00 that day, and you were making fun of me, Frank."

"How do you know anything about cars?"

"I was attending an auto-mechanic's school at the Los Angeles Adult Learning Center in Downtown, LA. Anthony and I were training for a smog certification. The instructor found that I was too young to be in his class."

"So, you're going to school and trying to get a trade?"

"Yes, I want to get out of this place as soon as possible."

"Where are you planning to go?"

"New York City."

"What! Why New York City?"

"I was there with my parents; I felt safe."

"So Ruben, are you going to give me a hand fixing my car?"

"Frank, we go way back. Of course I am. Let me clean up."

Frank had a '62 two-door Chevy Impala V8, and they are easy cars to work on. "It should be a breeze to tune up, Frank."

"Ruben, get in. I'm going to stop by Timmy's and pick him up."

"Frank, don't you think it would be better if we work on your car here?"

"No, I have all the tools and parts at my place."

"I am going to take the tools we are going to need for a tune-up. Here is an adjustable ratchet, five-eight swivels, a spark plug socket, and a feeler gauge. This way, we do not have to come back here."

Frank and I took off to Timmy's house; it was two blocks away. From there, it was another five blocks to Frank's place. Frank lived in the Elysian Park area, which happened to be non grata for me.

"Before we get started working on the car, let the engine cool down. I'm not getting burned. Frank, I don't know how you and your brother Roy survive up here. Every time I come up here, I am stopped by some of the homeboys in the area asking what I am doing here. I have a friend on Morton Avenue, almost got my ass handed to me the other day. Luckily, some guy said he saw us together in school and told the other that we were brothers and to leave me alone.

"Let's check the engine to see if it is cool enough to work on. Frank, this is how it's going to work. I'm going to instruct you on what to do. You're going to follow the distributor wires making sure that they are lined up to the spark plug that it leads to. The cables have to go back on the same spark plug that you removed it from. You are going to have to gap the new spark plugs first; this way, you do not double the work. Once the spark plugs are gapped, start removing the old spark plugs, replacing them one at a time. You're going to do this for all eight spark plugs. Once that is done, move on to replacing the points and condenser.

"Frank, whatever you do, don't move the distributor! I did not bring a timing light with me, and the engine is not going to start if you move the distributor."

Within two hours, Frank's '62 Low Rider was ready to go. The first time he turned on the ignition and turned over the engine, it started. It was idling as if a car dealership did the work.

"Ruben, I never believed that you knew what you were doing."

"Frank, I would never steer you wrong. I help you out, the way that I would want someone to help my little brother out."

"Ruben, you're a good friend."

"Frank, we're done here. Take me back to my place."

"Ruben, let me buy you lunch at Pioneer Chicken. It's on the way back to your house."

"I'd take you up on your offer, but I'm exhausted. Just drop me off at my place."

"Okay, but I owe you one, Ruben. You did for me what my brother would not help me do."

"Frank, Roy's a senior in high school, what do you expect? He does not want his little brother by his side 24/7. I'll see you at school."

The next day, as I was having lunch in the bleachers at school, Frank asked me to meet him after school.

"Frank, I'd like to, but I have to finish working on Charles's car. Anthony and I have this deal that we split the labor down the middle. I want to be there when Charles pays him. Lately, it's been 40/60, and I'm going to have to look for other prospects for work."

"The whole neighborhood thinks you and Anthony are friends."

"Frank, if there is one thing I learned from my grandfather, it's that friends and business do not go hand in hand. Never call your business partner, your friend. If Anthony believes that, it's on him.

"Anthony and I were going to open up an auto repair shop, but the way this 60/40 is working out is what I don't like. Today is 60/40; what's going to happen if we open a business? 70/30! No, it's not for me. I am glad to find out the way the real world works now instead of later."

"Ruben, I thought that you and Anthony were friends!"

"No, it's all about money for me; that's all money! Frank, I consider you a friend, and I would like to remain your friend for life."

"Ruben, don't get heavy on me, man!"

"Frank, we met in grammar school, now we're in high school. One more year, and we're out of here."

The 3 o'clock bell rang, and I was out the door. I made it to the house in 10 minutes. There was only one thing on my mind, and that is, I want my money. I changed into my work clothes and got over to Anthony's as fast as I could. Anthony had already put the front brakes on Charles's car. He had the back brakes left to replace.

Anthony was coming across the alley with the back-brake shoes. I made it there just in time to put the back brakes on.

"Wow! Anthony, what happened to your hand? Why is it all banged up?"

"I had hell trying to put the front brakes on the car this morning."

"Yeah, those tension springs get you every time. You really have to be careful.

"Man, Anthony, I see why you don't like working on brakes. I'll do the back brakes, that way you can finish up with the tune-up."

It did not take us long to get Charles's car on the road. The one thing we did have a problem with was adjusting the brakes. Once the self-adjusting brakes kicked in, it was all squared away. Charles test drove the car and was pleased with our work. Charles paid the bill, and Anthony and I split the proceeds.

It was still early, and I wanted something to eat. I went back to the house, trimmed my beard, and took a bath. I was still feeling blasé about my immediate prospect for the future. Just what was going to happen to my life? How was I going to get out of this place? I was not going to feel sorry for myself. I was going to do what the songs suggest and Go Downtown. I'm going downtown to check it out, maybe have dinner.

I walked to Temple Street and got on the bus and got off in front of the May Co. Department Store. I walked across the street into May Co. to do some shopping. The idea that I was going to purchase something and have to carry it did not sit very well with me. No, better not buy anything. I'll probably throw it away or lose it before I get back to the house. I stayed browsing in May Co. all of 30 minutes. I decided it was time to eat. I exited on the Broadway side of the store.

I walked up Broadway to Clifton's Cafeteria for dinner. Clifton's was a cafeteria in every sense of the word. It was one of the places that soldiers stopped off before shipping off to war during World War II. Once in a while, I ran into the ladies that U.S.O. set up to entertain the soldiers that were going overseas to fight in World War II. They were dressed the same, in hats and white gloves. If you were a movie buff, you would see a movie star from the Silver Screen. Back in its heyday, it was the place to be seen. I like to believe that is why people from all over the world visit here. For me, it was all about the food they served here; it was outstanding. I had the turkey, mashed potatoes, gravy, cranberry sauce, corn, and for dessert, *bread pudding*, my favorite dessert. I was in Hog Heaven! The beautiful thing was that I did not have to eat alone.

I had my tray full and walked into a full dining room of potrions. I felt like I was in another world. Clifton Cafeteria brought out the best of my dining etiquette. I sat in my favorite spot next to the waterfall. I enjoyed the sound of the river as it flowed by while I was having dinner. I had a clear view of the waterfall. I noticed the busboy was escorting two ladies to an empty table.

I was sure that this was a mother and a daughter coming down the aisle with the busboy. I was marveling over how sophisticated the daughter look. I did not want to make it evident that I was staring at her. I kept my head straight, my eye focused on the waterfall as they were walking towards my table.

I now had a bird's eye view of the "Daughter." She was dressed in El Couture, walking with one foot in front of the other. I noticed her high heels were just the right height for her. Her legs were perfect, not a flaw on them; the skirt came just above her knee. The skirt took the shape of her body; she looked as if she just stepped out of a vogue article.

The busboy sat the duo at the next table next to me. The busboy escorted the daughter back to the cafeteria. I looked over at the lady sitting at the following table and nodded to say hello, hoping to break the ice. It worked, and the lady gave a polite smile back. I said hello, my name is Ruben, she answers.

"I do not speak English, but I understand the language. My name is Mercedes Santizo De Tobias. Nice to meet you, Ruben."

"Excuse me, but are you alone?"

"No, I'm here with my daughter." I did not want to start eating until someone arrived with her meal.

I knew that would be impolite. "Mrs. Tobias, where are you from, what country?"

"I am from Guatemala. Are you from here?"

"Yes, I was born here." All that grade-school Spanish that I learned was flowing out of me without trepidation.

As we were talking, I looked down the aisle; again, she with the busboy carrying her tray. She walked with a sophisticated attitude and swagger. As if she was a debutante coming out for her debut. One foot right in front of the other. Her eyes moving ever so slowly from left to right, she put on a display of pure elegance. Her semi miniskirt, just right below the kneecap and high heels. Her legs looked as if they were made to an angel's specification. I stood up as she sat down at a small table on the left of me without even glancing at me. I noticed the busboy was nervous as he placed the tray on the table.

"I would like you to meet my daughter Hilda." She said to her daughter, "We have been chatting while you were getting our dinner." I was not accustomed to shaking anyone's hand, so I nodded my head ever so slightly to jester hello as she took her seat.

I noticed her green eyes, sandy brown hair, and milky white skin. She was pleasant enough, but she still would not look at me. I seemed to have won over Mrs. Tobias, but her daughter Hilda was not interested in me in the least. Mrs. Tobias and I talked while Hilda took her time eating her dinner. As I was sitting there talking to Mrs. Tobias, I was thinking about how Hilda would fit right in with the jet-set at dinner. She would engage in conversation but take her time to enjoy her meal.

Trying to get Hilda's attention, I had no other recourse but to offer her my bread pudding. I did not know how I was going to build a conversation around bread pudding, but I did. I was lucky in the sense that Clifton serves the best bread pudding in town. I broke the ice with the offering of my bread pudding.

I walked them back to the Alexander Hotel, where they were sharing a room with friends. Mrs. Tobias kissed me on the cheek and said goodbye, and Hilda shook my hand and said good night. I did the California thing and said, "I'll see you later."

I made it back to the house while all the time thinking of Hilda. I had got enough information on where they were going if I wanted to see them again. I walked into the house, and Mary and Tony were there sitting in Mary's bedroom. As I was walking past Mary's bedroom, she yelled out, "Where have you been?"

"Since when do you care where I go or what I do? I have not seen you in a month of Sundays! And I mean that literally! You know, you make me laugh, Mrs. Gonzales! You care now!"

"Ruben, I was just wondering."

"Oh! Your famous last words."

"Come in here, mijo."

"Why do you call me mijo? My mother never called me mijo; why you?"

"I know you're upset that I have to babysit, but I have to make money."

"What do you want, anyway?"

"Oh, nothing. I wanted to see how you are doing, that's all." Mary had a tabloid in her hand; the caption read Marilyn Monroe gives birth to a baby boy in 1959. This time, there was no beating around the bush. She just came right out and asked me, "Do you know what Marilyn Monroe did with the child?"

"Yes, I know where the child is, but why do you want to know?"

"I was just wondering."

"You are doing a whole lot of wondering this evening."

"So, it's true."

"Yes, it's true."

"Where is the child?"

"Tell me why you want to know where the child is, and I'll tell you where he is."

"I don't believe you know where the child is Ruben."

"Oh, I do!"

"Why won't you tell me where the child is?"

"First and foremost, it is none of your business, and second, look around you. Do you want to find my brother and have him living in the same manner that you have me living?"

"Ruben, you do not know where he is, do you?"

"I am going to put it the way my mother put it when someone asked her that same question. He is in your eyes, and I don't mean me. He is literally and utterly in your eyes! Now I'm going to bed!"

The next day was the same old humdrum. The one thing that was nagging me was, Why was Mary so interested in finding out about my little brother? I knew that if I did not keep him under wraps that it would be the end of his life. Now, this is one more thing on my plate that I have to worry about: JonJon's fate. First, Jacqueline and Onassis tried to kill my brother and sister off the waters of Acapulco. Now, Mary wants to know the whereabouts of my little brother. She did not realize that JonJon was not really Jacqueline's son. Does it ever end? There really is *no honor among Thieves!*

There is nothing like being in school; it's rewarding, and I leave my problems behind me. The day turned out to be worthwhile. I ran into Frank in the hallway.

"Ruben, I've been looking for you during lunch. I want you to help me work on my car after school."

"Okay, I'll meet you here after class."

"In front of the school?"

"Yes, right in front of the church."

3 o'clock came around. There was Frank in front of the church.

"Frank, what's up with your car?"

"It is overheating."

"Let's go to the parts house on Glendale and pick up a thermostat."

"How do you know it's the thermostat?"

"The car runs, and the water pump is working?"

"Yes."

"So the next thing to change is the thermostat. Look, it should cost about $3.50 for a new one and make sure to pick up a gasket too. I'll meet you at Anthony's place and change it there. The gasket sealant is the most expensive, and Anthony has plenty on hand."

"I want to go to Tommy's hamburger stand first for a hamburger."

"Okay, but on the way there, you'll burn up your car motor."

"Ruben, I made it here this morning without a problem."

"Frank, it was cold out this morning, if you did not notice. Let's buy the thermostat first and eat later."

"Okay, let's go."

We took off to the parts house and went on to Anthony's.

"Frank, let your car engine cool down; it should not take more than 10 minutes."

"Ruben, I'm going to see my mother, you get what we need from Anthony."

"Frank, if you leave me here any longer than 10 minutes, I'm going. I have to meet a friend."

"Okay, 10 minutes."

The car cooled down, and I showed Frank how to change the thermostat and place sealant on the gasket.

"Let's go inside Anthony's place and place the old thermostat in boiling water. We have to make sure that this is the reason your car is overheating."

I put a pot of water on to boil and went back outside to watch Frank change the thermostat.

"Frank, make sure you use a putty knife to remove any residue from the manifold and thermostat housing. Let me see how you are placing the thermostat back in place.

"The flat end goes in the manifold, and the point has to point upwards. If you put the thermostat in backward, the thermostat will not open, and you'll fry the engine. Let's go back inside and place the old thermostat in boiling water. When I drop the thermostat into the water, if it does not open all the way, then that is the reason your car is overheating."

Sure enough, the thermostat did not open all the way.

"Frank, this is your problem right here. Had you went to Tommy's Hamburger Joint, you would have needed a tow truck to get your car home. Put water in the car radiator, and you are ready to go."

"Ruben, let's go to Tommy's. I'll pay."

"Frank, I have too many things on my mind right now, but thanks for the offer. I'll see you tomorrow at school."

I don't know if my parents' death turned me into a heartless S.O.B. like the Gonzales's like to call me, but the only thing I could think of was Hilda and how to get to San Francisco. Luck would have it, divine intervention came into play. I was doing gardening work for some of the neighbors, and the auto repair business was picking up. The money I was making, I gave it to Mona to save for me. I saved $500.00 in no time.

Anthony happened to catch me at the right time and asked if I would like to take a trip. We had seen Sequoia National Park and Yosemite National Park with the Gonzales's a few times. This time he wanted me to go to San Francisco with him. Being that I was looking to take a trip up there myself, I jumped at the chance to go.

I took my best dress clothes to Holloway's Cleaners and told the owner that I needed my clothes for Thursday. I paid the laundry bill in advance to make sure I did not spend the money on something frivolous. I spent the next five days working and trying to attend school. Mary made sure that there were no free lunches or a discount for this underprivileged child. It was work for your next meal, or don't eat. Man, Thursday was here, and it was time to walk to Holloway's Cleaners to pick up my glad rags for the weekend in San Francisco.

I made it to Anthony's place, where he was waiting for me. We worked on the T-bird, getting it ready for the trip. We tuned it up and changed the oil, oil filter, and air filter. By 7:00 PM, the T-bird was running like a clock. The only thing I had left to do was get the grease and black oil from under my fingernails. Once I did that, it was time to see Mona for my money. Mona happened to be outside doing gardening.

"Ruben, I know what you are looking for. I put 250.00 dollars in your blue shirt pocket in the back room."

"You are a sweetheart, Mona!"

Anthony and I did not want to stop for breakfast, so we had a big dinner.

We were on our way to Frisco at 6:00 AM; we did not want to stop for anything but fuel, coffee, and to make pit stops. We pulled into San Luis Obispo about 11:30 AM; we were making good travel time. This was the fourth time we filled up for gas and decided to have lunch. I had to pick up the tab. The friendship was beginning to become one-sided, and I was growing tired of it.

If I could convince Mrs. Tobias that I have her daughter Hilda's best interest at heart, she'll marry me or at least have her move to Los Angeles.

We got back in the car and drove for the next two hours. We were just outside San Jose. I asked Anthony where we were going to stay.

"We are going to stay with my aunt in Berkeley."

"What! I'm not staying with your aunt! I want to go to a hotel in San Francisco. I did not come all this way to hang out in Berkeley."

"Ruben, I have to take care of some business with my aunt for my parents."

"That is the very reason why I should stay in a hotel and not with your aunt." What I was trying to accomplish was to keep Anthony from meeting Hilda and her mother. The one thing I learned about Anthony was his loyalty as a friend is questionable. For some reason, he wanted Mary to be my mother. Regardless of what I say or the neighbor tells him, I am Mary's son, and that's it.

"Anthony, I'll tell you where to drop me off in downtown Oakland, and I'll take the bus into San Francisco. That way, you can stay with your aunt and take care of the business at hand, and you don't have to look for a hotel."

"No, I'll drive you into San Francisco. I want to stay in the same hotel on Market Street that we were at the last time we were here."

We made it into San Francisco before rush hour started. I knew the moment Anthony got off the 101 Highway that he would want to stay in the city.

We pulled in the alleyway to the hotel and went into the hotel. We registered and paid for three days. I made sure that my name was on the register if Anthony wanted to leave a day early. I was able to get the room with a view of Market Street with two beds. The only thing was this hotel was more of a flap house as Old Man John would call it. There were three restrooms and a shower on each side of the hallway, which was communal. I came here for one reason and one reason only, and that was to see Hilda.

I hoped that Anthony would leave and stay with his aunt. Once he saw that I paid for the room for the weekend, he decided to stay in town. I had always been resourceful, and this time, I needed to trim my beard and shave around my neck and cheeks. Up to this point, I would not let a barber touch my beard; I would have to trim it myself. The problem I was having was the room was too dark. I would have to sit by the window overlooking Market Street if I was to do an excellent job on my beard. The only scissors I had were big seamstress scissors. They'll have to do; I'm not going to go out and pay 25 dollars to a barber for a haircut and a shave, besides I do not have the time.

I took a facial washcloth and ran it under hot water. I placed it on my face and neck to soften the hair. I shaved the hair that was on my neck. I followed the jawline from left to right, making sure the line was even on both sides of the jawbone. I next moved on to my cheek area, creating a clean carved shape as if I were a barber; he could do no better. I'm shining like a 20 dollar gold piece. Just like my dad, President John F. Kennedy, if I say so myself.

I went into the darkly lit hallway and on into the shower. I came out of the shower, feeling and smelling as if I had a May Spring Shower. I slapped on just enough British Sterling Cologne, making sure not to overdo it. I was ready to go to town. The only thing that was keeping me from leaving was Anthony. I did not want him to be a part of my quest.

"Anthony, shouldn't you be on your way to Berkeley? Your aunt may be worried about you."

"No, I called her and told her I was staying with you here." If this was not the end-all to be all!

"Well, I'm going out to check out the sights."

"I'm going with you."

"Not dressed like that. Put on some glad rags. Anthony, I'm not going to be stopped at the door of a night club just because you are not dressed appropriately. I'll leave you standing outside waiting to get in."

"Ruben, just who do you think you are?"

"I'm the same person that's been looking at you for the last 10 minutes, that's who. Anthony, I'm on a mission, and nothing is going to stop me from finding what I came here seeking. Not even you! Now get changed if you want to tag along."

It took Anthony a good hour to get ready, but the bad thing was he looked no different than before he started. He was clean, and his clothes were ironed. Now, all we both had to do was have our shoes shined.

"Anthony, take money with you. Whatever you eat or drink is on you tonight."

We stepped out onto Market Street around 9:00 PM. It was lit up as if it was New Year's Eve! And I was on my way to the GRAND BALL! What a sight! I was reminded of when I walked this very street with my mother, Marilyn Monroe, what a feeling! I'm on top of the world!

"Anthony, there is a place I want to go to; it's within walking distance from here. I want to make one thing clear: we are going to a dance and dinner at a Superclub. You are not going to order an alcoholic beverage of any sort, Anthony. I mean any kind, is that understood? If you try it and I have to leave the premises, there is going to be Cane to pay. Do I make myself clear! All I'm asking you is to carry yourself with some self-discipline."

"Ruben, where are we going?"

"Anthony, my mother, Marilyn Monroe, would say 'follow the limelight. When you come to an end, that is where you need to be.' So when we arrive there, we'll know."

As I was walking down Market Street, the glitz and glamour of San Francisco were engulfing my very soul. There I was in the middle of the very city of social change. The haven of "Hey buddy, do you have any spare change?" and you gladly hand it over. We finally found the hotel I was looking for; it was just one more ride to finding the limelight that my mother said was there. We had arrived. The elevator door opened, and there it was — the Starlight Room at the top of Sir Francis Drake Hotel.

I felt as if I had arrived home. Here is where I belong; this is what I had ripped away from me. I was going to stay here until I found what I came for, Hilda! I knew just how much money I had to spend, and I was not going to blow my budget on one night at the Starlight Room. It was not very crowded for a Friday night. The maître d' sat us at the table closest to the dance floor.

"Will you gentlemen be dining alone, or are you expecting company?"

"We are waiting for our dates to arrive. Just give us a small table for two in the event we are stood-up."

"Would you like a cocktail?"

"No, thank you. I'll have a club soda with a twist of lime, and Anthony was going to have the same."

"Ruben, do you know that the soda is just as much as a drink?"

"Anthony, take a step back; you cannot handle your liquor, and you know full well I do not like the taste of alcohol. So stay with the club soda for now!"

Anthony and I were having our dinner, and the music started to play. A lady was singing the song, Granada. I've heard the song in both English and Spanish. The atmosphere and music were intoxicating. There she was walking across the dance floor with that same sophisticated walk that I noticed while we were in Clifton's Cafeteria. Spontaneously, I pointed and turned to Anthony and said, "There goes the future Mrs. Kennedy!"

"Ruben, what did you say?"

Without hesitation, I repeated it.

"There goes the future Mrs. Kennedy. I'm going to marry that girl."

"How? You don't even know her name."

"I don't have to know her name to know that I'm going to marry her! Now you can have your drink, so long as you pay for it, Anthony. I found what I came here for, now get lost; I'll see you later or stay here I don't care."

I got up from the table and asked Hilda to dance with me. She was still aloof and unsympathetic to the long distance that I had traveled to find her. She was unimpressed with my plight. It was apparent to me that I was fighting an uphill battle.

After Hilda turned me down for a dance, I headed back to my table, where I sat contemplating my next move. I waited for the next opportunity and asked Hilda how her mother was. This seemed to hit a chord with her. She said she was fine, and thank you for asking. After making small talk, I asked if she and her mother would meet me for lunch the next day.

"I am going to have lunch at Woolworth's on Powell and Market where the cable cars stop. You and your mother are more than welcome to join me. I'll be there at 1:00 PM. I hope to see you there."

Hilda and her chaperone were out the door before midnight, just when the party started rocking. Hilda never agreed to dance with me that night. Anthony and I walked back down to Market Street. To walk the streets of San Francisco was like an open-air theme park. It was the place to be seen—the people dressed in psychedelic clothing, trying to hold on to the '60s.

Here I was walking down the street with a brown double-breasted jacket and beige baggy bell-bottoms that hugged the waist. I did not know if Hilda was paying any attention to me or not. I was not even sure if she heard me asking her to meet for lunch. The only thing I knew was that I was smitten with her.

The next morning, Anthony left for Berkeley, and I stayed behind. It is helpful when fate steps in, but it is the devil when you have no cooperation with the parties involved. It was still too early for Woolworth's. I did the next best thing: pray on both knees that Hilda shows up.

Where could I find a Catholic church? I needed the Saint of the impossible Saint Jude to help me in my quest. I need him to bring Hilda, and her mother, Mrs. Tobias, to Woolworth's, and I would do the rest myself.

Around noon I walked into Woolworth's and looked around the lunch counter; there was no sign of Hilda or Mrs. Tobias. I was anxious and sad that they were not there.

I walked back outside and pretended to wait for a bus. The thing about San Francisco was the people were amiable. I recalled what I had read in grammar school, that the people in Guatemala had their main meal for lunch; it is equivalent to our dinner hour here in the U.S.A. But in Guatemala, they stop work at noon and start back to work at 4:00 PM. If I have to wait until 4:00 PM, that is what I'm going to do.

It was around 1:00 PM when I saw Hilda and Mrs. Tobias walking down Market Street. Hilda was wearing a dark, navy blue ensemble with a white blouse and high heels. Mrs. Tobias was donning a blue flowered dress that was handmade. To witness the two of them come down the street was something you only see in a European Vogue Magazine. Just how unorthodox of me to ask Hilda if she and Mrs. Tobias would join me for lunch at Woolworth's, just what was I thinking? I hid behind a telephone booth to keep out of their line of sight as they entered into Woolworth's.

I caught a glimpse of Mrs. Tobias's face as she was entering the store; she did not look too pleased. I waited for them to take a table. Before they could take their seats, I walked up. "Oh! Good afternoon. How are you this afternoon?"

Here I was once again speaking Spanish. The language was rolling off my tongue as if it was my own. I've heard of divine intervention, but where my language skills have come from, I had no idea. I was too embarrassed to shake their hands, so I nodded my head. I recalled I read it in some book; it's what a gentleman does.

Hilda and Mrs. Tobias took the bench directly across from me. Not wanting to give an everlasting impression that I was a pauper without means of supporting myself, I suggested a cup of coffee and to head down to Fisherman's Wharf. It seemed that Mrs. Tobias was upset and was not interested in anything but staying put. Trying not to pry, I asked if there was anything I could do to help. Hilda, for the first time, took a good look at me and began to speak. "My mother thinks I should leave San Francisco."

"Oh, really, why? If you don't mind me asking."

"She does not want me to stay here alone with my cousins."

Once she said that, I sat back looking concerned and willing to help out.

"Mrs. Tobias, I have a suggestion. Why don't you come to Los Angeles? The rent in Los Angeles is inexpensive; there are single apartments in the downtown area. These apartments come with gas and electricity; the only other expense Hilda would incur is the telephone bill. The same $70 a month that she is paying to your cousins for a room. She'll have a single apartment with a kitchen and a bathroom." The second I mentioned the kitchen, Mrs. Tobias smiled!

I continued. "It would be my pleasure to look in on Hildita from time to time. You'll not have anything to worry about; I'll take care of her.

"I have one problem: my parents are deceased. And my stepmother and her husband left me with a very evil person. Otherwise, I work and attend school. I'm willing to meet you in Los Angeles and help you find an apartment. Finding a job should not be a problem; there are several offices and department stores in downtown Los Angeles that need people who speak a second language. Hilda should fit right in the workforce."

"Ruben, I worked for the United Nations in New York City. I also have secretarial skills and retail skills!"

"Wow! You worked for the U.N. in New York. Impressive.

"Whatever work you are doing here, you can find in Los Angeles."

Mrs. Tobias said, "It's kind of you to offer a helping hand, but we have to think about it. I do not want to leave my daughter here in San Francisco with her cousins. If she does not leave San Francisco, she'll have to return with me to Guatemala."

"I'll drive you to the airport in Los Angeles if you decide to return to Guatemala. I will take care of her if she decides to move to L.A. I'll make sure she is not alone."

"We have to leave now. It's getting late."

"It was nice to see you again, Mrs. Tobias. I hope to see you and your daughter in Los Angeles."

Hilda was picking up the tab when I reached for it. I was just a little faster and was able to touch her tiny little hand. "I'll take that if you would allow me." The way that Mrs. Tobias smiled at me, I knew that I hit a home run with Hilda's mother, but Hilda, on the other hand, was hard to read. The loving care that Hilda had for her mother reminded me of just how much I missed my mother.

I walked out of Woolworth's Department Store, not knowing if I would ever see them again. I had faith that somehow, we would meet again. I walked back to the hotel, feeling as if I had lost my best friend. I had to look on the bright side of things. I was alone in San Francisco, free of the Gonzales's, and I had met with beautiful people. What more could I ask for out of the afternoon?

Anthony arrived at the hotel about an hour after I did. "Ruben, let's go out and go downtown."

"No, I'd rather walk around and soak up the atmosphere if you don't mind." We took the cable car to Fisherman's Wharf; all I was doing was killing time. If I could leave this place, I would, but I'm stuck here till the morning. San Francisco is a beautiful city with charm and splendor, but now I hate to love it here. Damn! When am I going to find peace in this place? "Anthony, let's head back to the hotel and leave early in the morning."

We were dressed and out the door before sunrise. Heading back to L.A., it was a long ride back, almost a dead silence in the car, if not for the radio. I was feeling despair but not discouraged.

Anthony was trying to pry into my activities while he was visiting with his aunt in Berkley, but I kept changing the subject.

I did not want to arrive in L.A. too early, so we stopped off at Pismo Beach and had lunch. We stayed on US Highway 1 down to L.A. The Pacific Coast Highway is the scenic route of the California Coastline. It took us 12 hours to make it back to the house.

I went into the house, and no one was there. The one thing about living in this house is that I did not need a key to gain entrance.

There is nothing like a weekend retreat to clear your mind and move on to one's next project. I knew that it was only a matter of time before I was free of this dungeon that I was trapped in.

As I was walking to school, I was weighing my options; do I get married and start a family, or do I join the Armed Forces? Joining one of the armed forces would make it easy for my family to take me out, so that was definitely out of the question. For me to start a family, I'd want my wife to be someone that Mary or my fraternal family does not know. I'd like to marry Hilda; she was so innocent and gentle. I think she was not even aware that I existed.

There is nothing like walking into a school building full of talking students to take your mind off my predicament. I sailed from one classroom to another. My fourth-period teacher was waiting for me at the door.

"Ruben, I would like to discuss your test with you. Your answers are not hitting the mark, and I am not sure I should let you in the darkroom anymore."

"Mr. Collins, just what does that mean? Mr. Collins, it's all about mixing the chemicals together."

"Ruben, you're going into the darkroom to develop a roll of film. I'm going to watch you."

We walked into the darkroom with five other classmates and closed the door behind us. The first rule was no light in the darkroom at all! Once I developed the file without exposing it to light, Mr. Collins left the darkroom. I finished up by hanging up the negative to dry. Once the negative had dried, I took it to Mr. Collins to get his opinion on my work. I handed him the negative, and he looked it over.

"Ruben, it's apparent that you know what you are ( I do not understand is what happens to you when you'

"Mr. Collins, it's an enigma that I face with each jects. It's because probably I'm malnourished most of the time. I cannot think straight when taking a test."

"Ruben, you look far from malnourished now. Take your seat and make sure you eat something for lunch."

The lunch bell rang; I was no different from any other high school student. I found no nutritional value in the school lunch that was served in the school cafeteria. On my way to the cafeteria, I ran into Frank, Larry, and Bogart. The four of us lined up in the cafeteria. I took a bowl of white rice with brown gravy and a salad with Thousand Island dressing. Frank took one look at what was on my tray. "Ruben, is that all you are going to eat?"

"Frank, believe it or not, white rice is one of my favorite dishes. It's not that I live off of rice, but it's just one of my favorite foods. The only time I eat white rice is in a Chinese restaurant or here in school. Now let me have my rice and eat it too! Do you guys realize that next semester we start our last year of high school?"

"Ruben, you sure know how to kill lunch. This food tastes like cardboard."

"Yes, Larry, I agree with you; it does taste bland."

Frank looked at me. "Ruben, are you really going to eat all the rice?"

"Yes, that's the plan."

We finished up lunch and headed out to the courtyard.

There across the yard was Frank's brother Roy. He had just come back from Tommy's Hamburger Stand. I walked over to Roy to find out how he was, and he copped an attitude.

"Hey Ruben, don't you know that you're in the eleventh grade, and I'm in the twelfth grade? Oh!"

"Don't give me that B.S. I attended grammar school with you, Roy. This social pecking order you have going on with your brother Frank may work fine with him, but not you and me. If my little brother and I were in the same school, I'd make damn sure he was standing right next to me and not on the other side of the field as if he were some outcast. You're going to look back on your high school days and not see your little brother in your life, Roy. I'll feel sorry for you when that happens, dude."

Roy's friend said, "Ruben is not Frank's friend, he is his brother. Damn Roy! Roy that is your friend Ruben talking to you. We are saying the same thing. Show your brother Frank a little brotherly love, dude."

I turned and walked back to where I had left my homeboys sitting.

"Hey, Ruben, let's meet after school and go to Tommy's for a burger."

"Frank, Tommy's does not have French fries; all they sell is burgers, hotdogs, and chile tamales."

"Okay, let's meet up after school, and we'll hang out."

"I have a gym class next, after that math class, so I'll meet you in front of the main building."

"Are we going to pool our money, or are we each going to pay for our own food?"

"We'll see!"

"Okay, I'm going to gym class."

I finished up my last two classes of the day. I met Frank, Larry, and Bogart out in front of the main building. The four of us started to head down to Tommy's Hamburger Stand. Timmy decided to join us.

"Timmy, where did you come? I did not know that you attended Belmont High."

"Oh, well, now you know, Ruben."

Frank looked at me. "No, Ruben, he's still going to Virgil Junior High School. He just ditched school today. Oh, only today!"

"Timmy, how is your brother Tommy doing? I have not seen him around."

"He's doing fine."

Frank piled us all into his '62 Impala low rider for the drive to Tommy's Hamburger Stand. Anybody who was anybody that attended Belmont High School stopped there after school; it was the place to be seen. If you did not arrive in a low rider, you did not belong here.

We made it there before the crowd from Belmont did. We landed a parking space right on the corner of Tommy's. It was the spot that if you were anybody, you would want to park in this spot, right in the middle of all the action. There is enough parking for twelve cars. If you don't park there, there is also the parking lot across Rampart Blvd. Frank was lucky, we faced Beverly Blvd. Frank got the last parking space, the sweet spot.

We each pitched in two bucks, and Frank stood in line to order our food. I had the chili cheeseburger, chili cheese dogs, and a tamale with the works. The guy at the cash register looked at Frank and me and said, "The two of you are too skinny to eat all this food!"

"No, it's not all for us; there are three of our friends standing over there by the beige Impala." The cashier took the money; we walked off with our goods.

The food was wrapped in yellow and white cellophane paper. The top of the burgers had American cheese on the meat with a fat slice of tomato and chopped onion on a grilled toasted bun. These chili burgers were calling out to be eaten. The ecstasy to bite into one of these burgers is pure heaven. Who needs the fries? Gents, that's not even a question. Too bad summer is arriving next month.

"Ruben, I don't believe you'll finish off even the tamale."

"Yes, but I'm going to have dinner tonight. I should make it until morning without eating again."

Frank, Timmy, Larry, and Bogart finished their chili burgers and chili cheese dogs while I was still working on my chili cheese dog. Not being one that liked to ride shotgun, I told the guys to get in the car.

I finished up my chili cheese dog and got in the back seat of the car. I was sandwiched between Bogart and Larry. Frank pulled out onto Beverly Blvd. and made a left turn going up Beverly Blvd. There were office buildings on the left side of us and Coronado Street on the right. Once we passed that, there was a hundred-foot hill until we arrived at Park View Street.

I was watching Frank's eyes going back and forth once we passed Park View St. Timmy was looking at the reflection in the side mirror on the passenger side. Frank was still heading down Beverly Blvd. in the right lane. Timmy seemed annoyed by what he was viewing in the mirror. I was looking back and forth at the two of them and got this eerie feeling.

"Frank, what's going on?"

We made it across Alvarado Street, which is a main fairway! As Frank was rounding the corner onto Mountain View Avenue, I could see a black and white police car right on our tail! Just as Frank made the left turn onto Mountain View, the red cherry lights on the top of the patrol car came on in all their glory!

"Frank, I want you to pull all the way over to your left as if you are parking! Make sure you turn off the engine! Keep your hands at 10 and 2 o'clock on the steering wheel, and whatever you do, do not move! If anyone in this car disrespects the police officer, I am going to kick the living crap of you! Do I make myself clear! Timmy that goes for you too!"

"Ruben, lighten up."

"Frank, tell him I mean it."

"Timmy, when Ruben says he means it, you do not want to mess with him!"

The policeman walked up to the driver's side of the car. "Where are you boys headed?"

Frank looked up at the police offer with this aloof expression on his face. "Why did you stop us?"

"Where are you guys headed to?" asked the officer again.

Frank looked right into the police officer's eyes, "Why did you stop me?"

The officer answered, "A routine stop."

"There is no such thing as a routine stop, Officer."

"Let me have your registration and license, please." Frank reached into his back right pocket while keeping his left hand at 10 o'clock on the steering wheel. Frank complied with the policeman's orders.

The officer was sizing up Timmy and Bogart and kept one hand on his gun holster as he took Frank's driver's license with the other hand. "Boys, I'm going to walk around to the other side of the car." Before walking away, he took a good look at the license and Frank.

The officer walked around the front of the car with his hand still on the gun itself. As if he was itching to shoot one of us.

"Frank, do not do anything stupid. That cop is not playing around! He is dead ass serious!"

The officer gets to the right side of the car, which seemed as if it took him forever to get there. I had my eyes fixated on his trigger finger on the gun. He got to the other side of the car and leaned in the car window. The officer took a good look at Bogart and me. He sized up Frank, Larry, Timmy, and Bogart one more time. He looked directly at me and points at me with his forefinger! And says, "I'll shoot him first if you guys do anything stupid, if you so much as move!"

My heart started racing. "Frank, he means what he is saying. I'm telling you, don't move!"

The officer looks at Frank. "I'm going back to my vehicle to run your license."

The officer did what all police do. That old standard pose with one foot in the car and the other foot between the car door frame on the pavement with the car radio receiver in one hand. Frank seemed relaxed. Timmy, on the other hand, was getting restless. Larry was sitting as still as if he was a deer caught in oncoming headlights. My good friend Bogart was making light of the whole thing. I, on the other hand, saw things differently; why me, Lord, why me!

The police officer walked back to the car. Before the officer handed Frank his license. He asked Frank, "Why didn't you tell me your father is Whitey and was a police officer with the Venice Beach Police Department?"

"What the hell does my father have to do with you pulling me over!"

All the time that this was going on, I had both hands on the seat in front of me. Once Frank said that I slumped back in my seat. I had never given it much thought about Frank's father as a police officer, but this officer was right!

"Next time you get pulled over, Frank, inform the officer about your father."

"Sir, you still have not answered my question! What does my father have to do with you pulling me over?" I could see the red around the whites of Frank's green eyes.

"Hey, Frank, chill out, and let's get out of here when we are free to go."

The officer told us we were free to go. As Frank was pulling away from the curb and we were underway, I said, "Boys, that police officer was right; this is a bad combination we got going on here. Five high schoolers riding in one car does not look good. Why he singled me out, I don't know. But let me out of this car!"

"Ruben, why are you panicking? You chicken." There were other choice names that they called me that I don't want to remember. All I wanted was to get out of the back seat of the car. Frank came to a complete stop at the corner of Mountain View Ave. and Court Street. He still did not want to let me out of the car.

"Frank, if you don't pull this car over, I'm going to take Timmy's head and smash it into the dashboard, and I mean it. So pull the hell over and let me out of this car now!" Frank drove to the middle of Mountain View Ave. and Temple Street and pulled over to the left and let me out.

I started walking as Frank drove off. I could feel the warm sun on my back and saw nothing but blue sky ahead of me. I never saw Larry or Bogart again after that day. I learned that day to keep Timmy an arm's length from me. He was bad news. Frank and I stayed friends. I still thought of him as my little brother.

School had ended, and it was summertime. It was time for the month-end sales in all the stores located in downtown L.A. and time to get ready for summer. The month-end sales were a bargain hunter's dream. Being that I was always financially embarrassed, it was a penny pincher's lottery. I was in May Co. looking to purchase my allotment of Levi Strauss jeans and maybe some dress slacks. I told the salesclerk what I wanted, and in no time, I had what I came to purchase. I paid for the items and was out of there, going up Broadway.

I was hungry and in a hurry to get to Central Market. All I could think about was the fried shrimp, a dollar twenty-five for a dozen. The fried shrimp right out of the fryer smothered in red pepper sauce. I was in for a heavenly feast.

I was doing some high-power walking on my way to Central Market. I was perspiring profusely by the time I made it to 5th and Broadway. I had to stop for the red light. I looked up the block. Lo and behold, it was Mrs. Tobias. I could not believe my eyes! God does work in mysterious ways!

I waited to cool down before walking across the street. I must have taken five-light changes before I cooled down enough to step up and talk to Mrs. Tobias! I did not want to seem as anxious as I was. I walked up to Mrs. Tobias and smiled at her as I hugged and kissed her on the cheek. I did not know how I was going to marry her daughter, only that I was.

"Nice to see you again!"

"How have you been?" Her sweet and kind voice made me feel as if I was talking to my mother once more. Never speaking above a soft motherly tone.

"Y tu hija Hilda?

"She is coming now."

I looked up, and there she was. "Oh! You again," she said.

Mrs. Tobias said, "Hija!"

I answered Hilda, "Yes, me again. How have you been? Do you work here, Hilda?"

"Yes, I do. It is nice to see you again."

"So you took my advice and moved down here?"

"Yes, I did."

"Did you find a place to live?"

"Yes, just a few blocks from here."

"I was on my way to have something to eat. Would you care to join me?"

"No, thank you."

I did not want to press my luck, so I said, "Have a good evening, and I hope to see you again."

Hilda took her mother by the arm and walked away. It was one of the most adorable displays of mother and daughter affection I have ever witnessed. I never took my eyes off them as they were walking away. I ran across Broadway and followed them to make sure they got home safe.

They walked down to Seventh Street and turned onto Seventh Street and kept on walking. I made sure to stay on the opposite side of the street in the middle of the block. They walked up Seventh Street to Grand Ave. onto Wilshire Blvd. up to Bixel Street. I watched as Hilda and her mother walked into a brownstone four-story building on the corner of Bixel Street and Ingraham Street. The only thing I did not know was on which floor their apartment was located.

I spent the next two days trying to accidentally run into Hilda and Mrs. Tobias. Finally, Hilda and I broke the ice, and she started talking to me. There was a coffee shop on 7th Street that closed early. It was Hilda's day off, and I happened to follow them inside the coffee shop. We each had coffee and a piece of cake. It was funny, but we shared tasting each other's cake. Mrs. Tobias cut the cake into three equal parts. It reminded me of when my mother Marilyn did the same thing for me and my father, President John F. Kennedy. It brought tears to my eyes, just watching Mrs. Tobias cutting and placing each piece of cake on the plates with all the love and care a mother had to offer. Hilda looked at me and asked if I was okay.

"Yes, I am fine; my mother would do the same thing that your mother is doing now for my little brother and me in hopes that we would learn to share."

We finished our coffee and cake. Mrs. Tobias was insisting on paying for the three of us.

"I came here with money, hija, and you have not. Let me pay for anything. I'm going to leave here with the same amount of money I left Guatemala with." There was no sense in me arguing the point. Mrs. Tobias had her mind made up that she was going to pay for late afternoon coffee.

Once we were out the door, I took Mrs. Tobias by her arm, and the three of us walked back to their apartment. Up Bixel and onto Ingraham Street, they had the second apartment on the first floor on the right side of the building. It was a single furnished apartment with a kitchen separate from the living area, a Pullman bed, a walk-in closet, gas, and electricity included for 70.00 dollars a month.

Hilda was savvy enough to look for an apartment with a pay telephone right across the hall from her apartment door. Who would not want a payphone outside their door? The telephone company has a $125.00 deposit to turn on the phone. So it was convenient having a payphone across the hall of her apartment.

It was a lovely apartment for a single person or newlyweds. Either way, I felt that this was a safe place for Hilda and her mother to live for now. It was walking distance to Hilda's job, and her mother was able to meet Hilda after work.

I did not want to overstay my welcome; I was there all of ten minutes. I hugged and kissed Mrs. Tobias, and Hilda held her hand out to shake my hand goodbye.

"There is something that you should know about people from California. We do not like to say goodbye, but instead, we say 'I'll see you later,' which doesn't mean that we'll literally see you later, just that we hope to see you again soon. So I'll see you later."

I walked back to Hill Street, where I caught the 42 Temple bus back to the house. I knew that Mrs. Tobias had a fondness for me, but I was not sure about her daughter Hilda.

What was going on with me? Oh my God, I hope my hand was not sweaty when I shook Hilda's hand. By the time I made it to the house, I felt as if I had just come back from my first date. There was even a chaperone. I was sure of one thing: I was going to find a way to marry Hilda, even if she did not want to marry me. I knew enough about biology that she was the one for me! The next morning, I was up and on my way to see Mona for the other half of my money.

Once I had seen Mona, I took the bus downtown. I got off the bus at May Co. It was 10:00 when the doors opened. I asked the sales clerk where the personnel department was located. I tried Bullock's, Broadway, and Robinson's to get a job, but the personnel managers told me the same thing. If you do not have a parent or guardian's approval to work, you need not apply. Not only did I require a parent's permission, but I also needed support from the school I would be attending in the fall. There was no way on God's green earth that Mary was going to put her John Handcock on any work form so that I could work. I'll have to make do with working on cars and doing gardening work for the neighbors until that birth certificate that Mary gave me says I am eighteen. That does not mean I am going to live my life as if I am eighteen years old! I'm going out there to fight for what I want.

I waited around downtown until Hilda was off work. I didn't see Mrs. Tobias anywhere, so I walked Hilda to her apartment. We took our time walking along the same path that we walked with her mother. This time, I could see Hilda was more relaxed and was up on current events. The earthquake and the damage that she saw on the way down from San Francisco, she told me her experience. Yes, for me, it was the same as an E-ticket at Disney Land. She smiled and said that she and her mother had just visited Disney Land. We came around the corner, and Miss. Tobias was there waiting for Hilda.

To witness the greeting that Miss. Tobias displayed when her daughter Hilda arrived home from work, brought tears to my eyes. I saw that little boy of long ago, how he, too, would greet his mother as she returned home from work. Miss. Tobias invited me in for coffee.

As we were having coffee, Miss. Tobias was telling Hilda that maybe it was time for both of them to return to Guatemala. "I don't want to leave you here alone, and I think you should return home with me."

"Momma, I would like to stay here. I have an apartment close to my job, and I have met some friendly people at work. It would be easier to make money to finish the second floor in the house and open the school."

"Mija, you speak two languages, Spanish and English; I'm sure you'll find a good-paying job back home."

I said, "Hilda, Mrs. Tobias, I feel as if I am intruding, so I'll bid you good afternoon; thank you for the coffee."

Mrs. Tobias looked at me and asked, "What were you doing downtown? Do you live close?"

"Yes, I do; in walking distance from here. I was looking for work at the department stores but had no luck finding it. Perhaps tomorrow I'll have better luck. I'm exhausted, maybe I'll see you tomorrow, but I have to go. I'll see you later!"

As I walked up Wilshire, a smile came over my face! Yes, it is within walking distance; that's no lie. If one is one hell of a walker. I stood on the corner for a moment or two thinking, I'll walk down Wilshire Blvd. to MacArthur Park. It's the easiest way to get to the house. It cuts out the hills and zigzag streets that I'd have to walk. Which would give me time to think over the conversation that Hilda and her mother had had. By their conversation, I knew that I was running out of time. If I were going to convince Mrs. Tobias, to let Hilda stay here in the United States, I would have to work fast!

The next morning, Anthony came by. He wanted me to help him work on Charles's sister-in-law Ann Goldberg's '69 Ford pick-up. The one thing about work with Anthony was he started work at 8:00 AM and ended his workday by 2:30 PM. That would give me plenty of time to get cleaned up and head downtown. Staying busy working would also keep me from watching the clock tick away.

By 4:00 PM that afternoon, I was dressed and on my way downtown. If there was one surefire way to make sure no one followed me, it was to pay the 35 cents for the bus. Once I was on the bus, I was off in no time at 5th and Hill Street just before Pershing Square Park. I walked down 5th Street to Spring Street, made a right on Spring Street, and strolled down Spring Street onto Broadway Arcade Building.

I paced back and forth, waiting at the Spring Street entrance, to see if Mrs. Tobias was going to meet Hilda after work. I did not have too long of a wait. I saw Mrs. Tobias entering the coffee shop right across the street from Broadway Interior Department Store, where Hilda was employed.

I walked past the coffee shop window as if I did not know Mrs. Tobias was already there. I stopped at the window, hoping that Mrs. Tobias would ask me to come in. Which she did. I was becoming accustomed to kissing Mrs. Tobias when we greeted one another.

I sat down, and we began to talk about how she was enjoying her stay in Los Angeles. Their trip to Disney Land, the Hollywood Wax Museum, and their adventures to Santa Monica Beach. I finally got up enough nerve to bring the conversation to when she thought she may be leaving back to Guatemala.

It was the part of our discussion that I paid close attention to. "I don't want to leave my hija Hilda here alone. I'm thinking of taking her with me."

"Mrs. Tobias, if you decide to let Hildita stay here, I'll look in on her from time to time; she'll not be alone. I'll look after her. If she wants to return home, I'll accompany her on the trip to Guatemala. I have no family of my own, and it would be my pleasure to look out for her."

"Your parents, where are they?"

"Mrs. Tobias, both my parents are deceased. I have a sister and a brother, but they are back east. I'm here with many eyes that watch me, but that is it. I feel as if I am an only child, but unlike my parents, I am here, and they are not."

"Mijo, you seem like an honest person, but I'll have to talk to my husband about this, and thank you for your offer. You are well-meaning and sincere, but I still have to think about it."

A week later, my future mother-in-law was on a plane to Guatemala. I kept my word. I sometimes took the bus downtown, or I would borrow a car to meet Hilda when she finished working. I stayed in contact with Mrs. Tobias via the telephone outside Hilda's apartment. The one thought that my future mother-in-law left me with is I had to ask Mr. Felix Tobias for Hilda's hand in marriage. I was pushing a boulder up a steep hill. Hilda and her mother had no idea that I wanted Hilda's hand in marriage. All they knew was that I was a well-mannered, concerned, all-American young man.

However, do I explain to Mr. Tobias that his future son-in-law is the son of President John F. Kennedy and Marilyn Monroe? The United States Legal System has broken down, leaving me with a birth certificate that belongs to a deceased child — taking 5 years of my childhood from me. How was I going to put this in my own words?

# POSTFACE

**IT WAS A SPRING** day in Beverly Hills, California, a little chilly. My mother had picked up her last passenger. Next, on to buy snacks for our three-hour drive to Western White House to visit my dad. It was the last item left on her itinerary to do. She pulled into Ralph's Market on Wilshire Boulevard and Crescent Ave. She parked. Suddenly, we were blocked in by a car stopped behind us.

Everything took mere seconds to unfold. Two men came rushing out of the car that had blocked us in our parking space. The man with the blue eyes grabbed me and pulled me out of the vehicle. The other man had a gun to my mother's bosom. He told her, "If you scream, I'll kill your child." There was no time to say, "I'll see you later" to my mother. I looked at her and said, "If my father's family has anything to do with this, I will not stop. I give you my word!"

That was the last time I saw my mother alive. I walked among the elite to scrounging around for my next meal, day in and day out, fighting to stay alive!

This one day changed my life forever. It took more than half a century to write my biography. There are many people to thank for helping make this book possible, impossible to tell you about each one.

Hilda was assaulted on October 6, 2014, and then a bus crushing her on November 17, 2014, this book would have been published much earlier. After *John Fitzgerald Kennedy v The Trustees of the Testamentary Trust of the Last Will and Testament of President John Fitzgerald Kennedy* took six years of our life, my wife spent 7 days in intensive care, 19 days in rehabilitation, and 77 days in private care. I spent 7 days sleeping in the intensive care unit. Our son returned home from his engagement. The combination of these events makes an unfortunate delay.

Thank you to Dr. Richard B. Islinger. He was on call, and it was his last day at AtlantiCare. This had to be divine intervention. He is an Orthopedic Surgeon from Walter Reed Medical Center. I would also like to take this time to thank him and the staff at AtlantiCare Regional Medical Center. Also, Bacharach Institute for Rehabilitation, and Egg Harbor Care Center for the excellent job during my wife's recovery. It was the best treatment money could buy, heartfelt.

There was no justice for my wife and me in the American justice system. In July 2018, Judge Nelson Johnson, writer of The Boardwalk Empire, noted that there were seven reasons why our Attorney Randy C. Lafferty of Cooper Levenson should have never taken on our case. It was common knowledge in the Atlantic City Superior Courthouse. My cousin Congressman Patrick Kennedy, son of my Uncle Edward Moore Kennedy, had an office or maybe a partner in his firm. Judge Johnson rendered his decision and sealed the records. It was the sealing of the court files that made me more determined to move forward with publishing my writings.

Thank you also to my son William who has made tremendous sacrifices. He once spent two years trying to find out if there was ever Ralph's Market on the corner of Wilshire Blvd and Crescent Ave. The ridicule that he has endured, unsurmountable, yet he can still laugh and make others smile. My PTSD and Dyslexia did not make it easy on him. He wrote an article, which I include next. He lit my fire and kept it burning with his sheer will.

I would like to thank the publisher of the West View News, George Capsis. He brought journalist integrity back from its death in my life a long time ago. And you, the reader.

This book will answer your questions. The purpose of this book is to bring about justice. It is a work in progress. People reading it, sharing it, make it interactive. Thank you.

I would also like to thank the hidden good people, like Hugh Hefner, who desperately wanted me to live to write a book about my kidnapping with proof. Thank you from the bottom of my heart. I am sure my mother and father would have said the same.

Before anything and after everything, I would like to thank God Himself for allowing me/us to live to bring about goodness by His grace.

My own words start with my parents and end in 1972. This is the first book of a series of five books that chronicle my will to survive and have a family, albeit with suffering, while remaining true to myself. The upcoming book is titled *The Kennedy's of Massachusetts Re-Emerge*. To be continued...

John Fitzgerald Kennedy

John F. Kennedy and Hilda T. Kennedy

Happiness

Safety

Fear and Anxiety

Printed in the USA
CPSIA information can be obtained
at www.ICGtesting.com
CBHW061152080524
8241CB00024B/335/J

9 781642 375206